THE RIGHT TO BE COUNTED

SOUTH ASIA IN MOTION

THE RIGHT
TO BE COUNTED

The Urban Poor and the Politics
of Resettlement in Delhi

SANJEEV ROUTRAY

STANFORD UNIVERSITY PRESS

STANFORD, CALIFORNIA

Stanford University Press

Stanford, California

© 2022 by Sanjeev Routray. All rights reserved.

Printed in the United States of America on acid-free, archival-quality paper

Library of Congress Cataloging-in-Publication Data

Names: Routray, Sanjeev, author.

Title: The right to be counted : the urban poor and the politics of resettlement in Delhi / Sanjeev Routray.

Other titles: South Asia in motion.

Description: Stanford, California : Stanford University Press, 2022. | Series: South Asia in motion | Includes bibliographical references and index.

Identifiers: LCCN 2022005970 (print) | LCCN 2022005971 (ebook) | ISBN 9781503630840 (cloth) | ISBN 9781503632134 (paperback) | ISBN 9781503632141 (ebook)

Subjects: LCSH: Poor—Political activity—India—Delhi. | Poor—Civil rights—India—Delhi. | Citizenship—India—Delhi. | City planning—India—Delhi. | Land settlement—Political aspects—India—Delhi.

Classification: LCC HV4140.D4 S58 2022 (print) | LCC HV4140.D4 (ebook) | DDC 305.5/69095456—dc23/eng/20220228

LC record available at https://lccn.loc.gov/2022005970

LC ebook record available at https://lccn.loc.gov/2022005971

Cover design: Rob Ehle

Cover photo: Alleyway in Dehli. Sanjeev Routray

Typeset by Newgen in Adobe Caslon Pro 10.75/15

For
Dharashree Das
Sanoh Aranya

CONTENTS

TABLES AND FIGURES

ACKNOWLEDGMENTS

This book attempts to document the experience of poor migrants in their quest for citizenship entitlements in Delhi. Each page written in this book reflects the generous sharing of knowledge and the magnanimity of my research collaborators in the field. Over more than a decade, my collaborators have taught me about the tenacity, imagination, and vision needed to fight for social justice, especially in their struggles to claim a home and life in the city. I hope that I have done justice in interpreting and translating their life stories herein.

Jennifer Chun, John Harriss, Tom Kemple, and Renisa Mawani have continuously motivated and supported me in writing and revising this book. Tom Kemple has shown unparalleled dedication and has commented on multiple drafts of various portions of this book. John Harriss introduced me to a vast body of Indian scholarship and has always encouraged me to write sharply. I have also learned a great deal from my friends, colleagues, and mentors at the University of British Columbia (UBC; some of whom have already moved on from the university), especially Bonar Buffam, Dawn Currie, Sherrie Dilley, Junrong Du, the late John Friedmann, Gaston Gordillo, Amy Hanser, Abidin Kusno, Nathan Lauster, Rohit Mujumdar, Anand Pandian, Becki Ross, David Ryniker, Leonie Sandercock, Sumayya Syed, Ana Vivaldi, Rafa Wainer, Rima Wilkes, and Sophia Woodman. Whenever I hit rock bottom, Jennifer Chun and Renisa Mawani lifted my spirits. Benita Bunjun, Geraldina Polanco, and Fang Xu have remained steadfast friends and have always inquired after my well-being. In Vancouver over the span of many years, my friends Mandeep Basi, Jayasree Basivireddy, Ajay Bhardwaj, Mary Ann Chacko, Marian Gracias, Neelu Kang, Raksha Karki, Raj Khadka, Mosarrap Khan, Prajna Rao, Naresh Reddy, and Tanvi Sirari have provided formidable companionship in studying, hiking, movie-watching, karaoke singing, and partaking in the simple pleasures of life on an everyday basis. The late Chinmoy Banerjee, Patricia Gruben, and many comrades of the Hari Sharma Foundation and the South Asian Network for Secularism and Democracy (SANSAD) have offered me kind words and succor during this long journey.

Gavin Shatkin hosted me at Northeastern University, Boston, when I received an Urban Studies Foundation postdoctoral fellowship. He showed an admirable openness and provided encouragement during our weekly meetings when I rehearsed many of the ideas discussed in this book. Parts of the manuscript were discussed in two different workshops at Northeastern University and Harvard University. I thank Jonathan Anjaria, Doreen Lee, Gavin Shatkin, and Liza Weinstein for their comments regarding revisions for the manuscript in the workshop at Northeastern University. The comments of participants at the Political Anthropology and Political Ecology Working Group workshop at Harvard University—especially those provided by Namita Dharia, Sahana Ghosh, and Ajantha Subramanian—have helped me in revising the Introduction of the manuscript. Additionally, my Boston days would have been lonely without the friendship of Haytham Khalil, Jaspreet Mahal, Pradeep Mahale, Vivek Mishra, Dadasaheb Tandale, Alice Verticelli, and Suraj Yengde. I am indebted to Suraj Yengde for introducing me to the Boston Study Group and to Dadasaheb Tandale for routinely singing to me: "*Apna* time *ayega*" (My time shall come!).

A myriad of encounters, experiences, and events have shaped me as a person and as an academic over the years. Vinod Jairath, N. Purendra Prasad, and Aparna Rayaprol taught me the essentials of social sciences in my formative days in Hyderabad. Sasheej Hegde, who introduced me to sociology and has mentored me since then, has remained instrumental in shaping my academic career. Imrana Qadeer introduced me to the topic of displacement of the poor, for which I will remain forever grateful, and, along with Ghanshyam Shah, provided a direction for my research in Delhi. Amid the excitement of visiting monuments, parks, and bazaars as a new migrant in the capital city of India, I was fortunate to work with Mary E. John on a research project entitled "Gender and Governance in Two Cities," which exposed me to various contrasting neighborhoods in Delhi. In the spring of 2003, she gave me a photocopy of the paper entitled "Are Indian Cities Becoming Bourgeois, at Last?" that Partha Chatterjee had presented at the Center for the Study of Developing Societies, New Delhi, and in early 2004 she advised me to attend the first Winter Institute of Partners for Urban Knowledge, Action, and Research (PUKAR) in Mumbai. I met a dazzling group of young scholars at the PUKAR Winter Institute and returned with multiple notes and names of scholars to look up and read. Subsequently, I was introduced to an extraordinary array of critical literature by teachers and mentors including Dwaipayan Bhattacharyya, Partha Chatterjee, Rosinka Chaudhuri, Keya Dasgupta, the late Anjan Ghosh, Janaki Nair, and Manas Ray.

I had the opportunity to present my work and receive deeply engaging comments at seminars and workshops. I thank the following people for inviting me to attend these events: Naveen Bharathi (Center for the Advanced Study of India Seminar at the University of Pennsylvania), Grace Carswell and Geert de Neve (University of Sussex workshop on documents, cards, and paperwork in South Asia), Ratheesh Kumar and Tanweer Fazal (Thursday Colloquium at the Center for the Study of Social Systems, Jawaharlal Nehru University), Keisha-Khan Y. Perry and Beshara Doumani (Brown International Advanced Research Institute, or BIARI, workshop on "Displacements and the Making of the Modern World"), and Gavin Shatkin (School of Public Policy and Urban Affairs Seminar at Northeastern University). I am grateful to the following people for commenting on portions of the final drafts of the manuscript: Partha Chatterjee, Ankur Datta, John Harriss, Sasheej Hegde, Tom Kemple, Llerena Searle, and Claire Snell-Rood. I especially thank Karthik Rao-Cavale for commenting on the entire manuscript, and to Gary Fields (whom I had merely met at the BIARI workshop) for his kind support in commenting on a major part of the manuscript. I also had the privilege of discussing and receiving comments on my work from many generous scholars including Solomon Benjamin, Kushal Deb, Thomas Faist, John Flint, Shubhra Gururani, Patrick Heller, Ravinder Kaur, Roland Lardinois, Peggy Levitt, Jules Naudet, and Stacy Pigg at different times. A fortuitous meeting with Jinee Lokaneeta, who provided important advice on how to turn a PhD thesis into a book manuscript, has proved salient in finalizing the manuscript.

Many friends have sustained me emotionally and intellectually over the years. I extend my gratitude to Rosemary Abraham, Ramesh Bairy, Anita Barik, Omlata Bhagat, Karthikeyan Damodaran, Swati Das, Suneetha Eluri, Hadeel Fawadleh, Dhivya Janarthanan, Madhura Lohokare, Rekha Konsam, Lulufer Korukmez, Leah Koskimaki, Chris Mary Kurian, Nisha Mathew, Byasa Moharana, Camalita Naicker, Nitesh Narnolia, Swapna Nayani, Madhurima Nundy, Sumati Panikkar, Redento Recio, Sadananda Sahoo, Alpen Sheth, Pradeep Shinde, Gurram Srinivas, Shobha Surin, Vikramaditya Thakur, Amit Upadhyay, and Himanshu Upadhyaya for their affection and encouragement. Rakesh Kalshian, a beautiful soul, always had my back in Delhi. Saravana Raja has shared the camaraderie, humor, and tribulations of academic life on an everyday basis.

Satish Deshpande facilitated my affiliation with the Department of Sociology at the Delhi School of Economics during my fieldwork. Ranjana Padhi offered constant insights, encouragement, and affection, and introduced me to many grassroots activists in Delhi. Among them, Birju Nayak was instrumental in helping me decide on my field sites and providing me with an understanding of the local dynamics of different neighborhoods. The activists of Jagori, Jan Chetna Manch, Lok Raj Sangathan, and Delhi Shramik Sangathan and the planners at different state institutions contributed to my knowledge of governance and politics in Delhi. Lalit Batra, Anita Juneja, and Ramendra Kumar offered important perspectives on the issues of displacement and politics in Delhi. Deeba Moin and Abdur Rahoof provided valuable research assistance during my fieldwork. Sanghmitra Acharya's warmth and generosity is legendary. Without her support, it would have been difficult to establish key connections with various state officials in different institutions during my fieldwork.

My research and writing were made possible by the grants and fellowships I received from the University of British Columbia in Canada, the Paul Foundation Scholarships in India, the Foundation for Urban and Regional Studies in the UK, ZEIT-Stiftung in Germany, the International Development Research Center in Canada, Dr. Hari Sharma Foundation in Canada, and the Urban Studies Foundation in the UK. I am indebted to the selection committees and administrators for showing faith and offering me these grants at various stages of my project. As part of the Zeit-Stiftung Ebelin und Gerd Bucerius PhD Scholarship program, I had the unique experience of meeting and traveling with fellow researchers across different parts of the world. This opportunity was invaluable in teaching me about the complexities of migration issues across the globe and in giving me some terrific friends, especially Anna Boucher, Anne Koch, Onur Komurcu, Noora Lori, Muhammad Arafat bin Mohamad, Leonie Newhouse, and Luna Vives. Thank you, Muhammad Arafat bin Mohamad, for your graciousness and investment to see me succeed in life.

Thomas Blom Hansen and Marcela Maxfield immediately took interest in the manuscript when I submitted it to Stanford University Press in August 2020 and shepherded the entire process in the most understated manner. And then after a year, I realized that the book was really happening! In the summer of 2021, Dylan Kyung-Lim White took the reins from Marcela Maxfield and guided the process with the help of Sunna Juhn. Thank you very much to everyone at the press. I have been lucky to receive generous and deeply thorough comments from two anonymous referees. I offer my sincere gratitude to them for helping me to sharpen my arguments in the book. The manuscript has benefited from the copyediting of Julie Jenkins, Aiden Tait, and Anita Hueftle at various stages of writing.

My brother Diptendu Routray, sister-in-law Mausumee Bal, and cousin sister Snigdha Behera have offered their help as my unofficial research assistants for quite some time. They have transcribed and photocopied field notes, scanned documents, and mailed materials across the globe without ever doubting the importance of my work as I have tried to gain a foothold in academia. My parents, Mahesh Chandra Routray and Sumitra Routray, have often worried about my lack of social mobility despite living in Canada for all these years. They have expressed concerns about the constraints of making it in academia for people from my social background. Nonetheless, of late my mother has vicariously enjoyed my progress and self-indulgence in academia. It has been a long, arduous, exhilarating, and (at times) brutal journey from the early days of my education in Kainthipokhari village school in Jajpur district, Odisha, to my navigation of the world of elite academia. For a major part of this journey and since I met her, Dharashree Das has provided rock-solid support, encouragement, and unconditional love. Sanoh Aranya, our little daughter—a powerhouse—has already taught me a thing or two about resilience and determination. Thank you for teaching me the fundamentals of life and everything!

Some of the ideas discussed in this book have also appeared in my article "The Postcolonial City and Its Displaced Poor: Rethinking 'Political Society' in Delhi," published in *International Journal of Urban and Regional Research*.

ABBREVIATIONS

AAP	Aam Aadmi Party
APL	Above Poverty Line
BJP	Bharatiya Janata Party
BPL	Below Poverty Line
BSP	Bahujan Samaj Party
DDA	Delhi Development Authority
DJB	Delhi Jal Board
DSLSA	Delhi State Legal Services Authority
DSS	Delhi Shramik Sangathan
DUAC	Delhi Urban Arts Commission
DUSIB	Delhi Urban Shelter Improvement Board
DVB	Delhi Vidyut Board
FAA	First Appellate Authority
FDI	foreign direct investment
GNCTD	Government of National Capital Territory of Delhi
IAS	Indian Administrative Services
INC	Indian National Congress
JCM	Jan Chetna Manch
JNNURM	Jawaharlal Nehru National Urban Renewal Mission
LRS	Lok Raj Sangathan
MCD	Municipal Corporation of Delhi
MLA	Member of the Legislative Assembly
MoUD	Ministry of Urban Development
MP	Member of Parliament

MPD-I	First Master Plan of Delhi
MPD-II	Second Master Plan of Delhi
MPD-III	Third Master Plan of Delhi
NCRPB	National Capital Region Planning Board
PDS	Public Distribution System
PIO	Public Information Officer
PPP	Public Private Partnerships
PWD	Public Works Department
RoW	Right of Way
RTI	Right to Information
RWA	Resident Welfare Association
TCPO	Town and Country Planning Organization
UID	Unique Identification Number

THE RIGHT TO BE COUNTED

NUMERICAL CITIZENSHIP STRUGGLES
IN CONTEMPORARY DELHI

THE URBAN POOR WORK against difficult odds to incrementally stake their claims to a home and a life in the city. Across the globe, rural-urban migrants, refugees, and other communities of poor and marginalized people are exercising political agency[1] in pursuit of entitlements associated with citizenship. Among the poorest residents of Delhi, the recognition of citizenship claims by the Indian state is increasingly contingent on their struggles for visibility and entrenchment in urban living spaces. These citizenship projects are highly contested and take place incrementally over time through the deployment of a remarkable variety of *rann-nitis* (tactics and counter-tactics). Approximately 76 percent of Delhi's population lives in "unplanned," "illegal," and "informal" settlements (Bhan 2016: 19). Over 1.5 million people have been displaced in the last three decades in the city. Despite these alarming figures, the poor have incrementally advanced their citizenship projects and political claims in the city, gained a foothold, and managed to attain a "precarious stability" (Weinstein 2014). In this context, *The Right to Be Counted*[2] contributes to scholarly and public debates on the contradictions between state governmentality[3] and the citizenship projects of the poor themselves. The book explores how the planning process contributes to social suffering, but also the logic of negotiations and the cultural idioms of political mobilization that emanate from the processes of displacement and resettlement in Delhi.

Delhi's poor remain embedded in various social, political, and economic relationships even as they forge and build kinship networks and develop alliances of solidarity across a political and social spectrum in their struggles to gain a foothold in the city. Their overlapping struggles to build *jhuggis* (hutments—that is, a group of huts), to obtain access to welfare and to provide for basic needs, but also to stop displacements, gain eligibility for resettlement, and secure "proof documents," constitute a distinctive mode of advancing material claims and political belonging in the city. At the core of these struggles lie incremental efforts to become visible to the local state. *The Right to Be Counted* describes this process of claims-making as the struggle for "numerical citizenship," or the struggle to be "counted" in order for a political community of the poor to assert its numerical strength. Struggles over numerical citizenship constitute the systematic, protracted, and incremental political process by which the poor become entrenched in the city. It is not merely a "politics of presence" (Bayat 2010: 128), or the assertion of a right to exist, but also a struggle to be visible, to be identified, and to be recognized, and to be made eligible for food, shelter, and basic amenities and infrastructure in the city (see also Anand 2017: 16; Routray 2014: 2299–300).

This book provides a contemporary history of urban citizenship as seen from the vantage point of some of Delhi's poorest residents. Many of Delhi's poor transition from being migrants in the city, to residents in unidentified *jhuggi jhopri* settlements (that is, precarious and improvised hutments), to residents in state-recognized *jhuggi jhopri* settlements or re-settlement neighborhoods.[4] Once they settle in a state-recognized *jhuggi*, they come under the purview of state calculative governmentality—state regulations and calculations. Their struggles then shape the degree to which they may gain access to sets of entitlements, especially the provision of housing, rudimentary infrastructure, and basic amenities, which constitute citizenship in Delhi. In analyzing citizenship, the political theorist Niraja Jayal provides a succinct analysis of how the three dimensions of citizenship—"citizenship as legal status, citizenship as a bundle of rights and entitlements, and citizenship as a sense of identity and belonging"— are imagined and practiced in India (Jayal 2013: 2; see Jayal 2019). In this book, I primarily focus on one aspect of citizenship by examining the complex *rann-nitis* of the poor in obtaining a range of social rights and entitlements in the city.

In order to compare and contrast the modalities of state calculative governmentality enshrined in the urban restructuring processes and to trace the logics of political mobilization among the urban poor, I have chosen three sites: a *jhuggi jhopri* settlement (Gautam Nagar *jhuggi jhopri* settlement), a transit camp (Sitapuri transit camp), and a new resettlement colony (Azad resettlement colony) for ethnographic study. (I use pseudonyms for these neighborhoods throughout the book.) The three neighborhoods are all state-recognized settlements in that the residents all possess documents proving residence. In other words, they are relatively well entrenched in the political landscape of the city compared to the poor in other types of social spaces such as pavements or unrecognized *jhuggi jhopri* settlements, who are considerably less able to claim housing rights in the city. (The planning and political dynamics of the most vulnerable and excluded populations are briefly discussed in Chapter 2 by way of comparison.) I make my arguments about numerical citizenship based on twenty-five months of ethnographic research—twenty-two months from November 2009 through August 2011 and three

FIGURE INTRO.1: *Gautam Nagar* jhuggi jhopri *neighborhood. A cement road bisects two rows of hutments in the neighborhood.*

months from June through September 2017—in these three neighbor-hoods.[5] Throughout the book, I use vignettes from these three field sites to advance the empirical and theoretical arguments I make.

DOCUMENTING RESIDENCE: GAUTAM NAGAR
JHUGGI JHOPRI CAMP

In the early 1970s, a few residents took over an inhospitable patch of land near an industrial area to build *jhuggis*. They cleared part of a jungle near their workplaces to build shacks made of gunny bags, plastic sheets, straw, bamboo, and other materials. Their numbers grew gradually after more people started building huts, clearing and refilling the land as necessary. The settlement then expanded further into an industrial area, which in turn adjoined several urban villages. Soon, police started intervening by either tearing apart these partly built structures or by demanding payments to leave the residents alone. Self-styled strongmen eventually emerged from the neighborhood to negotiate with the police for protection against demolition in exchange for money. The strongmen even enclosed a portion of the land and distributed land parcels within it for a price while building more *jhuggis* to rent out or sell to newer residents. In addition to harassment from the police, the residents encountered hostility from people in the already established villages. The strongmen negotiated with these residents, especially regarding issues related to thefts and property damages. Gradually, the settlement gained leverage through its increased numbers, and as residents asserted themselves at key events, including elections, to demand infrastructure and recognition of their neighborhood. Once the residents got into the electoral database of the state, the settlement became enmeshed in "vote-bank" politics, that is, patron-client politics, wherein the clients vote for particular parties in exchange for recognition and extension of services. Thus, the "migrants" became *jhuggi* residents or owners over the years and the unrecognized *jhuggi* settlement became a state-recognized *jhuggi jhopri* colony, the Gautam Nagar camp.

When a part of Gautam Nagar was demolished in 2009 for a road-widening project, the residents fought a protracted battle with courts and the Government of National Capital Territory of Delhi (GNCTD). On

August 22, 2017, the Delhi Urban Shelter Improvement Board (DUSIB) decided to resettle the residents of Gautam Nagar. Aware that the board could reject their claim to resettlement on the slightest pretext, the residents decided to meet their member of the legislative assembly (MLA) to seek guidance and support in fixing any minor errors in their documents. The MLA, P,[6] had served as an elected councilor from Bahujan Samaj Party (BSP) in 2009–2011 (during my first round of fieldwork). In 2017 (during the second round of my fieldwork), he served as an MLA from the Aam Aadmi Party (AAP). Although from a Gujjar community from a nearby village, he spent considerable time socializing with the residents even before he entered politics. The residents claim that he was mentored and encouraged to join politics by one of their local leaders, a *pradhan* (chief) who was familiar with the political processes and landscape of Delhi. P was immensely popular in the neighborhood, but the residents distanced themselves from him after the demolitions in 2009 because he was not very helpful in their resettlement battles. By 2017, he was not only an MLA from the ruling party in Delhi but also an elected board member of DUSIB. Understandably, the residents recalled their past closeness with the MLA to me with some ambivalence, if not bitterness.

As we walked toward P's office, the local *pradhan* reminisced how "he gives us respect, acknowledges our presence, and even shares our *bidi* [a cigarette filled with tobacco and wrapped in a leaf] if we smoke one. We feel good that he is our own." The MLA's office sat nestled between a newly built community toilet and a well-maintained park. As we entered his office, he arranged chairs for us to sit while simultaneously watching a professional league *kabaddi* match broadcast on TV. The office had a makeshift gym, chairs for visitors, a TV, and a pair of millstones for grinding cattle feed. As more people streamed into his office, the *pradhan* bantered, "See, MLA sahib is very fond of building his body. He also raises cattle as a hobby. Look at those millstones; he grinds cattle feed every day." At this moment, the MLA instructed a caretaker to provide cattle-feed and medicines to the cattle in a shed at one corner of the park. The residents were in good spirits thanks to the informal atmosphere, the news of the board's decision to resettle, and the prospect of rectifying the *kami* (gaps or errors) in their documents with the help of the MLA.

After all, their own P-*ji* (the suffix *ji* is uttered as a mark of respect), who had learned politics playing and socializing in the neighborhood, was at the helm of political affairs that directly affected them. He narrated what occurred during the board meeting, answered their questions, and later invited everyone to a meeting to scrutinize the documents regarding their resettlement.

The meeting was called for the following Sunday to address the alarming documentary challenges that beset them. The documents, which are referred to as "proof documents" by both residents and various state officials, provide knowledge about the numerical presence of the residents from a particular year and are necessary for them to be "eligible" for resettlement and basic amenities. The intermediaries (neighborhood chiefs, social workers, and government workers who mediate issues with state and various non-state agencies) claimed that perhaps only 40–50 residents might possess error-free documents. Hence, they called for a meeting of all 223 eligible residents listed in the High Court case. In early September, the residents gathered in the park again. A resident asked me to read out the names of the people, their father's name, their *jhuggi* number, and their ID numbers, mainly from ration cards or voter IDs. I read out the names and details of the 223 residents listed. Many residents were conspicuously absent and untraceable. I tried contacting a few of the absentees but was unsuccessful. Their old phone numbers did not work and their neighbors had no knowledge about them.

Many residents whose names did not appear in the court case vehemently contested the list. A few of them verbally slandered the intermediaries who made the list for the court. SD exclaimed: "There were many Rajasthani residents [residents who originated from the western state of Rajasthan], but I do not see any of them here. I do not see many from the *Kabadda* camp [a part of the neighborhood known for recycling of *Kabadda*, or scrap materials] either. I see the names of many whose *jhuggis* have not been demolished yet. PB [one of the *samaj sevaks*, or social workers] must have included their names after taking money. All this happened because the *sarkar* [government] did not carry out any survey prior to the demolitions. The government people thought they would get away without resettling us. This is sheer injustice." To this accusation a *samaj sevak* argued: "These things happen. I was one of the five petition-ers, but my name was deleted from the list because I could not go to the court to sign the petition. Those of you whose names did not ap-pear must not have turned up that day. We will ask MLA sahib to add your name during the survey and verification process. We will request the government officials to verify only one document instead of a slew of documents."

Many documents consisting of photocopies were illegible. The resi-dents had surrendered their old ration cards but were required to produce photocopies of the old ration cards. A few residents produced photo-copies that were too light or too dark and at times had portions miss-ing around the edges. Eight years had passed since the neighborhood was demolished, and thus the documents and their photocopies had been subjected to rain, rats, and the ravages of time. The government staff had also made errors. For instance, in one document the staff had written over

FIGURE INTRO.2: *Sitapuri transit camp. Residents have built additional floors on the houses to accommodate their increasing family size.*

FIGURE INTRO.3: *Laxmi colony—a middle-class "planned" neighborhood as seen from Sitapuri transit camp. A lush green park separates Sitapuri transit camp and Laxmi colony.*

the misspelled name of a resident but had forgotten to sign and authenticate the document. An eligible resident's son appeared with his mother's document displaying her misspelled name. In his claim for authenticity, the son reminded the MLA about the school bag he had received from him as a gift when he joined grade five almost twenty years ago. Other residents debated the sequence of the arrival of residents, the involvement of particular residents in major events, and the details about individual biographies and the life history of the communities. They were concerned that some residents could be excluded from receiving flats if they had any *kami* in their documents.

RENAMING THE NEIGHBORHOOD: SITAPURI TRANSIT CAMP

In 2010, the residents of the Sitapuri transit camp attempted to reclassify themselves as "regular," "resettled," and "legal." Sitapuri transit camp was developed as a temporary measure to resettle residents from *jhuggi* settlements on so-called prime land in the mid-1980s. Between 2003 and 2010, the residents had successfully fought court battles against impending displacement after the Resident Welfare Association (RWA) of Lakshmi "colony" (a middle-class neighborhood) petitioned the court for the demolition of the transit camp. Since 2006, the primary political effort of the residents has been to contest the "temporary" status of their resettlement. The state enunciation or sanctioning of categories like "transit," "temporary," "illegal," and "encroacher" not only invested various populations of Sitapuri with contradictory meanings but also determined the legal status of their neighborhood. It then became incumbent on the residents to challenge these categories through renaming and reclassification. The categories of "transit" and "temporary" implied their lack of numerical entrenchment in the city. Here, the legality of their neighborhood depended on the number of years they had lived in the neighborhood. In this case, the documentation of their presence in the neighborhood since the 1980s bolstered their claims for permanent resettlement. The residents attempted to rename their locality for one of the former prime ministers of India who ruled during their "temporary" resettlement. The effort signaled the mutual endorsement of residents and the Congress party. The removal of "transit" and "camp" from the neighborhood's name and its replacement with the former Congress party prime minister's name and "colony" ("colony" is a commonly used term for "planned," "legal" neighborhoods in Delhi) were seen as legitimate efforts toward regularization and permanence.

After negotiations with various politicians and government officials, the residents were successful in renaming their neighborhood. On August 20, 2010, the residents decided to celebrate the occasion by organizing a ceremony for the unveiling of a stone sign, which also coincided with the birthday of the former prime minister. The residents had cleaned up the area and erected a makeshift stage. The floor of the stage was composed of a carpeted wooden plank, and the ceiling was a white cloth that rested on steel poles and was adorned with marigold flowers. Since there was a drizzle, the residents sat in chairs facing the stage with umbrellas in their hands. Revolutionary and nationalistic Hindi film songs extolling the contributions of soldiers and farmers blared from loudspeakers. The residents patiently waited and occasionally asked the intermediaries about the arrival time of their leaders. The councilor arrived at 10:00 a.m. to oversee the arrangements and quickly left in his car. Finally, the member of Parliament (MP), the MLA, and the councilor arrived at 11:30 a.m. and walked toward the stone sign. The unveiling of the stone sign was followed by the felicitation ceremony, during which the politicians were garlanded and extolled in generous terms by key members of the neighborhood. However, a sudden downpour truncated the celebration, and the politicians and residents rushed back to their homes. Despite being cut short, the renaming ceremony contributed to a semblance of regularization in the neighborhood, which in turn created optimism for the poor. After all, the Congress party MP, the MLA, and the councilor were the ones to officially rename and unveil the stone sign bearing the new name. I was asked to take pictures of the event and circulate them to two or three key members of the locality. When I went to meet some residents with printed copies of the pictures, a *pradhan* noted: "The day they [the members of the government] come to demolish again, I will show these pictures to the MLA and ask him why he had to carry out this drama of renaming before." As this remark illustrates, the practice of

FIGURE INTRO.4: *Azad resettlement colony. Residents have built precarious additional floors on homes on their tiny plots of land.*

auto-archiving of the events by collecting and storing pictures, newspaper clippings, and other artifacts steadily propelled the claims of the residents for more visibility and a secure foothold in the city.

DEMANDING SERVICES: AZAD RESETTLEMENT COLONY

The residents of the Azad resettlement colony, who are considered displaced, "eligible" residents of *jhuggi jhopri* settlements across the city, have held countless *dharnas* (peaceful gatherings) in front of the chief minister's house since they were resettled in 2000, demanding various basic amenities including water, bus services, and garbage disposal. The residents note that the gradual provisioning of various facilities in the neighborhood was made possible only after a protracted period of struggle.

On March 17, 2011, I joined a few residents who had congregated at a *halwai* shop (an Indian confectionary) in the evening to debate the dismal state of infrastructure in their neighborhood. The *halwai* shop owner, BC, squatted on the verandah and fried samosas in a deep and circular cooking pot. A portable TV rested on a glass-door fridge that stored soft drinks behind him. The residents watched the proceedings of the Lower House of the Parliament and debated the state of affairs in the country. The *halwai* shop faced a road that connected the neighborhood to the main square. Street vendors and myriad grocery shops and businesses plied their trade beside the road. The hustle and bustle of the neighborhood was evident as many residents descended from the main square and lanes and by-lanes of the neighborhoods to shop or make their way home. A garbage dump in an enclosed concrete structure stood across a park, which was barely 100 meters from the *halwai* shop. The residents covered their faces to avoid the putrid smell and flies from entering into their nostrils and mouths while crossing the garbage dump. Dogs and pigs rummaged through the garbage strewn across the park. Young men ferried cycle trollies with plastic containers to sell potable water in the neighborhood.

The *halwai* shop owner was visibly upset and expressed his anger to other residents. He had returned from the Delhi Development Authority office without being able to meet with officials to speak about the problems that beset the neighborhood. Despite incremental provisioning of services in their neighborhood over the years, the residents were appalled by what they perceived as the treatment of their neighborhood like a stepchild. As resident SS remarked, "The water line runs close to our neighborhood, but it supplies water to the distant Sarita Vihar [a middle-class neighborhood]. However, our neighborhood has not received potable water yet."

At *dharnas* in 2010 and 2011, residents warned that the politicians could lose as many as 36,000 votes, the number of voters in the Azad resettlement colony, if the politicians were to ignore their demands. As the *halwai* shop owner argued, "We invited the member of the Parliament of the area to the neighborhood to discuss our problems. He called us to his office instead and said that he did not like the *neta-giri* [leader activities] of *jhuggi* people. Instead he told us that he would do whatever was within his ability. I retorted by telling him that no one knew him in this neighborhood, although we had campaigned for him in order to garner votes during the elections." The MP's derogatory way of addressing the intermediaries and leaders of the neighborhood as *jhuggi* people upset residents. SS argued, "We [intermediaries and residents] have been spreading carpets and hoisting flags of the parties during various events. But we would never get party tickets to contest elections." At the time of my fieldwork in 2011, residents were contemplating the nomination of their own candidate in the future councilor elections: "We are tired of filling up vehicles with party supporters and public displays of numerical strength for candidates. We want to challenge the politicians in elections." By 2017, the population of the Azad resettlement colony had increased to almost 250,000, although the eligible voting population remained approximately 42,000. Nevertheless, the resettlement colony along with a nearby unauthorized colony[7] constituted a municipal ward. In the municipal elections of 2017, the residents successfully elected a councilor from their own neighborhood, thereby demonstrating their numerical strength. However, the election of a councilor from the neighborhood has not yet dramatically improved infrastructure of the neighborhood. Furthermore, the assertion of numerical strength and "demographic calculus" (see endnote 2) by neighborhood residents has yet to serve the interests of the entire community uniformly. Nevertheless, this ongoing struggle highlights the incremental—although uneven—entrenchment of the poor into the political landscape of the city on their own terms.

The three ethnographic vignettes discussed above offer ample evidence of the struggles for numerical citizenship that the poor residents of Delhi engage in to claim the right to the city by asserting their numerical strength. The legibility—the proof of existence of people that is tied to the process of decipherability of their proper documentation in a specific neighborhood—visibility, and gradual entrenchment of these poor urban residents lie at the heart of a variety of incremental struggles. The poor build and navigate a multitude of relationships and social divisions and forge political connections in their claims-making endeavors. In the course of this book, I offer other ethnographic vignettes to illustrate my theoretical analyses and to support my empirical arguments, including *rann-nitis* such as the mediated politics of intermediaries; the countertactics of enumeration among residents; a range of legal struggles; and myriad resistance tactics. Thus, although recent scholarship on Delhi has addressed the processes of dispossession,[8] my primary focus is on the political agency of the poor themselves.

CALCULATIVE STATE GOVERNMENTALITY
AND NUMERICAL CITIZENSHIP

The political economy of urban planning reflects particular historical conjunctures (see also Chari and Gidwani 2005; Hall and Massey 2010) and expresses particular kinds of "calculative rationality." Simply put, the agencies of the state enumerate, collect statistics, and categorize populations in order to extend welfare to the poor who are deemed "eligible." Each conjuncture produces a set of state rationalities and practices that define, enumerate, and categorize the urban poor in ways that underpin how the residents are deemed eligible and legible for citizenship. I discuss the details of these emerging calculative rationalities with respect to the changing political economy of urban planning in Chapter 1. Spatial surveillance, restructuring projects, demolitions of *jhuggi* neighborhoods, the resettlement of eligible poor, and the provision of infrastructure and amenities are entwined with these calculative rationalities of the state.

The processes of enumerating residents, compiling statistics on citizens, and bureaucratically documenting settlements reflect the operation of power at multiple levels in modern liberal settings, as many scholars have argued (Appadurai 1996; Cohn 1987; Foucault 1991; Hacking 1990; Rose 1999; Stoler 1995).[9] In general terms, the technologies of modern government lead to the unequal distribution of material resources and cultural life outcomes and produce forms of psychic and material subjugation (Cohn and Dirks 1988; Stoler 1995),[10] creating conditions for structural violence and social suffering (Farmer 2003; Gupta 2012; Kleinman, Das, and Lock 1997). Calculative state practices depoliticize political decisions insofar as they offer technical solutions to complex social and cultural problems (see also S. Benjamin and Raman 2001; Rose 1999: 198).[11] In exercising its own mode of governance, the state has offered resettlement, welfare services, and basic amenities to what it considers to be members of "eligible" populations in ways that simultaneously disenfranchise and ameliorate the conditions of the poor residents in the city.

In a recent work, Stephen Legg has systematically explored the effects of "practices, modalities and projects" of the calculative colonial state on the colonized populations in Delhi (Legg 2007: 20). Legg deploys a rigorous analysis inspired by Michel Foucault to evaluate the utilitarian rationalities that underpin improvement, management, and regulation of such populations. Although he does not provide an analysis of how the colonized have encountered state practices, Legg's analysis nevertheless challenges the assumption that colonial subjects are passive by exposing how the colonial administration is not only powerful but also in a state of "flux and indeterminism"[12] (Legg 2007: 211). By contrast, my focus is primarily on the consciousness and agency of the poor in their tactics against state calculations.

In another approach to these issues, Asher Ghertner (2015) argues that the aesthetic norms and visual codes enshrined in planning and judicial regimes—as opposed to calculative governmentality—have shaped urban space and political processes in contemporary Delhi. According to Ghertner, the logics of calculative rationality enshrined in surveys and maps are being replaced by the logics of aesthetic rationality. Seen through this lens, the *jhuggi* demolitions become possible because the *jhuggis* appear to be neither formal nor aesthetically pleasing. Ghertner provides illuminating evidence of how aesthetic norms, "nuisance talk," and the appropriation of the aesthetic sensibilities by the poor who have no citizenship rights shape the space of Delhi. His sophisticated account of state governmentality examines how the poor appropriate codes and standards in order to participate within the dominant urban aesthetic. In contrast, I argue that the calculative rationality of the state continues to shape the lives and politics of the poor, especially as these practices are embodied in planning measures and the judiciary arm of the state. This approach helps us to understand how marginalized residents encounter calculative governmental systems and politically mobilize on their own behalf. The technologies of statecraft produce unanticipated effects that allow for a myriad of negotiations by the marginalized residents of Delhi. In responding to state calculations, the poor engage in various struggles to build settlements, obtain voting rights, establish rudimentary infrastructure, procure subsidized food and household items, access basic amenities, and secure their livelihood. In this regard, Solomon Benjamin's conceptualization of "porous bureaucracy" is instructive in foregrounding how the poor negotiate with a seemingly non-transparent, complex, and local bureaucratic and political arrangement in their pursuit to access a range of entitlements (discussed in S. Benjamin and Raman 2001). Like Benjamin and Raman, I pay attention to the vital, messy, and deeply politicized local democratic practices (see also Sundaram 2010) to analyze the dense and entangled *rann-nitis* of the poor in obtaining citizenship rights. In this respect, and in line with what Emma Tarlo (2003) has shown, I contest the idea that the poor are passive victims of calculative governmentality; instead, I argue that the poor systematically contest the arbitrary and exclusionary processes of state calculations through an extraordinary array of *rann-nitis*.

In analyzing the practices of marginalized residents and governmental systems, post-colonial scholars highlight the peculiar nature of democracy and modernity in India (Chakrabarty 2000; Chatterjee 2004; Kaviraj 2005).[13] In his influential body of work, Partha Chatterjee argues that, in addition to considering the repressive functions of the state, one also has to examine how populations become "subjects of power" through subtle processes in which they are drawn into various government policies (Chatterjee 2008a: 93).[14] He theorizes that the features and dynamics of "civil society" and "political society" result from the establishment of modern governmental systems (Chatterjee 2004). Although in principle civil society is the domain of equal rights and citizenship, in reality "most of the inhabitants of India are only tenuously, and even then ambiguously and contextually, rights-bearing citizens in the sense imagined by the constitution" (Chatterjee 2004: 38). Hence, Chatterjee introduces his concept of political society to capture the terrain of politics where the government has a moral responsibility to take care of its poorer members according to the terms of political expediency. Political society, then, is the domain of populations which resort to various illegal and paralegal activities for their sustenance. He develops a further analytical distinction between "populations" and "citizens" by arguing that citizens share in the sovereignty of the state, while populations are merely enumerable categories subjected to the governmentality of the state (Chatterjee 2004: 40).

Chatterjee has provided influential and innovative conceptual methods for understanding the hegemonic and bourgeois parameters of the state in which dominant classes secure the consent and submission of subordinate (or subaltern) classes as well as the locational disadvantages and improvisational practices of the poor.[15] Nevertheless, the binaries between state and society, legality and illegality, "civil society" and "political society" explicitly or implicitly articulated in these theories remain largely schematic (Baviskar and Sundar 2008; Datta 2016; Fernandes 2006; Lemanski and Lama-Rewal 2013; N. Menon 2010; Routray 2014). That said, post-colonial concepts such as "political society" should be considered primarily for their heuristic value in situating the political activities of urban poor people within larger structures of power, including contemporary advanced capitalism; structures of class, caste, community, and gender; the hegemony of party politics; and neighborhood dynamics (Routray 2014: 2296). State policies and practices may replicate historicist assumptions about how subaltern groups must be educated in order to participate as fully fledged citizens (Chakrabarty 2000: 10). By contrast, a focus on local practices allows for a more nuanced understanding of the features and processes that define the developmental state in the Global South.

My empirical insights concerning everyday political practices and citizenship struggles do not advance a normative theory of citizenship. Instead, I consider how the practices of the poor challenge such a universal theory of citizenship. This challenge is especially pronounced when the locational disadvantages of the poor in various settings call for empirically grounded theorizations. Although I draw on the work of Partha Chatterjee in this respect, I go beyond the binary of "population" and "citizen" to explore how the poor interact with both the planning and judiciary bodies by claiming citizenship rights. In this light, I argue against fetishizing the state as the dispenser of normative rights as conceptualized in liberal political theory. Instead, I contend that the state is neither the fountain of the "rule of law" and social justice nor an unaccountable entity from the perspective of the poor. To be sure, the nature and character of the Indian state has evolved over time and often responds to the improvisations in different historical settings, as suggested by Kaviraj (2005). The perception that the "rule of law" may not be justified informs the moral rhetoric used to protect the poor as a matter of political expediency, even as aspects of the law are also marshaled to claim citizenship rights. Rather than the application of a normative set of rules and rights, I observe a shifting conception of rights and social justice with respect to the governmentality of the state. In particular, I assess post-colonial concepts for their empirical relevance. In the vein of I. Roy (2018), I show the deep entanglements between the improvisational tactics and the systematic negotiations with various state, political, and dominant actors in both informal and formal avenues on the part of the poor.

In this respect, the improvisational tactics deployed by the poor are addressed through a relational and processual approach (see also Bourdieu 1986; Bourdieu 1998: 4; de Certeau 1984: xi; Massey 2005: 10; A. Roy 2003: 78). Rather than looking at the supposed intrinsic properties of social groups in a determinate social space (Bourdieu 1998: 4), I demonstrate that scholars must understand the ensemble of social relations, such as non-institutional and institutional arrangements in Delhi, in order to fully understand the politics of the poor. I examine how the agency and political consciousness of the urban poor help them claim citizenship entitlements. As I show throughout this book, the struggles of claiming citizenship entitlements are historically contingent and contextual. The right to be counted remains a pivotal aspect of what has been called "subaltern urbanism,"[16] whereby the processes of improvisation and the everyday negotiations with law and politics are executed by the poor in Delhi. Numerical citizenship is a mode of "insurgent citizenship" that emerges through struggles to advance occupation of land, demand a multitude of rights, and extend solidarity (Holston 2008). However, unlike the context of Brazil in Holston's analysis, the poor in Delhi do not demand citizenship rights as taxpayers, consumers, and property owners (Holston 2008: 260). Instead, the poor in Delhi demand citizenship entitlements by foregrounding their numerical strength and community solidarity and by resorting to a multitude of non-institutional and institutional *rann-nitis* in their encounter with the state.

By drawing our attention to both the institutional and non-institutional activities of the poor, the concept of numerical citizenship both builds on and departs from the works of other scholars and their concepts, including "political society," "occupancy urbanism," and "the quiet encroachment of the ordinary." Through his concept of "occupancy urbanism," S. Benjamin (2008) demonstrates how the local and territorial practices of the poor subvert planning regimes, challenge elite attitudes, and undermine processes of global capital accumulation. Like the concept of occupancy urbanism, the framework of numerical citizenship draws on a bottom-up understanding of the expediency of local political and bureaucratic structures. However, it does not share the optimism of occupancy urbanism in contesting capital, non-governmental organizations (NGOs), and state power. The power of capital and state often circumscribes the space of occupancy urbanism (Weinstein 2017: 525). Furthermore, numerical citizenship struggles often engage the judiciary and well-meaning activists in more ambiguous ways. As I show, the poor develop their own *rann-nitis* in their negotiations with the judiciary and middle-class activists. Often, the members of the most marginalized communities are forced out of political negotiations as a result of the machinations of the *rann-nitis*. However, the struggles are articulated both as moral injunctions to care for the poor within the parameters of "political society" (Chatterjee 2004) and as constitutional obligations on the part of the state. Similarly, Bayat (1997) analyzes "the quiet encroachment of the ordinary," particularly with respect to housing and livelihood options in the Middle East, which he defines as the "silent, patient, protracted, and pervasive advancement of ordinary people on the propertied and powerful in order to survive hardships and better their lives" (57; see also Bayat 2010: 14–15). My focus is more on collective struggles that engage institutional and non-institutional resources in discreet as well as visible ways in the post-colonial democracy of India, in contrast to what have been called "social nonmovements" as represented in "the collective actions of noncollective actors" in a discreet manner under authoritarian regimes of the Middle East (Bayat 2010: 14). Most importantly, I offer a nuanced understanding of the agency of the poor by examining numerous *rann-nitis* that subvert or partake in the quotidian practices of the state.

THE *RANN-NITIS* OF NUMERICAL CITIZENSHIP

Drawing on numerous ethnographic observations, I illustrate and analyze a range of *rann-nitis* that the poor deploy to negotiate with established technologies of the state in the city (see de Certeau 1984; Kaviraj 1997).[17] The *rann-nitis* are complex and labyrinthine mazes of tactics and counter-tactics. If statecraft is marked by absurd, exclusionary, and arbitrary bureaucratic procedures, the poor then operate to ensure that they are indeed counted to stake claims to a panoply of citizenship entitlements. While the politics of numbers, or the assertion of numerical strength or "vote-bank politics" (Auerbach 2020; S. Benjamin 2000; S. Benjamin 2008; S. Benjamin and Raman 2001; Bjorkman 2014b) is the precondition for exercising political agency on the part of the poor, I emphasize that the numerical citizenship struggles spearhead claims for recognition, visibility, and legibility.[18] In other words, residents consistently struggle to be identified, enlisted, and counted in their quest for citizenship entitlements.

Demographic calculus is a significant *rann-niti*, but it does not exhaust the concept of numerical citizenship. I am not just trying to establish a relationship between arithmetic calculus and political outcomes in low-income neighborhoods in cities in India. I am also not arguing that if the neighborhood has a specific number of people and dense party networks, then it will be more successful in gaining recognition or obtaining basic amenities, especially when compared with another neighborhood with fewer people and sparse networks of party workers (cf. Auerbach 2020). Along with the politics of numbers and stronger party networks, other contingent and contextual factors play a salient role in shaping the struggles of numerical citizenship. Furthermore, the imperatives of neo-liberal restructuring, judicial activism, and political regimes at particular historical conjunctures shape claims-making and redistributive politics on the part of the urban poor in specific neighborhoods in the city.

Nevertheless, my arguments (which draw on but also depart from the studies discussed here) resonate with the political dynamics in cities in India as well as in other megacities in the Global South. As the poor experience social suffering, humiliation, and indignities due to exclusionary planning and bureaucratic regimes, they foreground their right to be counted through a myriad of ingenious, improvisational, and dense *rannnitis* to prove numerical presence in cities across the globe. In this regard, I emphasize how certain theoretical issues have direct relevance to the question of political agency in other contexts, in particular, the mechanics of locality building and mediated tactics (against state surveillance); the counter-tactics of enumeration; legal struggles (which may result in reclassification and recategorization); and the performance of citizenship (including spectacles and ceremonies).

Rather than keeping the "state at arm's length" (Scott 2009: x), the poor attempt to embed their citizenship struggles within various structures of the state. To be state recognized, a *jhuggi jhopri* settlement needs to include at least fifty households to begin with.[19] In building their numerical strength, the poor engage with the vagaries of the police and municipal authorities initially and then steadily enter into the field of electoral politics to advance citizenship claims. Displaying numerical strength remains an important aspect of mediations in the field of vote-bank politics. In this regard, the poor struggle to be listed on the electoral rolls to be part of political processes. Demographic calculus does not merely imply that the additive force of atomized individuals—who assert their numerical strength during elections, demonstrations, and events—determines political outcomes. Rather, I show how the politics of numbers converts the passive processes of state calculations into active processes of locality building. Thus, along with demographic calculus, I show how numerical citizenship struggles draw on the processes of forging kinship and collective solidarity. In this regard, my focus is on the temporal dimensions of citizenship struggles by highlighting the transformations in state calculations and political regimes. In response to the shifting nature of the roles of multiple interlocutors at different conjunctures, I examine the permutations and combinations of the *rann-nitis* of the poor.

It is pivotal to map a range of counter-tactics of enumeration across cities in India and the Global South to understand how these *rann-nitis* foreground democratic and citizenship struggles across various contexts. In asserting numerical strength, the struggle for citizenship is premised on the documentation of a population's numerical presence in the city. The poor become eligible for a panoply of citizenship rights in the city only upon the production of the proof of their presence from a particular date (Bjorkman 2014a; Routray 2014). The reiterative acts of naming and fixing identities (Hansen 2005b: 2) define state practices with respect to welfare provisions. The poor deploy ingenious strategies to obtain "proof documents" and contest arbitrary methods of classification that divide potential beneficiaries as eligible or ineligible. In this regard, I have listed a range of documentary and inscriptive *rann-nitis* but focus especially on the processes of authentication and counterfeiting, which contest numerical calculations of eligibility, as well as processes of self-enumeration, which challenge the fraught processes of state enumerations. I have also shown how mnemonic and auto-archiving *rann-nitis* are deployed to recall the past sequence of events to prove legitimate residency in particular neighborhoods, which play a significant role in shaping the struggle to be counted.

To be legible and counted, there is also a need to constantly challenge the processes of state mapping, classification, and categorization. The state enunciation of categories like "transit," "temporary," and "illegal" indicate the poor's lack of numerical entrenchment in the city. I show

how the *rann-nitis* of the poor draw on legal struggles to undermine state classifications and categorizations through the efforts at renaming, auto-archiving, un-mapping, and counterclaims in courtrooms and neighborhoods. The poor contest legal classification through mundane struggles in addition to performative and spectacular demonstrations in front of government offices, street corners, neighborhoods, and public spaces. In these demonstrations, which are simultaneously peaceful and militant, as I discuss in Chapter 6, the poor make use of their affective ties to manufacture specific cultural idioms of protest. Such performances subvert the imposed categories and subjectivities of illegality and ineligibility and draw on a repertoire of forms of protests (Tilly 2008). As I show throughout this book, numerical citizenship struggles constitute a performative politics that engages various idioms of speech acts and public spectacles (Bjorkman 2015; Guha 1999; Hansen 2005b: 232; Holston 2008; Postero 2017) to demand recognition, legibility, and entitlements.

Numerical citizenship struggles draw on the commissions and omissions of different state agencies. Ethnographies of the everyday state in India have analyzed the routinized presence of state power and how the poor implicate themselves with the activities of state institutions (Fuller and Harriss 2009: 25; Gupta 2012; Hansen 2005b; Mathur 2016; Tarlo 2003). They show how the poor imitate the state procedures and rituals in their quotidian struggles to realize substantive citizenship (V. Das and Poole 2004; Datta 2016; Gupta 2012; Hansen and Stepputat 2001; Hull 2012b; Srivastava 2012; Tarlo 2003). In contributing to this scholarship, this book documents citizenship struggles that span government offices, the judiciary, and non-governmental organizations. The contingent working of modern liberal institutions shows contradictory intentions and goals (see also Abrams 1988; Gupta 2012: 47; T. Mitchell 1991). Their response to the activities within the sphere of political society remains uneven (Routray 2014). Often, the practical implementation of state policies remains open-ended, indeterminate, and dynamic (see also Abrams 1988; Gupta 2012; T. Mitchell 1991). The various organs of the state adhere to different principles of governance at different points in time, thereby creating a space for participation, negotiation, and resistance to state policies in numerical citizenship struggles.

To sum it up, on the one hand, the lives of the poor are constrained by the numerical calculations of the state. On the other hand, the poor participate, negotiate, and resist the technologies of the state through a myriad of counter-calculations understood as citizenship struggles. These numerical citizenship struggles encompass a range of dialectics including the monitoring and surveillance of the poor versus locality building; the politics of enumeration versus the counter-tactics of enumeration; legal classification and categorization versus popular processes of renaming and reclassification; and projects of planning and legal erasure versus the lived politics of auto-archiving, mnemonic strategies, public performances, and speech acts during political and legal negotiations and resistance demonstrations. These struggles are shaped by forms of spatiality, social cleavages, and community networks, and by the involvement of activists and interlocutors. Thus, numerical citizenship struggles involve an ensemble of individual and collective contentions that draw on the expediency of political mediations, negotiations over documents and inscription, legal battles in the courts, and a variety of performances of popular resistance. These struggles encompass a universe of politics that is (counter) calculative, and they draw on shifting affective ties, interactions, and demonstrations among poor people, their allies, and their representatives. As I illustrate, the social relationships and affective ties among community members change over time. The dynamic spatial and temporal dimensions of these struggles shape the transformation of social relationships, political arrangements, and domestic bonds that emerge from demolitions and resettlements (see also V. Das 1996: 1510; Datta 2016: 9; Snell-Rood 2015). The political subjectivities of the poor are continuously reconfigured in a dialectical relationship with state policies, especially when welfare and resettlement policies are being enacted. Furthermore, the change in political regimes and legal discourses and practices underpin the modalities and outcomes of politics.

India is poised to undertake a humongous and historically unprecedented counting exercise to build a database of residents, called the National Population Register, and a database of citizens, called the National Register of Citizens. This book contributes to a timely analysis of how the state actually enumerates, documents, or counts its citizens. It illustrates the complex bureaucratic processes of legibility, counting, and error-prone documentation and the intricate *rann-nitis* the poor must deploy to be counted, especially to claim urban citizenship entitlements. I am not suggesting an ineluctable march of migrants to claim citizenship status, entitlements, and belonging in the city; rather, I show how the migrants continuously attempt to close the chasm between their statuses as residents and citizens through an extraordinary array of *rann-nitis*. The book underscores how the fraught counting exercise is poised to inaugurate unprecedented structural violence not only against immigrants and refugees but also against Indian citizens in the city.

A METHODOLOGICAL FRAMEWORK FOR STUDYING DISPLACED PEOPLE

The state technologies of planning and the politics of the poor sketched above draw our attention to spatial contexts, the social heterogeneity of the urban poor, and the role of activists and interlocutors in urban politics. I have argued that the fundamental aim of the poor is to incrementally lay claims to urban housing and other entitlements in the city. The gradual entrenchment of the poor in various social, political, and legal relations and arrangements potentially shifts their urban status from migrants to residents, and from *jhuggi* residents in a state-recognized *jhuggi jhopri* settlement to citizens with legal rights to a house. Throughout the course of this book, I show how this process is not homogeneous or unilinear but rather uneven and multi-level.

Spatiality and Politics

In order to understand the nature and scope of the politics of the poor, we must consider the intersection of urban space and politics. While the exigencies of urban life with respect to everyday structural and symbolic violence are often similar, the spatial settings both enable and constrain the political agency of the poor. The low-income neighborhoods in Delhi under study here are marked by distinct yet overlapping regimes of planning and by diverse social, political, and legal relations and arrangements. These distinctive but overlapping relations that underpin the nature of spatiality (cf. Lefebvre 1991; Massey 2005) precipitate specific political modalities and outcomes. While the identities of the urban poor are marked by economic, social, political, religious, and legal relations, to explore these intersecting dynamics I focus on how these identities arise out of their embeddedness in particular spaces.

The urban poor in contemporary Delhi can be heuristically mapped in terms of the social space they inhabit in a descending order from most to least precarious and vulnerable: the urban homeless; the urban poor in unrecognized, unidentified, and un-surveyed settlements; the urban poor renting rooms in villages, unauthorized colonies, designated slum areas, or planned colonies; the urban poor in government-recognized *jhuggi jhopri* settlements; the urban poor in old resettlement colonies and transit camps; and the urban poor in new resettlement colonies established since 1990 (see Chapter 2). The social spaces of the poor listed above are not survey categories or inert spaces that merely correspond with the mental and abstract faculties of planners and the physical realm of nature (Lefebvre 1991); rather, they are historically and socially produced. In other words, they are social spaces that provide settings embodying a range of social relations at particular historical conjunctures. My focus in this book is on a *jhuggi jhopri* settlement, a transit camp, and a resettlement colony, that is, those at the "top" of this list of precarious and vulnerable groups. These social spaces provide me with an analytic anchor to examine the processes of displacement and resettlement in the specific settings I have studied. After careful consideration, and in order to be as representative as possible, I chose these three neighborhoods with the aim of understanding the politics of claiming a "legal" home (along with basic amenities) on the part of the urban poor. The residents can claim a legal resettlement plot or flat upon displacement only if they reside in a recognized *jhuggi jhopri* neighborhood. Thus, while urban poverty is spatialized in different social spaces (pavements, unauthorized colonies, urban villages, etc.), it was only the poor in state-recognized *jhuggi jhopri* settlements who could claim resettlement housing in an old resettlement colony, a transit camp, and a new resettlement colony in the past. By looking at the incremental aspects of entrenchment, I examine how the temporal politics of citizenship relate to the processes of displacement and resettlement. As a consequence, this book shows the conjoint relationship of spatial and temporal practices of the poor in claiming citizenship entitlements. I discuss the nature, features, and instability of these state-designated categories and spaces in more detail in Chapter 2.

Gautam Nagar *jhuggi jhopri* settlement was incrementally established and developed in the 1970s (Chapters 2 and 3). A part of the settlement was demolished for the construction of an underpass in early 2009. Even after the demolitions, Gautam Nagar residents were not provided with resettlement plots because the government invoked the Right of Way clause of the Municipal Act. The residents have fought court cases in the High Court of Delhi and Supreme Court of India since 2009. Their legal fate has oscillated as judges delivered both favorable and unfavorable judgments between 2010 and 2017. In February 2010, the residents received a favorable decision from the High Court of Delhi, only to have government officials file a review petition, which was later dismissed by the High Court in January 2011. Subsequently, the residents filed a contempt petition in 2013 for the delay in resettling the residents. However, in a twist of fate, the petition was dismissed by the High Court in December 2014. Following the unfavorable verdict, the residents filed a Special Leave Application in the Supreme Court of India in early 2015. Ultimately, the favorable verdict of the Supreme Court was delivered on December 12, 2017, but only after the Delhi Urban Improvement Shelter Board (DUSIB) decided to resettle the residents on August 22, 2017, representing a complete reversal of its earlier decision.

Approximately 300 residents who were considered to have "encroached" on a road were displaced from Gautam Nagar in early 2009. Although I also conversed with non-displaced residents and intermediaries, my research primarily focused on the displaced residents of the area. After displacement, the residents rented *jhuggis* in Gautam Nagar, lived in makeshift huts beside the dug-up road, or rented houses in nearby areas. Most of the displaced people who moved away visited the area for work, social contact, and resettlement-related struggles almost daily. My analysis therefore focuses on how residents have gained recognition from the local state in order to receive infrastructure, services, and basic amenities through their struggles against displacement and to receive resettlement plots or flats. The political and judicial struggles of the poor in Gautam Nagar bring to light how the commissions and omissions of the various agencies of the state become critical for the citizenship projects of the poor. The residents continue to be actively engaged in a struggle to prove their resettlement eligibility by producing proof documents.

The general struggles to prove residence and recognition are similar in informal settlements given their precarious legal status across various contexts. Along with the politics of numbers, the claims for resettlement and basic services are predicated on documentary and inscriptive tactics of proving existence in particular neighborhoods (along with the other tactics that I outline in the book). Although an ethnographic study in another state-recognized *jhuggi jhopri* settlement would have allowed us to understand its contextual specificity, the findings are likely to be similar between another state-recognized *jhuggi jhopri* settlement and Gautam Nagar *jhuggi jhopri* settlement. An ethnographic study in an existing unrecognized settlement could have yielded further specific insights. But my general argument about the process of the establishment of a *jhuggi jhopri* settlement would still hold, as I also analyze the pre-recognition history of Gautam Nagar. The struggle is primarily aimed at occupying and distributing land parcels, fighting antagonistic host populations, and dealing with the vagaries of police and municipal authorities (see Chapter 3 for an analysis of these issues).

The state recognizes a *jhuggi jhopri* once it has fifty households. However, other factors—the location of a settlement, political patronage in the initial years (for instance, an MLA who instructs the police officials to leave the fledgling settlement alone), the urgency of cleaning up city spaces at different conjunctures on the part of various state agencies—shape the existence or demolition of the settlement. Most importantly, the collective struggles to navigate the bureaucratic and municipal authorities explain why a settlement will manage to grow precariously and gain recognition at some point. As a part of Gautam Nagar is still undemolished, this case also provides an opportunity to understand the politics of claiming basic services by residents still living in a *jhuggi jhopri* settlement. And, of course, the case offers insights into post-demolition hardships and the struggles to claim resettlement. Thus, the struggles of the poor to build a locality, resist demolition, claim resettlement, and obtain basic amenities in Gautam Nagar resonate with other cases elsewhere.

The case of the Sitapuri transit camp demonstrates how the poor are pitted against the middle classes. Transit camp residents were displaced in 1984–85 from *jhuggi* settlements on "prime land" that was designated as urgently required for various projects in the city. Sitapuri has two blocks, named simply Pocket A and Pocket B. The land use for Pocket A is "recreational" and Pocket B is partly "recreational" and partly "residential." The Sitapuri transit camp adjoins the Lakshmi colony, a planned colony of middle-class residents. The Resident Welfare Association (RWA) of Lakshmi colony petitioned the High Court of Delhi to demolish Sitapuri in 2003, a legal battle discussed in Chapter 5. However, the case was dismissed in 2010. While the fate of the neighborhood remains uncertain, the residents have steadily advanced their claims to remain and obtain basic amenities in the same neighborhood against the abstract imagination of planners and judges. This case exemplifies the widespread phenomenon of middle-class RWAs making use of the judiciary to initiate the demolitions of *jhuggi* and low-income settlements across Delhi and beyond in recent years. Class-based antagonisms (as epitomized in court battles) between low-income neighborhoods and middle-class neighborhoods could be analyzed by considering any other type of low-income settlement. But I achieved two objectives by choosing the case of Sitapuri transit camp: (1) map the temporal struggles to access basic amenities over the decades under the norms of the earlier resettlement policy and (2) examine the dynamics of class-based struggles between the poor and middle-class residents.

To elaborate on these two points, transit camps are fewer in number compared to old resettlement colonies. However, transit camps that do not face any immediate threat of demolition can be regarded as old resettlement colonies. In fact, both the residents and state officials designate transit camps and resettlement colonies interchangeably according to their own convenience. (The state has also designated Azad resettlement colony as a transit camp, thus alerting us to the uncertainty of this massive neighborhood in the future.) Thus, the case of Sitapuri transit camp illuminates how the poor staked their claims and availed themselves of basic amenities since they were resettled in the 1980s prior to the inauguration of the new resettlement policy and the establishment of new resettlement colonies. It also allows us to understand the changes in state calculations with respect to the housing of the poor over the last decades, especially if we compare old resettlement colonies, transit camps, and new resettlement colonies. Furthermore, this case illustrates how a middle-class RWA may wage a court battle against a low-income neighborhood. The case provides insights into the vexatious relationships and spatial practices of the poor and middle-class residents living in the adjoining areas. Here my aim is to show how the lived space of the transit camp is a joint product of spatial practices of the poor, the middle class, and the planners. Like the Gautam Nagar case, this case also underlines the intersection of planning and legal relations, representations, and arrangements that shape particular modalities of politics.

Finally, I provide an illustration of the production of social space through coping strategies and struggles in Azad resettlement colony. Through this case, I analyze the stakes of the poor in claiming housing and basic amenities in new resettlement colonies, especially in light of massive demolitions and the establishment of new resettlement colonies since the 1990s. Azad resettlement colony was established in 2000 to accommodate "eligible" poor people displaced from various parts of the city. Most of the residents had fought unsuccessful battles (including legal battles) against demolitions at their earlier places of residence. On a brighter note, the residents did succeed in procuring resettlement plots according to the resettlement policy. The case provides insight into the effects of impoverishment after displacement, and it raises questions about the lived practices of political struggles that the poor engage to start a new life in the city. The cases of Gautam Nagar *jhuggi jhopri* settlement, Sitapuri transit camp, and Azad resettlement colony underscore the dynamic process of public decision-making and the abstract imagination of planners that contribute to impoverishment in Delhi (see Baxi 1988: vi). However, the case of Azad resettlement colony also draws our attention to the coping mechanisms, the inventiveness, and the political tactics necessary in beginning a life in the abandoned spaces of the city through the assertion of a community's numerical strength. Although a unique case with its own specificity, Azad resettlement colony is also representative of the new resettlement colonies in Delhi.

These different kinds of social spaces reflect overlapping yet distinct planning, political, social, legal, and organizational arrangements. These arrangements mark specific patterns of displacement and generate unique kinds of struggles. Furthermore, the cases discussed reemphasize the point that the transition from being a migrant to being a resident in a legal resettlement/transit neighborhood in Delhi is not a unilinear and homogeneous process. The complexity of different social spaces is mind-boggling, and each specific social space (as listed in Chapter 2) will tell us something uniquely interesting. In choosing not to do ethnographic work in other social spaces, I was able to employ a longer temporal frame to understand the complexity of the issues in three sites rather than a shorter temporal frame to understand more sites. At the same time, the general theoretical arguments that I make still hold for informal settlements to the extent that the state actors use similar tactics of surveillance and enumeration across Delhi, elsewhere in India, and in the cities of the Global South. In this respect, my arguments may provide a broader comparative framework for understanding a myriad of *rann-nitis* of claims-making by poor communities.

Social Cleavages and Political Tensions

Before considering the logic and cultural idioms that inform the political practices of poor people in the city, we must scrutinize the category "urban poor" itself. Delhi's poor are differentiated along the lines of caste, income, gender, and regional origin. These divisions among communities must be taken into account in order to fully understand the struggles surrounding their citizenship and thus their right to claim space in the city (Datta 2016; Doshi 2013; A. Roy 2003). A majority of the urban poor, especially those living in *jhuggi jhopri* settlements, belong to marginalized castes and communities (Datta 2016: 14). The diverse experiences and identities of these impoverished communities give rise to distinct neighborhood-specific political struggles. Nandini Gooptu's (2001) methodological argument for the category "urban poor" instead of "working classes" or "labor" is useful. Gooptu avoids the latter categories as they connote "organized, formal sector industrial workers," while the term "urban poor" avoids suggesting "a distinct social class arising from a particular set of production relations" with a singular identity arising from "shared interests and plight." Gooptu deploys the term "urban poor" to "encompass various occupational groups and to highlight the diversity and plurality of their employment relations and working conditions" (Gooptu 2001: 3). Thus, the category "urban poor" must be qualified since it intentionally implies specific vulnerabilities associated with varying social locations, even among urban poor populations themselves.

The vulnerability of the urban poor originates from economic relations among different occupational groups as well as non-economic relations among groups identified by caste and religious affiliations (Breman 2004; Gooptu 2001: 2–3; Harriss 1986; Saberwal 1977: 15). However, the precarious and vulnerable situation of the urban poor in contemporary Delhi is also related to the legal definition of the neighborhoods where they reside, to whether one possesses proof documents for resettlement and welfare eligibility, and to the nature of patronage structures. Thus, the most vulnerable poor in the neighborhoods I studied are oppressed castes and Muslim women engaged in casual work without permanent jobs living in *jhuggi jhopri* settlements without requisite proof documents, and who therefore lack eligibility for future resettlement. Their vulnerability is compounded if a rival politician wins the election and shows lukewarm interest in extending basic amenities to members of the neighborhood.[20]

Most poor residents in the three settlements earned between 2,000 and 10,000 Indian rupees per month in 2010 (approximately US$45–$220).[21] In 2017, the earnings ranged from 5,300 to 18,000 rupees (approximately $80–$275). During my research between 2009 and 2011, the lowest daily wage was between 70 (for women) and 100 (for men) rupees (approximately $1.50–$2.20). The corresponding figures were 170 and 300 in 2017 (approximately $2.60–$4.60). The income among the poorest also varied when both parents and their children contributed to the family incomes. Extensive unemployment was also a factor. The highest-paid residents among the poor were the intermediaries, petty contractors, and traders who typically earned between 10,000 and 50,000 rupees per month in 2010 (approximately $222–$1,111) and between 20,000 and 70,000 rupees in 2017 (approximately $308–$1,077). Most often they lived outside the neighborhoods but possessed *jhuggis* or houses and actively participated in neighborhood politics.

The population of Gautam Nagar is predominantly composed of casual workers, daily wage laborers, contract factory workers, and construction workers. This is the most vulnerable population in the city, apart from the homeless and destitute groups, which include street performers, petty workers, and abandoned residents who are often physically and mentally challenged. The only housing option for the latter is in one of the night shelter facilities, which remain chronically insufficient in size during inclement weather. The urban poor residing in Gautam Nagar have managed to gain access to some form of shelter. Thus, the primary aim of their struggle for survival following the demolition of their neighborhood in 2009 is to delay further demolitions, obtain basic services, and procure resettlement plots or flats. Generally speaking, inequalities and political mobilizations in *jhuggi jhopri* neighborhoods like Gautam Nagar are defined by the ability to procure proof documents, appropriate scarce resources, acquire or exchange suitable plots or flats upon resettlement, build additional structures, and carry out local business activities. In this respect, the intermediaries and other residents with political and social connections often position themselves favorably in accessing rudimentary infrastructure and basic amenities in the city, as I elaborate in Chapter 3.

While income differences exist among the urban poor living in informal settlements prior to demolitions and relocation, other factors become more pronounced over time when residents are relocated to "transit camps" or "resettlement colonies." Without access to work nearby, many poor people are forced to sell their resettlement or transit camp plots to cover living expenses and emergency medical care, as discussed in Chapters 2 and 5. As resettled neighborhoods become integrated as a result of adjacent land acquisition and city expansion, families with relatively higher income move into these neighborhoods. New resettlement neighborhoods like the Azad resettlement colony have become affordable places for small contractors, lower-rung government workers, and service providers in private firms. These new entrants to the neighborhoods must coexist with the original allottees, who are often initially looked down upon by newcomers. Inequalities of income in transit camps and resettlement colonies become more pronounced over time, shaping the politics of accessing resources and infrastructure. The politics of the poor are likewise shaped by the ideological and political affiliations, the status of allottees or purchasers of houses in the transit camps and resettlement colonies, and the location of houses in the neighborhood.

There is a constant process of upward and downward mobility in these low-income neighborhoods. While employment in the new economy, relative job security in factories, and successful entrepreneurship may contribute to upward mobility, such advances are often thwarted by retrenchment, factory closures, losses incurred in businesses as a result of lack of political patronage, precarious relocation upon demolition, and the lack of proximal work resulting from urban-restructuring policies. The majority of residents in these neighborhoods barely make a living from daily wage labor, even after living there for fifteen to twenty years. Most of the residents navigate both the formal and informal sectors of work in the city (Breman 1996; Gooptu 2001; Holmstrom 1984). Survival in Delhi demands flexibility, adaptability, and the ability to cope with unexpected exigencies and the constant threat of downward mobility. Even in this context, there are rare cases of upward mobility. Upward mobility is experienced most often by transport operators, scrap dealers, and construction-related contractors. Most often these residents start off as daily wage laborers in scrap-dealing and construction sites, or as drivers for transport operators. However, significant upward mobility may be afforded by social and political connections, funds from trusting moneylenders, risk taking, and entrepreneurial skills. The residents who acquire significant economic capital, who cultivate social and political connections, or who create dependencies to control and manage other residents are often the ones who manage to shape specific political outcomes at the individual and community levels in the neighborhood.

Differences along caste, community, and gender lines precipitate distinct modes of political negotiations in each of these sites. For example, neighborhood residents refer to Muslims using global and local terms that are often Islamophobic. These characterizations include Muslims' perceived uncontrollable fertility; predisposition for fighting, terrorism, and slaughter (referring to the profession of meat cutting); how they celebrate Pakistan's wins over India in cricket matches; how the Hindus feel insecure in predominantly Muslim areas like Batla House, Turkman Gate, Okhla Mandi, Jamia Nagar, and Seelampur; and the daily disruption caused by offering *namaz* (the ritual prayer of Muslims) over loudspeakers. Islamophobia distorts their perceptions of the numerical strength (or numerical insignificance) of Muslims in these neighborhoods and contributes to the civic and political marginalization that Muslims face in the city. In neighborhoods like the Azad resettlement colony, which has a numerically significant Muslim population, residents often articulate their citizenship struggles in redistributive terms as well as along identity lines, as discussed in Chapter 6.

The neighborhoods are also characterized by caste-specific *gallis* (lanes or alleyways) such as the *Kabadda* (scrap) camp in Gautam Nagar, where Dalits[22] engage in "scavenging" and recycling work. Residents prefer intermediaries from their own caste, although they attest that the *gallis* are not as homogeneous as they once were. A sense of superiority exists among many upper-caste residents who secretly divulge details about the caste identities of other residents. As a resident in Gautam Nagar expressed his caste bias, "People do a lot of *dikhawa* [showing off]. They are of lower caste, but they would use surnames like *Singh* to hide their own identity." The rise of the Bahujan Samaj Party in local municipal elections has also challenged the hegemony of upper-caste interests. One resident remarked that "*bhangi ka raaj hai*" (the *bhangis* [Dalits engaged in scavenging work] rule). Similarly, alarming casteist comments are also widespread, such as when residents defend the pride of Rajput (the dominant military caste of northern India) or Brahmin (the dominant priestly Hindu caste), mock the "lowly" occupations of Dalits, or recall disproportionate punishment and violence by upper-caste police officers working in the neighborhoods.

Bhed-bhav (discrimination), antagonisms, and fighting can also be observed along caste and community lines. Petty quarrels over the distribution of water and electricity, garbage disposal, and fights among children often end in name-calling or deepening suspicions and hatred for

other castes, religions, or regions. It is not uncommon to flaunt one's caste
identity and the propriety of voting for a party that supports a particular community (mostly the Bahujan Samaj Party or the Bharatiya Janata
Party). The real and imaginary sense of historical injustice experienced by
members of each community adds a further layer of mistrust among residents that often compounds their suspicion of neighbors, activists, and
state officials.

Despite the survival of caste prejudices and discrimination, evidence
of a crumbling caste hegemony exists in how the leaders of the oppressed
castes engage in political battles. As a resident of the dominant Rajput
caste in the Sitapuri transit camp remarked, "I would like to return back
to my village. I do not like it here. There is so much *gandh* [dirt] here.
Back in my village the *bhangis* will bow, take off their shoes and touch
my feet, and utter a respectful form of greeting from a distance. But here
they want to sit with you." This resident, whom the other residents refer
to as mad, is unhappy with the political agency exercised by oppressed
caste residents and feels helpless to the point of considering a return to
his village where his brethren reproduce familiar caste prejudices, exclusions, and violence.

Despite differences in caste, religion, and regional origin, there is a
palpable feeling of solidarity among residents concerning critical issues
affecting their shared locality. As one resident in the Sitapuri transit
camp noted, "Politicians, factory owners, or religious leaders may try to
divide us, but the reality is that we need to have *bhai-chara* [brotherhood]
to survive here. Unless we have *bhai-chara* we cannot exist and bargain for
our rights." Building *bhai-chara* often involves a display and performance
of strength and solidarity in the neighborhood, which also entails various
kinds of exclusions. Residents are thus aware of their marginality in the
larger urban economic and political landscape. The coexistence of various social groups necessitates solidarity and unity in mobilizing for basic
services. As Auyero (2000b: 70) in the Argentinean context has observed,
"Clientelist problem-solving involves constructing personalized ties, an
imaginary solidaristic community, and a protective and predictable network that buffers the harsh everyday reality of the slum." Residents build
community through compromise and relations of trust in order to deal

with the exigencies of life. Solidarity is required to confront the police; to get an electricity connection from a neighbor, especially if paying for a connection from the company is outside one's means; to reciprocate favors by standing in a queue for water; and for babysitting or lending money during times of emergency. As one resident in Gautam Nagar put it, "In *galli-mohalla* [lane-neighborhoods], the neighbors are more important than your own relatives." Despite the divisions that separate them, residents share a common identity that stems from living in the marginalized niches of the city. While in some cases the social divisions may produce favorable outcomes for certain groups or individuals in these neighborhoods, residents nevertheless consistently forge a common identity and assert their numerical strength in resisting displacement, claiming resettlement, or obtaining infrastructure and basic amenities in the city. However, the collective solidarity is often contingent, tenuous, and disrupted. The disruption of collective solidarity was evident after the Government of India passed the Citizenship Amendment Act in 2019 (discussed in the Conclusion), which in principle extends citizenship to persecuted Hindus in three neighboring countries but excludes non-Hindu persecuted minorities (both religious and non-religious) in neighboring countries and people of foreign origin, especially Bangladeshi Muslims residing in India. Furthermore, the plan to build an official National Register of Citizens (NRC) based on proper documentation and family legacy data (Birla, Jha, and Kumari 2020) has increased the suspicion and anxiety of poor Muslim residents in these neighborhoods.

The Urban Poor and the Activists

Ranajit Guha's seminal work calls for investigating the politics of subalterns on their own terms. He suggests that assuming subaltern politics are pre-political, spontaneous, or lacking consciousness is not only erroneous but also elitist (Guha 1999: 4–5). Like Guha, I analyze the politics of the urban poor on their own terms by illustrating highly coordinated, systematic, and politically conscious patterns of thought and action among individuals and groups in particular contexts. Of course, such thoughts and actions also reflect contradictions, ambiguities, and conflicts in various scenarios. The politics of the urban poor intersect with the interventions of activists, lawyers, and politicians in the city who often do not share their life experiences. Nevertheless, these alliances are celebrated despite being fraught and contested. The contribution of activists and interlocutors to their struggles is significant and entails complex and contradictory logics in contemporary Delhi. On the one hand, the political strategies of Delhi's urban poor are independent of outside activists and the well-meaning interventions of interlocutors. On the other hand, these strategies benefit from active mediation on the part of the activists. The poor actively seek certain interventions from "experts" and activists as a response to the structural difficulties they experience with the judiciary, the Delhi Development Authority, and other state bodies.

While many activist organizations and NGOs are working in these neighborhoods, three organizations have figured prominently: Lok Raj Sangathan, Delhi Shramik Sangathan, and Jan Chetna Manch. Lok Raj Sangathan is an organization run by human rights activists, trade union leaders, retired judges, and people with socialist leanings from various walks of life.[23] The organization has a local office near the Sitapuri transit camp. Local Lok Raj Sangathan activists organize the poor around a range of issues, including struggles to procure ration cards and voter IDs in Gautam Nagar and in the Azad resettlement colony. The organization played an important role in the road blockade demonstrations in Sitapuri (discussed in Chapter 6). The activists of Lok Raj Sangathan continued to organize and intervene energetically in everyday politics in Gautam Nagar, although their activities had diminished in Sitapuri by the time of my fieldwork in 2009–2011 and 2017. Delhi Shramik Sangathan, another important organization, is a federation working among the poor in Delhi.[24] The organization works in nearly one hundred low-income neighborhoods and holds cycle rallies to raise awareness about rights, policies, and legislation. During my fieldwork in 2009–2011, the organization facilitated a range of activities in Gautam Nagar especially related to the High Court case. However, in the course of my fieldwork in 2017, the organization had retreated from the neighborhood to a considerable degree. Finally, V. P. Singh, a former prime minister of India, established Jan Chetna Manch in the mid-1990s. The organization campaigned against *jhuggi* demolitions and industrial closures in Delhi. After the death of V.

P. Singh, Jan Chetna Manch became inactive, but there were periodic attempts to revive it during my fieldwork. The residents of Gautam Nagar, Sitapuri, and the Azad resettlement colony often recalled Jan Chetna Manch's active role with appreciation.

Three phrases used by residents were commonly associated with the work of well-meaning activists: *marg darshan* (path-showing or guidance), *chetna badhana* (consciousness raising), and *rann-nitis. Marg darshan* and *chetna badhana* may connote an element of condescension when understood in abstract terms in the sense that the poor receive guidance in a passive manner. Nevertheless, their usage in everyday contexts usually connotes a positive meaning, especially when the *marg darshan* and *chetna badhana* work of activists is solicited as part of the general *rann-niti.* Thus, it was only after losing hope in the politicians that Gautam Nagar residents reached out to the activists for *marg darshan* and a fresh *rann-niti.* Activists may often be understood to be an integral part of a particular *rann-niti.* However, *rann-niti* connotes an open-ended dialogical act and usually requires the appraisal of multiple possible routes for collective action, some of which may not require the activists or experts. Further, *rann-niti* connotes an act of evaluation based on one's own experiential knowledge. As a result, the advice components of *marg darshan* and *chetna badhana* are selectively adhered to on the basis of a community's own calculations and affective considerations, especially when members recognize the structural barriers or inadequate knowledge they encounter in appealing to state policies and in taking legal recourse.

In other words, not all the advice provided to residents as part of *marg darshan* and *chetna badhana* is considered useful, sometimes to the bewilderment of the activists. In Gautam Nagar, for example, suggestions by activists to avoid politicians (or what is regarded as vote-bank politics) and to wage independent struggles were carefully calibrated in order to appeal to skeptical residents. While *marg darshan* and *chetna badhana* constitute important components of political mobilization on a local level, the poor in Gautam Nagar and Sitapuri routinely reach out to politicians as part of a tactic of resistance or *rann-niti.* The efforts of activists are praised at times, but the failure of a particular *rann-niti* can also invite censure of those same activists. Further, certain groups of residents sometimes reach out to Dalit and Muslim activists or leaders who work primarily for these marginalized groups. Thus, while the course of political action may be coherently thought out, it may also present various ambiguities, contradictions, and conflicting feelings.

Thoughtful and coherent political action can also be illustrated with reference to the efforts of the poor at auto-archiving. Many residents I spoke to as part of my fieldwork showed me files of documents containing information and newspaper clippings about their neighborhoods, government policies concerning urban poverty, and pictures of themselves with activists and politicians during rallies. These residents had stored newspaper articles about their political engagements and performances, often spreading these files out for me to see, explaining the sequence of events, and identifying or evaluating the persons (mostly themselves) in the photographs that accompanied the news articles. This practice was most common among illiterate residents, which suggests that the poor archive their own stories despite their illiteracy (see also Auerbach 2018; Auerbach 2020; Bandyopadhyay 2011; Bandyopadhyay 2016). In fact, many times after they had told me stories, they asked me to read aloud certain portions of the articles and to examine the pictures to verify their accounts of the events. Auto-archiving thus creates a repertoire of potential collective action to pursue in the future as part of *rann-niti* while at the same time contesting the invisibility of the poor and consolidating their claims to citizenship in the city.

FINAL REMARKS ON CONDUCTING AN ETHNOGRAPHY
OF NUMERICAL CITIZENSHIP

Analyzed in the framework of numerical citizenship, the schemes and policies of the state underwrite the politics of planning and give rise to the politics of the poor. I have discussed some of the methodological and theoretical dimensions of my argument with respect to the general themes of spatiality and politics, social cleavages and politics, and the urban poor and the activists who form alliances with them. To conclude, I want to elaborate on my ethnographic approach to the study of planning, poverty, and politics. An exploration of numerical citizenship relies on a rigorous ethnographic approach that offers "thick descriptions" of the events and everyday realities of the poor, not just theoretical general-izations (Geertz 1973: 7). I record the layers of meanings, inferences, and implications of accounts by the urban poor of their own experiences of displacement, resettlement, and political engagements in particular social milieus. My ethnographic approach thus entails a "historically situated mode of understanding historically situated contexts" (Comaroff and Co-maroff 1992: 9) in particular by examining the calculative rationalities of the state in detail, the specific effects of recurring and emerging social inequalities in various contexts, and citizenship struggles at the intimate level of everyday and interpersonal experience. In understanding everyday experiences, I attempt to record those experiential and contextual realities with "empathy and mutuality" (Stacey 1988: 22) while at the same time documenting how the social relations and experiences of the poor are shaped by the contemporary history of urban restructuring and modes of political engagement (see Willis and Trondman 2000: 6).

More importantly, I examine how the poor "embody, mediate and enact the operations and results of unequal power" in their attempts to engage with political mediations, to document their legal struggles, and to stage performances of resistance (Willis and Trondman 2000: 10). Through sustained and ongoing ethnographic observations, I explore how affects and emotions mediate social and political relationships (Raf-fles 2002: 326) while remaining attentive to spatial politics over extended periods. In this regard, *The Right to Be Counted* shows how ethnographic sensitivity can be used as a tool to explore the richness of culture and pol-itics as well as the complexity of human agency (Ortner 1995; see also I. Roy 2018). My approach offers a middle ground that avoids the extremes of overly "abstract theoretical categories" and the "empirical fallacy" (Wil-lis and Trondman 2000: 12) in attempting to illuminate the local and larger significance of these struggles for numerical citizenship.

I carried out twenty-five months of field research—twenty-two months from November 2009 through August 2011 and three months from June to September 2017—in Gautam Nagar, the Sitapuri transit camp, and the Azad resettlement colony. In addition to my daily inter-actions with residents, I attended court proceedings, grievance-related meetings with councilors, and public events organized by the activists in these neighborhoods. My long-term involvement within these communities afforded me insights into the complex dynamics of numerical citizenship struggles spanning almost a decade. The temporal frame of my field research provided me with a critical vantage point for examining the processes of planning and the politics of the poor (see Cerwonka and Malkii 2007; V. Das 1996; Stoller 1989). To document the effects of displacement, the experience of social suffering, and the logic of political mobilization on the ground, my ethnographic research entailed interactions with approximately 140 residents across the three neighborhoods. My work involved ethnographic observations among twenty-five households in both Gautam Nagar and the Sitapuri transit camp, and in the Azad resettlement colony, I carried out ethnographic work among twenty households.

On average, I interacted with two members of each family through conversations, informal interviews, and discussions. While I met some residents repeatedly on an everyday basis over the course of my fieldwork, non-participant observations and informal discussions with many of my research collaborators were occasionally restricted to only two to three encounters. I did not live in any of these neighborhoods. Rather, I traveled to the neighborhoods by appointment. While I usually met residents in the morning before they left for work or in the evening after they came home, there were times when I visited in the afternoon. Mostly I sat in front of eateries, grocery shops, and teashops to discuss issues that concerned the residents. These were popular places where residents congregated, played cards, and conversed about common problems. In the winter, residents burned sundry materials to produce improvised fireplaces at various sites in the neighborhoods. At times I joined these gatherings to discuss issues regarding their displacement and the difficulties they had in accessing basic amenities.

My ethnographic work also involved visits to a range of offices, including the Food and Supply Department, Sub-divisional Magistrate's Office, Public Works Department, Delhi Urban Shelter Improvement Board, and Delhi Secretariat. In addition, I joined monthly meetings of grassroots organizations, events hosted by state bodies in the neighborhoods, political rallies, and a range of demonstrations and celebrations.

My firsthand observations at these events animate my empirical arguments in the chapters that follow. In addition to ethnographic research, I conducted interviews with twenty-four planners of various planning institutions, ten activists, and four representatives of Lakshmi colony's Resident Welfare Association (RWA). I spoke with planners, activists, and RWA representatives in English mostly, though we also switched to Hindi at times. In contrast, I always conversed in Hindi with the residents of the three neighborhoods. My activist friends introduced me to key residents from various groups and communities in the neighborhoods I chose to study, which are often divided along lines of caste, community, gender, regional origin, and political affiliation. I did not have survey records to analyze each demographic category, but I carefully designed my household study to be as representative as possible. My initial plan to follow the electoral rolls to identify residents proved too difficult once I realized the extent of under-enumeration in these neighborhoods and realized that this lack is itself an important topic of investigation. I selected households that reflected differences in terms of income, caste, community, political affiliation, and gender distribution in various streets and blocks of the neighborhoods.

I have drawn on a range of documents to analyze the politics of planning and the politics of the poor in Delhi:

a. *Delhi planning documents.* I draw on planning documents including Master Plans published by the Delhi Development Authority, a compilation of zonal plans in Delhi, and other reports published by the Government of India, the Planning Commission, and the National Capital Regional Planning Board. I have also taken recourse to Shah Commission reports to examine the planning process during the "Emergency" period.

b. *Archival documents concerning Sitapuri Transit Camp and Azad Resettlement Colony from the Delhi Development Authority, Vikas Sadan.* I have mostly used policy reports, letters, background information, minutes, handwritten notes, and quotes from various officials about the unfolding events regarding Sitapuri transit camp and Azad resettlement colony. Most of the information is repeated in multiple documents.

I have provided the document number, dates (where available), file name, and the name of the office where I found the document. Often the documents have handwritten notes and signatures from various officials on various dates. Some of the documents are excerpts of other documents (for instance, excerpts of court verdicts). Some documents are torn, and some others have not been paginated. The documents have been stored randomly without any order. Some documents do not have titles, as they are basically correspondence among various officials about Sitapuri transit camp and Azad resettlement colony. In the absence of a title, I have described the document's contents in parentheses in the endnotes. The notes and correspondence start randomly at times. Most documents have a number, which I refer to by the document number. The above description itself is an important point in analyzing the production of bureaucratic knowledge (a topic I do not take up in the book).

c. *Documents from activist organizations.* I have relied on newsletters, pamphlets, and a variety of letters collected from activist organizations, especially Jan Chetna Manch. Most of the documents at the Jan Chetna Manch office were previously part of the private collections of V. P. Singh, a former prime minister of India who started Jan Chetna Manch from his personal residence.

d. *Documents received from residents of the three neighborhoods.* I use information from letters and petitions to government offices and the Delhi Development Authority; Right to Information (RTI) applications and responses; proof documents; self-survey sheets; and court verdicts (mostly excerpts), all collected from poor residents of the three neighborhoods. The residents also provided me with pamphlets and newsletters from various activist organizations. I also draw on information from the websites of urban planning institutions, state bodies, and activist organizations.

Taking a cue from Ann Stoler, I use the documents as "sites of state ethnography." Thus, my documentary research does not merely entail the extractive collection of facts and data (Stoler 2002: 90). Rather, the documents provide an ethnographic perspective on the everyday functioning of state institutions and details on social relations in the neighborhoods. Through ethnographic and documentary research, I analyze the specificity of social life, everyday interactions, and power dynamics along the lines of class, caste, literacy, and gender relations. Thus, along with examining the effects of state power, I also investigate the embodiment of various kinds of capital in terms of the economic resources, cultural competences, social connections, and political power that shape each of these sites. I scrutinize the complexities of human agency in everyday life by illustrating the hopes, aspirations, contradictions, and ambiguities among individuals as well as collectives. I attempt to produce multiple perspectives that are coexistent and competing in particular contexts (Bourdieu 1999: 3). Following the advice of Bourdieu (2003: 281), I have tried to avoid perpetuating "pre-reflexive social and academic experiences of the social world" while carrying out research in these sites and writing up my findings. In this respect, in order to understand the complex logics of numerical citizenship struggles, I provide detailed and textured accounts of the poor, intermediaries, local leaders, middle-class residents, planners, politicians, bureaucrats, and activists in their negotiations with the technologies and practices of the state.

I provide a historical context for understanding the struggles for numerical citizenship among the poor in the first two chapters. In Chapter 1, by examining the political economy of Delhi, I explore shifts in the parameters of planning and technologies of the statecraft implemented through planning protocols. In Chapter 2, I investigate the effects of the structural violence of mass displacement and resettlement. Throughout the remainder of the book, I describe and analyze the political mobilizations of the poor. In Chapter 3, I examine the tactics and techniques of various kinds of intermediaries, who acquire a range of forms of capital in their political engagement on the terrain of numerical citizenship struggles. Chapter 4 develops a discussion of the documentary and inscriptive practices embedded in a range of counter-tactics of enumeration used by the poor in order to claim resettlement and food subsidies. In Chapter 5, I explain how the poor engage with the judiciary to explore how the law is lived, appropriated, encountered, and challenged by them in order to realize numerical citizenship. I show how the poor engage with the judiciary by contesting judicial classifications and by developing social relationships and alliances in order to maneuver legal outcomes in their favor. Finally, I delve into the cultural idioms and strategies of resistance among the residents of these neighborhoods by examining how they engage in a range of demonstrations. Throughout this book, I examine the double-edged idea of numerical citizenship in Delhi. On the one hand, the state addresses the poor through surveillance, enumeration, displacement, and welfare policies that entail residency requirements and "proof documents." On the other hand, the poor deploy numerous *rann-nitis* to realize substantive claims to citizenship and their right to the city.

Part I

THE POLITICS OF PLANNING

CHAPTER 1

THE POLITICAL ECONOMY OF
URBAN PLANNING, CALCULATIVE
GOVERNMENTALITY, AND THE URBAN POOR

THE CHANGING POLITICAL economy of urban planning and the shifting calculative rationalities of the state affect the lives of poor people in different ways at different times. In this chapter, I provide an analysis of the politics of urban planning, which serves as a backdrop to understanding the effects of planning in Delhi. I deploy a "conjunctural analysis" as advocated by Stuart Hall and Doreen Massey (2010), which examines "the different social, political, economic and ideological contradictions" (57) that shape a particular society to understand the politics of planning in different periods. The planning process in Delhi has descended from its original high-modernist zeal to a contemporary obsession with neo-liberal market rationality. Thus, I argue that while the initial post-independence Nehruvian era[1] urban-planning regime represents one conjuncture, the current neo-liberal urban-planning regime that replaced it represents another.

I examine the phases of urban planning processes by drawing on planning documents and my own interviews with planning experts. In so doing, I examine the state rationales and contradictory ideologies—including modernism, environmentalism, consumerism, and neo-liberalism—that underpin the planning discourses that have shaped Delhi since Indian independence, and the consequent history of displacements and resettlements of poor people in the city. The policy protocols informing the history of displacements and resettlements shed light on governmental efforts in managing, improving, and also marginally entitling the poor. These protocols also define the processes of impoverishment and social suffering that provide the backdrop to understanding the political agency of the poor in the city.

PASSIVE REVOLUTION IN URBAN PLANNING:
THE RATIONALE OF MPD-I

After India's independence in 1947, various planning institutions, including the School of Planning and Architecture, the Town and Country Planning Organization (TCPO), and the Institute of Town Planners, India, were either established anew or refashioned and renamed as versions of the older colonial institutions. Nehruvian modernism aimed to train a body of planning experts, technocrats, and bureaucrats in India. Later institutions, including Delhi Urban Arts Commission (DUAC), the National Institute of Urban Affairs, and the National Capital Region Planning Board (NCRPB), were established to manage urban issues in response to the bourgeois preoccupation with planning, technocratic expertise, and bureaucratic rationality in Delhi (see also Kaviraj 1988). In 1950, the G. D. Birla committee was constituted to examine the functioning of the colonial-era Delhi Improvement Trust, especially to evaluate its role in decongestion and sanitation projects in the city (Priya 1993; Sundaram 2010). The committee provided a staunch critique of the trust in addressing the issues of overcrowding, housing, and hygiene in Delhi (Priya 1993; Sundaram 2010). It also recommended that the government carry out civic surveys, draw up a master plan, and establish a central authority to address the question of urban planning in the city (Priya 1993: 826; Sundaram 2010: 55). As Ravi Sundaram notes, the elites of the city were worried about the threat of slums and an urban collapse. The jaundice epidemic in 1955 added fuel to the fire and the elites became preoccupied with the issue of pollution management in the city (Sundaram 2010: 34).

In 1956, the Raj Kumari Amrit Kaur, the minister of health and local self-government, invited experts from the Ford Foundation to advise city officials in the planning and development of Delhi (Priya 1993: 826;

Sundaram 2010: 35). Subsequently, the American planner Albert Mayer, representatives of the regional city movement, and the Ford Foundation experts arrived in Delhi to assist their Indian counterparts in developing a master plan for the city (Sundaram 2010: 40). As Sundaram notes, the Ford Foundation represented the philosophy of liberal internationalism against the threat of communism in the Cold War era (Sundaram 2010: 37). It was invested in spreading ideas of modernization, technocratic planning, behavioral change, and liberal ideas of "citizen participation" across the globe (Sundaram 2010: 38). The foundation espoused a depoliticized planning process, which elided the questions of structural inequality in planning Delhi (Sundaram 2010: 39). The Delhi Development Act (DD Act) came into force in 1957, laying the groundwork for the establishment of the Delhi Development Authority (DDA)—an organization entrusted with planning Delhi in a systematic way (Government of India [1957] 2011).[2] The DDA, composed of technical members and political representatives, was given the power to "acquire, hold, manage, and dispose of land and other property" in the city (Government of India [1957] 2011: 6).

The DD Act inaugurated a technical impulse to conduct civic surveys, formulate master plans, and implement zoning and land-use plans in the city (Government of India [1957] 2011: 6–7). The act also empowered the DDA to increase public participation in the formulation of master plans. In turn, the DDA invited "objections and suggestions from any person with respect to the draft plan" (Government of India [1957] 2011: 8). However, the formulation of master plans remained a centralized activity without full involvement of the public through political representatives. Public participation in the planning process was largely aimed at a presumably literate middle class, which could understand the technical jargon of the planning authority, while at the time of independence a vast majority of the population remained "illiterate," even in cities. The central government was entrusted with the task of acquiring and transferring land to the authority through the colonial Land Acquisition Act of 1894 (Government of India [1957] 2011: 11). In turn, the authority was empowered with near-absolute power to develop plans and monitor contravention in the city (Government of India [1957] 2011: 15).

The formulation of urban planning in Delhi was situated within the larger logic of development planning and state power in India. The logic of development planning and the nature of state power have been analyzed through the coalition model of class interests (Bardhan 1988; Chatterjee 2008b; Kaviraj 1988). Pranab Bardhan and Sudipta Kaviraj have identified the bourgeoisie or capitalists, landed elites or rich farmers, and the bureaucratic elites as composing the three dominant classes (Bardhan 1988; Kaviraj 1988) in the first few decades in post-colonial India. In his seminal essay titled "A Critique of the Passive Revolution," Kaviraj (1988) argues that the state has become bourgeois as it advantages the capitalist class by imposing capitalist planning in India. In this sense, the proliferation of planning institutions has been rendered compatible with bourgeois developmental perspectives in India. As Kaviraj argues, "Those directive functions that capital cannot perform through the market . . . the bourgeois state performs through the legitimized directive mechanisms of the state." Furthermore, he argues, "The Indian capitalist class exercises its control over society neither through a form of moral-cultural hegemony of the Gramscian type, nor a simple coercive strategy on the lines of satellite states of the third world. It does so by a coalition strategy carried out partly through the state-directed process of economic growth, partly through the allocational necessities indicated by the bourgeois democratic political system" (Kaviraj 1988: 2430). Thus, three social groups constitute the ruling bloc in India—namely, the bourgeoisie, the landed elites, and the bureaucratic managerial elite. In Kaviraj's schema, the bureaucratic managerial elite, which carries out the mediating role between other classes and the ruling block, is "culturally and ideologically affiliated . . . to the bourgeois order." As such, the bureaucratic managerial elite provides "the theory and the institutional drive for bourgeois rule" in India (2431).

There is a great deal of merit in Kaviraj's arguments if we look at the policies, plans, and schemes of the state and the interests they have subserved historically, especially in tracing the evolution of urban planning in the first period. The first Master Plan inaugurated what can be called a passive revolution in urban planning. In subsequent master plans, the planning process has aimed at capital accumulation in the city. As discussed in this chapter, the planning process has moved away from the redistribution of urban resources to a focus on capital accumulation, thereby exacerbating unequal class relations over the years. In this regard, we can highlight three distinctive urban planning designs and formats and their underpinning class interests (see Table 1.1).

The Delhi Development Authority prepared and released the first Master Plan of Delhi (MPD-I) in 1962 with the support of the Ford Foundation.[3] MPD-I was imbued with modernist ideals that planned the city for an estimated five million people in 1981 (DDA 1962). The MPD-I, which carried a legal sanction for development that conflicted with the plan, also envisioned the planning of roads, bridges, and a Ring Railway, as well as offices, shopping centers, and various institutions (DDA 1962: 5). The plan proposed large-scale land acquisition and public ownership. It aimed for a holistic linking of social, economic, and governmental factors and recognized the need for adequate housing to avoid overcrowding and unsanitary conditions in the city (DDA 1962: 5). While the plan proposed a mixed policy promoting public goals and private interests, the public ownership of land meant that the government had complete control of "slum clearance, redevelopment and subsidized housing and provision of community facilities" (DDA 1962: 7). Large-scale clearance and demolition were seen to be unfeasible, though the plan proposed decongestion and the management of population density in the neighborhoods. The planning framework still operated within the Geddesian logic of improvement and transformation.[4] Apart from the abstract technical exercises, this planning mechanism inspired by American liberal thought also aimed at socio-psychological changes in order to transform the people of Delhi into "better" urban citizens (Hull 2010; Srivastava 2014).

In other words, Albert Mayer along with his colleagues and their Indian counterparts—despite frictions among them—went on to develop a highly modernist, rationalized, and regionalist framework for Delhi's future growth (Sundaram 2010). As Sundaram argues, the Cold War–era liberal modernism of the US experts informed the design of the first Master Plan of Delhi (Sundaram 2010: 19). These experts abandoned the utopian dreams of modernist planning but espoused a pragmatic and technical rationality to address the problems of overcrowding and congestion in

TABLE 1.1: *Comparison of the Primary Features of Delhi's Three Master Plans*

Master Plan 1 (1962)	Master Plan 2 (1990)	Master Plan 3 (2007)[59]
1. Comprehensive plan considering social, economic, and governmental factors.	1. Migration control and restrictive legal and fiscal policy on employment.	1. Aim to make Delhi a global metropolis and a "world-class" city.
2. Recognition of housing shortage and consequent overcrowding.	2. National Capital Region Planning Board (NCRPB) established to monitor regional development and population dispersal.	2. Private sector involvement in land development. Focus on sustainable development, public-private partnerships, and community participation.
3. Large-scale clearance of crowded areas deemed unviable because of financial constraints on government and the poor.	3. Conservation and restoration of historical buildings and heritage.	3. Focus on redevelopment and densification of the areas.
4. Rural migrants allowed to build cheap houses on earmarked sites.	4. Focus on visual quality and integration, city personality, and urban design.	4. Zoning and participatory planning at local level.
5. Lack of developed land results in unauthorized construction in the city. Acquisition of land to provide for housing and other facilities.	5. Emphasis on transportation and communication systems, convention and exhibition centers, shopping arcades, and amusement parks.	5. Restructuring the city through mass transport, expressways, elevated roads, arterial roads, distributor roads, and relief roads.
6. Public ownership of land. Leasing land to private individuals and cooperative societies. Integration of housing and employment options. Emphasis on avoiding stratification based on income.	6. Envisioned public-private partnerships and the role of NGOs in service delivery.	6. In situ slum rehabilitation and involvement of private sector. Regularization of unauthorized colonies.
7. Delhi divided into eight zones. Land use according to zonal regulations.	7. Delhi split into fifteen zones. Three tiers of planning formulated in Master Plan, zonal plans, and layout plans.	7. Delhi divided into fifteen zones. Land use according to zonal regulations.
8. Development of riverfront, Delhi Ridge, and a greenbelt around the urbanizable 1981 limit.	8. Development of Yamuna riverfront along the lines of the Thames in London and the Seine in Paris. Proposal for an amusement park like Disneyland along Yamuna River.	8. Conservation of the Ridge, rejuvenation of River Yamuna. Provisioning of 15–20 percent of land for recreation or as lung space.
9. Relocation of non-conforming large and nuisance-causing industries. Proposed multistory buildings to accommodate small industries.	9. Small-scale non–nuisance and clean industrial development. Heavy, large, hazardous and noxious industrial units to be relocated out of Delhi.	9. Restriction of employment in industrial and distributive trades. Relocation of industries. Emphasis on pollution– and nuisance–free high-tech industry.

Delhi (Sundaram 2010: 19). Albert Mayer and his colleagues embraced "the model of the garden city designs of Ebenezer Howard," which justified dispersal of people and infrastructure in the city (Sundaram 2010: 40). The regionalist framework of the plan mirrored the decentralization plans in US cities, which systematically aimed at containing people, commerce, and industry in demarcated spatial zones (Sundaram 2010: 40). This framework provided the rationale for land acquisition, a greenbelt, and the relocation of industries and resettlement of "squatters" in the periphery of the city. Furthermore, the liberal paternalism of the experts was obvious when they attempted to educate the residents to give up their village-like habits and particularistic attachments in order to develop a sense of civic consciousness and urban community in their cellular neighborhoods (Sundaram 2010: 55–58).

Although the strategy of improving slums[5] as opposed to demolition and redevelopment was seen as a sounder alternative because of "the financial burden on public bodies, low rent paying capacity of slum dwellers, and for keeping slum dwellers near the place of their work," the plan developed schemes to relocate "*busti* squatters"[6] to suitable areas not far from major work centers (DDA 1962: 26–27). At one point the plan endorsed the provisioning of lower-income housing on account of what it called "the relentless push from the rural areas" by earmarking suitable sites for the poor to build cheap houses in the city. While the plan called for adherence to strict zoning regulations by proposing relocation of "noxious and nuisance industries and fire hazard trades," it also recommended relaxing building bylaws "to enable the construction of low-cost cheap houses or huts" (27). MPD-I revised the colonial segregationist policies by stressing that "zoning regulations are not to be used for nuisance control nor can they be used to accomplish any kind of human segregation like excluding certain communities, or income groups from certain areas" (44). The plan defended the relocation of non-conforming industries, though it emphasized the need for a "minimum amount of dislocation" and for addressing workers' hardships (46). In other words, it stressed that "physical plans should avoid stratification on income or occupation basis" (DDA 1962: ii).

MPD-I proposed to reserve 5 percent of housing for low-income service providers, including gardeners, domestic workers, and janitors. More importantly, it proposed integrating low-income groups within different neighborhoods and the provision of community facilities (DDA 1962: 72). It recognized the need to accommodate around 100,000 construction workers who migrated into the city after partition and independence (73). MPD-I argued for periodic revisions based on rational scientific studies, and it connected urban planning with the welfare activities under the five-year plans of the government (39). Its modernist ideals justifying adherence to land-use plans and zoning stressed the need to "promote public health, safety, and the general moral and social welfare of the community" (44). Thus, the first Master Plan in theory proposed gradual transformation of the cityscape and aimed at accommodating the poor through its reformist agenda. Despite these measures, the plan did not envision a reordering of the city by carrying out land reforms favoring the poor. It merely reserved a total of 5 percent of housing units for the service class. In the planners' vision, the city predominantly remained a set of open spaces, green "lungs" like Delhi Ridge, aesthetically pleasing architecture and offices, roads, bridges, and other conveniences. Nevertheless, planners recognized the need for social housing, mixed land use, and integration of the poor in the city. Just as Kaviraj (1988: 2441) argues that the state struggled even to carry out passive revolution in India, we can also say that Delhi's passive revolution in urban planning is largely marked by failure.

In fact, the history of urban planning in Delhi in the first phase includes incidences of "slum" clearance and the demolition of "squatter" settlements. Girish Misra and Rakesh Gupta's (1981) study of resettlement policies in Delhi shows that 57,368 "squatter" families were resettled in eighteen resettlement colonies prior to the Emergency period.[7] The study also shows that around 141,820 families were resettled in sixteen resettlement colonies during the Emergency period between 1975 and 1976 (Misra and Gupta 1981: 6). Drawing on a study by the Town and Country Planning Organization (TCPO), Misra and Gupta argue that "29 percent of the land occupied by the 'squatter' settlements was meant for residential uses as per the records of the Master Plan" (26). They go on to argue that the resettlements in far-flung areas were carried out not because of the scarcity of land but because of an elitist approach to the housing problem (8). Thus, contrary to the specifications of MPD-I, the poor were banished to inhabitable land outside the limits of the city (27). As Priya (1993: 827) notes, reviewing the first Master Plan, the TCPO noted the increase in housing deficits, slow progress in low-income housing, and substandard community facilities and housing in slum areas. Evaluating the implementation of plans, the TCPO also remarked that the plans in practice emphasized higher-income housing and beautification drives in Delhi. Priya, discussing the TCPO report, notes that the lands cleared from the heart of the city were used for developing "parks and picnic spots specially around historic monuments, commercial centers, and some for residential areas" (Priya 1993: 827).

The declaration of Emergency sped up demolitions all over the city. Indira Gandhi assumed authoritarian power while her son, Sanjay Gandhi, became what a former municipal commissioner called the "de facto ruler of the Municipal Corporation" of Delhi (Shah Commission 1978b: 79). The conjuncture of the Emergency, accompanied by a contradictory culture of sycophancy, dictatorial impulse, and populism, represented an absolute form of authoritarian rule. Those executing the Emergency consecrated themselves as de facto rulers in ways that even challenged the legitimate symbolic order of the ruling regime (cf. Bourdieu 1991: 209). As the Shah Commission (1978b) report observed, "The general policy of caution and concern for the people affected by demolitions gave place to a measure of reckless speed in cleaning and clearing up the areas" during the Emergency period (77). For example, around 1,800 structures were demolished between 1973 and 1975 prior to the declaration of Emergency. After the proclamation of Emergency, some 150,105 structures were demolished between 1975 and 1977 (78). Consequently, during the Emergency the Master Plan specifications were violated with impunity and without adhering to the basic protocols of rehabilitation.

Subhadra Joshi, the chairperson of the Minorities Department of the All India Congress Committee, in her poignant letters to the prime minister, pointed out the human suffering brought about by the lack of rehabilitation, the cutting off of the water supply to slum localities, the removal of rickshaws from the bazaar areas, and the general unsanitary conditions during the period of Emergency (Shah Commission 1978b: 79–80). Joshi wrote to the prime minister that a "human touch" was lacking and insinuated that Sanjay Gandhi was controlling the entire thing (Shah Commission 1978b: 80). Muslim neighborhoods like Jama Masjid and Turkman Gate were especially targeted for demolitions (81). In her letter, Joshi argued that, upon learning about the Muslim neighborhoods, the Hindu policemen acted with brutality toward the residents. Joshi also maintained that many poor residents fled back to their villages (Shah Commission 1978b: 81) as a result of the demolitions and the coercive character of family planning programs. The report noted that "Jagmohan's [vice chairman of the DDA during the Emergency] pet phrase was that no second Pakistan could be permitted to exist" during the period (Shah Commission 1978b: 82). Various depositions and testimonies to the commission confirm that the implementation of these schemes violated the Master Plan's land-use specifications (83).

In this way, demolitions continued unabated during the attempted passive revolution in urban planning while the living and environmental conditions of low-income neighborhoods remained dismal. The plot sizes offered were progressively reduced from 80 square yards in the 1960s to 25 square yards during the Emergency period (Priya 1993: 827). Evaluating the environmental conditions and provisioning of basic amenities in resettlement colonies, Priya has called these neighborhoods "planned slums" (828). Similarly, Misra and Gupta's (1981) study brought to light the harsh conditions in the resettlement colonies. Drawing on their research and quoting a newspaper article, Misra and Gupta dubbed the resettlement colonies "real monuments of misery" (quoted in Misra and Gupta 1981: 5). Thus, a constant process of displacement and resettlement in the outskirts of the city without adequate basic amenities came to define the larger housing policy of the state. The second Master Plan, which came into effect in 1990, noted a shortage of three hundred thousand housing units in the city (DDA [1990] 1996: 5).

RECASTING URBAN PLANNING AS CAPITAL
ACCUMULATION: THE RATIONALE OF MPD-II
AND MPD-III

Where MPD-I inaugurated a revision of the colonial policies of segregation by ensuring social housing in mixed neighborhoods, the second Master Plan (MPD-II) reversed these initial measures by making way for the increasing participation of the private sector. MPD-II was formulated according to Rajiv Gandhi's policies for downsizing state investments in the social sector. The period was marked by the growth and assertion of the middle class in India (Corbridge and Harriss 2001). Additionally, the second Master Plan was framed in such a way as to enhance leisure spaces for the members of the middle and upper classes. Whereas MPD-I recognized the inability of the urban poor to build houses, MPD-II stressed systematic monitoring of unauthorized colonies,[8] squatter settlements, and the informal sector (DDA [1990] 1996: ii). MPD-II envisioned the dispersal of the city's population, thereby propounding regional development of the metropolitan area by restructuring settlement patterns and transport networks (iii). The plan emphasized beautification measures, pollution control, city aesthetics, the development of riverfront and recreational areas, and the visual integration of the city. The core principles at the heart of urban design were intended to accentuate "road geometrics, landscaping, street furniture," and the removal of "unsightly" structures (39). The plan envisioned the development of the Yamuna riverfront along the lines of the Thames in London and the Seine in Paris to provide limitless ecological improvements and recreational opportunities (4–5). It also envisioned the conservation of urban heritage, the decentralization of city centers, and a multi-modal mass transport system. According to MPD-II, "A city is an assemblage of buildings and streets, system[s] of communication and utilities, places of work, transportation, leisure and meeting places. The process of arranging these elements both functionally and beautifully is the essence of urban design" (38). This abstract, technical, and aesthetic definition did not take into account the lived realities of all the city's inhabitants, however.

One of the integral ideas of the plan was "aspirational" planning to develop a distinct city personality. On the one hand, MPD-II accepted a shortage of 300,000– 350,000 housing units (DDA [1990] 1996: 5, 122) by clearly recognizing the failure of the planning machinery to provide adequate housing in the city. On the other hand, the plan endorsed neo-liberal diktats by emphasizing public-private partnerships (PPP) and the role of NGOs in delivering services in the city. MPD-II also laid out a blueprint to relocate "noxious and hazardous industrial units" outside of Delhi (10). Following this logic, the Supreme Court of India, between July 8 and December 19, 1996, called in six different orders for the closure of 1,328 industrial units in Delhi (for details see NCRPB 2005: 58; Sundaram 2010: 29). Further, in its 2004 judgment, the Supreme Court ordered the relocation of all non-conforming industrial units that had been established in the city after August 1, 1990 (NCRPB 2005: 59). Baviskar (2003: 90; Baviskar 2020) argues that the "bourgeois environmentalism" underpinning this logic threatened around two million workers in 98,000 industrial units in Delhi. Scholars, trade union activists, and grassroots movements have already documented the magnitude of industrial displacement and the plight of the workers rendered jobless after these verdicts (Baviskar 2003; Nigam 2001; Padhi 2007; D. Roy 2000). While the planning machinery was relatively tolerant of *jhuggi* settlements after the Emergency, after 1990 this tolerance was replaced with a drive to demolish such neighborhoods.

There is a great deal of overlap and continuity between MPD-II (1990) and the third Master Plan (MPD-III), which was introduced in 2007. In short, the foundational assumptions underlying the first Master Plan to provide a blueprint for equitable urban development were challenged by the ideologies guiding subsequent planning processes in the city. These ideologies subvert the supposedly participatory and democratic nature of the planning process. The provision allowing statements of objection and suggestions at the drafting stage of the plan continues to be a mere formality. MPD-III unequivocally envisioned making "Delhi a global metropolis and a world-class city" (DDA [2007] 2010: 2). It abandoned the principle of urban development as a "public sector led process" that was enshrined in MPD-I and instead aligned with the economic reforms launched since the early 1990s. The plan emphasized involvement of the private sector "in the assembly and development of land and provision of infrastructure services." It set out to tackle *jhuggi* settlements and authorized colonies by "redevelopment and densification of the existing urban areas" (3). MPD-III thus made a case for housing by in situ rehabilitation and mandatory provisions for the economically weaker sections, and by proposing to reserve 50 to 55 percent of the total housing for the poor (6). In fact, MPD-III recognized a backlog of four hundred thousand dwelling units and admitted that housing needs are largely met through non-institutional sources in informal settlements in the city (31). As a planning document notes, 64.5 percent of people in Delhi have obtained accommodation in *jhuggis*, slum-designated areas, and unauthorized colonies (Planning Commission 2009: 33). Another 11.9 percent of the population in Delhi continues to reside in rural and urban villages without many civic amenities (33). In fact, brutal demolitions without resettlement continue across the city despite the proposed new schemes for the poor. In other words, despite making provisions for housing the poor in the city, unabated demolitions call into question the legitimacy of the Master Plan as a legal document.

MPD-III proposed demolition only if the land was required for public purposes. However, "public purpose" has been defined in a contentious way. While many demolished sites remained vacant for years after eviction, demolitions contributed to the formation of new *jhuggi* settlements and the densification of the existing ones (Dupont 2008: 85). After surveying demolished sites, Bhan and Shivanand (2013) note that the "four primary uses are vacant land, road and related infrastructure, parks and playgrounds, and government infrastructure" (57). They state that 25 percent of the demolished sites remained vacant or unused after demolitions (Bhan and Shivanand 2013: 57). Simply put, it is clearly a futile exercise on the part of the state to clear and vacate sites productively used by the poor in the city (Bhan and Shivanand 2013: 57). These are striking findings, as the idea of "public purpose" largely appears to be an excuse for intolerant policies of clearing spaces that are seen to be incongruent in a "world-class city" (see also Ghertner 2008: 66). In fact, the ideology underpinning the definition of "public purpose" in this context exposes the presumption of "disinterested knowledge" in the production of space (Lefebvre 1991: 9). Dupont's and Bhan and Shivanand's meticulous surveys of land use in demolished sites may not establish a direct relationship between demolition and the conversion of sites for commercial purposes or capital accumulation. However, vacant lots, road infrastructure, and green areas produce spaces of leisure and facilitate the accumulation of capital in the city. As such, the attractiveness of spaces can be directly connected with the setting up of hotels, shopping malls, and offices for service sector industries. A five-star hotel was established just a few months after the demolition of a portion of the Gautam Nagar *jhuggi jhopri* settlement. The hotel also adjoined the Sitapuri transit camp that faced the threat of demolition in the neighborhood. Furthermore, the underpass that was built eased the traffic in the area particularly for the occupants of the hotel, but the poor still struggled to obtain amenities and receive resettlement compensation as this book went to press in early October 2021.

REMAKING DELHI AS A "WORLD-CLASS" CITY

The process of globalization and the associated restructuring of space, economy, and labor have highlighted various forms of inequity.[9] MPD-III was framed alongside the new national economic policies in India, thereby accentuating retail and allied services and the entry of multinational corporations into the economic structure of the city (DDA [2007] 2010: 50).[10] The National Capital Region Planning Board (NCRPB) was at the forefront in its presentation of Delhi as an important destination for foreign direct investments (FDIs) (NCRPB 2005: 36).[11] FDIs are sought to develop integrated townships, which include investments in housing, commercial premises, hotels and resorts, roads and bridges, and mass rapid transit systems (37). MPD-III has advanced a narrow understanding of industrial development by focusing on computer, information, and telecommunication technologies; commercial packaging; electronics and repair; textile design and fabric testing; biotechnology; and the gems and jewelry industries (DDA [2007] 2010: 73–74).

Consequently, the role of the state in urban planning, developing infrastructure, and providing social services has shifted toward facilitating both foreign and indigenous investments in the city. The desire is to represent

Delhi as a model "e-city," with the NCRPB arguing that Delhi is on its way to becoming an "e-governed, e-citizen, and e-services city" (NCRPB 2005: 49). Today, Delhi is emerging as a key agglomeration of Export Processing Zones (Dupont 2011). Dupont has scrupulously listed the multinational firms and business process outsourcing units and foreign direct investments to argue that the Delhi metropolitan region has emerged as a major hub of offshoring and outsourcing activities (Dupont 2011: 539–540). The unreasonable planning tools aimed to turn Delhi into an "e-city" erode the rights and potential of the poor to participate in the economic, cultural, and social spheres of the city. Instead, as the NCRPB (2005: 49) report envisions, the thrust of this strategy is toward developing Delhi along the lines of Singapore and Hong Kong by expanding export-oriented and service sector industries, including finance, hotel, tourism, international travel, and retail shopping. As is evident from the discussion above, the planners have been instrumental actors in fostering such "inter-place competition."[12]

MPD-III has continued the policy of legal and fiscal measures "to restrict employment in industries and distributive trade" (DDA [2007] 2010: 10). In particular, the policy of restriction of employment in industries has negative effects on the poor. Planner RM of the NCRPB[13] told me about some of the outcomes of this planning regime:

Our avowed objective is to develop a regional plan in order to restrict migration into the city. We only got funding in the mid-1990s. But look at our performance. The population growth rate and migration ratios into the city have declined in a major way since the mid-1990s. We've collaborated with various state governments to develop a regional plan in the Delhi region. We raise finances from the market and advise state governments about land acquisitions for various purposes. Our main purpose is to create more jobs outside Delhi. It is only due to our report that the Supreme Court gave a series of orders to close down and relocate the non-conforming industries outside Delhi. Our work has led to the development of huge industrial estates in the region, including Manesar, Greater Bhiwadi, Neemrana, Loni, Tronica City, and Bawal. The NCR [National Capital Region] is number one in terms of foreign direct investment. We invite foreign delegations to visit the areas and invest in ventures around the region. We have convinced a delegation from

Japan to invest in the area. A delegation from Singapore has decided to shift their investments from Bangalore to the market-friendly region of the NCR.

The avowed policy of migration restriction stated here has paid off, as is apparent in the declining rate of migration into the city (see DDA [2007] 2010: 13). Industrial planning followed strictures around pollution control and land use in the city. The plan called for technology-intensive, high-tech, low-volume, and high-value-added industries in the city (67). In this regard, by continuing with the industrial policy enshrined in MPD-II, MPD-III laid out various incentives and disincentives to relocate industries in non-conforming areas (67). While there is a significant decline in the manufacturing sector in Delhi, the city is poised to expand its base of services, including "accountancy, law, advertising, finance, research and development, consultancy etc." (NCRPB 2005: 49). A recent Planning Commission report states that the share of the manufacturing sector in Delhi alone declined by 8 percent between the 1980s and early 1990s (Planning Commission 2009: 51).[14]

Industries catering to the consumer needs of the people are encouraged in the city (NCRPB 2005: 50). As a consequence, urban citizenship is related to the "aspirational consumption" potential of the people (Baviskar 2020; Mazzarella 2003: 99; Srivastava 2014). Delhi is poised to become a city for consumers—a city that has turned into a spectacle of consumption, leisure, and sporting events. Additionally, the process of "surplus consumption" is accelerated through recourse to "cultural symbols, meanings, and strategies generated across a number of time spans" (Srivastava 2009: 341–342).[15] The trends are toward the construction of corporate hospitals, upscale residential complexes, and theme parks in the Delhi metropolitan region (Dupont 2011). Around one hundred shopping malls have been built in the last twenty years to offer international consumption spectacles in the Delhi metropolitan region (Baviskar 2020: 4; Dupont 2011: 543).[16] Comaroff and Comaroff (2000: 294) have argued in more general terms that "consumerism . . . [is a] material sensibility actively cultivated, for the common good." Ironically, spaces of leisure and consumption advertised as promoting "the common good" have been established in Delhi after the destruction of city commons.

MPD-III earmarked 15 to 20 percent of the total land in Delhi for developing what it called "lung spaces," recreational areas, and a greenbelt (DDA [2007] 2010: 6). City planners aspire to transform Delhi into a clean and green city with high aesthetic value (Planning Commission 2009: 41). The desire is also to turn Delhi into a "World Class Heritage City" (309). As a Planning Commission report suggests, "tourism is the 'industry of industries'" (317–318). Consequently, the government has made financial promises for infrastructure development in the tourism industry. According to MPD-III, Delhi remains an important center for national and international sporting events, and so the plan encourages sports infrastructure development in the city (DDA [2007] 2010: 95). Thus, the landscape of Delhi is rewritten through the active marketing of a variety of consumption spectacles.

MPD-III presents arguments for urban restructuring around mass transport, expressways, elevated roads, arterial roads, distributor roads, and relief roads (DDA [2007] 2010: 5, 8). The Metro Rail lines through the city have contributed to the planners' expectations of visual integration in Delhi. Metro Rail was expected to transport 108 *lakh* (10,800,000) passengers daily in a network of 250 kilometers by 2021 (115). The international airport at Delhi has been restructured massively so as to compare with the major high-tech airports around the world. The airport is expected to handle over "1,000 lakh [100,000,000] passengers and 3.6 million tons of cargo" annually by 2036 (122). The expansion of the Indira Gandhi International Airport, however, led to the demolition of Nangla Devat village (Bhan and Shivanand 2013: 57). In addition, the regional plan has developed a blueprint for the Mass Rapid Transit System (MRTS) around Delhi (NCRPB 2005: 65). These "signature projects" designed as a facelift for Delhi have often led to the displacement of the poor, especially with the expansion of the Metro Rail.

Delhi's changing skyline attests to these transformations with respect to the spaces of leisure and the revitalization of River Yamuna and heritage structures. MPD-III argued for the need to revitalize Yamuna by checking untreated sewage flowing from *jhuggi* settlements (DDA [2007] 2010: 100). Many court judgments preceding the plan have argued for *jhuggi* demolitions specifically to manage pollution of the Yamuna River.

As a result, approximately 150,000 to 200,000 people have been displaced in riverbank beautification drives alone (Baviskar 2020: 81; Bhan 2009: 127). In fact, subsidies and a bailout were extended to a Dubai-based real estate company to build the Commonwealth Games Village on the riverfront (Baviskar 2011: 51; Baviskar 2020: 91; Housing and Land Rights Network 2010: 2). Thus, the commodification of the riverfront for profit has also accompanied concerns for city aesthetics and national prestige (Baviskar 2011; Baviskar 2020).[17]

On the eve of the Commonwealth Games in 2010, the government proposed to develop, renovate, and promote various sites in Delhi. Various projects including bridges over River Yamuna, flyovers, improvement and beautification of roads, upgrades to the airport, railway services and bus stations, grid stations, and a hospital for the Games Village were planned as part of refurbishing the city (Planning Commission 2009: 312). A report published by the Housing and Land Rights Network estimated an expenditure of up to 30,000 *crores* (300 billion rupees, or approximately US$6.7 billion) for the Commonwealth Games (Housing

FIGURE 1.1: *The refurbished Jawaharlal Nehru Stadium to host the Commonwealth Games in 2010.*

FIGURE 1.2: *Posters of Commonwealth Games adorning a newly built flyover in Delhi.*

and Land Rights Network 2010: 2). The report carefully documents the wanton waste of public money, raising questions about the democratic process and the perpetuation of poverty. It also underlines the accompanying disenfranchisement of the poor through *jhuggi* demolition; the removal of beggars, the homeless, and street vendors; and ecological degradation (Housing and Land Rights Network 2010: 2). Many of these projects violated Master Plan norms in the city. More importantly, these practices of planning violation contributed to "territorialized flexibility," which are predicated on state informality, power, and exclusions (A. Roy 2009: 81). The Delhi Urban Arts Commission (DUAC)—a government statutory body that validates the aesthetic and functional aspects of specific projects, such as the Commonwealth Games—was not even consulted prior to the implementation and flexible regulations concerning the development projects. Planner AM (DUAC) commented:

> Metro Railway never sought our suggestions regarding the aesthetics and functional aspects of their projects. This violation is tantamount to illegality.

Most often we are not even aware of the projects, as we do not have the mechanisms to monitor, so there are violations concerning alignment of roads and construction activities, particularly in the Ridge area. During the Commonwealth Games many projects have come up. Some of them did not submit their proposals to [the] DUAC. Now if the construction is at an advanced stage, we will not be able to intervene.

Leisure and religious spaces often violate the planning norms (Baviskar 2011; Ghertner 2008: 65; Housing and Land Rights Network 2010; Srivastava 2009). For example, the Games Village and Akshardham temple were established on the demolished site of the Nangla Machi *jhuggi* settlement (Srivastava 2009: 339). The upscale temple is modeled along the lines of Disneyland and Universal studios (Srivastava 2009: 340). Additionally, the "politico-spiritual clout" enjoyed by the temple complex vests it with legal status, which was denied to the demolished *jhuggi* settlement (Srivastava 2009: 341). As a result, the emphasis on turning Delhi into a world-class city has propelled the state authorities to promote spaces of leisure and sports, heritage conservation and tourism, and new technology. However, the state planning bodies have also violated their own planning protocols and undermined the interests of the poor in the city.

Today, the focus has shifted to the private sector and corporate social responsibility with respect to providing housing for the poor. As planner M (DDA) notes:

> The poor do not have a dignified life in *jhuggis* or resettlement colonies. These neighborhoods are filthy spaces harboring criminal activities. We have followed the British policy of segregation. There are stark differences between the neighborhoods of the rich and the poor. Our past policy of mixed land use has failed in the city. In the future the state and the private sector should be able to build and rent out housing units to the poor. We must also work on corporate social responsibility. We can have a rigorous rent recovery system to make the planning process effective.

Likewise, ideas around corporate social responsibility and a rent recovery system also challenge ownership claims and housing entitlements among the poor. On the one hand, urban design is deployed to clear encroachments and filth in the city. On the other hand, it is represented as a dignity-restoring tool, which is expected to inculcate a renewed civic ethos among the poor. Furthermore, new governance policies are extolled—namely, policies concerning public-private partnerships (PPP) and the *bhagidari* (partnership) program, which will shape urban governance in Delhi's future (Dupont et al. 2014; Ghertner 2011; Srivastava 2009). In particular, public discourses concerning sustainability, decentralization, participation, and local planning have become fashionable in recent times. For instance, the "twelfth schedule" of the Constitution (Seventy-Fourth Amendment) Act (Government of India 1992) lays out measures for the devolution of power from national and state governments to municipal governments. It emphasizes the participation of municipal bodies in a range of activities including urban planning, regulation of land use, building of bridges and roads, slum improvement, and the alleviation of urban poverty.

As planner VD (National Institute of Urban Affairs) noted:

> The urban local bodies do not have the competence to prepare plans in Delhi. The Seventy-Fourth Amendment requires the local government to be involved in the planning process, but Delhi's governance structure is different from the rest of India. Here, the DDA plans and the MCD implements without even understanding what has gone on [that is, without either of them understanding what the other has done]. The DDA and other parastatal bodies control the   city resources, including the land. They don't want their autonomy to be eroded, but they also don't want to be subservient to the local bodies. The amendment has happened on paper. The local bodies have not been provided financial or manpower resources in Delhi. Local bodies should be empowered by training and [through the provision of] fiscal facilities.

Similarly, planner M (DDA) characterized the DDA as a

> government developer that purchases, develops, and disposes land or property for a profit on a leasehold basis. We have a social commitment even when we are making profits for our organization. We provide land to different agencies

like Delhi Metro Rail Corporation for public purposes. We also involve private players to facilitate social commitment goals. But we do not have mechanisms to check. For instance, we have given land on a lease to Apollo hospital with the agreement that a certain percentage of beds be reserved for the poor. But I am not sure if they follow the agreement. The Seventy-Fourth Amendment allows for public participation and local level planning, but the central government has to repeal the Delhi Development Act in order to make the DDA accountable to the state and local governments.

As these planners acknowledge, the Seventy-Fourth Amendment Act does not apply to Delhi. Hence, the democratic potential of local planning is automatically outside the ambit of urban governance models in Delhi. Nevertheless, the planning ideology in Delhi reflects the broader ideology of the Indian state. In the absence of the Seventy-Fourth Amendment, the prescriptions of participation and decentralization have been taken up through public-private partnerships and the *bhagidari* program. In particular, grandiloquent neo-liberal doctrines of efficiency, grandeur, and performance-oriented appraisals are accentuated in the policy prescriptions, while involvement of the private sector remains at the core of planning.[18] The idea is to involve the private sector in land development and housing for the poor, rather than to manage social and economic inequalities through state interventions alone. The current policy focuses on in situ development of *jhuggi* settlements instead of demolition.

The first-ever in situ slum development was undertaken in Kathputli colony in Delhi. The project raises critical concerns about the process of participation and the role of NGOs and community-based organizations in representing a heterogeneous community as well as issues concerning consultation and transparency (Dubey 2016; Dupont et al. 2014). At the time of my fieldwork in 2011 and 2017, activists in Gautam Nagar raised critical questions about affordability under the new rehabilitation schemes. Obviously, the poorest of Gautam Nagar residents would not be able to afford a beneficiary contribution.[19] Furthermore, the flats are in five-story buildings.[20] Activists have already voiced concerns regarding the impossibility, after relocation to these multistory buildings, of retaining the small trades and businesses that the poor engage in. As activists

R and A remarked, "It is impossible to hoard materials and carts in multistoried buildings, especially for street hawkers. Further, a sizable poor population raises animals for milk, eggs, and meat in the city." Inviting builders to develop *jhuggi* land in order to provide housing for the poor anticipates a slow process and is widely considered a contentious issue in Delhi.

While the third Master Plan aims at making Delhi "slum-free" through such schemes, it is unlikely that the DDA will find potential builders for the less lucrative sites. Additionally, the DDA will have to respond to the demands of the poor, especially the "ineligible" and excluded poor. Displaced "eligible" residents of Gautam Nagar will most likely get flats in the resettlement colonies soon. However, it is difficult to predict the fate of the undemolished part of Gautam Nagar, which has been developed in an industrial area. In contrast, there are proposals to redevelop the Sitapuri transit camp along the public-private partnership model, but most residents contest this redevelopment plan since there is no clear-cut rehabilitation policy.

The Delhi Development Authority, under the jurisdiction of the central government, is the primary nodal agency for initiating land development, involvement of the private sector, and rehabilitation of the low-income neighborhoods under public-private partnership. In contrast, the innovations around the provision of basic services at the municipal level involve the Delhi state government. The Delhi government inaugurated what it called the *bhagidari* program in 2000 to address the concerns of elite residents through their Resident Welfare Associations (RWAs). Elite schemes like the *bhagidari* program have been framed within the ideological terms of neo-liberal discourse.[21] In fact, the *bhagidari* scheme was inspired by the World Bank prescriptions of participation and governance (Dupont 2011: 537). The participatory approach is seen as revising a top-down model of urban planning. The RWAs represent the "new politics" of India in the latest post-liberal phase. These new politics intensify the antinomies of uncritical faith in the market, "transparency," and "accountability" instead of democratic politics and questions of redistribution (Harriss 2007). In this regard, the third Master Plan lays out provisions for including Resident Welfare Associations and Traders' Associations in the formulation of development plans to enhance the public participation of citizens in Delhi (DDA [2007] 2010: 26). The participatory governance protocols inherent in schemes like the *bhagidari* and the Seventy-Fourth Amendment disproportionately favor the wealthy and the better educated (Shatkin 2014: 8). In turn, the consuming middle class attempts to redefine citizenship through the *bhagidari* scheme (Srivastava: 2009). In Ghertner's (2011) apt words, the *bhagidari* scheme has led to the "gentrification of state spaces" (505) and the "gentrification of political participation" (526). In other words, the *bhagidari* program opens up access to the state based on property ownership.

The *bhagidari* scheme aimed to address the concerns of "public participation in various utility and civic services" (Planning Commission 2009: 160). A 2009 planning commission report claimed that there were about "1,600 RWAs, traders' bodies, and industry associations" participating in the *bhagidari* program. It further claimed that the program was expanding "numerically, spatially, and thematically" (Planning Commission 2009: 160), although low-income neighborhoods remained excluded from the program. Clearly, the Gautam Nagar *jhuggi* settlement and the Azad resettlement colony remained outside these models of governance. However, as discussed in Chapter 5, the traders along with the upwardly mobile residents of Sitapuri formed their own Resident Welfare Association. Their attempt to organize and legitimatize the organization has not been successful. The organization, which modeled itself after RWAs in elite colonies (neighborhoods), could not address the day-to-day problems of the neighborhood. Instead it merely focused on regularizing the neighborhood.

In contrast, the Lakshmi colony RWA slowly emerged as a powerful force in the area. The *bhagidari* program had created a parallel system of urban governance in Delhi: the elites had direct access to state officials through monthly meetings and personal connections, whereas the poor relied on the old grievance-redress routes (Ghertner 2011: 520). Although the Lakshmi colony RWA did not participate directly in *bhagidari* programs during the period of my fieldwork, the representatives debated and planned to get actively involved:

REPRESENTATIVE N: *Bhagidari* policy has helped dispose of garbage in the city. It has also facilitated hiring gardeners to carry out park maintenance. The Municipal Corporation of Delhi (MCD) gives money to RWAs for park maintenance on the basis of acreage. We should be actively involved in the local layout of the planning process. The DDA and MCD should tap the potential in civil society. *Bhagidari* is better than nothing. Our neighborhood is not actively involved but we should be part of it; we could initiate many projects if the DDA and MCD intend to cooperate.

REPRESENTATIVE A: The RWA deals with water, electricity, and security-related problems. We maintain relationships with the politicians, officials of the state, and the police. It's very difficult to arrange for the security of your neighborhood. Security is directly related to the number and quality of the guards. The RWA hires security guards who guard the gates in the neighborhood. The *bhagidari* system is really cumbersome and bureaucratic. At this stage we are not involved. The scheme needs to be improved a lot by further involvement of the people.

As these remarks suggest, the seemingly innocuous provision of participation raises questions about the distribution of urban resources and an extra-constitutional mode of urban governance. Residents often misconstrue the rhetoric of decentralization and participation among city planners as the privatized ability to guard one's neighborhood. As representative A's comments make clear, the aspiration is to manage security of the neighborhood in an extra-constitutional and privatized manner (see also Hansen and Stepputat 2006). In fact, the security guards in Lakshmi colony were arbitrarily directed to control who can enter the neighborhood, especially the residents from the Sitapuri transit camp, usually making judgments on the basis of physical appearance.

In theory, the *bhagidari* scheme promoted partnerships between the RWAs of mostly planned colonies and various departments of the state, including Delhi Jal (water) Board (DJB), Delhi Vidyut (electricity) Board, and the Delhi Police. One of the themes of the scheme was to prevent encroachments in the neighborhoods (Planning Commission 2009: 413). Often these programs accentuated class-based antagonisms in the city. Thus, the "'reform oriented' elite civil society" had targeted low-income neighborhoods in the name of "citizen participation" (S. Benjamin 2008: 721; Ghertner 2011). This sort of vigilantism and arbitrary extra-constitutional surveillance (Hansen and Stepputat 2006) had the potential to shrink the space of citizenship claims of the poor in the city. The activities of the poor in the low-income neighborhoods, especially in their attempts at building *jhuggis* and carrying out economic activities, do not strictly fall under the legal domain of zoning and planning in Delhi (see also Chatterjee 2004). In contrast, the RWAs have called for the demolition of low-income settlements (see also Ghertner 2011). Consequently, the politics of RWAs coincide with the politics of planning that accentuate surveillance and monitoring of "encroachment."

While the clamor for adherence to legal and planning norms on behalf of the middle class has become paramount, it is often noted that they themselves carry out blatant violations of legal and planning provisions (Baviskar and Sundar 2008; Verma 2002). The *bhagidari* program also demands a disproportionately high share of urban resources for the middle class (Verma 2002). Furthermore, the *bhagidari* program weakens the role of the local representatives, which is the primary reason councilors contest it in Delhi (Ghertner 2011: 523). It must be emphasized that the local political representatives, especially the councilors, are seldom taken into account in the events of demolition and resettlement of *jhuggi* settlements (see also Ghertner 2011). The issues discussed above concerning decentralization, participation, and partnership currently in vogue raise critical questions about the future of urban citizenship in Delhi. Additionally, the implication of public-private partnership in providing housing for the urban poor will have to be studied systematically.

CALCULATIVE GOVERNMENTALITY AND THE URBAN POOR

As discussed above, various conjunctures have propelled particular calculative rationales of the state. To begin with, urban planning in post-colonial Delhi inaugurated a reformist agenda, which contested segregation and stratification policies of the colonial era. The passive revolution in urban planning was ruptured by the conjuncture of the Emergency—a period that witnessed demolitions at a reckless speed and the targeting of specific vulnerable populations. In the decade and a half after the Emergency ended, the planning process aimed for the improvement of populations in the *jhuggi* neighborhoods rather than large-scale displacements of populations. Next was the move toward neo-liberal planning, which accentuated new technology and the service sector economy, public-private participation, elite participation, heritage conservation, and aesthetics integration in the city. The motifs of "aspirational planning" and "distinct city personality" integral to making a world-class city engendered a particular mode of calculative rationality. While MPD-I desisted from "nuisance control," the two later Master Plans attempted to rewrite nuisance laws (see also Ghertner 2008). MPD-III proposed the removal of "unnecessary controls [like height]" and the promotion of "'signature' projects" (DDA [2007] 2010: 6), which also fomented large-scale planning violations in the city.

Delhi has a population of fourteen million, and approximately three million live in *jhuggi jhopri* settlements in six hundred thousand *jhuggis*.[22] The Delhi Urban Shelter Improvement Board (DUSIB), the nodal agency established in 2010, is mandated to carry out routine surveys and enumeration, and to decide whether to resettle and rehabilitate or carry out in situ development of the area.[23] It routinely—especially in its board meetings—sets the protocols for the removal of the *jhuggis* in Delhi.[24] It defines eligibility and verifies the documents for eligibility by consulting various agencies such as the Department of Food and Supplies and the Department of Revenue of the GNCTD.[25] It periodically organizes "eligibility determination camps" at its Raja Garden office.[26] However, the calculative rationality of the state has aimed at surveillance and enumeration of poor populations in recent years. MPD-III envisions increasing surveillance of the poor through remote sensing and geographic information system (GIS) technologies to control "unauthorized" development and "encroachments," and the protection of green spaces in the city (DDA [2007] 2010: 192). The current policy requires that the GNCTD must take all steps to prohibit *jhuggi* building in Delhi.[27] The clear intention is to prohibit the building of any new *jhuggi* after January 1, 2015—the cut-off date for the current resettlement policy. In this regard, the policy calls for surveillance and periodic satellite mapping, joint inspection of the land along with the land-owning agencies, and immediate removal of previously unidentified *jhuggis*. The state policy also aims to recruit volunteers from the neighborhoods who could inform or "act as eye and ear of the government" in thwarting attempts to seize land in the city.[28] Thus, the state agencies attempt to enlist potential neighbors in their espionage tactics to restrict building of *jhuggis* in the city. As planner DS of the DDA put it: "The inventorization [*sic*] of land is not proper in Delhi. We established the GIS unit only recently. This will help us build a database of land parcels and better monitor encroachments." In fact, the land management department of the DDA has recently taken active steps to improve surveillance using GIS mapping. Moreover, the ominous aim "to make Delhi slum free within a time frame" (DDA [2007] 2010: 210) begs some urgent questions. As past experience shows, this objective necessarily means large-scale demolition and displacement of the poor out of the city. Furthermore, these espionage and surveillance state technologies challenge the democratic and redistributive potential of *jhuggi* building and land utilization on the part of the poor.

MPD-III developed a three-pronged strategy for *jhuggi jhopri* settlements: (a) the demolition and relocation of settlements if the land is required for "public purposes"; (b) in situ upgrading according to specific parameters; and (c) environmental upgrading to ensure minimum basic services as an interim measure (DDA [2007] 2010: 37). The in situ upgrading scheme envisioned providing the poor with 10- to 12.5-square-meter plots by redistributing and realigning existing *jhuggis* along with basic amenities in the neighborhoods. In situ upgrading of a *jhuggi* cluster is carried out only if the land-owning agency provides a No Objection Certificate.[29] However, the current Delhi Slum and JJ (*jhuggi jhopri*) Rehabilitation and Relocation Policy of 2015 invites the residents to participate in the public-private partnership (PPP) schemes of in situ development, as modeled in the Kathputli colony "slum" rehabilitation project, which was developed by the Delhi Development Authority.[30] Even so, the residents are relocated to resettlement flats if the occupied land is required for a "public purpose." Under the Pradhan Mantri Awas Yojana (the Prime Minister Housing Program) introduced in 2015, DUSIB carries out in situ rehabilitation of residents on land belonging to Delhi government and its agencies, whereas DDA carries out in situ rehabilitation on land belonging to the central government.[31]

In situ upgrading schemes are definitely preferable to brutal demolitions and resettlements; however, only about 5,583 families had been covered under this scheme by 2010.[32] In 2017, DUSIB claimed to have only covered 46,212 families in ninety-nine *jhuggi jhopri* clusters as part of this program in Delhi.[33] Furthermore, as A. Roy (2005: 150) notes, these upgrading schemes necessarily entail "aesthetic upgrading" without bringing about substantial changes in the livelihood and political capacity of the poor. The policy of Environmental Improvement in Urban Slums aims to improve the living standards in the *jhuggi jhopri* clusters in the city. Yet even a preliminary survey of these settlements can convince anyone of the dismal environmental conditions of these neighborhoods. Since 1990, the resettlement policy has targeted "eligible" populations with proof documents from 1990 and 1998 for relocation onto plots measuring 18 and 12.5 square meters, respectively, in the outskirts of the city.[34] As the number and size of plots offered have been progressively reduced from earlier periods, resettlement colonies have been established in far-off areas, including Dwarka, Rohini, Narela, Bawana, Holumbi Kalan, Bhalswa, Molar Band, and Madanpur Khaddar.[35] Further, as Bhan and Shivanand (2013: 59) observe, resettlement colonies like Bawana, Bhalswa, Bakkarwala, and Savda Ghevra have been established outside the urban boundaries demarcated by MPD-III.

The resettlement policy has been revised periodically since its inception. In April 2016, DUSIB approved the Delhi Slum and JJ Rehabilitation and Relocation Policy of 2015, which was substantially shaped by progressive court judgments and the populist measures of the Aam Admi Party (AAP) that formed the Delhi government.[36] Following are the most salient features of eligibility for resettlement:

a. The residents need to prove that their neighborhood has been in existence prior to January 1, 2006. In other words, their neighborhood should have gained official recognition prior to January 1, 2006.

b. They also need to produce "proof documents" that were issued before January 1, 2015. The eligible resident needs to produce one of the designated state-recognized documents and should be able to provide biometric authentication.

c. The resident should appear in at least one of the voters lists between 2012 and 2015.

d. The resident should appear in the survey list for rehabilitation.

The beneficiary is required to contribute 112,000 rupees, along with a maintenance fee of 30,000 rupees for five years after receiving the resettlement flat.[37] After the launch of Jawaharlal Nehru National Urban Renewal Mission (JNNURM), the state policy envisions abandoning the provision of plots in resettlement colonies (DDA [2007] 2010: 37). Gautam Nagar residents who lost their houses in 2009 were covered under the old resettlement policy to receive plots upon the production of documents issued before 1998. However, the protracted struggles delayed their resettlement, and the government has decided to resettle them in flats in accordance with the new resettlement policy. The new policy advocates the provision of flats—through the active involvement of the private sector—measuring 25 square meters with common areas. In turn, the private builders could lease out land for commercial use in premises constructed under the JNNURM program (DDA [2007] 2010: 37–38). JNNURM, the flagship program that has aimed at overhauling cities in India, seeks governance reforms and investments in infrastructure development, notably in public transport and basic services.[38] The Rajiv Gandhi Awas Yojana was announced in 2009, which created the mandate to provide resettlement flats for the residents.[39] The idea was to extend property rights and include the poor within what has been called a "formal system" that is in the domain of state regulation.[40] As A. Roy (2005: 148) argues, these policy prescriptions, which constitute a euphemism for capital accumulation, align with the Peruvian economist Hernando De Soto's call for asset building, self-help, and the legalization of settlements for the poor.

The involvement of the private sector in housing for the poor raises critical questions around accumulation strategies, affordability, transparency, and the viability of high-rise buildings for housing poor people.

However, as Comaroff and Comaroff (2000: 293) note, these capitalist housing policies project an image of messianic, salvific, and magical transformation. The effectiveness of subsidizing housing for the poor by leasing out land or plots for commercial purposes and housing for the middle class needs to be examined once the projects come into fruition. Housing activists have already voiced concerns about the unequal exchanges, appropriation, unbridled profits, and viability of these schemes. In the recent past, planners have actively negotiated with various private sector agencies to provide housing for the poor, though the pace of implementing such schemes has been slow. Further, DUSIB officials note that they encounter problems related to the availability of land, identification of beneficiaries, and court litigations to implement the Rajiv Awas Yojana.[41] Within the mandates of the current policy, the residents receive a lease for the flats for ten years initially. It is envisioned that the leasehold will change to freehold after a period of ten years.[42] The board promises to support the residents to procure loans to defray the costs of resettlement. In keeping the neo-liberal spirit intact, the board requires the resettled people to constitute RWAs in order to self-provision and bear the costs of maintenance in the neighborhoods (see also Graham and Marvin 2001).[43]

The current policy is even more stringent in determining eligibility by requiring biometric authentication and voter list registration of residents, although the policy requires only one of the twelve documents listed as a proof document. The struggle over authentic documents and determination of eligibility is paramount. The board routinely constitutes an appellate authority to redress grievances. A multitude of minutes of the DUSIB meetings (available on the official DUSIB website) uphold that a substantial number of residents are not able to produce the documents. A significant number of the poor become ineligible after living in the settlements for a long time. Through the Gautam Nagar case, I illustrate throughout the book that the displaced residents have struggled to receive resettlement since their *jhuggis* were demolished more than ten years ago. Although the current policy looks more humane than the earlier resettlement policies, the pace of relocation upon displacement has been extremely slow, thereby undermining housing rights in the city.

TABLE 1.2: *Resettlement in Delhi (1990–2009)**

Year	Number of Resettled Families**
1960–85	240,000
1985–90***	—
1990–91	1,570
1991–92	356
1992–93	1,078
1993–94	216
1994–95	839
1995–96	2,353
1996–97	705
1997–98	2,412
1998–99	2,590
1999–2000	4,220
2000–2001	11,045
2001–2002	13,028
2002–2003	6,984
2003–2004	3,811
2004–2005	1,753
2005–2007	11,624
2007–2009	211
Total (1990–2009)	64,795

* Delhi Urban Shelter Improvement Board (DUSIB), 2011, Delhi Resettlement Data, November 23, response to Right to Information (RTI) application (R-3253/Dir/ Rehabilitation) by author. (See also DUSIB, "Present Policies and Strategies," http:// delhishelterboard.in/main/?page_id=128, accessed May 23, 2014.)

** Total annual counts of resettled families include some errors. It is not clear, however, whether officials failed to note each and every demolished *jhuggi*, or if they made calculation errors. Nevertheless, these numbers give an approximate official figure.

*** The focus was on improvement rather than eviction during this period. Data on evictions carried out during this phase are unavailable.

As shown in Table 1.2, between 1960 and 1985, approximately 240,000 families received resettlement plots. In contrast, only about 64,795 families had been resettled as of 2009 after large-scale demolitions began in 1990. As also shown in Table 1.2, the response to a Right to Information application that I filed in 2011 did not provide the details of resettlement between 2009 and 2011.[44] Despite large-scale demolitions, the number of *jhuggi* settlements has steadily increased, underlining the need for housing and also the gradual entrenchment of the poor in the city. In 2010, DUSIB had estimated that there were 685 *jhuggi* settlements in Delhi. The settlements accommodated approximately 2,500,000 people in 419,887 individual *jhuggis*.[45] In 2014, the number of *jhuggi* settlements increased to 701,[46] and the most recent data revealed that there were about 757 *jhuggi* settlements by the year 2019.[47] As stated earlier, there are about three million residents living in approximately 600,000 individual *jhuggis* in Delhi. Thus, these residents struggle to lay claims to citizenship in the city.

Furthermore, unidentified *jhuggi* settlements, or settlements where demolitions happened without any resettlement, are clearly not documented. The state recognizes or identifies a settlement only if it has fifty households, thereby excluding the significant number of settlements with fewer than fifty households.[48] However, at times the planners may incorporate individual *jhuggis* close by into a recognized settlement. As planner RD of DUSIB claimed, "Any *jhuggi* near a settlement may be amalgamated into the recognized cluster once the board and the Delhi government approve such a proposal."

In 2010, it was estimated that only 20 to 30 percent of the displaced population was deemed "eligible" for resettlement among a group of settlements earmarked for compensation.[49] If we take an average of 25 percent, then only about one-fourth of the displaced populations have received resettlement plots prior to the establishment of DUSIB in Delhi. This figure suggests a staggering estimate of 259,180 families displaced (out of which only 64,795 families have received resettlement plots, as argued above) between 1990 and 2009. In other words, approximately 1,295,900 people have been displaced if we assume an average of five members per family. Thus, the housing policy has led to the displacement in the city of approximately 1.3 million people over a period of nineteen years between 1990 and 2009. Additionally, the number of families eligible for resettlement may not tally with the number of actually resettled families. The DUSIB figures indicate the number of "eligible" families, or at best the families that were issued resettlement slips. However, the actual possession of plots or flats was dependent on availability in the

TABLE 1.3: *Resettlement in Delhi (2010–2019)*

Area	Total Number of Flats Built	Total Number of Resettled Flats	Agency
Dwarka	980 (site 1) 736 (site 2) 288 (site 3)	823	DUSIB
Bawana	704 (site 1) 893 (site 2)	266	DSIIDC
Baprola	3,424 (phase I) 3,144 (phase II)	847	DSIIDC
Bhorgarh	1,272		DSIIDC
Ghogha	3,680		DSIIDC
Narela	1,184 (phase I) 228 (different site)		DSIIDC
Pooth Khurad	3,840		DSIIDC
Total	20,373	1,936	

Source: DUSIB, July 30, 2019.

resettlement colonies and the financial ability of the beneficiary to pay resettlement fees. In other words, based on my own field observation, I argue that resettlement plots are not always available, and many or some families cannot afford the deposit. Even in 2019, after nineteen years of displacement, a significant population did not receive resettlement plots and lived in tents in the open spaces in the Azad resettlement colony. Similarly, by the time this book went into production in early October 2021, Gautam Nagar residents had not received their resettlement flats and still waited for the land-owning agency to deposit its share of resettlement costs. A huge backlog of residents have not received resettlement plots or flats after their *jhuggis* were demolished prior to the establishment of DUSIB, as evidenced by numerous court cases.[50]

Under the new policy, the government has provided merely 1,936 resettlement flats between July 1, 2010 and July 30, 2019 (Table 1.3).[51] The Delhi State Industrial and Infrastructure Development Corporation Limited (DSIIDC) and DUSIB have built a total of approximately 20,373 resettlement flats. If the number of resettlement flats represent the eligible recipients or the estimated 25 percent of the total displaced families, then a total of approximately 81,492 families have been displaced between 2010 and 2019. In other words, another 407,460 people have been displaced if we take an average of five members per family between 2010 and 2019. And these figures do not include displaced people from un-surveyed, unidentified, and ineligible *jhuggi* settlements. Thus, there is a solid reason to believe that over one and half million people—1,295,900 between 1990 and 2009 and 407,460 between 2010 and 2019—have been displaced in Delhi. During my visit in July 2019, the planners at DUSIB claimed that they envisioned resettling the poor from the neighbor-hoods of Dhobi Ghat 7 and 9, Vishwas Nagar, and Sunheri Bagh Lane by the end of August 2019. Consequently, while the magnitude of dis-placement has been enormous in the recent past, the rate of resettlement has declined significantly. As previously discussed, the issue of eligibil-ity determination underpinning the calculative rationale of the state is vital. Resettlement produces horrendous consequences for the poor, as discussed in Chapter 2, but the experience of the people displaced with-out resettlement is even worse. Furthermore, the process of resettlement raises critical questions around eligibility and misappropriation of the plots. As planner SR (DUSIB) remarked to me, the Survey, Upgradation [*sic*], Relocation (SUR) section of the DUSIB conducts surveys at the request of the landowning agency: "We collect data about the households with the staff of the landowning agency. The analytical report based on our survey guides the implementation of the policies of relocation and in situ upgradation [*sic*]. During surveys, difficulties arise when the *jhuggis* are being rented, locked, or occupied by the relatives of the residents. We need to exercise responsibility during surveys." Since 2010, the Eligibility Determination Committee of DUSIB has arbitrated on a range of eli-gibility issues concerning the displaced residents in various parts of city. The problem of eligibility and identification remains even during the im-plementation of the new policies. Planner PR (DDA, Vikas Sadan) notes that there are two types of *jhuggi* clusters: identified clusters and uniden-tified clusters. "The Delhi government identifies the *jhuggi* clusters and provides services. If the landowning agency requires the land for 'public purposes,' we take the help of the police commissioner to demolish the cluster. Now we are planning for in situ rehabilitation under the PPP [public-private partnership] model. But it is a big challenge to identify eligible residents. There was a big scam. Malhotra alone had purchased 5,500 plots, most of which were in the resettlement colonies."

Thus, apart from critical questions around eligibility, the issue of misappropriation of plots was significant until 2010. Planners BH and MS (DUSIB) noted in 2011 that the Slum and JJ Department[52] has relocated *jhuggi* clusters before: "There was a lot of *hera pheri* [swindling]. The Central Bureau of Investigation seized the papers related to misappropriation of plots during relocation. You must have heard about the Malhotra scam [Malhotra was accused of purchasing thousands of resettlement plots]. Some government officials and land mafia people were also involved. The poor misuse the policy. We should not provide them houses or plots; we should provide them rooms on a rental basis." Likewise, planner AD remarked in 2019, "In earlier times, the officials in charge of resettlement worked in connivance with the ineligible residents to provide resettlement plots upon the production of *farzi* [counterfeit] documents. A few have been jailed and there are ongoing court cases against some of them."[53]

The distinction between "eligible" and "ineligible" residents creates an atmosphere of desperation. Yet the planners resort to victim-blaming in the absence of adequate housing provisions in the city. The challenge of identifying "eligible" residents creates a space for discretion among planners and the perception of arbitrariness from the perspective of residents. The misappropriation of plots and the influence of state officials and land mafia in manipulating the poor are recurring risks inherent in the implementation of this program. Further, as discussed above, the plots exchange hands and a few people are able to secure multiple plots with the active connivance of a range of agents. Sometimes the poor sell off their allotment documents to *dalals* (touts), as they lack the financial ability to build houses in the colonies. Therefore, the number of actual beneficiaries is fraught with uncertainty. Furthermore, the arbitration concerning eligibility and resettlement raises questions about the heterogeneity of state structures and omissions and commissions of the state that have differential effects on the poor. The state agencies are guided by contradictory rationales and conflicting interests in the projects of resettlement. The demolition and resettlement of the *jhuggi* settlements often involve multiple state agencies: landowning agencies (for example, the Public Works Department or the Indian Railways), DUSIB (the nodal agency responsible for carrying out surveys, resettlement, and eligibility under the state government), the Government of National Capital Territory of Delhi (the state government that makes decisions regarding resettlement), the Ministry of Urban Development and its agencies (central government and their agencies that shape housing policies), and the judiciary. The agencies of the state are not in agreement with each other; they have different intentions and operations concerning the same issue at different points in time. Often the landowning agencies, which are mostly state agencies, do not adhere to the protocols of the state policies of resettlement. They frequently hesitate or procrastinate in providing the required amount of money for rehabilitation as per the policy. At times, they carry out demolitions with the support of the Delhi Police (a state agency under central government in Delhi) without carrying out proper surveys and informing DUSIB.[54] Thus, although DUSIB—guided by the populist measures of AAP and progressive judgments of the court in the last ten years—has attempted to resettle the displaced residents, the landowning agencies have shown lukewarm interest in the resettlement of residents. For instance, the Public Works Department (PWD—the landowning agency—had not committed its share of the financial contribution of resettlement for Gautam Nagar residents even as this book went to press in early October 2021, thereby considerably delaying the resettlement of the residents.[55] As I argue throughout the book, the calculative rationality of the state is often contradictory; various state agencies simultaneously enfranchise and disenfranchise the poor.

At times there are bottlenecks in the implementation of housing policies due to political differences between the state government and central government. In the past, the judiciary has both attempted to subvert the redistributive intentions of the state as well as bolster the populist measures of the state agencies. While the judiciary played a critical role as a "slum demolition machine" (Bhuwania 2017) in the two decades beginning in 1990, it has reversed some of these intentions in forging redistributive goals in the recent past. In fact, the draft protocols of rehabilitation enshrined in the recent populist measures of the state have been shaped in accordance with the court orders.[56] As a result, while the focus in recent times has been on accumulation through urban design and development, the new Aam Admi Party (AAP) has attempted to reverse the effects of these policies through populist politics (cf. Chatterjee 2011). The populist politics of AAP steers clear of any ideological affiliation[57] and accentuates the need to provide better urban governance. A pragmatic party, AAP remains non-committal to some fundamental principles enshrined in the constitution of India, namely secularism; nonetheless it is geared toward revisiting the framework of passive revolution in urban planning. In other words, its agenda is primarily to redistribute the accumulation of profits and revenues through populist measures of providing resettlement flats and providing subsidized or free public goods including electricity, water, public transport, and school education.

Thus, the changing political regimes have shaped the policies and the contents of the draft protocols of resettlement. In the latest resettlement policy of 2015, there is an emphasis on the economic indispensability of the poor, the requirement of subsidized public housing, and willingness to adhere to the humane judgments of the judiciary.[58] A longer view about the citizenship struggles of the poor needs to take into account the changes in the planning protocols, political regimes, the nature of the judiciary, and the politics of the poor in the city. In this chapter, I have traced various conjunctures that have shaped the planning rationales as well as the calculative governmentality of the poor. A primary planning focus was to make Delhi "slum free." In this respect, the planning agencies have concentrated on planning demolitions and resettlements in the city. I turn to the issue of planning of demolitions and resettlements and the social suffering that have accompanied these initiatives in the next chapter. Following an analysis of social suffering that is inherent in the policies of demolitions and resettlements, I analyze the politics of the poor in their citizenship struggles in the remainder of the book.

CHAPTER 2

THE PLANNING OF DEMOLITION
AND RESETTLEMENT
Structural Violence and Social Suffering of the Poor

THE PROCESS OF URBAN restructuring in the last three decades has inaugurated a planning desire to make Delhi "world class." As discussed in Chapter 1, there is an accentuation on building a "distinct city personality." The aesthetics and aspirations that have underpinned these abstract planning imaginations have led to the emergence of an ensemble of calculative rationalities. The fundamental aim is to restrict migration into the city, clear congestion, and to make Delhi "slum-free." While the predominant motif of urban planning is to build a world-class city, I have also argued throughout the book that the planning regimes and states are multifaceted. The rationales of state apparatuses are often divergent (and at times incommensurate) in "world-class" city-making. To give an illustration, when the judicial arm of the state (with the implicit support of the then chief minister of Delhi) justified decongestion and cleaning of retail shops across Delhi in its pursuit of world-class city-making in 2006–2007, the Government of India enacted new laws and suggested amendments to the Master Plan to allow mixed land use as a response to widespread protest and violence on the part of the retail traders in the city (Mehra 2012: 84). In other words, the central government eventually undermined the judgments of the court and actions of the executive in responding to these logics of world-class city-making. As I show, the acts of commission and the omissions of various state agencies serve as the sine qua non for understanding the tactics and counter-tactics of numerical citizenship.

Nonetheless, the demolition of *jhuggi jhopri* settlements and a strict enforcement of eligibility for resettlement have shaped the urban planning regimes in Delhi in recent decades. In this chapter, I analyze the ideological and practical motivations that underlie the planning of demolition and resettlement to begin with. Then I examine the social suffering endured by the poor as a result of the structural violence of demolition and resettlement in order to provide the context to analyze the numerical citizenship struggles in Delhi.

PLANNING REGIMES AND THE PRODUCTION OF SOCIAL SPACES

The social spaces of *jhuggi jhopri*, transit camp, and resettlement colonies do not merely provide a "passive locus of social relations" but also actively shape relations of production and social reproduction (Lefebvre 1991: 11). Henri Lefebvre introduces a conceptual triad of "spatial practices," "representations of space," and "representational space" as a model for understanding the range of social relations that produce social space in particular historical periods. Spatial practices refer to how people perceive and act in spaces in their daily routines of producing and reproducing themselves. For example, spatial practices of the poor entail migration from the rural hinterland to the city in search of work and shelter, movements within the city, and the everyday activities they engage in to sustain life (see Gidwani and Sivaramakrishnan 2003: 341; Kudva 2009: 1619). Likewise, the spatial practices of the owners of capital and planners include investment decisions, restructuring processes, demolitions, and resettlement in the city. The representations of space, or conceptualized space, include the space of planners who express an abstract conception of the city in their imaginations, written plans, and policies. Finally, representational space is the actual lived space produced through spatial practices with their associated symbols, aspirations, and protocols of resistance. For example, the tactics of the poor in Gautam Nagar to claim resettlement or the tactics of Sitapuri residents to rename their neighborhood to gain a foothold in the city epitomize the representational spaces in Delhi. In the vein of Lefebvre, I examine the "dialectical relationship which exists within the triad of the perceived, the conceived, and the lived" (Lefebvre 1991: 39). Social spaces are constituted by and constitutive of relations of social reproduction, including the biological reproduction and reproduction of labor power to sustain life over generations, and the relations of production that define neoliberal capitalism in megacities like Delhi. Although Lefebvre focuses on Western capitalist modes and relations of production, his model can be extended to examine how social spaces entail capitalist relations and non-capitalist relations of production (see Chatterjee 2008b; Sanyal 2007) as well as relations of social reproduction underpinned by caste, gender, religious, and ethnic differences.

As discussed above, the production of social space is underpinned by social, legal, political, and economic relations in the city. Thus, planning protocols, political regimes, the nature of the judiciary, and the politics of the poor and the activists shape the social spaces in the city. Let us examine the ideological and practical motivations of the planners. Of course, the interventions of the planners are not autonomous and independent of the spatial practices of various constituencies in the city. Nevertheless, the planning knowledge, ideology, and rationale play a salient role in the restructuring of urban spaces (Lefebvre 1991: 42). An analysis of their ideological and practical motivations will allow us to understand the production of specific social spaces, including Gautam Nagar, the Sitapuri transit camp, and the Azad resettlement colony, in more detail.

The planners largely view the planning process as an impartial technical exercise. In this regard, the planners continue to reiterate the need to keep the planning process free from politics:

Planner BS (Delhi Development Authority [DDA]):
The DDA functions according to the mandate of the Delhi Development Act. The DDA is the technical authority that approves land-use plans, which are later ratified by the central government. However, there are often delays due to conflicts of interests. The state government may initiate projects but cannot go ahead on its own without the approval of the DDA; the state government does not have the authority to change land use in the city. The politicians may protect short-term objectives, as they aspire to be reelected

after five years. But planning is a slow, gradual, and long-term process. The politicians often pressure the DDA to regularize unauthorized colonies, but they seldom talk about low-cost housing. A particular project may be technically sound, but it has to be backed by financial and administrative resources and political will.

Planner JK (Town and Country Planning Organization):
The DDA is a giant organization controlling land in the city. The government of Delhi does not have much power when it comes to land use in the city. In one sense, vested political interests are avoided in the effective planning and development of different neighborhoods. Otherwise, the members of the legislative assembly will promote vested interests concerning their own constituencies.

Planner MD (Institute of Town Planners, India):
The political interference in the planning process is the major obstacle against plan implementation. For instance, the politicians even intervened to change road alignments when a particular group of people was affected during construction work prior to the Commonwealth Games. The politicians intervene during plan preparation, plan implementation, and plan enforcement. See, the vice chairman of the DDA is an Indian Administrative Services [IAS] officer, who has to listen to another IAS officer, the chief secretary of Delhi, who in turn reports to the chief minister of Delhi. So the state government has political influence over the planning process.

Planner BC (Delhi Development Authority):
The politicians come to us with their demands, but we try our best not to deviate from planning protocols. The Supreme Court of India treats the Master Plan as the bible and also supports our non-partial expertise.

Planner BJ (National Capital Region Planning Board):
The implementation process is shoddy, especially in its inability to restrict the encroachment of government land, which in turn is largely due to political interference.

Planner SD (Delhi Development Authority):

The *jhuggi jhopris* are vote banks of the political parties. If we try to demolish these during BJP rule, then the Congress politicians come with their flags to protest and if we attempt to demolish during the Congress rule, then BJP politicians come with their flags to resist.

These planners highlight the relative autonomy of the planning process, administrative complexities, and political bottlenecks. They also view politics as a major obstacle to the effective implementation of plans. As shown above, the issues of development, enforcement, implementation, and monitoring preoccupy the planners. While one particular planner (planner BS) showed concern for low-income housing, the rest of the planners argued for strict adherence to planning protocols. Efforts to regularize unauthorized colonies are often cited as examples of political interference. The political class is seen as bypassing the planning regulations in the city. The planners think that they alone should have autonomy regarding land management in the city. In contrast, the planning process responds to a complex reality with respect to land management, powerful interests, and political expediencies. There are innumerable cases of planning violations concerning farmhouses, religious structures, Metro Rail stations, and shopping malls (Baviskar 2011; Baviskar 2020; Soni 2000; Srivastava 2009). In this respect, the planning machinery improvises and subverts its own planning protocols. On the one hand, the violations accommodate the interests of the rich, promote the signature projects of the state, and expand spaces of leisure and accumulation for the middle and upper classes. On the other hand, the violations provide spaces for settlements of the poor in the absence of low-income housing in the city. In other words, the planning regime in India is marked by a "state of deregulation, ambiguity, and exception" (A. Roy 2009: 76). As Roy argues, the "idiom of urbanization" is not necessarily anti-planning in India; rather, the planning regime is produced through state informality (A. Roy 2009: 80). Furthermore, while bringing politics to the fore provides a standpoint for critiquing the abstract rationale underpinning planning expertise and representations of social spaces, it is also important to analyze the nuances in the exercise of political power and the process of urban development on a case-by-case basis.

Along with the spatial practices of various constituencies, the abstract planning ideologies shape various kinds of social spaces in Delhi. Before I turn to an analysis of abstract planning rationales shaping Gautam Nagar, the Sitapuri transit camp, and the Azad resettlement colony, let me provide an analysis of the production of social spaces that the poor inhabit in the city. As I argued earlier, the poor inhabit various spaces in terms of their incremental entrenchment in the city. Consequently, they inhabit the social spaces of pavements/shelters; unrecognized, unidentified, and un-surveyed settlements; villages, unauthorized colonies, designated slum areas, or planned colonies; government-recognized *jhuggi jhopri* (JJ) settlements; old resettlement colonies and transit camps; and new resettlement colonies. The social spaces are neither abstract survey categories nor stable entities and are instead historically produced and remain unstable and mutable. Yet these spaces provide the material casing of social life for the poor (Harvey 2008; Lefebvre 1991).

a. **Pavements and shelters:** The homeless, who are mostly migrants from the rural hinterland, occupy the spaces of pavements and night shelters in the cities. Thus, the social space of the urban homeless is shaped by agrarian relations and rural dispossessions and urban dis-entitlements (G. Menon 2018). Simply put, the spaces of the homeless represent the social relations of the rural hinterland that spill over to the pavements of the cities. At times, the patriarchal intra-family relations epitomized in unequal age and gender relations and intimate violence underlie the neglect and abandonment experienced by the homeless. The urban homeless are the most vulnerable and marginalized populations in the city. The life of the urban homeless or destitute is marked by everyday violence and philanthropy (Bornstein 2012), which intersect with planning and political regimes in the city. The social spaces of the homeless are constantly reconfigured: they are underpinned by regimes of police violence, political patronage, and philanthropic relations. While most of the urban homeless live on the streets, a few of them are under the purview of state governmentality when they secure porta cabins or night shelters[1] during inclement weather conditions. The category of "homeless" is not a fixed category, as a few of the homeless may secure a foothold in unrecognized *jhuggi jhopri* settlements over the years but largely remain outside the mechanics and dynamics of housing entitlements in the city. In other words, their lack of spatial and at times temporal entrenchment excludes them from the dynamic politics of displacement and resettlement. For the homeless, the fundamental struggle is to survive everyday violence, hunger, and harsh weather.

b. **Unrecognized, unidentified, and un-surveyed settlements:** The unrecognized, unidentified, and un-surveyed *jhuggi* settlements are of relatively recent origin compared to the state-recognized *jhuggi* settlements, many of which date back more than fifteen years in the city. These spaces are produced as a result of production relations and inventiveness of the poor in the city. To begin with, some of these spaces accommodate the workers of myriad industries, which lowers the costs of the reproduction of labor power and increases the profit margins of capital. The unrecognized settlements emerge in the interstices of city spaces amid factories, construction sites, and abandoned sites. The poor also use their inventiveness to meet the basic requirements of shelter and other concerns of social reproduction in order to sustain their lives. Living in unrecognized settlements, the poor experience everyday demolition of certain kinds in these spaces. Like the homeless poor, the urban poor in the un-surveyed settlements are mostly excluded from activities concerning housing entitlements in the city. Once displaced, the residents of these settlements do not receive alternate resettlement plots or flats. The primary struggle of the poor in these neighborhoods is to secure state recognition and protection by enmeshing themselves in the political relations in the city. While the poor may receive minimal patronage from the police and local municipal officials during the fledgling years of the neighborhood, the strengthening of political relations with the political and bureaucratic structures of the local state offers possibilities of gradual entrenchment in the city. In other words, the lived space is a product of the struggles associated with temporal aspects of subsisting and claiming citizenship in the city.

c. **Villages, unauthorized colonies,**[2] **designated slum areas, or planned colonies:** These spaces are marked by different colonial, planning, and social relations. For instance, the urban villages were demarcated in terms of inhabited areas and farm areas—the latter under the purview of taxation regulations during colonial rule (Chakravarty 2016: 113). As the inhabited areas of the urban villages are exempt from building and planning regulations, in continuation of colonial policies, a spirit of entrepreneurship has shaped the efforts at speculation, rent maximization, and densification of these spaces (114).[3] The unauthorized colonies are social spaces on the land outside designated legal zones for development and for residential use (Bhan 2013; Sheikh and Banda 2016). Nevertheless, they are an outcome of planning, legal, and social relations in the city. The Slum Improvement and Clearance Areas Act of 1956 designates the slum areas—social spaces that are "unfit" for human habitation. Nevertheless, the designated slum areas are considered legal and entitled to various state services. Thus, various planning, legal, and municipal regimes intersect in shaping the social space of designated slum areas. Finally, the planned colonies are "legal" social spaces that have been envisioned and developed by state agencies. The urban poor living in these four types of social spaces rent their houses and do not face imminent displacement and resettlement. These renters may enjoy certain benefits with respect to basic amenities by renting in social spaces that are relatively better serviced than the three types of settlements listed below. However, some may be even poorer than these other displaced residents, particularly insofar as the renters do not have the possibility of ever procuring resettlement plots or flats. The upwardly mobile poor may at times be able to purchase houses, especially in the villages and unauthorized colonies. The nature, range of property values, and built structures of these settlements vary greatly. The residents owning property in unauthorized colonies usually do not face the problem of displacement. The spatial practices and collective struggles in unauthorized colonies cut across the poor, the lower middle classes, and even the wealthy landlords who may or may not live in the neighborhood. It should also be noted that many poor also rent houses in *jhuggi* settlements, old resettlement colonies, transit camps, and new resettlement colonies without many prospects for procuring current or future housing under relocation schemes. The poor residents of planned colonies mostly reside in "servant" quarters. As a result, caste and class relations determine the spatial practices of social reproduction of daily life in the planned colonies/neighborhoods, wherein the poor and mostly oppressed caste residents carry out a range of social reproduction work (see also Froystad 2003).

d. **Recognized *jhuggi jhopri (JJ)* settlements:** The urban poor in state-recognized *jhuggi jhopri* neighborhoods are embedded within various structures of the state. While the spatial practices of the poor in these neighborhoods are similar to those of the unrecognized settlements with respect to production and social reproduction, the residents are engaged with numerical citizenship struggles, especially with regard to housing in the city. Most of these neighborhoods are targets of demolition at some point, except for those covered under in situ upgrading (as discussed in Chapter 1). The primary struggle of the poor is to resist or delay displacement and fight to secure resettlement plots or flats upon demolition of *jhuggi jhopri* neighborhoods. The *jhuggi* residents of recognized settlements have been surveyed and identified in the government database. Thus, the neighborhoods have a temporal privilege—they have gained state patronage and the residents have incrementally laid claims to infrastructure and other basic amenities. As argued earlier, the processes of numerical documentation of the number of years spent and assertion of numerical strength in the neighborhoods strengthen the claims of citizenship in these neighborhoods. Usually, the Municipal Corporation of Delhi (MCD) provides minimal infrastructure and basic services in these neighborhoods. Most of the residents in these settlements are eligible to procure subsidized food and other household amenities and resettlement flats if they can produce proof documents (ration cards and voter IDs) that were obtained before pre-determined cut-off dates. As previously pointed out, the current cut-off date for eligible resettlement is January 1, 2015. However, a significant number of the urban poor living in these settlements do not possess proof documents (an issue discussed in Chapter 4). Some residents rent out a *jhuggi* in these neighborhoods, making them ineligible for compensation upon demolition.[4] Some of the residents who reside outside the *jhuggi jhopri* settlements may still own a *jhuggi*. *Jhuggi* owners possessing proof documents usually receive resettlement plots/flats upon demolition.

e. **Old resettlement colonies and transit camps**: The old resettlement colonies and transit camps were established at various times in the city's history, as discussed in Chapter 1. These neighborhoods were primarily an outcome of the abstract imagination of planners, which ignored the lived realities of the poor. Most of the old resettlement colonies were established in the 1970s with a ninety-nine-year lease, and the poor there are provided with basic amenities. In 2013, the government extended freehold or ownership rights to the residents of forty-five resettlement colonies in Delhi.[5] The transit camps were mostly developed after the Emergency period and prior to the implementation of the new resettlement policy in the 1990s, and they were designed to accommodate displaced populations on a temporary basis during the 1980s. The future of these "temporary" existing transit camps remains uncertain in terms of tenure, security, and legal regularization, thereby precipitating certain modalities of politics. The transit camps that do not face any immediate demolition can be regarded as old resettlement colonies in terms of legal status.

f. **New resettlement colonies:** The new resettlement colonies have been established since 1990. The squeezing of resettlement plots, provisioning of services, changes in tenure security, and the process of displacement mark shifts in the policy of resettlement. The new resettlement colonies only had a tenure security of five years to begin with, but tenure security has been renewed upon expiration. However, the new resettlement policy aims at providing flats instead of plots of land to the displaced residents in resettlement colonies (as discussed in Chapter 1). The variations in the provisioning of resettlement draw our attention not only to the different kinds of housing and infrastructure, but also to the associated processes of physical and social mobility. Furthermore, the social relations with the host populations and the emerging gender relations remain prominent in shaping these social spaces. It should also be noted that the complexities around housing, land titles, and the struggles of the urban poor are heterogeneous and diverse. Even the most careful classification and categorization of these social spaces must make room for anomalies. (For instance, the poor also rent properties in regularized unauthorized colonies, *lal dora* extended areas, and rural villages, and the upwardly mobile poor may be able to buy properties in these social spaces.)[6] Nevertheless, these social spaces have overlapping features with respect to various abstract imaginations, spatial practices, and lived struggles. Moreover, these typologies provide an analytical anchor to examine the processes of entrenchment that define displacement and resettlement and the concomitant numerical citizenship struggles. Thus, I have chosen a *jhuggi jhopri* settlement, a transit camp, and a resettlement colony to examine the intersecting aspects of incremental entrenchment, contradictions of state governmentality, and the numerical citizenship struggles of the poor.

PLANNING AND THE PRODUCTION OF GAUTAM NAGAR, SITAPURI TRANSIT CAMP, AND AZAD RESETTLEMENT COLONY

To illustrate the conceptual points about the production of space, let us turn again to the chosen field sites, which are produced through spatial practices, abstract ideologies, and lived practices. The case of Gautam Nagar yields insights into the *spatial practices* of *jhuggi* building among migrants, practices which are a primary mode of claiming urban space, housing, and livelihood in the city. This case also raises issues about the arena of abstract imagination and *representations of space* on the part of planners, lawyers, and judges. My analysis therefore focuses on how residents, through their struggles against displacement, have gained recognition from the local government in order to receive infrastructure, services, and basic amenities and to receive resettlement plots or flats. The political and judicial struggles of the poor in the *lived space* of Gautam Nagar bring to light how the commissions and omissions of the various agencies of the state become critical for the citizenship projects of the poor. The residents continue to be actively engaged in a struggle to prove their eligibility for resettlement by producing proof documents.

The establishment of Gautam Nagar entailed an incremental process of entrenchment in the city. According to letters to politicians and state officials demanding basic amenities in the neighborhood, residents have been living in the area since 1973. A part of the neighborhood was demolished in early 2009. It was argued that the residents "encroached" on a road and were not entitled to resettlement (the legal battle concerning Gautam Nagar from 2009 to 2019 is discussed in Chapter 5). Located amid an area of many other *jhuggi* settlements, Gautam Nagar lacks neatly demarcated borders. Careless surveys and haphazard documentation of the residents often lead to errors regarding residence status in the area. For instance, the residents living in X *jhuggi* settlement often show up in the electoral roll of Y *jhuggi* settlement. Similarly, unscrupulous documentation of survey answers has resulted in errors on ration cards and voter IDs (struggles around these issues are discussed in Chapter 4). The demolition was carried out in spite of the Delhi Law (Special Provisions) Act, 2006, which prohibits demolitions in the city. However, *jhuggi* demolitions have continued unabated to make way for the construction of "public projects,"[7] as permitted under the act.

The production of social space was also evident when the Sitapuri transit camp was established to accommodate people displaced from "squatter clusters." Built between 1984 and 1985 after an order by the lieutenant governor of Delhi, the Sitapuri transit camp was constructed as one of six transit camps established around that time.[8] The Sitapuri camp was developed on an area of 11.93 hectares to accommodate 2,094 families in a "green zone" or district park area.[9] The residents were settled on a temporary and nominal license fee basis. In fact, while deliberating on the future course of action, the Delhi Development Authority officials recapitulated several salient features of transit camps from a report titled "Transit Camp: A New System of Rehabilitation of *Jhuggi* Dwellers." The report stipulated the following:[10]

- "Transit camps will be of temporary/semi-permanent nature."

- "Each unit shall not be more than ten square meters."

- "Services namely water, sewer and electricity will be [provided] on [a] community basis."

- "*Jhuggi* dwellers will only reside for a period of six to ten months and then will be shifted . . . to dwelling units in an area of eighteen square meters."

It was assumed that residents could be moved to resettlement colonies within a few months, at which point the original Master Plan land-use stipulation could be restored.[11] However, the government neither resettled the population within the stipulated time period nor showed an active interest in changing the land use. This policy illustrates the ad hoc planning regime, especially for a resource-starved city, to house a population in tenements before relocating them just six to ten months later. Further, the DDA violated planning norms when a significant portion of the transit camp was established on designated "recreational" land instead of in a "residential area." This is a case of unplanned planning or "planned illegalities" (Bhan 2013) insofar as proper deliberation on the transit camp's future was not taken into account. In this case the planning regime did not demonstrate a standardized, legally binding, and modernist rationale. Furthermore, the members of the RWA of the adjoining Lakshmi colony petitioned the court for the demolition of the neighborhood in 2003. Settling the poor in a "green zone" and targeting them again for demolition after twenty years reflects not only the arbitrariness but also the tentativeness and ad hoc character of the planning machinery. The case illustrates the informal and improvised character of a state that subverts its own authorized rules through a process of deregulation (A. Roy 2009: 80). While the DDA changed the land use of a particular pocket of land to establish a middle-class school,[12] similar rezoning efforts led by transit camp residents have been unsuccessful. The resettled populations remain "transitory encroachers" in the imaginations of the middle-class residents who aim at reclaiming the use of the area for their own purposes. Here, state informality has exclusionary effects (A. Roy 2009: 81). Further, the planners claim that the original inhabitants have sold their plots to "rich" people. As planner M notes, "We do not find original beneficiaries in these neighborhoods anymore. The transit camps are inhabited by 'rich' people who have built multistoried buildings."

In the cases of both Gautam Nagar and Sitapuri, the issue of the power and protection of dominant interests remains integral to the abstract planning process that inform the representations of space (see also Flyvbjerg 2002; Flyvberg 2004), as the issues of development of infrastructure and zoning adherence disproportionately benefit particular sections of the population. Gautam Nagar and the Sitapuri transit camp fall under the F planning zone. According to Delhi zonal plans, the F zone is particularly marked by low-density population, green and open spaces, the Ridge area (Delhi Ridge), and "posh residential localities" (Puri 2010: 2.8). The zone is also unique for encompassing three important industrial districts in Delhi. In particular, the zone contains Okhla Industrial Area, Mohan Cooperative Industrial Area, and the Small Industries Service Institute (SISI) complex (Puri 2010: 2.10). The surroundings of these industrial areas become a destination for the poor looking for employment opportunities. Furthermore, a sizable section of poor women find jobs in the middle-class households located in this zone. Without adequate housing provision in the city, the spatial practices of the poor are aimed at gradually settling in various *jhuggi* settlements in the area. Many of the *jhuggi* settlements in the zone have been demolished as part of urban restructuring drives since the early 1990s. The remaining settlements, including the undemolished part of Gautam Nagar, are insecure with respect to their existence in the future.

In 2001, prior to massive demolitions, the population of the F zone stood at 1,717,000 (Puri 2010: 2.9). The planning machinery has projected a population- holding capacity of 1,975,000 for the year of 2021 as a result of re-densification (Puri 2010: 2.8). The class logic of planning is blatant as the projected plan aims at re-densification after massive demolitions of low-income households in the area. As discussed in Chapter 1, the protocols of the first Master Plan, which envisage mixed land use and the integration of work and housing opportunities in the neighborhoods, have been subverted by the contemporary urban planning regimes. In contrast to the first Master Plan, the current plans emphasize infrastructure development as part of the urban restructuring drives in the city. For instance, the third Master Plan has proposed "urban relief roads all over Delhi" (Puri 2010: 2.18). The materialization of the abstract "relief roads" policy has led to the construction of an underpass that rendered approximately three hundred residents homeless in Gautam Nagar.

The Azad resettlement colony was planned for about ten thousand families in an area of about 51 hectares[13] and was developed in three phases. The different blocks in the colony accommodate displaced residents from different *jhuggi* settlements in Delhi. The Azad resettlement colony was established in the O zone, thereby violating the prescriptions laid out in the third Master Plan. The O zone is alternatively designated as the Yamuna River zone, specifically developed to maintain ecological balance, control pollution, and preserve flora and fauna around the river. While the brutal demolitions of Yamuna Pushta *jhuggi* settlements were carried out with a stated objective to promote the sustainability of the river, the Azad resettlement colony was developed a few meters away from the river in contravention of this same policy. I chose the Azad resettlement colony for study as it is the nearest resettlement colony to the *jhuggi* settlements in the F zone. The resettlement policies explicitly state that populations should be resettled near the place of their earlier residence. According to this policy, the Azad resettlement colony should have taken displaced people from Gautam Nagar. While I attempt to examine the experience of displacement in a particular zone (the F zone) and the process of resettlement in the nearest resettlement colony, in many instances the displaced poor have been resettled in far-away resettlement colonies.

It is ironic that the planning authority decided to resettle a population in the damp, marshy, inaccessible area of a riverbed. This example of "informality from above," where the state violates its own specifications to manage territories (A. Roy 2009: 84), has grievous consequences for the poor, as discussed below. The change of land use required the approval of the Yamuna Action Plan committee.[14] The DDA was aware that silting had already reduced the carrying capacity of the soil, thereby increasing the risks of flooding in the riverbed, and officials had stipulated that "no residential, commercial, industrial, or public/semi-public facility requiring permanent structures should be provided on the riverbed."[15] Moreover, a committee of experts from the National Environmental Engineering Research Institute strictly advised against developing the resettlement colony in the riverbed after carrying out a ground-level study.[16] The committee warned about the hazardous health effects of emissions from the Thermal Power Plant in the vicinity. Further, it argued that the LPG bottling plant to the north of the proposed site posed a major fire hazard in the area. In addition, "*samadhi* [tomb/mausoleum] complexes, crematorium grounds, sports complexes, thermal and gas power stations, bathing *ghats* [riverbanks], sewerage treatment plants, fly-ash ponds and fly-ash brick plants" feature prominently in the O zone (Puri 2010: 3.87). Resettling a population in a low-lying area inundated with treatment plants and crematorium grounds further exposes the class logic of urban planning in the city. In fact, the planners themselves concede that the resettlement colony should not have been located in the area:

> PLANNER U (DDA): The high power committee chaired by the lieutenant governor had concluded that no construction should be allowed in Yamuna zone. But I guess some changes were made at the last minute to accommodate the resettlement colony.

> PLANNER M (DDA): The DDA wants to develop Yamuna zone in order to rejuvenate and channelize the Yamuna River. It also wants to develop the riverbed as a green recreational space. Then how did it develop the resettlement colony there? What can we expect from the private sector if the DDA itself flouts the rules? The DDA is well aware that the zone is prone to flooding. Only the Commonwealth Games village and Akshardham temple, which have been built in the zone, have been suitably cordoned off. Our [the planners', including his own] recommendations were not taken into account.

These statements do not tell us clearly if the planners are worried about the resettled population, the failure of the objective of creating a leisure space in the riverbed, or both. While the leisure and religious spaces were safely cordoned off, the resettlement colony for a proposed population of ten thousand families was developed without much attention. The planners' comments also reveal their disagreements, even concerning impartial "technical expertise." In other words, the establishment of the Azad resettlement colony illustrates a curious case of conflicts arising from power dynamics among the planners. Furthermore, the construction of leisure and religious spaces in addition to the resettlement colony reaffirm the extra-legal character of the state implementation of urban planning.

The transfer of *jhuggi* residents to the Azad resettlement colony was carried out in haste without proper plotting. The total area was mostly designated as an "agricultural and water body [Yamuna River zone]."[17] Thus, there was a need to change the land-use designation from an "agricultural and water body" to a residential area.[18] The residents were transferred even before plots were developed in the neighborhood. The contentious land acquisition process created animosity between the residents and the host populations in the nearby villages. The poor were left to fend for themselves against the wrath of the host populations (discussed in the next sections).[19] The provisioning of services in the neighborhood was complicated, as the land-use changes had not been initiated before the colony was established. The DDA considered the establishment of the Azad resettlement colony a "liability."[20] It further argued that the task of developing the colony was "thrust upon" the authority.[21] What is also intriguing is that the neighborhood is labeled and referred to as a "transit camp" developed for temporary accommodation,[22] thereby highlighting the ad hoc planning.

The planners do not require clearance from the Delhi Urban Arts Commission (DUAC), which approves the aesthetics and functionality of projects, prior to developing the resettlement colonies. As planner MA (DUAC) noted, "It is not within the mandate of DUAC to suggest aesthetic norms for the resettlement colonies. For this reason, we do not receive proposals with respect to resettlement colonies." The planning logic described above illustrates how housing for the poor need not abide by requirements prescribed for other planned neighborhoods. In other words, the planners do not consider whether the poor may also require the aesthetic and functional integration of their neighborhoods. Or it may be the case that the experts always regard the resettlement colonies as temporary, capable of conveniently being removed during times of urban restructuring. In a nutshell, the cases reflect ad hocism, that is, the tentativeness and improvised character of the implementation and violation of planning protocols in the city. The three cases described above raise critical questions about democracy, the mechanisms and effects of state power, and urban development (Flyvbjerg 2002: 356).

The abstract rationale of the planners has accentuated city aesthetics, migration control, and removal of the poor from the urban spaces. The process of urban restructuring has often resulted in the displacement of the urban poor from valuable land, which Harvey (2008: 33–34) has evocatively described as a process of "accumulation by dispossession." Demolition has remained the cornerstone of the current planning apparatus. The poor have endured enormous social suffering as a result of demolitions and resettlements.

With this backdrop of planning regimes and calculative governmentality, I turn to an analysis of the structural violence of demolition and resettlement and the social suffering experienced by the poor. An analysis of social suffering in the three low-income neighborhoods provides the context to understand the struggles associated with numerical citizenship in the following chapters. In recent years, Paul Farmer has popularized the idea of "structural violence," a term he uses as a "broad rubric that includes a host of offensives against human dignity: extreme and relative poverty, social inequalities ranging from racism to gender inequality, and the more spectacular forms of violence that are uncontestedly human rights abuses" (Farmer 2003: 8; see also Farmer 2004). Drawing on my own ethnographic observations and the accounts of my respondents, I show how displacement and resettlement produce a range of experiences of social suffering caused by the structural violence of planning regimes for the poor.[23]

PLANNING REGIMES AND THE STRUCTURAL VIOLENCE OF DEMOLITIONS

The tentativeness, ad hocism, and class basis of demolition and resettlement practices, described above, define the central features of planning in

Delhi. In fact, Delhi's housing policy promising "shelter for all" through the spatial integration of economic activities, social services, and urban activities (Planning Commission 2009: 108) has been systematically abandoned in its everyday implementation. The structural violence of demolitions is marked by top-down and non-participatory practices that often violate basic citizenship entitlements in the city. In Gautam Nagar, the residents were warned to vacate the premises peacefully the night before the impending demolition. Those who made some attempt to protest against the demolition were beaten ruthlessly. The intermediaries were unconstitutionally rounded up and taken to the police station to prevent residents from inciting violent protests. As S *pradhan* remarked, "We were merely told that there was an order and taken to the police station." Cell phones were snatched to interrupt communication with the activists, politicians, and the media. Often the demolitions happen without any notice and with the use of force. At times, there are no records available of these demolitions. As activist R of Delhi Shramik Sangathan (DSS) told me, "The resettlement policies are not followed, surveys are not conducted, and procedures are not abided by during demolitions. To give you examples, we [the activists] had to intervene in R. K. Puram in March 2011, as the *jhuggis* were targeted for demolition to construct a drain without following any procedure. Similarly, in Karolbagh, the Gayatri colony was demolished using force."

When I visited Gautam Nagar a few days before the demolition in late January 2009 during a preliminary field visit, the residents remarked that the demolitions would be carried out due to the urgency of preparations for the Commonwealth Games. A resident remarked, "*Iss desh ka nagarik bas kothiwala aur videshi hai*" (The true citizen of this country is the one who owns a house or is a foreigner). The resident aptly remarks how Delhi has become a city of *kothiwala*[s]. As Sundaram has argued, the planners of Delhi have historically envisaged building Delhi, as demonstrated in successive Master Plans, in line with the post-war American imagination of suburban planning (Sundaram 2010). Like the suburban vision in the US, the Delhi plans imagined *kothis* (mansions on gigantic plots) for the wealthy, but systematically banished the urban poor and "rural forms of work and life to the periphery" (Sundaram 2010: 65). A

FIGURE 2.1: *The construction of a luxury hotel near the demolished site of Gautam Nagar just prior to the Commonwealth Games of Delhi in 2010.*

luxury hotel opened a few months after the demolition, barely 200 meters away from the demolished site. Residents argued that the hotel opened just in time to accommodate the Commonwealth Games guests. The police prohibited the street vendors and scrap dealers from working in order to temporarily clean up the neighborhood during the games (Routray 2021). Most often, these petty entrepreneurs were evicted from the area after their carts and weighing machines were seized. Thus, the desire to present a world-class city to tourists and foreigners during the Commonwealth Games was taken to be the primary reason for the demolition of Gautam Nagar and the eviction of street vendors.

Similarly, a demolition drive against street vendors was launched when I was doing fieldwork in Sitapuri. I was having a conversation with one particular vendor in late August 2010. The vendors sold vegetables, spices, clothes, junk jewelry, and trinkets, which they had arranged on their carts. Many had temporary makeshift structures, usually made of tarpaulin sheets supported by four bamboo poles. Each vendor had a demarcated space, informally decided by the vendors plying their trade. These temporary structures protected vendors from harsh summers and monsoons. All of a sudden, there was a commotion and vendors screamed and alerted others about an approaching Municipal Corporation of Delhi (MCD) vehicle. The vehicle had indeed arrived to raid the vendors who were "illegally" plying their trades on the road. The vendors uprooted the bamboo and dismantled the partial structures to save their valuable belongings. They quickly drove their carts into the *gallis* (lanes) adjoining the street. Children accompanying the vendors ran frantically, carrying their belongings into the *gallis*. Those who could not move fast had to bear the brunt of the MCD officials. Their makeshift structures were torn apart, carts and gunny bags containing vegetables were seized, and their names were noted. Some vendors who had their carts farthest away from the road were spared.

When I objected to the raid, the MCD officials—who themselves belonged to the lower rungs of the corporation—argued that they were only following orders. A group of vendors sarcastically remarked, "Yes, we had bombs in those gunny bags. MCD had to take those away." The vendors barely made 150 to 200 rupees (US$3.33 to US$4.44) per day by selling fresh vegetables in 2010.[24] Destruction of property, seizure of vegetables and carts, and routine public humiliation were features of their everyday lives.[25] The MCD raids became more frequent prior to the Commonwealth Games. During the games the vendors could only ply their trade in the crowded *gallis* adjoining the road, which significantly reduced their daily earnings. The games wrought havoc on the lives of the poor. On my way back home in September 2010, an auto-rickshaw driver in Sitapuri noted, "If there is another such game, all the poor would be out of this city. But the poor have already cursed the city. See, it's raining incessantly even in September this year. You will see, the games will be a total disaster."

The presence of a dense low-income neighborhood like the Sitapuri transit camp amid middle-class posh neighborhoods depresses local real estate values. Further, crowded streets around the new luxury hotels are an inconvenience for the bourgeois guests. Thus, the beautification drives that target the poor have been correlated with middle-class activism in recent years. The Sitapuri transit camp residents have invested substantially in their building structures. Almost all the residents have built additional floors to accommodate growing families. Many depend on *kiraya* (rent) from subletting their property, especially in the context of rampant unemployment.[26] The residents have also made enormous emotional investments in the neighborhood. As resident V remarked, "I was a small kid when we came here. I got married here. My brothers and sisters got married here. Meanwhile we have erected three floors and we all live in the same house."

The economic conditions and uncertainty of living in *jhuggi* settlements under the threat of demolition prevent the poor from investing in the *jhuggis* in the long term. Hence, the *jhuggi* structures are precarious and ultimately unfit for habitation. Nevertheless, the poor slowly augment their *jhuggis* with valuable building materials and structures. Residents in Gautam Nagar described with a certain amount of pride the bricks, asbestos or tin roofs, wooden doors, cots, water coolers, and other possessions they had accumulated over their years in the city. During demolitions, many residents could not collect their belongings, as they were forced to leave the premises. Later the residents retrieved partly destroyed belongings and building structures from the debris. As resident K noted, "The demolitions were over in a few hours in the morning, but we were busy retrieving our belongings until late in the night. Children ran helterskelter and did not have food. Some residents volunteered to buy biscuits and tea for the children." Often the residents lost household materials and tools that had been accumulated over many years.[27] More importantly, the residents note that some lost valuable documents, including their ration cards, during the demolitions. An added challenge was to store the retrieved materials after demolitions. The residents who rented houses were not allowed to carry broken building structures into their rented houses. Those who lived in the makeshift huts could not pile their belongings out in the open. Furthermore, those residents who were absent during demolitions lost valuable materials, especially the proof documents, which remain the most salient component of numerical citizenship struggles. As resident S recalled, "They started bulldozing early in the morning when people were still sleeping in their *jhuggis*. Those who had gone to their villages lost everything. Actually, many also returned back to their villages after their *jhuggis* were demolished." The hardship experienced immediately after demolition compels many to return to their villages in the months following demolition. Gautam Nagar residents fought a protracted battle to win a case for resettlement (discussed in Chapter 5). When I visited the neighborhood in late August 2017, I could not trace several residents who were entitled to resettlement in the city. In other words, the violent and non-participatory nature of demolitions and delaying tactics of the state foreclosed the possibility of housing and other citizenship entitlements for residents who could not negotiate hardships and stay put indefinitely in the city.

While the residents who could afford to rent places found alternative accommodation, the poorest still lived in makeshift huts with plastic covers over their heads during the biting cold of February. The improvised arrangements were often torn apart by the police, who routinely chased the poor out of the area. Old men and women who did not have caretakers remained on the demolished sites at the mercy of the police. During the time of my fieldwork, they adjusted their precarious huts according to the progress of the digging work at the construction site. Rubble, especially broken concrete with protruding iron rods and dug-up land, made the place dangerous for everyday activities. Women left their babies in the care of older children to go look for work. Such makeshift arrangements particularly posed a threat to younger children, who often crawled out of the huts. Accidents and deaths are common at demolished and resettlement sites (see Menon-Sen and Bhan 2008: 9, 136–37; Padhi 2007: 81–82). A resident of Gautam Nagar remembered that "a young boy fell into the ditch merely few days after the demolition and we could only retrieve his dead body."

Gautam Nagar residents noted that when they approached a politician for help, he replied, "Return back to the place you came from." Demolitions and resettlement not only threaten the citizenship entitlements in the city but also dash the aspirations of the poor for upward mobility. The stigma of extreme poverty after demolitions further burdened the residents, who experienced a range of mental crises. Many residents stopped inviting friends and relatives to their place of residence near the

FIGURE 2.2: *A makeshift hut after demolition of homes in Gautam Nagar. The residents carefully adjusted their huts according to the progress of construction work.*

demolished sites. A resident once asked me, "What will people think of us back in our villages when they hear that we live like this?" The sudden decline in income after demolition exacerbated the problem of hunger in the neighborhood. New residents in particular faced enormous hardship if they had purchased *jhuggis* only a few months before the demolitions. Suddenly, they had not only lost their most valuable investment but also remained ineligible for resettlement plots. According to the activists, the humiliation associated with being displaced has also been linked to suicides in Delhi (Padhi 2007: 82, 89).

Residents' incomes declined dramatically after demolition. Those residents of Gautam Nagar working in the recycling business experienced extreme downward mobility after demolition. Since contractors could no longer hoard scrap materials on the demolition site, residents who had previously worked recycling scrap materials could not find gainful employment in the neighborhoods (see also Routray 2021). Similarly, residents who ran roadside eateries and shops were also adversely affected after their properties were demolished. Renting houses added a further burden of 800 to 1,000 rupees (US$18–$22) per month for many soon after displacement, while people who could afford to rent went in search of rooms in low-income neighborhoods like Meethapur, Pehladpur, Zaitpur, Thekhand, Khadar, and Harkesh Nagar.[28] Along with options for making a living, provisions of basic life necessities were also terribly jeopardized by the demolitions. Tube wells were uprooted prior to the demolitions in Gautam Nagar, which further obstructed access to the neighborhood's water supply. Those who previously had electric lighting now relied on kerosene lamps in their makeshift, post-demolition *jhuggis*. Confiscation of ration cards prevented the poor from obtaining subsidized food commodities. Increased tensions and conflicts over scarce resources, especially water supply, became acute, which resulted in frequent fights among residents. As Scheper-Hughes (1992) notes in another context, the nervous-hungry often explode into rage against one another (211). Many returned to their villages, as they could not afford to rent, with the hope that they would return to the city once they were allotted resettlement plots. The stigma of losing a house and returning to the village without any visible upward mobility bothered many residents. Deaths from diarrhea and accidents were also common. Indebtedness, too, is a serious problem after demolition, with loan sharks frequently taking advantage of the poor by offering money at usurious rates. Ultimately, residents' accounts document experiences of social suffering that result from the contemporary history of urban political economy and restructuring (see also Farmer 2003).

PLANNING REGIMES AND THE STRUCTURAL VIOLENCE OF RESETTLEMENT

The resettlement colonies concretize and express the prevailing social relations in the city. Resettlement colonies express specific forms of spatiality and their accompanying conflicts in the context of post-colonial cities like Delhi.[29] Furthermore, the process of resettlement must also be seen as a temporal phenomenon. Seeing resettlement in temporal terms analytically allows us to capture the dynamics of mental health, environmental risk, the role of the state, and coping mechanisms over time (V. Das 1996: 1510–11). As noted above, often the resettlements are carried out without following official procedures. Sufficient notice is not provided prior to displacement, and adequate means of transportation are usually not provided to carry the residents' belongings. The sight of displacement resembles a revenge drama, as activist R once told me. The process of resettlement not only involves involuntary settlement in un-inhabitable lands without basic amenities, but also destroys the networks, relationships, and patronage of key leaders and politicians. The decontextualized free-floating expertise underpinning such technical solutions (Ferguson 2006: 275) does not take into account the lived realities of the poor. A lifetime is needed to build various kinds of relationships, networks, and support systems. The poor engage with the contradictory rationales of the state and straddle myriad social relationships in their efforts at emplacement and homemaking in a new neighborhood (Read 2012; Read 2014).

The residents of low-income settlements neither possess substantial amounts of social capital nor experience any significant social mobility (Krishna 2013). The process of displacement and resettlement tears down these social networks further and exacerbates vulnerabilities in the city. The residents of the Azad resettlement colony lost friends, neighbors, and acquaintances who had helped them in various ways in the past. According to one resident, all residents were resettled in eight pockets. The attempt was to resettle the residents coming from the same *jhuggi* settlement together. However, many residents were scattered after the demolitions and had to start new lives with displaced residents brought from faraway *jhuggi* settlements in Nehru Place, Alaknanda, Sarita Vihar, Okhla, Lajpat Nagar, Batra Hospital, Tughlaqabad, Rajnagar, and Green Park. Furthermore, the lease tenure of a mere five years initially created confusion and uncertainty among the residents. The resettled residents remained perplexed by the brutality and urgency of demolition. The displaced residents of the Ambedkar camp in Nehru Place attest that the cleared-up area was later used as a parking lot. As resident M remarked, "Our *jhuggis* were demolished between 2000 and 2001. Some of us demolished the *jhuggis* on our own to salvage valuable building materials.

FIGURE 2.3: *The Nehru Place metro station and parking lot were constructed after the demolitions of the homes of poor migrants living at the site. The residents were resettled in the undeveloped Azad resettlement colony.*

Later we realized that the government built a parking lot on our demolished homes."

The Azad resettlement colony was developed in a *daldal* (marshy) area without any basic amenities. The varying plot sizes of 22, 18, and 12.5 square meters for different groups of people created confusion. This also produced a fertile ground for the seizure and inequitable exchanges of plots. Those who were allotted plots measuring 12.5 square meters could barely manage to fit a *charpai* (woven jute cot) in their homes. When I conducted fieldwork in 2011, many displaced residents who were eligible for resettlement were still running around the MCD offices trying to procure plots. Resident AR noted in 2011 that "approximately 600 to 700 eligible residents have not received their plots yet." Similarly, resident T stated, "Approximately 500 eligible Ambedkar camp residents have not got resettlement plots yet. Many other residents have illegally occupied plots here." Without resettlement many have fought protracted court battles to avail themselves of resettlement plots/flats.[30] In 2017, a significant number of residents eligible to obtain resettlement plots were instead renting houses in the Azad resettlement colony as well as villages near the neighborhood. The planners of Delhi Development Authority have argued that they were unable to resettle eligible residents because of the paucity of land in the city.[31] However, during my field visit in late August 2017, the DDA officials carried out raids and demolitions of houses that were built on unallotted plots of land in the neighborhood. In other words, the DDA showed unwillingness to allot the remaining vacant plots in the neighborhood, which in turn motivated the "big men" to carry out fraudulent transactions by seizing the government land in the neighborhood. In some cases, the "big men," who fashioned themselves as *pradhans* (chiefs) of the neighborhoods, had built houses and sold them to residents. When I spoke to them, they argued that the land (approximately 300–350 plots) remained unused for a long time, motivating them to help the needy who could not receive resettlement plots yet. Thus, the ad hocism and tentativeness of the state turned the unallotted plots of land in the Azad resettlement colony into sites of profiteering and inventiveness, which entitled some but disenfranchised those "eligible" people who could not afford to negotiate for the land. Many residents were forced to sell their plots and search for new accommodation because work was not available in the neighborhood. Those who were unable to pay the resettlement fees at the time of allotment could not procure their plots. Exchanges of plots, misidentifications of beneficiaries, and usurpation of plots by local "big men" who deceived the most vulnerable residents with token payments were all rampant.

Without adequate material and social resources in the initial years, most of the resettled people were unable to build houses. Initially the residents could only manage to live in makeshift *jhuggis* at the sites. The financiers extended loans to the residents at exorbitant rates by keeping their allotment slips and ration cards as collateral. The residents gradually built their houses after borrowing money. However, widespread indebtedness was the major reason that allotment plots were sold by the poorest residents. As resident B told me, "I have seen the land dealers buying plots for 50,000 rupees [US$1,111] and selling them for 500,000 rupees

[US$11,111]. It was a time of desperation." Activist R recalled, "There was a major scandal in 2006 and 2007 regarding the allotment of plots, misidentification of beneficiaries, and *dalals* owning multiple plots in the resettlement colonies." Ursula Rao (2013b) identifies the experience of resettlement as a negotiated process, wherein the poor improvise ways of owning plots in the face of their lack of material resources. The residents took an average of three to four years to build their houses on the allotted plots. In the meantime, they lived in huts in an isolated marshy land exposed to rodents, snakes, and animals:

RESIDENT A: We put our huts in the allotted areas. Sometimes the strong wind just blew our huts away in the middle of the night. The fight was no longer with the Delhi Development Authority. After resettlement, the territorial battle was fought between humans on one side and animals, including rodents, insects, and snakes, on the other.

RESIDENT B: Big rodents roamed around the area and bit the residents regularly.

RESIDENT J: You could see blankets, tin shades, and buckets flying around. Sometimes we just huddled together in the public toilet in the night.

RESIDENT H: It was raining heavily the day we were brought here. After we were dumped, we realized that our allotted plot was flooded with water up to the waist.

RESIDENT BC: If you dug a bit, you hit the water. This was a jungle area. The drains often spilled over. The area was used as a burial ground before, so we would find bones everywhere.

The Azad resettlement colony, which was established by the DDA after violating planning protocols, resembles a "gray space" (Yiftachel 2009). Oren Yiftachel (2009) uses the term "gray space" to refer to "developments, enclaves, populations and transactions positioned between the 'lightness' of legality/approval/safety and the 'darkness' of eviction/destruction/death." While Yiftachel describes a completely different context (namely, the Beersheba metropolitan region), the resettlement colonies resemble such a gray space in constituting "pseudo-permanent margins." The residents of the Azad resettlement colony vividly narrated the process of the "creation of peripheral, weakened and marginalized spaces," as described by Yiftachel (2009: 243). The residents note that it was difficult to construct anything. The colony adjoins an effluent drain and the Yamuna River. The flooding of the river resulted in the stagnation of water in the neighborhood that created breeding grounds for mosquitoes. As a resident noted, "We have to burn a range of materials to produce smoke to ward off swarming mosquitoes and flies near our huts." Similarly, another resident observed, "Mosquitoes feast on us."

In the absence of water facilities, the residents installed hand pumps and drew contaminated water for drinking. The hand pumps were attached to pipes supplying water into the houses. (However, those who could afford to buy water resisted drinking hand-pump water.) There was no water supply in 2011 nor in 2017 during the times of my fieldwork. Young men ferried cycle trolleys carrying water in containers in the neighborhood.[32] The residents could not verify if the water bought was potable, though it was believed that the quality of purchased water was better than the water drawn from hand pumps. As resident B remarked, "The hand-pump water quality is very bad here. If you keep the water for fifteen minutes, it turns yellow." The politicians sent water tankers in the absence of clean water supply, but there were frequent fights over the distribution of water. During my visit in 2017, I saw that a few residents had turned into entrepreneurs by installing water filtration systems at their own homes in order to provide potable water in the neighborhood.[33] Ironically, there is a government liquor shop near the entrance of the neighborhood. Many residents without jobs, experiencing downward mobility and everyday violence, have become alcoholics, according to one resident.

I was perplexed when the residents complained about the lack of water facilities and of cremation or burial grounds in the same breath. Later on, I understood the normalization of death and the practical need for cremation and burial grounds as the residents shared poignant stories about the many deaths that had occurred after resettlement. In

FIGURE 2.4: *Residents installed hand pumps to supply drinking water in Azad re-settlement colony. The water drawn was often contaminated and known to contribute to death and a variety of illnesses.*

fact, diarrhea and dengue-related deaths were rife in the initial years of resettlement:

> RESIDENT BC: Guessing, 100 to 150 people died because of dengue alone when we came here. [Dengue continued to be a major cause of death in 2010 when I was doing fieldwork in Delhi.]

> RESIDENT B: Last year many people died of dengue here. The sight of cycle trolleys carrying dead bodies was commonplace. I guess around 1,000 people have died since we have been resettled in this neighborhood.

> RESIDENT T: I am the *pradhan*, so I know the number of deaths. Up until now 4,100 people have died in this neighborhood. Some families lost four to five members after relocating here.

While it was not possible for me to verify the exact number of deaths, these narratives reveal the enormity of death that has occurred since resettlement and the violence of state policies. Recurring statements like "half the population died" and "death was rampant" indicated the high incidence of death and the "routinization of human suffering"

(Scheper-Hughes 1992: 16) after resettlement. The residents note that many perished when they could not bear the harsh winter after being resettled in a low-lying open area. Resident BC stated, "The situation was bad. We would go to cremate a body, and by the time we returned back, there was another death in the neighborhood." Deaths were attributed mostly to hunger and the drinking of contaminated water. Furthermore, communicable diseases such as typhoid, jaundice, cholera, and malaria were widespread during my fieldwork. Skin rashes, stomach problems, and joint pain were other ailments that accompanied life-taking diseases. According to Resident B, "The prevalence of joint pain is common among residents." Without adequate income and transportation, most of the sick residents relied on informal medical practitioners.

The host populations attempted to use the colony as a site for generating profits of various kinds. In the absence of government services, the private operators of host villages provided a range of services, including water, electricity, and transportation. The planning machinery failed to initiate any dialogue with the host populations, and the residents of the Azad resettlement colony faced the wrath of the host populations if they resisted or organized to provide services on their own. It took four to five years for the residents to get electricity. Private suppliers provided electricity by running generators, charging 10 rupees per hour in the initial years. As a resident put it, "Some of the nearby village people lost land when the colony was established. Therefore, they felt entitled to make money by providing services and forcing the government to delay provisioning basic amenities."

Private operators provided the limited transportation available in the area. The operators ran mini-buses and charged more money than public transport for comparable distances. There were frequent fights between the operators and the travelers. Many residents noted that the operators instructed the drivers to load as many people as they could to increase profits. resident N observed, "They hiked the fares whenever they wished," while resident B remarked, "Until recently, they filled the vehicles as if residents traveling to the resettlement colony were animals." The hostile host population also took advantage of a surplus population living immediately next to their villages by offering extremely low daily wages compared to the prevailing wages for similar work done elsewhere. The lack of infrastructure, dismal living conditions, and stigma attached to the resettlement neighborhoods (see Coelho, Venkat, and Chandrika 2012: 55) obviates attempts at finding gainful employment, thereby reproducing poverty. In short, the planning ideologies underpinning resettlement betray the visions, aspirations, and images of social mobility among millions of people who throng the city to fight chronic rural poverty. These ideologies challenge the incremental struggles of citizenship. As discussed above, industrial closures in Delhi have further impoverished and created labor market insecurities while limiting work opportunities. Resettlement creates obstacles for the poor participating in both the old and the new economy (for a discussion of opportunities and constraints in the new economy, see Shatkin 2007: 12) because high transportation costs and inconvenient location combined with ongoing domestic responsibilities thwart employment opportunities.

The spatial relations produced through resettlement have created unequal vulnerabilities for women.[34] Women who worked in middle-class households as domestic workers or in vegetable wholesale markets before resettlement lost their jobs, as they could not reach their places of work early in the morning because of a lack of transportation. The residents had to walk 2 or 3 kilometers up to the highway before they could find any transportation.[35] Furthermore, the issue of safety for women walking in early mornings and late evenings prevented them from actively taking up work in far-flung neighborhoods. Often the residents were robbed of their bicycles, money, and belongings by petty thieves while returning from work in the initial years of resettlement. The neighborhood was dark and had no street lighting in the first few years.

Toilet facilities were limited, poorly maintained, and operated by charging user fees to residents. Additionally, the lack of toilet facilities at home or immediately near the place of residence created problems, especially for sick residents. Residents innovated by building pit toilets in crammed and fragilely built multistory buildings; the precariously built pits threatened to cause the entire building structure to sink into the ground. Furthermore, building additional structures to secure basic facilities and to accommodate increasing family size incorporated the poor into the web of patronage relationships. As these constructions are touted as "illegal," the poor must depend on their network of relationships to negotiate with the police and politicians in order to incrementally entrench themselves in the domain of citizenship. The areas marked for parks were used as dumping grounds, as the garbage bins overflowed in the neighborhood. During both rounds of my fieldwork, bins burst with rotten garbage, emitting a putrid stench in the neighborhoods. Animals rummaged the heaps, further scattering the garbage, and residents covered their faces while passing by. Sewer lines were also absent in the neighborhood, and engineers often dug up the area to build roads, which created problems with water logging.[36] Most portions of the Azad resettlement colony did not have proper roads in 2011. The muddy roads were washed away frequently, and water in the potholes stagnated and turned black. Often children threw stones, splashing the dirty water onto the street as a favorite pastime. During my field visits I often tiptoed around the neighborhood so as to avoid stepping in the mud. The Azad resettlement colony was not handed over to MCD, the agency responsible for providing municipal services, until 2012.[37] As planners BH and MS from the DUSIB remarked to me, "According to the rules, the resettlement colonies should be handed over to the MCD within four years of development. But the MCD slum wing does not accept the transference. It demands deficiency charges to augment substandard, depleted, and ill-maintained facilities in the neighborhoods. If DDA or any other government agencies decline to provide the deficiency charge, then the colony is unattended."[38]

As previously discussed, the DDA is responsible for planning and developing the resettlement colonies. Subsequently, the colonies are handed over to the MCD for maintenance work. Many of the problems in the Azad resettlement colony emerged because of the multiplicity of governance structures and uncoordinated policy implementation between the DDA and the state government. As a result of this delay, the physical condition of the Azad resettlement colony deteriorated. It was only in 2012 that the DUSIB drew up plans for repairing and renovating the existing roads and drains in the neighborhood. There was neither a school nor a dispensary at the time of resettlement. Children were forced to drop out of school after getting resettled in the neighborhood. According to one resident, the school was managed from makeshift huts until 2005. A school was constructed next to the sludge created by the effluent from the nearby power plant and residents reported that a few children had drowned in it. The area still did not have a dispensary during the time of my fieldwork in 2011, but the government had opened schools[39] and a dispensary by 2017. The land department had confiscated the ration cards of the residents,[40] and it took three or four years or more for residents to receive new ones after resettlement. As a result, the residents could not procure subsidized food commodities after resettlement. The loss of ration cards is especially worrying in the context of hunger-related deaths.

The above accounts and my field observations document "offensives" the poor have encountered as a result of the implementation of planning regimes. Depoliticized and abstract urban planning ideologies—especially through policies of demolition and resettlement—produce structured patterns of social suffering (see also Farmer 2003: 40). The structural violence and offensives experienced by the poor provide a context by which to analyze the numerical citizenship struggles in the city. The processes of displacement and resettlement embodied in urban restructuring projects of the state demonstrate the challenges of realizing substantive citizenship in the city. Nevertheless, the poor incrementally lay claims to citizenship entitlements through myriad innovations and improvisations. In the next four chapters, I analyze the logic of numerical citizenship mobilizations among the poor in response to the structural violence they face through the implementation of these policies. With reference to the three field sites, I consider the messiness of the politics and popular struggles that were engaged through the planning process regarding the displacement of the poor, lack of basic services, confiscation of ration cards, and struggles to acquire resettlement plots. In particular, the next four chapters deal with modes of political mobilization employed by the urban poor in their struggles for numerical citizenship in Delhi. I specifically examine their mediations through intermediaries, their negotiations with the state and judiciary, and their resistance to urban policies.

Part II

THE POLITICS OF THE POOR

CHAPTER 3

INFRASTRUCTURE AND INTERMEDIARIES
Mediated Politics of Pradhans, Samaj Sevaks,
and Sarkari Karmacharis

THE URBAN POOR participate in citizenship struggles through various
kinds of intermediaries, who help them negotiate to obtain various basic
amenities in the city. The foremost struggle of the poor migrants is to
gain a foothold in the city. As the urban poor build *jhuggis* and incrementally attempt to access rudimentary infrastructure and basic amenities
in the neighborhoods, the intermediaries originating from the informal
settlements become key actors in mediating the infrastructural questions
in the city. The numerical strength in *jhuggi jhopri* settlements becomes
the primary drive for the state to recognize an informal neighborhood.
To begin with, a *jhuggi* settlement needs to have at least fifty households
to gain state recognition. The state recognition of a settlement, the provision of basic amenities and proof documents, and the extension of infrastructure to the neighborhood are enmeshed with what is referred to as
vote-bank politics in the neighborhoods (Auerbach 2020; S. Benjamin
2000; S. Benjamin 2008; S. Benjamin and Raman 2001; Bjorkman 2014b).

In examining numerical citizenship struggles, as epitomized in the
resilience of vote-bank politics, I focus on the idioms and strategies of
intermediaries who offer personalized services and demand differential
treatment for their clients instead of abstract and liberal justice. The intermediaries' practices reveal the peculiarity of patronage politics in the city.
As a consequence, these practices "escape the gridlock of liberal political

heuristics" and offer us a framework to understand the horizon of mediated politics (Piliavsky 2014: 4). In this respect, a historical understanding of the contextual, structural, and relational features of mediated politics in Delhi goes against the current of liberal thinking about the state, rule of law, and abstract principles of modernity.[1]

The nature and model of neo-liberal urban policies and restructuring processes along capitalist lines in Delhi, as discussed in Chapter 1, have created an excluded constituency that lacks housing and adequate amenities and must resort to competitive vote-bank politics to redistribute urban resources. The marginalization of the urban poor and the current preoccupation with city aesthetics indicate conflicting class interests and give rise to distinct political and civic practices. These practices are not merely symptoms of cultural difference or inconsistency in modern statecraft (Fuller and Harriss 2009); the urban poor understand the class character, structural limits, and relative benefits of statecraft, and modify their political strategies based on careful calculations and political rhetoric. The governance and political structures of Delhi's low-income settlements still largely reflect old-style vote-bank politics, clientelism, and patronage structures. In fact, the combination of changing political cultures[2] and patronage structures gives rise to extra-constitutional authorities that remain to some degree enmeshed in state structures. This chapter focuses on the nature of patronage politics, gendered mediation and cultural styles, and options for income, housing, and basic amenities within the framework of the transforming political economy of Delhi and the emerging calculative state governmentality that address consequent impoverishment (see also Auyero 2000b; Jeffrey, Jeffery, and Jeffery 2008; Jeffrey 2009; A. Roy 2003). The features of the neo-liberal urban restructuring, urban opportunity structures, and everyday conflicts over scarce services are conducive to numerical citizenship struggles of vote-bank politics and clientelism. To begin with, the assertion of numerical strength and the associated process of vote-bank politics propel the strategies of locality-building—that is, building a common identity and strength based on shared locality. This strength can begin to be used against monitoring and surveillance of the poor. Although the struggles associated with locality-building involve various forms of exploitation and accumulation strategies, these struggles also redistribute the basic urban amenities.

THE FIGURE OF THE INTERMEDIARY

Mediated politics are at the heart of numerical citizenship struggles, especially struggles to build *jhuggis*, access services, and resist demolitions. Intermediaries between state and society take various forms and define themselves in various ways. For the sake of clarity, it is important to define the categories involved. While the services and strategies offered by intermediaries overlap considerably, their sources of legitimacy and motivations are different. *Pradhans* (chiefs), *samaj sevaks* (social workers), and *sarkari karmacharis* (government workers) all operate as intermediaries and provide myriad services. Each possesses "knowledge, skills, and attitudes" (Manor 2000: 819) that qualify them to meet people's everyday needs in their localities.

The intermediaries attempt but ultimately fail to occupy what Bourdieu calls the "intermediate regions of the social space."[3] Thus, their socially sanctioned desire to inhabit these intermediate spaces creates "tension and pretension" (Bourdieu 1991: 62), particularly when they confront the experts, caretakers, and personnel of the bourgeois class. While all three types of intermediaries carry out a host of functions in the informal settlements, the work of *pradhans* and *samaj sevaks* is much more pronounced; therefore this chapter focuses more on their activities. *Pradhans* are recognized for their political capital. Their legitimacy and symbolic profits are secured through connections with councilors, members of the legislative assembly (MLAs), and members of Parliament (MPs). *Pradhans* help solve local problems by forging *ristedari* (relationships), *jaan pehchaan* (acquaintances), or connections with *khaas aadmi* (special men) or *milne julne wale aadmi* (men who mingle) in state bureaucracy. *Pradhans* may belong to any caste, community, or gender, and each *mohalla* (neighborhood) may have its own *pradhan*. Most often Dalits and Muslims approach the *pradhans* belonging to their own caste or community. The *pradhans* are mostly petty contractors, owners of neighborhood grocery shops or eateries, or other small-business owners. If not illiterate, they typically have only basic primary or secondary school education. The *pradhans* secure their legitimacy, *himmat* (strength), and popularity by asking the *janata* (people) to demonstrate their loyalty. This legitimacy depends on their accessibility and indispensability: "The *pradhan* is someone whose interventions can help the residents and someone who could be accessible even in the middle of the night to stand by you during any possible emergency," noted one resident of Gautam Nagar.

Though arguments made by Reddy and Haragopal (1985) about rural contexts still hold for cities in many ways, the *pyraveekar* (fixers) in rural areas are characteristically different from *pradhans* in cities like Delhi. The *pradhans* in informal urban settlements are likely to share precarious living conditions with those they lead, despite possessing relatively more social, cultural, and economic capital. In this sense, the *pradhan* is organically linked to the settlement, and unlike a *pyraveekar* (fixer), who fixes other people's situations for personal favors and gain, the *pradhan* is directly concerned with his or her future in the informal settlement. Nevertheless, the *pradhans* act according to their whims and fancies without any accountability, and through dealings that are often private and personal (Reddy and Haragopal 1985: 1159).

Pradhans are typically affiliated with major political parties. Between 2009 and 2011, most supported the Indian National Congress (INC) or Bahujan Samaj Party (BSP), and some represented the Bharatiya Janata Party (BJP) in their neighborhoods. The Bahujan Samaj Party's popularity was increasing, at least in municipal elections in lower-income settlements between 2009 and 2011, but its influence in civic politics had significantly declined by 2017. Traditionally, the poor had favored the Congress party over the BJP in Delhi (Kumar 2009). However, the entry of the Aam Aadmi Party had cut into the vote shares of Congress and BSP, and the BJP had notable popularity among the poor by 2017. Many other poor residents argued that BJP was still not a viable party for the *jhuggi* poor; they argued that BJP won in 2014 because of an election wave (BJP *ka leher tha*). In 2017, AAP and BJP remained the two most popular parties among the poor in these neighborhoods. As a result of this new development, a significant number of *pradhans* had campaigned, advocated, and affiliated themselves with the AAP, while other *pradhans* gave their allegiance to other parties in these neighborhoods. Voting may happen along caste and community lines: residents often talk about voting for *biradari* (community) people.[4] Because of their detailed knowledge of the voting dynamics in their localities, the *pradhans* serve as key bridges between politicians and residents. They canvass for particular leaders and organize events during election time. Their work involves demonstrating numerical strength in election-day voter turnout, canvassing, and *naarabaazi* (sloganeering) in exchange for money, gifts, food, and alcohol crates. On average, the residents who participated in these election-related activities were paid 200 rupees per day between 2009 and 2011 and 300–350 rupees per day in 2017. *Pradhans* most often alert "the politicians to popular resentments or to constituencies that are available for cultivation" (Manor 2000: 818). There is no strong correlation, however, between receiving these favors and voting in the elections, as many residents testify.

The *pradhans* boast of their personal connections to politicians and ministers. They argue that the concerned politician will not entertain the neighborhood representatives without the *pradhan*'s involvement. Often the *pradhans* have pictures in their homes of themselves with politicians at rallies, meetings, and events. Usually they are pictured smiling, garlanding, and shaking hands with or standing very close to politicians or speaking at public events attended by key figures. Most pictures are carefully enlarged, framed, and conspicuously hung in their living rooms. These pictures have symbolic weight, signifying power through proximity to key politicians and mass following in the area. Likewise, letter-pads embellished with their names and the names of their politicians send a message about the authentic and formal character of the *pradhan*-politician relationship. Often the *pradhans* share anecdotes about their dealing with politicians, claiming they are considered family members who can even enter the kitchen and bedroom (the most private spaces of a household) and receive *guldasta* (bouquets) and letters for special occasions. In addition to official phone calls from politicians, *pradhans* receive invitations to key family events. These semi-public family events include birthday celebrations, nighttime prayer meetings (*jagrans*), and festivals where *pradhans* actively participate and are publicly referred to as *bhai* (brother) or *behena* (sister). Despite photographic and paper evidence, some residents believe the *janata* (people) are in *bhram* (a state of misconception) about the *pradhans'* actual political influence, that they are deluded or deceived.

While the *pradhans* carefully construct self-images that highlight their toughness, indispensability, and benevolence, rival *pradhans* and their supporters promote counter-narratives of how the neighborhood should function and be governed. The entry of new *pradhans* into neighborhoods also poses a threat to established *pradhans*. The ensuing turf battles and ego clashes often divide neighborhoods as *pradhans* vie for supporters and loyalty and engage in competitive image building. *Pradhans* are also pressured by political rivals to ensure that residents vote for a particular party. Bickering among *pradhans* and accusations of payments from rival politicians often invite mistrust from residents. Some *pradhans* claim they do not even charge money for *bhaag-daud* (running around) government offices and politicians' residences. While intermediaries earn money by providing services, they generally detest state corruption, as this leads to "implementation process disruptions" (Manor 2000: 821) that negatively affect their own lives. *Pradhans* are also wary of NGOs and activists, whom they perceive as hostile. The *pradhans* may grow increasingly insecure if their support base starts dwindling. Residents' independence directly challenges the power and authority of *pradhans* in the neighborhood. Knowledge of legal rights and bureaucratic protocols can diminish dependency on *pradhans* and cause their influence in the neighborhood to decline. *Pradhans* belonging to upper castes look down upon *dalit pradhans*, especially poor *dalit pradhans*. The division of labor relating to *pradhan*-led politics and governance also signifies caste fissures in the neighborhood, in addition to highlighting social cleavages along community, ethnic, and linguistic lines.

Samaj sevaks (social workers) are mostly upper-caste brokers, fixers, and mediators who rely on the advantage of their relative cultural capital in these neighborhoods. Most have intermediate or higher school degrees and a few are even college educated. They work in NGOs, run small shops, own businesses, run coaching classes in the neighborhood, or work in the service sector labor market in the city. *Samaj sevaks* are similar to *pyraveekars* (fixers); they are professional, polished, and shrewd individuals with a range of public powers (Reddy and Haragopal 1985). *Samaj sevaks* refer to their work as "public dealings"—solving the problems of the neighborhood mainly through negotiations with activists, lawyers, politicians, government officials, or other people of influence. The administrative arrangements are "known for their complexity, cumbersomeness, elitism, centralization, legalism, red tape, and inertia" (Reddy and Haragopal 1985: 1148–49). The literacy of *samaj sevaks* positions them to act as a bridge between state structures and the mundane day-to-day life of the poor. For example, one *samaj sevak* in Gautam Nagar volunteered to help interpret the electricity bills of all the residents in his locality. He would collect all the bills and read out the names, the amount owed, and the deadline by which it had to be paid. It then became a bimonthly event to gather in front of the *samaj sevak*'s home to collect bills, complain about rising electricity prices, debate the privatization of electricity, and refuse to pay bills in protest.

The *samaj sevaks* use their "caste-capital" (Deshpande 2013: 32) to secure petty clerical, temporary, and itinerant jobs. Thus, like *pyraveekar* (fixers), the *samaj sevaks* occupy the space between government service providers and poor people who lack adequate education and communication skills (Reddy and Haragopal 1985). At times they may be asked to tutor the children of lower-rung government officials. The *samaj sevaks* from these localities are also the first contact persons for social workers from abroad who come to intern, work, or evaluate the work of the NGOs they fund. With the increase in the visibility of the *samaj sevaks*, their children may benefit by receiving study kits and other paraphernalia. The *samaj sevaks* are able to articulate the nature of the nation-state, democracy, socialism, or plutocracy at various political events organized in the neighborhoods, creating friendships between them and the activists organizing in their neighborhoods. One *samaj sevak* wrote stories, poems, and polemical pamphlets to be published with NGO newsletters and bulletins in Gautam Nagar. Privileges like these may encourage a sense of superiority among the *samaj sevaks*, who in turn pathologize the behavior of their neighbors. The *samaj sevaks* typically accuse the *pradhans* of money laundering and corruption. However, very often the *samaj sevaks* also charge the poor fees for services. On the one hand, the *samaj sevaks* (often a title they give to themselves) do not call themselves *pradhans* to avoid negative publicity attached to the term; on the other hand, some may aspire to acquire the symbolic profit and political connections associated with *pradhan-giri* or *neta-giri* (activities of *pradhans* or leaders).

Finally, the *sarkari karmacharis* (government workers) derive legitimacy mainly through their contacts and networks within state bureaucracies and through their advice for accessing government services. They work in the lower rungs of various state departments and possess relatively more bureaucratic social capital than the other two kinds of intermediaries. Their legitimacy depends on their ability to solve local problems related to water supply, electricity connections, garbage disposal, and the legal system. They may provide valuable information about court cases, hearing dates, government facilities, and service provision in the city. *Sarkari karmacharis* may also provide important contacts and act as conduits that link ill residents with government hospitals (see also V. Das and R. K. Das 2007: 83–84). The *sarkari karmacharis* active in these neighborhoods may belong to various castes. While there are many vocal, articulate, and shrewd female *pradhans*, *sarkari karmacharis* are much less likely to be women, and *samaj sevaks* even less so. In addition to these three types of intermediaries, it should be noted that poor people also seek support from religious leaders, lawyers, and political activists who mediate citizenship entitlements, especially during difficult periods.

In analyzing mediation, I separate various kinds of intermediaries rather than grouping them as a homogeneous category. The source of legitimacy and motivations of intermediaries are different despite overlaps in their services and strategies. While the *pradhans* rely on their political capital (political connections and affiliations), the *samaj sevaks* possess relatively larger amounts of cultural capital and typically affiliate with activists and NGOs. The *samaj sevaks* shun politicians and do not typically carry out the activities that are associated with a *pradhan*. In contrast, the *sarkari karmacharis* derive their legitimacy through connections with state bureaucracies. However, they function not merely as public servants but as neighborhood leaders and intermediaries outside the parameters of liberal and normative logics. For instance, they leak information about court cases, mediate public dealings with various rungs of the bureaucracy, and facilitate various kinds of negotiations in favor of the residents. Nonetheless, as discussed next, the work of the *pradhans* and *samaj sevaks* is much more evident than that of government workers in these neighborhoods.

THE TECHNIQUES AND TACTICS OF INTERMEDIARIES

Intermediaries are set apart by their affiliations with particular politicians, activists, NGOs, leaders, police officials, or lawyers. Aware of the new-found legitimacy and power they enjoy in their neighborhoods, intermediaries continually show off their proximity to important leaders. A key aspiration of strong intermediaries is to be candidates in councilor elections or otherwise gain political power. Most often they are not successful, leaving them with tales of betrayal about their political patrons and bitterness over their bad luck. Personal aspirations to wield important positions in neighborhood politics are often contested by locals, especially in the urban villages that influence neighborhood politics and often in resettlement colonies, which are always outside the city precincts adjoining urban villages. The *pradhans* are aware of their own location and structural opportunities for political mobility. As one *pradhan* in Gautam Nagar argued, "See, this constituency for the councilor post has mostly *jhuggiwalas* (*jhuggi* residents). Maybe only ten percent of the constituency belongs to the villages, but the villages have money and powerful people. Even if I worked under any leader for years, this would not change. They think that *jhuggiwalas* are drain worms." Thus, despite their vigorous political activities, intermediaries know they are viewed with contempt and are consequently shut out from competitive electoral processes and formal institutionalized power. In fact, on one occasion, rival *pradhans* in the Sitapuri transit camp supported a leader outside the locality and paid another *pradhan*—who seemed powerful and popular—to withdraw from the election race. This example illustrates social divisions in these neighborhoods. Despite these structural difficulties, the growing numerical strength of a neighborhood, especially in resettlement colonies, allows for the representation of the poor in the electoral politics. In the 2017 municipal elections, the residents of the Azad resettlement colony elected a councilor from their own neighborhood.

Jha, Rao, and Woolcock (2007) rightly argue that the urban poor have more political agency, channels, and contacts than their village counterparts (232). However, intermediaries often reproduce cultures of dependency, exclusion, and, at times, exploitation. The intermediaries partake in everyday displays of power and benevolence, and tell dramatic tales of subverting authority, most often the police, through their connections with various powerful people. These tales serve to acknowledge the regular humiliation, indignity, and abuse suffered by the poor at the hands of police, contractors, and employers. A specific incident of the *pradhans'* dealings with politicians illustrates these points. I arrived early one morning in late November 2009 at the Sitapuri transit camp councilor's house in a middle-class neighborhood. I stood in front of the three-storied building of the councilor opposite an MCD (Municipal Corporation of Delhi) park. The road in front of the house was clean and two security guards patrolled the area. In the meantime, the councilor came out of the house and surveyed the area and people who were waiting for the daily hearing of complaints and grievances. He asked them all to enter the house and offered everyone a chair. Residents and *pradhans* from various informal settlements started whispering about their problems and greeted each other. A person, perhaps a "servant," brought water for everyone. When the councilor entered the living room, everyone stood up. He asked them to be seated and finally took his seat on a sofa. An assistant with a file sat beside him and people from various poor settlements sat near him. The *pradhans* started bantering with the councilor to ease their situations. The councilor looked grave and smiled occasionally, keenly surveying the room. People accompanying the *pradhans* with their grievances sat in rows behind them. This marked the social distance between the councilor and the residents and also between the *pradhans* and the residents. Some came to apply for voter IDs, ration cards, and old age pensions; others to ask for financial help for weddings, funerals, medical treatments, or home repairs. After each resident narrated their grievances, the councilor dictated to the assistant the course of action to be taken and occasionally made a phone call to solve the problem right away. He called someone to help with the wedding arrangement of one person, and asked someone else to help with some building materials. Then he started complaining: "See, what I do is a thankless job. I do everything possible to help everyone, even things that are not within the mandate of a councilor, but still people might be complaining about me." Reacting to this remark, one *pradhan* intervened immediately and affirmed, "There is no one like the councilor in the entire region—he is the true friend of the poor and no other politician from any other party makes the poor feel so comfortable and concerned for the poor as much as he does."

Following this, the *pradhans* asked general questions about the status of the neighborhoods (if they would be demolished or not), if they could hold religious *jagrans* (nighttime prayer meetings), and how they should go about solving problems related to local water supplies. The councilor responded to each and every query, and confirmed he had spoken to the relevant government officials and that the problems would be solved. He also informed the residents about the municipal rules that they ought to follow. The meeting was adjourned, residents touched the councilor's feet and paid respects, and *pradhans* shook their hands and left one by one. These practices mediated by the *pradhans* contribute to what Chatterjee (1997), in *The Present History of West Bengal*, calls the "daily renewal of legitimacy" of the councilor (144, quoted in A. Roy 2003: 18). The meetings also renew the legitimacy and symbolic power of the *pradhans*, who prove their closeness to the councilor/politicians in the presence of the residents by the "technique of ego-tickling and gratification of one's vanity" (Reddy and Haragopal 1985: 1153). Moreover, the episode confirmed for the residents that the *pradhan* truly cares for his neighborhood and can intervene to help the poor, thereby creating a relationship of dependency between the *pradhan* and residents. These practices do not only imply an enactment of feudal benevolence but also practical strategies of everyday problem solving. For instance, as Mushtaq Khan has pointed out, the "personalization of politics" is based neither solely on traditional deference nor on charisma, but on a rational calculation of benefits (M. Khan 2005: 712).

The intermediaries represent distinct cultural styles in their manner of authoritative speech, their dress at semi-formal occasions, and their articulation of critical issues in the neighborhoods. As Ferguson (1999) argues, such cultural variations do not reflect any deep-seated habitus, as

Bourdieu might suggest. Rather, Ferguson argues that distinct cultural styles function as "modes of practical action in contemporary urban social life." The intermediaries' cultural styles are an "achieved performative competence, an empowering capability acquired and cultivated over a lifetime . . . developed in relation to the demands and exigencies of day-to-day life" (Ferguson 1999: 221). The intermediaries might also organize road blockades independently or at the request of their political masters, bringing attention to recurring problems in their neighborhoods through the technique of assertion of numerical strength. To summarize, the intermediaries are well-known players of *jugaad* (fixing) who possess the "capacity to 'fix things' through bringing together unlike practices or materials" (Jeffrey 2009: 203). Similarly, one resident in the Sitapuri transit camp remarked on the definition and nature of *jugaad*:

> The name of India should be *jugaad-stan*. You need to have a *jugaad* system in place to thwart the attempts of government or police. People do a lot of *jugaad* to survive in Hindustan. Doing *jugaad* is not an easy option; you need to have some power to do *jugaad*, and that does not just mean economic power. See, I may not have money to run my shop, but I can do some *jugaad* to get flour, oil, and spices to start making samosas in my shop. Similarly, we need to solve, say, our problems around economic insolvency, toilet facilities, or garbage disposal through the *jugaad* system.

This resident identifies the nature of power, its multiple manifestations, and its economic and non-economic sources. He then uses a series of examples to discuss how residents navigate the *jugaad* system. Though *jugaad* is a "morally uncertain concept" and practice (Jeffrey 2009: 203), it figures prominently in Indian civic and political life given the limited nature of opportunities and availability of resources. As a result, the mediation of intermediaries, in their efforts at obtaining citizenship entitlements, engage the *jugaad* system in a myriad of ingenious ways, especially in their dealings with the politicians.

The popularity of a politician also depends on how effectively she or he performs in a patron-client relationship where the intermediaries, as clients, are messengers, canvassers, and image-builders for the politicians. The politicians enact these relationships through performative politics, mediating conflicts and providing people with scarce urban resources. These performative styles may take spectacular forms during displacements or road blockades, often leading to violence (see also Hansen 2005b). A *samaj sevak* in the Sitapuri transit camp became animated when we discussed politicians and their politics. He recollected his experience at the councilor's residence: "People around the councilor form a coterie and create problems and obstacles. I once went to apply for my mother's old age pension and the assistant wanted me to come back at a later date. The councilor shouted at the assistant, '*Uncle-ji*, [the suffix *ji* is uttered as a mark of respect], do you know who you are talking to? He is a very *khaas aadmi* (special man). You fill out his forms, submit them at the relevant offices, and get this work done as soon as possible.'" This incident is a remarkable example of the arbitrary nature of offering pension to a selected beneficiary. It demonstrates the access that intermediaries have to key state agents, and how their connections straddle the state-society binary. Most often, the residents are not even aware of the policies, constitutionally guaranteed rights, and government welfare schemes that affect them, which in turn makes political mediations through intermediaries indispensable to the urban poor.

Most *pradhans* recall legitimate elections that bestowed them with the authority to look after the neighborhood. Though their claims might be true in some cases, it is tricky to find out the details of particular elections. It may be that an election was held a decade back and the *pradhan* has since continued to proclaim his or her leadership. Residents agree that neighborhood consensus is necessary to consider someone a *pradhan*. In some *gallis*, there have not been any *pradhan* elections in the last fifteen to twenty years. Despite community preferences to select *pradhans* democratically, nepotism is widespread. Often the councilor or MLA will arbitrarily choose someone close to her or him to be the *pradhan*.

MEDIATED POLITICS OF *JHUGGI* BUILDING

The poor engage in slow and gradual occupation of land and house building across many contexts (Bayat 1997; S. Benjamin 2008; Caldeira 2017: 5; Holston 2008; Simone 2015: S16).[5] To gain a foothold and incrementally claim housing and a cluster of other citizenship entitlements, the poor

occupy abandoned and inhospitable land in the city. In the absence of adequate low-income housing facilities, taking over or slowly encroaching
on abandoned land is the only viable housing option for the urban poor
in the city. The survival of poor people is a tale of contingent conditions,
grassroots organizing, risk-taking, and forging relationships with various
actors.[6]

Building a *jhuggi* is the first step in claiming housing rights in the
city. The gradual *jhuggi* building efforts may appear as solitary acts, but
they very quickly become a collective effort. The *jhuggi jhopri* settlements are products of sheer hard work, monetary transactions, including
relationship-building with state agencies, and innovation in the inhospitable lands of the city: jungles, marshy lands, barren garbage disposal
areas, low-lying flood-prone areas, vacant spaces around *nullahs* (drains),
or hazardous factories. For instance, as discussed in the Introduction,
the Gautam Nagar *jhuggi jhopri* settlement did not just suddenly appear
in a major center of the city; rather, it was built over a few years. Migrants from various parts of India, but especially from the states of Uttar
Pradesh, Bihar, and Rajasthan, used their village networks to come to
Gautam Nagar in search of work. Village members introduced newcomers to the fledgling settlement most often along caste lines, and slowly
the settlement started to acquire "the moral attributes of a community"
(Chatterjee 2004: 57). To begin with, the settlement did not have state
recognition or patronage. Most often, the police provided the patronage
in the initial years, agreeing with the "moral rhetoric of a community
striving to build a decent social life under extremely harsh conditions"
(60). But often, the poor used their practical wisdom and enmeshed
themselves in bureaucratic and municipal structures through the intermediaries in order to claim the right to housing. As discussed in the Introduction, once the settlement gained numerical strength and became
salient in vote-bank politics, the self-styled strongmen turned into *pradhans* and encouraged the residents to build semi-permanent structures.
Pradhans played a significant role in the development and gradual recognition of the settlement, as they did during threats of demolition and
in arranging for basic amenities in the settlements. As a result of these

incremental struggles and mediations, the migrants from various parts of India claimed precarious housing rights in Gautam Nagar.

Once Gautam Nagar became a state-recognized *jhuggi* settlement, the residents built brick walls with asbestos or tin roofs and found innovative sleeping spaces given the tiny plots on which they built their *jhuggis*. Sometimes the asbestos roofs doubled as sleeping spaces. Building materials were acquired through the politicians, who in turn made arrangements with petty contractors in the neighborhood. This system of exchanging favors is intricately entwined with the *rann-nitis* of the urban poor, petty traders, and contractors, who inhabit a legal gray area. The adjoining factories provided employment to many residents, and a booming recycling industry, which thrived on factory wastes, soon emerged in the neighborhood (Routray 2021). The recycling of factory wastes made the *jhuggis* highly fire-prone, and the rudimentary house structures were often washed away during heavy monsoons. In a nutshell, fire-related accidents, structures washed away during monsoons, routine demolitions by police, and the consequent destruction of properties and thefts of valuables were all common features of *jhuggi* building strategies and risk-taking enterprises in Gautam Nagar.

Gautam Nagar residents often had to deal with harassment from the host population in nearby villages as well. As the strength of the neighborhood grew, the strongmen mustered courage to confront harassment and define the community on their own terms. This process of locality-building was "relational and contextual rather than . . . scalar or spatial." As is evident, locality-building was a "complex phenomenological quality, constituted by a series of links between the sense of social immediacy, the technologies of interactivity, and the relativity of contexts" (Appadurai 1996: 178).[7] Subsequently, the residents develop locality-based identity and kinship, which remain fundamental to collective solidarity and struggles (see De Neve 2008: 226). However, as discussed earlier, building a locality is contingent, contextual, and relational. The fragility of locality-building, as pointed out by Appadurai, is compounded by various obstacles, such as those illustrated above (Appadurai 1996: 179; Hansen 2005b: 13; Tarlo 2003: 13). Nevertheless, locality-building is the first step toward reworking the surveillance and monitoring strategies of the state—the incremental claims of the poor on the state through locality-building advance the citizenship projects of the poor.

Not only did the *pradhans* play an important part in the development of the locality of Gautam Nagar, they also had a role during demolition threats and following demolitions. In early 2009, a section of Gautam Nagar was demolished for a road-widening project. The neighborhood had survived demolitions many times before as a result of residents' successful bargaining and intermediaries' mediations with the elected politicians and ministers. Prior to the 2009 demolition, residents did not take the threats seriously. However, the demolitions happened without any resettlement and residents felt cheated by the politicians. Residents argued that the politicians misled them by denying them their right to go to court: *"Yeh neta log humme gumrah kiye"* (The politicians misled us). In response, the *pradhans* and *samaj sevaks* organized themselves and went to the councilor, MLA, MP, minister of urban development, chief minister of Delhi, and other politicians. The *sarkari karmacharis* provided vital information about planned demolitions, court procedures, and internal news of government offices concerning their settlement. While the MLA promised to intervene after the elections, he lost and was unable to follow through. Complicating matters further, the delimitation of constituencies resulted in changes that disqualified the residents' support for the ex-MLA. The rival MLA instead invited residents to join and support him in future elections before he could help the community as a precondition for their votes. There is a trend toward the declining numerical strength of the poor in many central constituencies in Delhi after they are displaced from these areas. The numerical decline of poor people in these neighborhoods will alter the political dynamics. Poorer populations in Delhi pursue their social and economic rights through political parties (Harriss 2005: 1041). However, current urban restructuring policies that displace poorer populations from central areas have the potential to undermine these citizenship rights by reducing the political significance of poor populations in the central parts of Delhi.

Back at Gautam Nagar, the *pradhans* continued to meet with the politicians, who in turn wrote letters to various lower officials, often in a cavalier fashion without assurance or commitment to residents. The *samaj sevaks* grew discontented with the *pradhans'* unsuccessful interventions and emerged as self-fashioned leaders of the neighborhood at this juncture. The strategy of *samaj sevaks* in the neighborhoods is markedly different from the politician-centered approach taken by the *pradhans*, as explained previously in the chapter. When the *samaj sevaks* took the lead, they received suggestions from activists visiting their locality and forwarded a case against the Government of National Capital Territory of Delhi (GNCTD) at the High Court of Delhi, thereby marginalizing the influence of the *pradhans*. Thus, the High Court, middle-class activists, lawyers, and *likhai-padhai ka kaam* (work related to writing and reading) were seen as more effective than a defeated MLA and his elected rival. The *samaj sevaks* with their relative sophistication were better suited for this job than the *pradhans*, who relied on the messiness of politics, muscle power, and a popular support base for their success.

Soon the residents organized a meeting led by *samaj sevaks* to discuss the High Court proceedings at the end of December 2009 (the details of this case are discussed in Chapter 5). The *samaj sevaks* gathered prior to the meeting and argued that people have *aham* (a false ego) and do not join them when there is a need to unite. "Only a handful of people go to the court and everyone is aspiring to get government resettlement plots for free," noted one *samaj sevak*. A plastic mat was quickly spread on the part of the demolished settlement that remained intact. The *samaj sevaks* sat on the *charpai* (woven jute cot) and seventy residents huddled together around them on the plastic mat. One of the *samaj sevaks* started collecting money, listed names on the register, and took the signatures or thumbprints of residents. Soon, conflicts and disagreements surfaced relating to monies spent, monies collected, and the *rann-nitis* used to solve their collective problem of resettlement. The *samaj sevaks* retorted with complaints about the thankless nature of their jobs, sacrifices they had made, and job loss from going to the courts. They made statements about their daily expenses for court hearings and meetings with politicians and officials.

The *samaj sevaks* informed the residents about their compensation, the need to organize and maintain unity, the proof documents required, and upcoming mandatory meetings. They also informed the residents about a survey to be undertaken by state bodies in order to bolster their numerical presence in the city. However, they were also evasive about their expenses, lawyer fees (the lawyer actually had not taken any money for this case), and about their exact strategies and possible resettlement timeline. The *samaj sevaks'* ambiguity was combined with reassurances about their indispensability. They were irked by recommendations demanding accountability on their part and threatened to quit their jobs. The residents intervened when things got out of control. On one occasion, a few residents argued, "You are our leader and we trust your discretion." One *samaj sevak* looked pleased and responded, "We are *sevaks* (workers) and we do selfless *seva* (service), but you should be aware of what happens in the courts. The lawyers are very vocal. When they debate, sweat streams down their faces. Then all of a sudden, they'll demand a particular document about our neighborhood, and I'll run out of the court to photocopy it and bring it back to the lawyer. This is a tough job and we have fought hard to win." These dramatic descriptions of the *samaj sevaks'* work ensure and legitimize their role in the neighborhood. The *samaj sevaks* vociferously made the point that if residents had initially organized with them and not the *pradhans*, the problem would have been solved already. In fact, they contemptuously accused the *pradhans* of *chamchagiri* (sycophancy). Further, they gently warned that they would only keep informed those residents who were part of the struggle and who contributed financially and morally to it. At this juncture, the role of *pradhans* is reduced to logistics, such as arranging meetings and commemorations with government officials, visitors, and NGOs by putting up makeshift stages. However, it should be noted that these activities often overlap with those of other intermediaries, blurring their roles and spheres of influence.

MEDIATED POLITICS OF PROOF DOCUMENTS

The procurement of "proof documents" such as ration cards and voter IDs is perhaps the most challenging task in the quest of numerical citizenship struggles for the urban poor. These proof documents are required to establish residency claims, procure basic amenities, and demand compensation upon resettlement.[8] The intermediaries' help in obtaining these documents creates an impression of indispensability. As residents in the three neighborhoods concurred, on average it takes more than ten years to obtain ration cards or voter IDs, as this process involves intricate bureaucratic procedures. One *samaj sevak* was committed to helping people procure ration cards and voter IDs. He made use of the Right to Information to point out irregularities in issuing ration cards and was successful in securing ration cards for almost sixty people in Gautam Nagar.

The *samaj sevak*'s congenial personality connected him with the people with ease. He had a wooden cot adjoining a wall on the extremely narrow *galli* in front of his precariously built brick house. The front part of the house served as a grocery shop and he often sat on his cot, a plastic sheet hung overhead, surveying the people and activities that went on in his *galli*. He also tutored small children in the neighborhood, which confirmed his level of literacy to the residents. Residents brought many documents for him to submit with their applications for ration cards, voter IDs, birth certificates, and other proof documents. The *samaj sevak* gently chided them if they made mistakes with the documents. His clientele were mostly women across caste lines, though he approached the oppressed castes in a condescending way. He charged a token amount of money to cover his expenses, which included buying forms, conveyance, and office supplies. He spoke fluent Hindi, Sanskrit, and a bit of English, and insisted that he was interested in *samaj seva* (social work) rather than monetary gains. On the one hand, he passionately expressed his views about rights and poor people's citizenship entitlements. On the other, he shared anecdotes, proverbs, metaphors, and poems that expressed patriarchal views on the changing role of women in the city.

The residents' reliance on *samaj sevaks* reflects the unequal distribution of cultural capital in Gautam Nagar. The *samaj sevaks* demonstrated a semblance of what Bourdieu (1991), following Pierre Guiraud, calls "articulatory styles" that did not make them complete misfits in different fields (86). Their accents, behavior, and bodily gestures are refined compared to other residents, but they fall short in the eyes of the agents they encounter higher up. As "all linguistic practices are measured against the legitimate practices, i.e. the practices of those who are dominant" (53), the *samaj sevaks*' confident articulation in their own setting waned, for example, in offices. They also possessed a semblance of bureaucratic linguistic capital (which can be considered a subset of cultural capital)—that is, the ability to articulate bureaucratic procedures, identify the rights and entitlements of the poor, and express democratic ideals enshrined in the constitution. Awareness of mundane bureaucratic procedures puts them in a position to unravel the mysteries of state policies. Intermediaries who lacked these bureaucratic linguistic skills were also considered to lack *kshyamata* (capability). The intermediaries play off the poor's vulnerability or lack of *kshyamata* by providing information, procedures, contacts, and, at times, "forged credentials" in order to help them procure proof documents. The *sarkari karmacharis*, along with *samaj sevaks* and *pradhans*, provide information about bribes to be paid, officials to be contacted, and the routes through which "legitimate" as well as "forged" credentials should pass for procuring proof documents. Thus, the irony consists in procuring what rightfully belongs to the urban poor, by virtue of their presence in the city or otherwise, while at the same time creating dependencies, exclusions, and arbitrariness in the process. These practices, which draw on historical attempts to build a community against the odds of power arrangements, provide insight into how the legal arms of the state can be negotiated and subverted. The embodied experiences of the urban poor reveal the nature of power and the constraints they face while trying to build a mutually supportive community in the interstices of the cityscape.

MEDIATED POLITICS OF BASIC AMENITIES

Once the *jhuggi jhopri* settlements gain the patronage of a politician and are incorporated into the voter list, residents feel politically enfranchised and articulate stronger citizenship claims in the neighborhood. In other words, once the neighborhood gains state recognition and is incorporated into the electorate, the politicians and municipal officials become responsible for extending basic amenities, such as water and electricity.[9] *Pradhans* initially arrange for water tankers and then convince politicians to install hand pumps, and later tube-wells, along with providing water tankers (cf. Banda et al. 2014). The water tankers and containers often bear the names of the political leaders or patrons, as occurred in the Sitapuri transit camp in attempts at futuristic appeal to the multitude of

FIGURE 3.1: *Water tanker supplied by a local politician in the vicinity of Sitapuri transit camp.*

FIGURE 3.2: *A water tank bearing the name of the MLA and the councilor in Sitapuri transit camp.*

residents to vote in their favor in the upcoming elections. Water facilities are often absent, however, in demolished sites and in the initial years of resettlement, as discussed in Chapter 2. As a female *pradhan* in Gautam Nagar noted, "After the *jhuggi* was demolished, we ceased to be a vote bank and now the MLA does not listen to our needs."

The *pradhans* and residents of the three neighborhoods also forge relationships with factory owners, roadside eatery owners, guards, temple priests, staff at public toilets, and state officials in order to collect water from their supply points. Women and children walk long distances with buckets, plastic containers (purchased or collected and reused from chemical factories), and other receptacles to collect water from supply points around the neighborhoods. Sometimes the supply water (available only two or three times a week) turns to a trickle or shuts off completely because of a power failure. Leakages at various points in the line also serve as water sources. The inability to collect water forces residents to drink tube-well water, which may be contaminated. Water availability is dependent on material and social relations (Anand 2011: 543; Anand 2017; Bjorkman 2015) in the city. In fact, the supply of water is the outcome of politics and social relations along with the topography in the city (Anand 2011: 543; Anand 2017; Bjorkman 2015). In the Delhi neighborhoods, the *pradhans* bargain and arrange for minimum water taps and mediate conflicts that arise over scarce water supply. Attempts to jump the water collection queue, disagreements about the amount to be collected, spills, and collisions often lead to bitter fights. The *pradhans* mediate between families when petty neighborhood quarrels arise over water collection at the neighborhood tap, garbage disposal, or minor sanitary issues. In all three neighborhoods, *pradhans* gave conflicting accounts of their "sole" responsibility for certain amenities. These accounts are difficult to verify, as even *pradhans* belonging to the same political party often have to bargain with their respective politicians.

At times, a *pradhan* in the Azad resettlement colony sat near the tanker and supervised, distributed, and disciplined the crowd collecting the water in 2011. Accessing water supply points or water tankers involves political struggle. As a *pradhan* in Gautam Nagar noted, "Just before the first Delhi state assembly election [1993], we had a big meeting in the neighborhood. The politician had come and promised us basic amenities if he won. We supported him and he won the elections and later he arranged for water tankers and hand pumps, electricity connection, garbage disposal, and public toilets." The *pradhan* also noted, "You need to have *talmel* (be in sync) with the politician, or else you are least likely to get anything here." One resident argued, "Usually the MLA does work in his first stint, but then if the rival MLA wins, the former may even facilitate the demolition of the neighborhood." Hence, residents must choose their leaders wisely and have *talmel* with them in order to procure various services.

While intermediaries mediate fights over water supply and availability, they may also appropriate disproportionate shares for themselves or their supporters. Thus, some of the residents, with the support of a particular *samaj sevak*, were able to get a direct water connection in their homes at the Sitapuri transit camp. As the intermediary argued:

> The councilor is a friend and he directed Delhi *Jal* (water) Board [DJB] to install a water line in my home. The DJB people told me that I should install the pipe on my own and they would take care of the rest. Initially, people did not dare to complain as they thought we were *hi-fi* people [people of higher status], but later they informed the police and when the police came, we just explained that we knew Rajesh Pilot [a Congress politician who is no more] well. Thinking about it, I did not help him during election trips in Rajasthan just like that—he and his party ought to exchange favors too.

When asked if this *jugaad* was appropriate, as it would diminish the scarce water supply in neighborhood hydrants used daily by residents, he argued, "See, thirty percent of residents have water pipes in their homes already and no one is complaining. People have enough water here and I was even instrumental in installing a water treatment plant, which is currently dysfunctional, with the help of an NGO called CASP-Plan in Delhi." Thus, the distribution of scarce resources like water reflects unequal power relations in the neighborhood itself (see also Snell-Rood 2015: 110). It is not uncommon for intermediaries to arrange meetings with politicians and government service providers like the *jal* board to lobby for preferred contacts, service delivery, and duties. This is why the intermediaries' streets and lanes, especially those of *sarkari karmacharis*, are often better maintained and serviced than the rest.

Residents of *jhuggi* settlements and transit camps owe a debt to a former prime minister of India for their electricity connections. Historically, the urban poor would tap into the main electricity supply for the minimum electricity required in their homes. This often led to electrocution, police harassment, and bribery. In 1990, Prime Minister V. P. Singh openly suggested that poor people could use electricity for free by tapping into the main supply around the neighborhoods. "The *netaji* (leader) had allowed us to use electricity for free but since it's been privatized, we have been using kerosene lamps," noted one resident. In some cases, neighbors will allow others access to an electricity connection from their homes at a reasonable price so that the residents who cannot afford it can have a bulb or two. The *pradhans* help broker such arrangements for a minimum fee. Further, the *pradhans* may benefit from the state schemes that subcontract services. For instance, prior to privatization in 2002,[10] a *pradhan* in Gautam Nagar managed to get *bijli thekedari* (contracts to distribute electricity) in the neighborhood. The contract required him to give a certain amount of money to the government after collecting the electricity fee from residents. The *pradhan* used his discretion to base charges on meter readings or the number of electric appliances in the homes of each resident. This scheme involved money laundering by the *pradhan*, and a benevolent supply of free electricity for the poorest residents. As one resident remarked, "The *pradhan* demanded money or meter installation based on one's *haisiyat* (capacity/status), though he also made *manmani* (arbitrary decisions) that often led to fights." The state withdrew the license once it was realized that collection through the *pradhan* was a major failure. However, the residents are quick to note that "all these factory owners use free electricity, tamper with meter readings, and use all kinds of means to evade raids or bribe government officials, but only the poor are seen to steal electricity. Look at how much the poor earn; how do you expect them to pay for such soaring electricity bills? The cost of electricity has become prohibitive since it was privatized." The residents paid prohibitive electricity bills between 2009 and 2011 but received a respite after the newly elected Aam Aadmi Party introduced the populist measure of subsidizing electricity connections in low-income neighbor-hoods in Delhi.[11] In 2017, most residents observed that only the problem of soaring electricity bills had been resolved by the government in the preceding few years. Thus, the nature of mediation has changed since the electricity was privatized and then later subsidized. Nonetheless, the in-termediaries often solve electricity-related problems regarding pilfering, raids, and out-of-court settlements.

From time to time, the *pradhans* also clear clogged drains, remove garbage strewn across lanes and by-lanes, and install public toilets in the neighborhoods. They negotiate with the politicians to install garbage bins, campaign for more toilet seats in public facilities, and distribute blankets at the onset of harsh winters. As one female *pradhan* in Gautam Nagar re-called, "I must have received at least five hundred blankets from the MLA and distributed them among the poor in this neighborhood." The *pradhans* also arrange to have the lanes paved and ask politicians to install lamp-posts at the corners. They may also negotiate with politicians to allow a portion of the municipal park to be used for wedding functions or reli-gious purposes. Sewer lines are usually conspicuously absent in *jhuggi jho-pri*, transit camp, and resettlement colony neighborhoods in Delhi. How-ever, in 2013, before the legislative elections, the councilor built a drain along the main road of the Sitapuri neighborhood. The idea was to allow residents to connect their own sewers to the main drain. However, this was designed primarily to benefit the residents who lived along the main road; it was difficult for the residents living in the narrow lanes to build sewers. The intermediaries, who mostly lived in the convenient parts of the neigh-borhood, benefited in a disproportionate way. The few intermediaries who lived in the narrow lanes, which barely separate rows of houses, could also bargain with their neighbors to lay out and connect their sewers with the main drain. As can be discerned, the intermediaries deployed their rela-tive economic capital as well as symbolic power to their advantage in lay-ing out fragile sewers. They were able to successfully negotiate with their neighbors even when there was a protest against the possibility of leakage from the sewers right beside the entrance of their homes.

The intermediaries also actively campaign for various social and welfare services for the poor in their locality. For example, when the government sanctioned a plot of land for Apollo Hospital, the *prad-hans* led a campaign along with politicians to reserve seventy hospital beds for the poor. However, it remains uncertain whether these beds are actually available to poor people in such a high-end hospital. *Pradhans* spread the word around about widow pensions, old age pensions, and other compensation available on compassionate grounds. Accessing these services involves intricate bureaucratic procedures, and the *pradhans'* mediation services and assistance in filling out forms are significant, as discussed above. Female *pradhans* primarily negotiate with their political patrons about poor women's eligibility for widow or old age pensions. One such *pradhan* claims to have arranged monthly pensions for approximately 350 women in the Sitapuri transit camp. The arbitrary nature of government service provisions makes the intermediaries' relationships indispensable.

MEDIATED POLITICS OF LIVELIHOOD ARRANGEMENTS

Many of the poor earn livelihoods through officially illegal means, such as street vending or offering ancillary services in residential neighborhoods (Chatterjee 2008b; Harriss-White 2003). Often the poor have to establish a range of relationships across state and non-state domains to pursue livelihood options in the city (Routray 2021; Schindler 2014). In fact, the rich have also resorted to illegal means to make profits, especially in factories that do not abide by minimum labor laws (Ramaswami 2012); the rich often flout legal norms, as demonstrated in the building of illegal additional structures (Kamath and Vijayabaskar 2014; Verma 2002: 157) or in the "urban conquest" of the countryside through the illegal building of luxurious farmhouses (Soni 2000). However, law-breaking has disproportionate disadvantages for the urban poor, despite the fact that it is often provoked by their structural location in society. This is why political patronage and connections with police and municipal officials are paramount to the basic citizenship entitlements of the urban poor. In fact, the power and efficacy of an intermediary, especially a *pradhan*, is directly correlated with their connection with police officials and with politicians near the settlement. The *pradhans* do not only provide protection from police brutality; they also hold contractors, factory supervisors, and owners accountable for salaries, working conditions, and work-site disputes (Routray 2021). The *pradhans* and other petty entrepreneurs in the locality run small businesses that require intense labor input to generate profit (Routray 2021). Self-employed entrepreneurialism among the poor often involves the exploitation of the very poor to survive in a fragile economy (M. Davis 2004: 21–22). Most economic activity in and around the neighborhoods is beyond the purview of a formal plan. Hence, these activities are rendered illegal, which creates space for secret dealings, *kharcha-pani* (bribe-related spending), and brokerage with the police.

Pradhans fiercely oppose the MCD-driven demolitions of temporary street vendor structures or cart vendors and the clearing of scrapyards, as *pradhans* are often the owners of these businesses in the neighborhood. Many of the economic activities that border on illegal give rise to rent-seeking in the neighborhoods. For instance, the *pradhans* are responsible for collecting illegal extortion of *hafta* (extortion of rent on a weekly or monthly basis) from petty traders at weekly fairs in the Sitapuri transit camp, which is then passed along to politicians and government officials. This ensures protection for the petty traders and allows them to evade regulations laid out by the MCD or Public Works Department. At times, the *pradhans* turn into moneylenders, charging usurious interest rates in the neighborhood. When doing so, they may forcefully seize proof documents as *girwi* (mortgage). Most often, the *pradhans* inform the police about new construction, sales, and renovations of structures, as well as running of businesses, including water filtration at homes in transit camps and resettlement colonies. The police officials endorse *pradhans* who act as real-estate brokers and sell houses or *jhuggis* in neighborhoods through pecuniary exchanges. Police involvement and mediations through *pradhans* form a fundamental part of the ritual to initiate building, buying, or renovating a *jhuggi*. In addition to informal property transactions, the *pradhans* help residents find compromise settlements for petty squabbles and for new constructions that threaten the existing ones.

Youth are led into drug peddling by their urban marginalization, the "structural violence of mass unemployment" (Auyero 2000a: 97), and impoverishment in the wake of displacements (see also Wacquant 1997). Police raids and drug seizures often render youth helpless, necessitating the mediation of *pradhans* to protect them from incarceration. In 2017, the problem of drug abuse in the neighborhoods had achieved dangerous proportions. Many residents were concerned about the abuse of smack (a variety of heroin), especially among children, as one of the major problems in the three neighborhoods. If there were thefts in the neighborhood, police often chased children who abused smack or sniffed a variety of solutions (especially a glue used to patch punctured cycle tubes). *Pradhans* mediated during such encounters to support neighborhood children and families. In fact, informal governance through a compromise settlement is the standard procedure for arriving at resolutions in these neighborhoods. The politics of compromise gives rise to grievances, doubts about the *pradhan*'s authority, and the potential defection to a different *pradhan* if a party is unhappy with the settlement. Thus, the mediation of concerns related to basic amenities and social reproduction is characterized by conflict and mistrust, as well as solidarity and practical survival wisdom. Most often, the *pradhans* arbitrate cases before they involve any *police ka chakkar* (dealings with police). This role has the potential to render them kind and polite or rude and malevolent.

GENDER AND MEDIATED POLITICS

The role of female *pradhans* is as significant as that of male *pradhans*. Female *pradhans* fiercely articulate neighborhood arguments, solve local problems, and resolve petty quarrels. Like their male counterparts, their power is derived indirectly from their association with a particular politician or police official. Female *pradhans* organize rallies for politicians, especially during elections, and arrange for ration cards and old age and widow pensions. While female *pradhans* engage in the same political activities as their male counterparts, their role in solving women-specific issues in the neighborhoods is striking.

Female *pradhans* frequently participate with *mahila mandals* (women's organizations) in the neighborhoods. These *mahila mandals* are often initiated by political leaders, NGOs, or government agencies. Others are organized by women residents themselves, who draw on lessons from other neighborhoods. Downward mobility and unemployment are constant features of contemporary city life marked by informalization of labor processes and relations (Breman 2004). Furthermore, displacements, seizures of ration cards, homelessness, and lost amenities upon demolition are accompanied by frustration and interpersonal violence. Thus, the "interconnectedness of factors leading to disruption of everyday life" and "threats to the security of economic activities" mutate into "domestic and other forms of intimate violence" (V. Das 1996: 1510). As key members of *mahila mandals, pradhans* mediate domestic violence disputes, marital conflicts, dowry harassment, and family property disputes, as well as child-rearing responsibilities, gambling, and drunkenness on the part of men in these neighborhoods. Female *pradhans* participate in and mediate *tehkikat* (investigation) and *sunwai* (hearing/trial) in weekly or monthly *panchayats* (councils). Female *pradhans* in the Azad resettlement colony address residents' needs and *dukh-dard* (pain-suffering). They arrive at decisions when mediating disputes.

Female *pradhans* also advise police sensitization programs run by NGOs in these neighborhoods. Female *pradhans* may tend to promote compromise, sometimes to the extent of asking parties to sign onto terms and conditions of a compromise formula arrived at through a resolution process. They decide between "good" and "bad" parties and exercise the freedom to punish or to refer cases to NGOs or the police. At times, female *pradhans* may subvert the NGOs that initiated them into this work. I once asked a female *pradhan* in the Azad resettlement colony what motivated her to do the job, why she cut ties with one NGO in the Azad resettlement colony, and if she ever felt scared to do this work:

> Well, this is *samaj seva* (social work). I work for the poor. I charge one hundred rupees [US$2.20] per arbitration or settlement. The NGO is my guru, but they do not understand the dynamics here. I was once arbitrating a woman's inheritance case, and the NGO demanded the woman's documents. You tell me, what right do they have to retain the personal documents of this woman? The NGO staff was cross with me and did not involve me much after that, but that was fine with me. I am not scared of anyone here. I know the police very well and they respect my work, and I also go to the court. Fear is a bad thing; people may bitch about me behind my back, but they dare not say anything in front of me.

This account indicates competing authority structures and the persistence of what Hansen (2005a: 179) calls "repertoires of authority." Though at times female *pradhans* work in solidarity as marginal leaders, the practices described above raise critical questions about the delivery of justice.

Male *pradhans* often characterize women's work in negative terms and deride them as insignificant. They argue that police and court intervention in private affairs fosters disunity in families. Articulate and fiery female leaders are seen as "*ahankar ki laxmi*" or "*ghamand ki devi*" (these expressions are adjectives for arrogant women). Male residents talk about female *pradhans* with caution, as they depend on them for various services, yet they still display gendered prejudices concerning their role in society. Women's authority and extra earnings from *pradhan-giri* (*pradhan* activities) are resented by male residents who encounter an uncertain labor market, impoverishment due to displacements, and masculinity crises when struggling to provide for their families. In another context, Ferguson (1999: 194) argues that "antagonism, mutual suspicion, cynicism, and misogyny" emanate from a changing "political economic regime of gender." While it is important to recognize women's subordination beyond the political and economic spheres, the "political economy of misogyny" (197–198) offers a framework to understand the attitudes, behaviors, and gendered norms in contemporary Delhi. Though character assassination is a common method of disparaging female *pradhans* by stating or inventing their obvious or purported relationships with politicians and police officials, residents are aware of the power of female *pradhans* and their indispensable role in solving day-to-day problems in the neighborhood. In the refrain of a particular male resident: "*Naari use bolte hain jiska koi shatru na ho*" (Real women do not have enemies). The same people who benefit from female *pradhans* are also suspicious of their proximity to the police. For example, one resident argued, "Tell me which *bhadra mahila* (genteel woman) would have contacts at the police?"

Clearly, female *pradhans'* achievements challenge the passivity that is often ascribed to women. Nevertheless, there is a tendency on the part of male *pradhans* in the neighborhood to contrast their own achievements in bringing progress and development with women's so-called minor successes in solving domestic problems. This binary of *vikas ka kaam* (development-related work) versus *gharelu samasya ka kaam* (work related to domestic problems) is fiercely contested by female *pradhans*, who cite their dealings with politicians and police and narrate the work they have done over the years with respect to gaining a foothold in the city. Thus, unlike Ananya Roy's (2003: 86) empirical findings about masculinized idioms of political participation in Calcutta, the context of Delhi provides empirical insight into women's active participation in politics as *pradhans* in low-income neighborhoods. Nonetheless, the vulnerabilities women suffer in negotiating an uncertain labor market and raising children in cases of abandonment are strikingly similar in Calcutta and Delhi. Thus, female *pradhans* remain at the forefront in solving a range of problems. At times they even disparage men's abilities to navigate politics, work, and domestic responsibilities. For example, a female *pradhan* constantly referred to her husband as a person with *mota dimag* (low intelligence) and asked me to speak only with her.

THE PITFALLS OF MEDIATED POLITICS

The preceding descriptions illustrate the complexity of intermediaries' activities in citizenship struggles. Intermediaries are not a monolithic group; they can be distinguished in terms of their political affiliations, income, caste, gender, religious affiliations, and educational and cultural capital, as well as their commitment to particular causes and the strategies they use. In addition, the diversity of caste, gender, income, and cultural and educational capital in neighborhoods should be understood along with the general vulnerability and poverty of all residents. The determination of the urban poor in fighting against unjust redistribution of resources and erosion of social, economic, and political rights creates the space for marginal leaders to emerge from impoverished niches of the city. Though intermediaries may foster identity-driven divisions, the residents themselves use their practical wisdom to forge alliances and solidarity before negotiating with state officials, the legal apparatus, and other influential persons. The intermediaries show both democratic potential and the ability to create dependencies and exclusions. Furthermore, the mediated politics of numerical citizenship can also have an underside and a reactionary nature.

The power of *pradhans* and their reactionary politics is most evident when they take on moral crusades in the locality. One female *pradhan* in Gautam Nagar remarked, *"Mere ilaake se koi ladki bhaag gayee, mera naam kharab hota hai* (If a girl runs away with a boy from my area, then it brings a bad name to me). Since I left *saashan* (rule), nothing is happening here. I have withdrawn from politics as the neighborhood is too fractured, and it is all about money and alcohol now." Thus, at times female *pradhans* echo patriarchal sentiments and attempt to police "wrong" women and their *rahan-sahan* (way of living). Jha, Rao, and Woolcock (2007: 234) found that *pradhans* fine residents and even ostracize inter-caste married couples. This points to the nefarious ramifications that may result from extra-legal and extra-constitutional authorities. The intermediaries also often make use of "nuisance value" to their own advantage (Hansen 2005b: 80; Jeffrey 2009: 199).

Pradhans often take advantage of vulnerable populations in the Azad resettlement colony, extending loans for selling off residents' plots for meager amounts, meeting family emergencies, and creating dependencies. Vulnerable populations with neither earnings nor savings are more likely to sell off their plots and return to city centers in search of work to survive. At the time of allotment, *pradhans* manage to be involved in *hera pheri* (swindling) by allotting themselves multiple resettlement plots, often with the connivance of state officials, as discussed in Chapter 1. This grave situation is compounded by a dearth of plots at relocation sites for other eligible residents, who are seen at government offices with their allotment slips to acquire new plots. Though *pradhans* help residents acquire the important documents that prove eligibility to get new plots in the wake of displacements, they may confiscate these documents, offer the most vulnerable residents money in exchange for them, and actively participate in arbitrary land allotment decisions with state authorities. *Pradhans* may also be involved in deals with state officials to exchange allotment plots, such as making those eligible for 12-square-foot plots get 18 square feet instead, and vice versa. Residents who lose out on bigger plots are most often resigned to their fate, since declining the smaller plots and navigating bureaucratic and judiciary hurdles may be more disastrous in the long run. *Pradhans, samaj sevaks, sarkari karmacharis,* and other influential residents more often than not receive corner plots, are selected in allotment lotteries, and own the houses facing the streets. This is a significant gain because houses in narrow lanes have inadequate ventilation. Further, there is a possibility of renting or starting home businesses if the location is ideal.

Emma Tarlo's (2003: 88) study of the Emergency illustrates how sterilization became a medium to negotiate one's housing rights in the city. Her study vividly analyzes how poor people underwent sterilization or encouraged others to do so in order to acquire, transfer, or regularize their plots. This process gave rise to a complex scenario where intermediaries helped the poor acquire sterilization certificates as proof documents, often violating the bodily integrity of the most vulnerable poor in the process. Similar evidence of swindling, unjust exchanges, plot seizure, and plot confiscation upon inability to pay back loans can be found in the Azad resettlement colony. Thus, the activities of intermediaries complicate the story of "innocent victims" versus "pragmatic opportunists," and of "victims" versus "victimizers" (Tarlo 2003: 93, 119).

The activities of *dalals* (touts/brokers) also figure significantly in the demolition of *jhuggi* settlements, the establishment of resettlement colonies, and property dealings in the resettlement colonies. The *dalals* forge or make *nakli* (counterfeit) documents, encourage property transfers, and arrange powers of attorney. They work closely with government officials, politicians, financiers, and *pradhans* to carry out their deals or bargains and pay commission for these property transactions. As activist R once noted:

> The *dalals* mislead and motivate the poorest to sell off their plots [allotment documents]. They play on the poor's fear of unemployment in the far-off neighborhoods without basic amenities. Then they produce a power of attorney and transfer the plot to someone else. This is a well-known thing and the *dalals* have a "setting" [understanding] with the *pradhans*. The *dalals* coordinate with the eligible resident and the financier. The financier gives them money to buy the plots. The state officials, politicians, *pradhans*, and a range of agents are involved and receive commissions. Later, the plots are sold for hefty prices. There have been Central Bureau of Investigation inquiries

against DDA officials and one particular agent, who ran a canteen in Municipal Corporation of Delhi premises and had many plots in the Bawana resettlement colony alone.

As a result, the resettlement sites and plots become vital components of the accumulation strategies of *dalals*, politicians, state officials, and *pradhans*. Pradhans are suspected of seizing vacant plots and are seen as *dalals* by some residents. Even the self-proclaimed *pradhans* make a distinction between their activities and the activities of *dalals*, who swindle poor people's money and property, erect multistory buildings, and bargain for profit with state officials. The *pradhans* of the Azad resettlement colony colluded with *dalals* from outside the neighborhood to transfer property in their names, forge documents, obliterate names of absentees during surveys for resettlement, and usurp their plots (cf. Simone 2015: S21). The most vulnerable in this scenario are the poor, who are unable to pay even the minimum resettlement fees to the Delhi Development Authority (DDA) and the absentees during the surveys. Thus, while many residents actively bargain, negotiate, and create relationships to survive, the most vulnerable members of these neighborhoods are excluded by default. Moreover, most of these activities involve some degree of physical violence. Though the *pradhans* do not claim to be *dada* (bullies), they may perform *dada-ism*—that is, "a style of exercising political and social power and protection that invokes images of a masculine, assertive, often violent local strongman, whose clout lies in self-made networks of loyalty rather than in institutionalized action and discourse" (Hansen 2005b: 72).

The *pradhans* have an ambiguous role in simultaneously helping residents procure money to build houses in resettlement colonies and helping moneylenders commit usury and seize plots. For this reason, there is a climate of mistrust vis-à-vis *pradhans*. Many believe the *pradhans* are dishonest or lack integrity, and accuse the *pradhans* of double-dealing and securing benefits, even alternate plots of land, from government officials and politicians. At times, the *pradhans'* diffidence or lack of interest in resettlement advocacy creates mistrust among the residents. One resident in Gautam Nagar remarked, "See, we are not present when the *pradhans* go and talk with the councilor, MLA, MP, minister, or any state official.

What do we know about the real story behind closed doors? We just accompany them until the doorsteps. But what they bargain, how they bargain, and under what conditions they agree are not in our control. So, either you have to trust the *pradhan* or resign to fate." The misappropriation of plots and houses in these circumstances significantly involves state officials, *dalals* outside the localities, and various intermediaries. Navigating bureaucratic hurdles (such as filling out forms and bribing officials to submit resettlement claims) and structural challenges to mere survival can saturate the day-to-day lives and aspirations of the urban poor. This raises critical questions about resettlement policies, the structural location of the most vulnerable, and the nature of citizenship struggles. Thus, what is needed is a situated understanding of the workings of citizenship struggles in the city.

The power arrangements and activities of various authorities and organizations evolve over time into hybridized forms of power with peculiar practices. In fact, the intermediaries' styles of authority are not distinct from those that characterize state sovereignty. These local actors interact and overlap with state structures through a multitude of practices. Krishna's study of *naya netas* (new leaders) rightly bemoans the absence of "institutionalized avenues" that affect the functioning of Indian democracy. *Naya netas* "are not a permanent and institutionalized force that can stand in place of well organized parties" (Krishna 2007: 157). While direct access to political resources and channels remains a cornerstone of citizenship practices, the liminality of these leaders grants them the potential to realize substantive citizenship, especially when the institutionalized parameters of planning, city governance, and unequal provisioning of services go against the interests of the poor. Urban restructuring initiatives in recent times have called for demolitions, the privatization of services, and increasing user fees. But the active political participation of the urban poor and their intermediaries has also subverted these trends through their accentuation of numerical strength and mediations to obtain a variety of basic amenities. I agree with Chatterjee (2004) that participation in political society expands freedoms for the poor, who lack the social, cultural, and economic capital to navigate the "sanitized fortress of civil society" (67, 74). However, it is evident that the domain of political society also expands various un-freedoms. Therefore, the biggest challenge is to temper the "squalor, ugliness, and violence of popular life" (74) through social justice and redistribution. In fact, it should also be noted, as pointed out by A. Roy (2008: xxxv), that "urban populism: a system of political bargains and negotiations through which informal vendors, workers, and squatters establish tenuous access to land, livelihood, and shelters" has not succeeded in converting "tenuous access into a secure and permanent right to the city."

It is obvious that the routinization of state activities (Fuller and Harriss 2009) is part of the consciousness of the poor. An ethnography of the mediation of intermediaries between the residents and the state reveals everyday politics and cultural forms used by the urban poor in negotiations to claim citizenship entitlements. *Pradhan-giri* (*pradhan* activities), *neta-giri* (leader activities), *jugaad* (fixing), and other cultural idioms that arise from political improvisations and dealings should be understood as a part of poor people's repertoire of citizenship *rann-nitis* given neoliberal economic restructuring and the limited availability of opportunities, resources, and basic amenities in the city. These *rann-nitis* of mediation entail patronage, exclusions, and dependencies, as well as solidarities. In analyzing the mediated politics of the urban poor when dealing with state policies and claiming citizenship entitlements, this chapter emphasizes not only the salience of vote-bank politics but also the complexities of locality-building, "public dealings," and navigation of the intricate bureaucratic and political arrangements to lay claim to a home, infrastructure, and public provisions in the city. In the next chapter, I examine how poor people foreground their citizenship struggles in claiming a range of documents. While the "proof documents" remain the cornerstone of urban dispossession and governance, the poor develop a range of *rann-nitis* concerning "proof documents" that establish eligibility for procuring welfare services in the city.

CHAPTER 4

DOCUMENTARY PRACTICES AND THE COUNTER-TACTICS OF ENUMERATION

TO BECOME ELIGIBLE to obtain basic citizenship entitlements including welfare services, the poor are required to produce numerical documentation of their presence in the city. As discussed in the Introduction, the state recognizes a *jhuggi jhopri* cluster only if the settlement has at least fifty households. The ability to subsist in a state-recognized neighborhood is the first step toward accessing citizenship entitlements. State recognition of the neighborhood vests the residents with political rights, whereby they become eligible to obtain voter IDs. Following this, the poor become eligible for numerous citizenship entitlements if they can produce documents issued by the state before particular cut-off dates. The poor work to procure a range of documents that code their status and mutually reinforce their claims to eligibility, undergoing documentary and inscriptive struggles that remain pivotal to the claims of numerical citizenship. This chapter examines the complexity of practices concerning the procurement of two key documents, namely ration and voter identity cards, and their lesser inscriptive substitutes that may fulfill the citizenship aspirations for material claims and political belonging.[1]

The state undertakes enumeration, collection of statistics, and bureaucratic documentation to determine eligibility for resettlement housing and subsidized food. The formal processes of state calculations exclude a significant population through the imposition of arbitrary classification categories. In turn, the poor adopt a range of counter-tactics of enumeration, namely letter-writing, office visits, claims through Right to Information, self-surveys, and counterfeit production. In this light, I explore both the practical and ideological motivations and the web of social and political relationships that shape the ingenious strategies of the poor in challenging exclusionary state technologies. I argue that these documents, inscriptive artifacts, and their counterfeits raise significant questions about arbitrary and official definitions of legality, illegality, and eligibility. The improvisational tactics of the poor at times challenge the state through the manipulation of eligibility lists and the production of counterfeits. However, these same tactics also engage the communities and the state actors in documentary projects of the state as well as citizenship claims of the poor. Through ethnographic vignettes from three neighborhoods, I illustrate how numerical citizenship is claimed, negotiated, performed, and realized by a range of documentary and inscriptive practices. I analyze how ration cards, voter IDs, and less-valued substitutes, such as V. P. Singh cards (issued by a former prime minister of India as an urban residential proof document), as well as allotment slips, Delhi Development Authority registration numbers, *jhuggi* tokens, electricity bills, vaccination certificates, child delivery documents, birth certificates, and school leaving certificates, are important components of citizenship struggles, especially in regard to housing and food security, among Delhi's urban poor. In this respect, the poor attempt to procure these documents independently or with the help of a range of intermediaries.

In analyzing the "regime of paper documents" and "graphic artifacts," I explore how documentary and inscriptive artifacts mediate "relations among people, things, and purposes" and how the residents desire, use, and contest these artifacts in myriad ways (Chatterji 2005: 199; V. Das 2011; Fassin and d'Halluin 2005; Hull 2012b: 1; Mathur 2012; Mathur 2016; Sadiq 2008; Srivastava 2012). Thus, the chapter explores how the documentary practices are felt, partaken, and subverted by the poor (V. Das and Poole 2004; Srivastava 2012). In his comprehensive review of scholarship on documents and bureaucracy, Matthew Hull (2012a: 253) has argued, "Documents are not simply instruments of bureaucratic organizations, but rather are constitutive of bureaucratic rules, ideologies, knowledge, practices, subjectivities, objects, outcomes, and even the organizations themselves." Drawing on this insight, I contend that documentary and inscriptive practices are also constitutive of innovations, ingenious tactics, and a range of improvisations on the part of the poor that constitute counter-tactics in their citizenship struggles. The documentary and inscriptive improvisations are a response to the material and cultural constraints of the poor. Consequently, the orthographic anxieties, experiences of humiliation, symbolic violence, and state condescension and protracted waiting that remain integral to state technologies necessitate a variety of innovations and struggles. My examination of the imbrication of state and community practices draws attention to the forging of contextual sociality, the potential of exclusionary logics, and the subversion of hierarchies in unanticipated ways. I acknowledge the role of activists and NGOs in documentary and inscriptive struggles, but unlike scholars like Appadurai (2002), my approach examines the complex modes of political agency beyond the vision and practice of NGO-driven politics. However, drawing on Appadurai, I show that some of the practices of the poor contribute to generating useful knowledge and constituting communities in these neighborhoods (Appadurai 2012), which remain critical for claims-making and citizenship struggles in the city.

ENUMERATION AND ELIGIBILITY

Prior to the economic reforms period, India had the universal Public Distribution System (PDS) through which subsidized food grains and essential commodities were supplied via Fair Price Shops across the country. Massive public spending cuts affecting food provisions began with the reform period in 1991, and since 1997, India has targeted its PDS at populations enumerated as Below Poverty Line (BPL) or Above Poverty Line (APL) (Corbridge, Harriss, and Jeffrey 2013: 107; Patnaik 2007; Swaminathan 2000). As observers note, the "poverty line" was an "arbitrary construct" that created enormous administrative challenges to supply subsidized grains to only the poorest populations (Corbridge, Harriss, and Jeffrey 2013: 107). In fact, many economists claim that leakages and inefficiencies have increased since the targeted PDS was introduced (110). Swaminathan (2000) has also discussed problems of misidentification and mis-targeting under the targeted PDS. She argues that universal programs produce "large errors of wrong inclusion (that is, include the rich) but small errors of wrong exclusion. On the other hand, narrowly targeted programs tend to have small errors of wrong inclusion but large errors of wrong exclusion" (Swaminathan 2000: 102). In other words, the targeted PDS system is more likely to exclude even the deserving poor. Further, PDS illegal sales, false entries on ration cards, short weighing of commodities, and the adulteration of goods are rampant (54). These claims raise significant questions about subsidized food. In this context, struggles over ration cards become even more acute, as corruption related to the issuance of various cards, underselling, and other forms of pilfering become increasingly rampant. For instance, I often came across APL (Above Poverty Line) cards among daily-wage Dalit residents working in the recycling business of the *Kabadda* camp in Gautam Nagar, while some relatively upwardly mobile residents could procure BPL cards (Below Poverty Line) or *Antyodaya* (designated as the "poorest of the poor") cards.

Like food subsidies, resettlement policies are linked to welfare in demolished informal settlements. It is these policies that form the most important component of the housing policy in Delhi today. Without substantial redistribution of land in the city or social housing programs and up until the introduction of the new housing policy in 2010, historically the right of housing was negotiated through the capacity to build *jhuggis*, gain state recognition, and acquire resettlement plots upon demolition in the vicinity of the city. As discussed in Chapter 1, the resettlement policy formally ensured plots of 18 square meters and 12.5 square meters for residents with proof documents dated from 1990 and 1998, respectively. The new housing policy ensured resettlement flats instead of plots, and the cut-off dates have been revised periodically since 2010, with the current cut-off date set at January 1, 2015. As pointed out earlier, Gautam Nagar residents struggled to receive resettlement plots on the production of proof documents issued prior to 1998 after their *jhuggis* were demolished in 2009. However, the government has decided to resettle them in resettlement flats instead of plots under the new resettlement policy.[2] In order to obtain a flat, Gautam Nagar residents have to produce documents issued before 1998. However, because the residents surrendered their old ration cards in order to get new ones, they are required to produce photocopies of the old ration cards to be eligible beneficiaries. Working in conjunction with the new housing policy and founded in 2010, the Delhi Urban Shelter Improvement Board (DUSIB) is charged with demolishing encroachments, negotiating compensation with landowning agencies, and determining eligibility for resettlement, as discussed in Chapter 1. The board carries out calculative tasks related to the enumeration, supervision, and surveillance of the areas, as well as the lottery for allotment of resettlement flats. The board's work gives rise to conflicts over the definition of neighborhoods, the responsibilities of the landowning agency in the event of demolition and resettlement, and the discretionary power of surveyors.

In this regard, the issuance of important documents like ration cards and voter IDs bolsters moral as well as quasi-legal opinions about the legitimacy of a particular neighborhood.[3] Proof documents help prevent arbitrary demolitions of transit camps, which ironically were established by government agencies as part of their planning apparatus. Proof documents are also bargaining tools for resettlement and state-sponsored benefits for *jhuggi* residents. For instance, the residents of the Sitapuri transit camp opined that they were issued ration cards and voter IDs, possessed a range of documents for many years, paid license fees regularly, paid for basic amenities, and produced bills whenever necessary as proof of their claim to the neighborhood. In our conversations, they reiterated their belief that they are proper citizens abiding by legal and constitutional norms. In their view, demolition of their houses would be not only absurd but also unjust and unconstitutional.

THE POLITICS OF ENUMERATION

As discussed above, enumeration, surveys, and various identification mechanisms constitute vital aspects of citizenship in the city, as state policy is written so that only the surveyed and identified *jhuggi* settlements can be relocated. In reality, identified and surveyed *jhuggi* settlements, such as Gautam Nagar, enjoy only minimal citizenship. As a result, numerous newer, unidentified, un-surveyed, and undesignated *jhuggi* settlements in various parts of the city removed from patronage structures remain outside the ambit of state policies of resettlement. They could be removed without any consideration or consultation, thus depriving the poor in these settlements of minimal basic amenities and also undermining any hope for their relocation. The issue of enumeration and related governmental activities is contentious and raises critical questions about literacy, the collection of documents, and substantive citizenship in the city. Problems arising from under-enumeration and anomalies in the production of government statistics are rampant. Under-enumeration often results from work- or travel-related absences at the time of surveys and the discretionary power of the surveyors regarding the details furnished by residents. It is a standard practice on the part of government officials to reject proof documents and render people ineligible on the slightest pretext. Resident B of the Azad resettlement colony, who was active with the feminist organization Jagori, noted:

> The DDA people rejected a lot of applications in the Alaknanda camp [one of the *jhuggi* clusters from which people were brought to the Azad resettlement colony] and people were running around various offices to claim plots. We filled numerous applications, arranged documents, and submitted them at Vikash Sadan office. I guess around 50 percent of the residents in Alaknanda camp were deemed "ineligible." But what is more important is that hundreds of "eligible" residents did not get plots. They came and had to build *jhuggis* in the open spaces and parks here. They made rounds at the offices but were told that the DDA can give them plots only after they acquire government-sanctioned land for resettlement.

Thus, the scarcity of plots and "proper" documents to establish eligibility grew more prominent. While the state officials acknowledged their inability to fully implement the resettlement policy, the urban poor developed a range of *rann-nitis* to circumvent these policies and their lack of proper documentation. Scott (1998) argues that legibility, standardization, and homogenization are central features of statecraft. For example, Delhi urban planners emphasize standardized procedures. The effort to standardize information sits uneasily with the aspirations of poor migrants in the city. Measurement of the area "encroached" on (discussed in

Chapter 5), arbitrariness in judging the nature of encroachment, eligibility guidelines, and the requirement of photographs of eligible couples taken together during the survey become battlegrounds in the lives of the poor. Further, migrants from Bangladesh and Nepal living in the city for decades are instantly denied these housing rights once the eligibility and physical surveys are codified, as these residents do not fulfill the citizenship conditions for eligibility. It should also be stressed, however, that post-colonial statecraft is founded upon *il*legibility and flexibility, which reflect the logic of the state (see also Ferguson 2005). From the comments of the Jagori activist quoted above, it is obvious that definitions are critical, especially in the absence of substantial land allotments for poor people's housing. Illegibility has serious implications, as some poor people are automatically rendered ineligible for various state-sponsored welfare measures.

Surveys and other techniques of enumeration do not remain impersonal or impartial bureaucratic technologies. They are sites for social relations to unfold and for appeals to the moral worlds of the surveyors. Sriraman (2013) argues that the enumeration, inspection, and regulation of welfare processes engage "the world of instinct, emotion, and conscience" for state officials (336). As a result, emotion, compassion, and vengefulness are integral to these state practices, which also reflect interlocking "kinship ties and cultural affinities" with welfare policies (345). However, it is critical to place power at the center to analyze how emotions are crucial to the production of benefits, profits, exclusions, and indifference. We need more ethnographic work to learn about the experiences of Dalits, Muslims, and other underrepresented urban poor communities navigating the bureaucratic world. As CT (a Muslim resident) in Gautam Nagar noted, "I cannot understand how they just listed eleven Muslim families in the survey before demolition. There were seven Muslim families in my street alone and there are many lanes housing Muslims here." It is difficult to determine whether this particular instance of under-enumeration was part of the general under-enumeration prevalent in these occasions, or if it involved an emotionally charged bias on the part of the enumerator. My ethnography suggests that, on the one hand, disagreements about survey attendance, proof documents, and enumeration slips can be

resolved locally through debates, leading to mutual recognition and acknowledgment by neighbors (in-person) and councilors (on the phone)
(see also Bandyopadhyay 2016: 708; V. Das 2011: 324). On the other hand,
in cases where the discretionary power of the surveyor disadvantages residents, influential community members, such as *sarkari karmacharis* (government workers), can facilitate negotiation. It is in this kind of context
that *sarkari karmacharis* collapse "the distinction between their roles as
public servants and as private citizens, not only at the site of their activity but also in their styles of operation" (Gupta 2012: 90). In other words,
they blur the boundaries between the state and society (Fuller and Harriss 2009: 15; Gupta 2012: 90).

The roles of intermediaries, government officials, and *dalals* in the numerous cases of *ghapla* (wrongdoings) are discussed in Chapter 3 . Those
roles come into play in demonstrating proofs, enumerating or register-
ing oneself, and procuring plots because those can become contingent
and tenuous projects among the urban poor. Let me illustrate this point
through a few ethnographic vignettes. I once arrived in the early evening in mid-December 2009 in Gautam Nagar to meet a few residents.
They had gathered in a particular *galli* (lane) in front of the house of a
samaj sevak and were discussing the enumeration process. Residents complained about irregularities in their voter IDs, arbitrary decision-making
on the part of government officials, and irresponsible lower-level bureaucrats excluding some residents from the surveys:

> RESIDENT B: Our neighborhood is in Phase I, but the voter IDs of
> some suggest that we live in Phase II of the neighborhood. How did
> our names crop up in a different electoral roll altogether? Will this
> discrepancy not lead to problems later, at the time of resettlement?
> The *babus* (state officials) may reject our documents if they say Phase
> II has not been demolished yet.

> RESIDENT M: HR, the booth level officer [who has already passed
> away], must have done this intentionally to harass us. There is
> no accountability, and this will result in bribery and malpractices
> now. Some residents are just happy that they got their documents

without checking if the details are correct. And some others cannot even read what is written on those documents.

RESIDENT P: I do not know if I should blame the intermediary or the government. I voted in the last election, but they deleted my name altogether from the electoral roll this time and I could not vote.

On a subsequent visit, resident P went on to show me a voter ID issued by the Election Commission of India in 2002. The residents made a claim that around 25 percent of the residents were either missing from the electoral roll or did not have correct voter IDs. Moreover, in neighborhoods like the Sitapuri transit camp, people who rent rooms are not able to obtain voter IDs for lack of "proofs," even after living in the city for many years. The owners of the houses do not allow the renters to procure these documents, as they fear that they may seize their property once they have proof documents. Often the residents would take out their proof IDs during discussions about displacement and resettlement in Gautam Nagar, as they knew that they would require these soon during the period for allotting plots. Gordillo (2006: 162) has shown how the denial of identity papers, and thereby the alienation of Argentinean Chacos from citizenship rights, led to the fetishization of these objects. Identity documents are "worthless without the social relations that produce them and give meaning to them as symbols of something else" (173). Indeed, the fetishism of proof IDs masks the social relations behind the production, authentication, and imitation of documents. The fetishization of documents, government-issued receipts, and correspondence letters is evident in the ways that the poor show great circumspection in retaining, preserving, and displaying them on particular occasions as part of their auto-archiving efforts. In fact, the proof documents are commonly considered to be the most valuable belongings to be saved during fires, demolitions, and heavy downpours.

Although the documents are valued possessions, irregularities in them threaten the entitlements of the poor. At times, the details of old documents do not match new ones. Some of the irregularities include misspelled names, wrong *jhuggi* numbers, incorrect information about age and gender, and other trivial anomalies. Sometimes, even residents' photographs on their documents are wrong. Women often visited villages to deliver babies with the support of family members, after which it was difficult to procure birth certificates back in the city. Most do not have bank accounts, proof of employment (employers often evade taxes and deny minimum wages and workers' benefits by making their workers invisible), or school-completion certificates. Failure to produce photo ID or attestation (notarization) of these documents reflects the small network of political and administrative contacts the poor have. Politicians' agents also struggle to procure voter IDs, as loyalty is rare in an atmosphere of competitive vote-bank politics among the major political parties. Residents confirm the link between politicians and booth-level officers (official representatives of the Election Commission of India who update and maintain the electoral roll of a local polling area), the affiliation of surveyors with particular politicians, and bribery in sub-divisional magistrate offices, as well as the rampant favoritism with respect to enumeration. On one occasion, I witnessed some minor fights and arguments regarding ration card renewal. One resident gave this description of problems with ration cards:

> RESIDENT B: It has become very difficult to obtain new ration cards or renew old ones. The ration verification office opens in the morning, but we congregate and sleep in front of the office the night before in order to avoid the long queue. Some of us were issued ration cards in 2007, but we did not receive them until 2009. So, we did not have access to ration shops for two years. It is frustrating if there still remains a discrepancy, spelling mistakes, or other irregularities committed on the part of government officials. One has to wait for long hours in the queue to buy rations at these shops. The shop owners do not have a timetable and arbitrarily operate based on their whims. In any case, the ration shop has also moved to a different location now.

As Bourdieu (1998: 37) argues, orthography, or "correct spelling, designated and guaranteed as normal by law, that is, by the state, is a social artefact only imperfectly founded upon logical or even linguistic reason." Thus, the state's orthographic techniques, seemingly founded on reason, create classificatory categories around social eligibility. These classificatory and orthographic techniques constitute the "realm of symbolic production" where the "grip of the state is felt most powerfully" (38). Orthographic anxiety is compounded by wage loss, dependence on intermediaries and scribes, and the additional costs incurred to rectify the associated mistakes. These problems are particularly distressing for the impoverished Dalit residents in Gautam Nagar, who remain tied to their employers by daily wages and who also depend on scribes and intermediaries to compensate for their low literacy levels.

Commenting on the tedious application process, a resident in Gautam Nagar remarked to me: "See, I have submitted the required documents four times, but the computer fails to add the correct details. There is some deficiency in my application even when I involve the intermediaries." Literacy skills distinguish people along the *padhe-likhe* (literacy) continuum, while also disguising other forms of social relations and power. Once, a resident in Gautam Nagar recited the following refrain: "*Yeh sab babu log angrez ke aulaad hain!*" (These *babus* are the children of English people!) Although the forms, information about various protocols, signs, and insignia of bureaucracy are also available in Hindi, the English language has a spectral presence in the lives of the urban poor. Bureaucracy is equated with Englishness, and therefore the intricate procedures for navigating the offices and fastidious efforts to find faults in the documents are scoffed at by the urban poor. In a country where the ability to speak English is perhaps the greatest divider, the comments that people make regarding language skills for navigating bureaucracy make sense.

In fact, the concerns about documents while negotiating with scribes, intermediaries, and various levels of bureaucracy are a manifestation of the effects of symbolic power—a "misrecognizable, transfigured, and legitimated form of the other forms of power" (Bourdieu 1991: 170). The language-based (especially English-language-based) "distinction operators" (Bourdieu 1998: 8) have led subaltern-caste activists and scholars to demand compulsory English education because of its capacity to open up symbolic and material opportunities (see also Kothari 2013). Higher levels of literacy—in particular, English language skills—reflect a person's social origins and associated possibilities of symbolic prestige, as well as promote the capability to navigate bureaucracy. One has the option to navigate paperwork in Hindi (which also assumes and expects that all Delhi residents are Hindi speakers). However, a bifurcated system of governance frequently emerges, with the lower-level government officials mostly dealing in Hindi and upper-level government officials mostly dealing in English. Because engaging with upper-level officials is more efficient, English speakers have a systemic advantage over Hindi speakers. In other words, access to and comfort with the *babus*[4] high up in the hierarchy can directly improve one's problem-solving ability.

Whenever I accompanied the residents to *daftars* (offices), the *babus* invariably spoke to the residents in Hindi, but also initiated conversations with me in English in their presence. This is why even a smattering of English-speaking ability gave confidence to the *samaj sevaks* (social workers), who help the poor in procuring documents. As Williams (1973: 166) reminds us, "To be face-to-face in this world is already to belong to a class." Class relations substantially shape access to officials higher up in the bureaucracy and thereby determine the capacity to solve problems. Repeated failed applications for the same proof IDs are common. For instance, disputes often arise concerning the legal heirs of deceased *jhuggi* owners. Negotiations in these cases reflect not only local power dynamics but also a degree of arbitrary and impromptu decision-making. For example, most rejected residents in the Azad resettlement colony are still trying to figure out the *kami* (lack) in their documents and eligibility. Moreover, the inscrutability of census-recording procedures creates an economy of symbolic prestige in the neighborhood. Some residents blame others for their inability to properly record their personal details. For example, one commonly finds proof documents without the surnames of the person or of his or her parents. Another ethnographic vignette illuminates the complexity of surveys and enumerations to highlight this point. I arrived at Gautam Nagar in the afternoon in early May 2010 to meet with my interlocutors. A few people had gathered in the narrow *galli* and vociferously argued with the enumerator regarding the confusion and arbitrariness related to the enumeration process. The enumerator, DN, who otherwise worked as a polytechnic college instructor, was on special duty to carry out the enumeration in the neighborhood. The residents were anxious and confused about the nature and goal of the survey. The enumerator looked visibly irritated as the residents debated the necessity of providing surnames and other personal details during the survey:

ENUMERATOR DN: What is your mother's name?

RESIDENT A: It is difficult to understand why we need to provide details about our mothers' names. Some do not know their mother's name, as they just call them Ma. Is it necessary for you to know the names of our parents? Will you make the documents for our parents too? We call them Ma or Papa and various people call them by various names depending on the context.

ENUMERATOR DN [after putting a hyphen in the space for recording the mother's name, turns to me]: You are doing a PhD, see the situation here; they do not even know the names of their *janamdata* [creator].

RESIDENT B: At least you should know the names of your parents.

RESIDENT C: What if the person was orphaned as a child?

And, on another occasion:

ENUMERATOR DN: What is your caste?

RESIDENT R: My caste is *Chauhan*.

ENUMERATOR DN: What caste is *Chauhan*?

RESIDENT R: I do not understand your question and you can fill in whatever you feel like.

Usually, the facts and data are decided after active negotiation with the enumerator. Biographical details are tentatively determined and recorded on the sheets. The residents collectively record the building information and the availability of certain amenities, like water. In this process, state naming practices often contradict customary or local naming practices, producing intelligibility problems (Scott, Tehranian, and Mathias 2002) for the enumerators. The state's desire to record permanent surnames also forms part of its legibility project (Scott 1998: 65). In fact, the "conquest of illegibility" (Scott, Tehranian, and Mathias 2002: 7) entails the effacement of the fuzziness of communities, castes, linguistic divisions, and identities (Kaviraj 2010). However, "the politics of caste identities is not infinitely fluid and malleable, whether at the level of the individual or the group. For most Indians, caste is an interrelational identity embedded in the politics of everyday life" (Deshpande and John 2010: 41). Enumeration and its associated practices are not only welfare and surveillance strategies of the state, but are also sites of dignity, state condescension, and struggles over symbolic meanings.

Scott, Tehranian, and Mathias (2002) argue that these state practices constitute a "cultural project" to train populations for citizenship (18). Most often, enumeration is not followed by the redistribution of substantive resources. However, despite the merit of their observations, it is difficult to agree with their "ethical-philosophical case that no state ought to have such panoptic powers" and their call to forgo the panoptic state (38). While it is essential to confront the menace of the panoptic state, the advantages of information generation make it impractical to give up surveillance altogether, as it promises to provide leverage for addressing the material regulations of modern society. For this reason, social justice observers in the Indian context have recently called for a caste census and for linking caste disadvantages with public policies.[5] In fact, Deshpande and John (2010) have called for a rejection of "caste-blindness" after considering the nuances of various arguments for and against caste census.

(COUNTER-)TACTICS OF ENUMERATION I: LETTER WRITING AND OFFICE VISITS

Uncertainty about eligibility for voting rights and other welfare entitlements is a constant feature of citizenship for the urban poor. In this section and the following two, I analyze poor people's political imagination and agency when negotiating with state structures in their quest for numerical citizenship. Recent attempts have tried to view culture through an analysis of "collective identity" and "collective aspirations" vis-à-vis poverty (V. Rao and Walton 2004: 9). According to Appadurai (2004: 59), the "capacity to aspire" is embedded in and nurtured by culture. Breaking away from static models of culture and dichotomies of culture and economy, Appadurai argues that it is within the domain of culture that an orientation to the future can be conceptualized. This in turn has radical implications for fighting poverty (Appadurai 2004). In fact, this perspective can help us examine the numerical aspirations of the poor by drawing attention to culture-inflected worldviews, actions, constraints, exclusions, and—most importantly—collective aspirations.

One common strategy in these negotiations is to seek reference letters from a range of politicians, bureaucrats, and civil rights activists. These letters include appeals for compassion, to ethical obligations to protect the poor, and to constitutional principles of justice. At times, politicians write letters indicating a political vendetta against their voters during demolitions. After examining the letters preserved by the residents, I concluded that officers tend to devolve responsibility down the hierarchy, with requests for utmost care and adherence to the official resettlement policy invoked as alibis. Delegations of the poor collect letters from residents addressed to DDA or Municipal Corporation of Delhi (MCD) officials, especially the MCD Additional Commissioner. These letters include requests for proper survey procedures and resettlement for members of the deserving poor who were excluded from past surveys.[6] In the past, many of the letters were drafted under the guidance of V. P. Singh and activists from Jan Chetna Manch. Residents often self-enumerate in the letters, including details such as *jhuggi* numbers, signatures, ration cards, and voter IDs to lay claims to visibility. This is logical, since the official survey list, in the words of an additional commissioner, is the "guiding bible for eligibility for allotment."[7] To contest under-enumeration, the poor often attend public grievance hearings or deposit copies of bills and previous proof IDs at various offices.

A gendered division of labor emerges in the struggle for proof documents, wherein men tend to undertake office visits while women invest emotionally in sustaining relationships with key neighborhood actors. Repeated visits to *samaj sevaks*, forging kinship relationships with key actors, and informing partners about possible procurement routes define women's gendered responsibilities in these neighborhoods. Of course, there is no neat division of labor and women also occasionally visit offices for proof documents, especially with contingents led by female intermediaries. Once, a few residents told me the story of having their ration cards confiscated in Gautam Nagar:

> In 2007–2008, we had to submit our old ration cards in exchange for slips. They told us that you could procure rations [subsidized food and other commodities] on production of these slips. Of course, many residents stopped going to ration shops as there was a lot of confusion and they thought the government had stopped giving rations. But then we organized ourselves, collected reference letters from *netas* (leaders), and collectively went to the food and supply officer in early 2009. He said that the *jhuggis* have been demolished and we were no longer eligible to procure rations. Then we went to the MLA, and he sent us to the assistant commissioner [Food and Supply Department] with a letter directing him to issue us ration cards. The assistant commissioner wrote a letter to the officer in charge of circle office number thirty-five, and the officer instead said our locality is in circle thirty-six. We went to circle thirty-six and he did not show any interest in helping. We then went to the MP and he wrote a letter and directed us to meet the minister of food and supply of the Delhi Government. We had already spent a lot of time in *bhaag-daud* (running around) and it was election time. We knew they could not entertain requests before elections due to the Election Commission rules. So, we asked for an official in the office to receive our request letter on a back date. After a lot of hard work and rounds to the offices to remind the officers of our letters, delegation, and minister's referral, our pressure to obtain rations finally succeeded. We started getting rations by producing slips again from the month of April 2009.

This story highlights the *bhaag-daud* (running around) and *dhakka khao*[8] (shoving and pushing/struggling) that poor people encounter to procure welfare provisions in the city. In the process, they incur extra expenses, lose time and wages, and sometimes abandon the pursuit. The most vulnerable populations, including Dalit daily wage laborers, often give up as they lack time to navigate the bureaucracy, money to spend on intermediaries, or patience to engage with hostile officials. As the letters traverse files, desks, and a field of interpretations and actions, the poor encounter an economy of favors and disfavors depending on how officials interpret and respond to their letters. Their source of support is not a single individual, nor is their target a single bureaucrat. Thus, they maneuver through the heterogeneous state structures by appealing or supplicating to a multitude of officials in different agencies, which do not always exhibit similar intentions and goals (cf. Abrams 1988: 79).

This argument is reinforced by my own lived experience of class-based degradation and humiliation during an office visit. This particular incident occurred during a visit to a sub-divisional magistrate's office. I accompanied two residents along with a *samaj sevak* to the office on a hot summer afternoon in mid-May 2010, to seek an update on their applications for voter IDs and birth certificates. We were supposed to take two buses to reach the office but had no luck after waiting thirty minutes at the bus stop. The temperature was around 45 degrees Celsius and we decided to rent an auto-rickshaw in the unbearable heat. We arrived at the office and joined the other visitors inside. As soon as we entered, we noticed an antagonistic atmosphere. A visitor, MC, perhaps in his sixties, had come to inquire about his voter ID. He argued that the office had sent him the document but that his landlord had declined to receive it, as the landlord feared the man might seize his property if he had proof of residency. The official, perhaps in his late forties, denied having his document. Persistent in his requests, the man argued that since he had the government-issued slips, the official was irresponsible for not providing the requisite document. The official was annoyed by this accusation and started to verbally abuse him. The official said things like: "*Tu apne aukaad mein rah!* [*aukaad* connotes one's social location determined by a range of capital or identity]; *Kya naam bol tera, kya jaanta hai?*; *Nikal yahan se!* ("Be where you belong!"; "What's your name, what do you know?"; and "Get out of here!"). There was no utterance of honorifics for the older man requesting his documents. The disrespectful informal pronouns like *tu/tera* (informal you/yours), which mark either endearing closeness or disrespect for a particular class of people, replaced the more culturally appropriate *aap/aapka* (formal you/yours). This mode of address was not a manifestation of "hidden injuries of class" experienced as a result of status hierarchies of class relations (Sennett and Cobb 1972), but a direct affront to the dignity, respect, and humanity of the poor.

Palshikar (2009: 82) makes an important point while analyzing the humiliation of the weak by the mighty. He argues that elites insist on a "protocol, demanding a privilege, drawing distinctions," and therefore "a sudden and momentary reversal of relations of hierarchy produces the experience of humiliation for them." The above scenario demonstrates the varying intensity and nature of humiliation experienced by both the official and the residents. The official could not bear that a poor man could question him in his own office. In the official's mind, the poor man's so-called incivility contributed to inappropriate behavior in the office, and his illiteracy contributed to his lack of knowledge about government procedures and rules, crystallized in his lack of "*aukaad.*" Similarly, another visitor wanted to correct the wrong address on his voter ID. The official tore his form, arguing that there were errors, and shouted that he should contact a different official. In turn, the resident pleaded with the official to reconsider, as he had done enough *bhaag-daud* already. As Palshikar argues, the powerful speak of "slight, offence, rudeness, temerity, whereas the subalterns complain of callousness, neglect, and inhuman treatment. Having fewer resources to immediately undo the damage to their self-respect, they ask for kindness, compassion, etc." (Palshikar 2009: 82). Yet, in this case, the state official refused to show mercy or kindness and the group of visitors left the office one by one. The *samaj sevak* tried politely to engage with the official by referring to the councilor but did not pursue the matter further, as the situation had become too antagonistic.

Afterward, the visitors gathered in front of the office under a tree to protect themselves from the sun and to discuss their maltreatment and the bribery and corruption rampant in these offices. One visitor argued, "They find the slightest error and reject our forms and applications. I want a birth certificate for my child and submitted the documents eight months ago, but I have not been able to procure it yet." Another visitor argued, "We wander around, wait endlessly in the long queues, and are humiliated, but we are still not able to procure these documents. They are asking me to show a bank account. I do not have money to eat and they are asking for my bank balance." As they excitedly discussed this, they opened their bags and started exchanging *roti*, onions, chilies, pickles, and curries rolled in plastic bags. Everyone shared their feelings of helplessness, maltreatment, and indifference. At this point, the visitor MC, who was verbally abused, started screaming in the direction of the office:

Dil jal jata hai, kasam se, saala yahan aoo, dehadi chhodo, kaam hota nahin hai! (My heart burns, to be honest. I come here, leave my daily wage-labor, but cannot get the work done!) I am a *darzi* (tailor) and not well [he coughed intermittently]. People know me for twenty years—you can go and ask in the Lodhi area—but here they would not even acknowledge my requests. *Bhagwan samjhte hain khudko, do kaudi ki tameez nahin hai, aadmi ko chor bana rahe hain saale, bal bachhon ki hamdardi nahin hoti to kaleja phaad dete hum* (They think of themselves as gods. They lack the minimum decency. They are turning people into thieves. If I did not care about my children, I would have ripped them apart today).

As he walked toward the bus, he continued to scream about his health and his inability to avenge himself. The other visitors developed instant friendships and affective ties through their collective pain. They discussed future *rann-nitis* and debated whether they should meet their respective councilors or other leaders. As Palshikar argues, "Solidarities and friendships lessen the hurt caused by insults." He maintains that the presence of those sharing the hurt with you "turn the traumatic situation into a battle and that is the first move from solitary and purely psychological suffering to collective action" (Palshikar 2009: 83). In fact, the *samaj sevak* suggested that things are not as bad as they look. Apparently, he had successfully elicited responses regarding the proof documents and expedited action through Right to Information (RTI) applications (discussed in the next section). He also volunteered to write applications for the visitors.[9]

Of course, this is not a typical experience for the urban poor in government offices. The encounter discussed above was perhaps the most extreme symbolic violence I witnessed in all my trips to *sarkari daftars* (government offices) with the residents as part of my fieldwork. Even so, in every official interaction that I witnessed, the treatment of the poor by the *babus* ranged from indifference to outright hostility, from frisking at the gates to symbolic violence in the *babus'* air-conditioned offices. In the

Argentinean context, Auyero (2011: 6) has examined the welfare office "as a site of intense sociability amid pervasive uncertainty." However, in recent times, the government offices in metropolitan Delhi have modeled themselves along corporate lines and have instituted measures such as surveillance cameras, entry registrars, and various other unwelcoming devices in the offices.[10] At times, entry into the offices is dependent on an appointment, security inspection at the gate, referral by a "big person," and the ability to articulate one's reason for the desired meeting. Yet it is also important to see how the poor perceive the state practices and engage with inscriptive tactics as they deal with documentary practices in their quest for citizenship.

(COUNTER-)TACTICS OF ENUMERATION II: SELF-SURVEYS AND THE RIGHT TO INFORMATION

Poor migrants use self-surveys as a technique to challenge government-produced figures that determine compensation. Self-surveys are most often carried out on the eve of demolition or upon a failure of government bodies to resettle populations. Self-surveys serve as the semblance of legitimate survey figures against deflated state numbers; they also provide important data for court battles. In a different context, Appadurai (2002: 36) evocatively describes these processes of self-enumeration as "counter-governmentality"—a form of "governmentality from below." In fact, just after the demolition of their houses, the residents of Gautam Nagar came together under the banner "Gautam Nagar Sangharsh Samiti" (Struggle Committee) to make a list of residents eligible for resettlement. They were aware of the competition among various intermediaries to procure multiple plots, the underside of *jugaad* (fixing) on the part of *dalals* (brokers) and "ineligible" residents, and the arbitrary judgment of official resettlement applications (Jeffrey 2009; cf. Manor 2000). For these reasons, there was an overwhelming response to the Delhi State Legal Services Authority's (DSLSA) call on April 24, 2010, to debate enumeration, proof documents, and eligibility. As mentioned in the Introduction , the High Court of Delhi had delivered a favorable verdict in February 2010. It had also directed the DSLSA to assist the residents in the resettlement process. The DSLSA meeting was held at the usual *peepal* tree courtyard. The *pradhans* provided chairs and tables for the visitors and decorated the table with a golden-yellow cloth. They hung a red sheet in the tree as protection against the sun and laid out a plastic mat on the cleanly swept mud floor. Women sat on the right side of the mat facing the table while the men sat on the left. The whole atmosphere had a carnivalesque feeling. The residents came armed with their proof documents, ready to tally their names against the list of names on the self-survey. The committee of five persons from the authority arrived and briefed the residents about slum policy. One of the visitors explained:

> We are from the authority; the High Court has a writ now. The PWD [Public Works Department] and MCD did not provide resettlement plots before the demolitions. So, now you should be ready with the key documents to prove your residence for resettlement plots. The two critical documents are your voter ID and your ration card. If you do not have those, the procedure will be different, and you will need to collect as many documents as you can to have a strong case. So, I suggest that you collect the following if you have them: Employees' State Insurance cards, children's birth certificates, V. P. Singh cards, and *jhuggi* tokens. I read through your self-survey list. I suggest that you make a group of twenty to thirty people and submit your applications along with proof documents. Make sure that you mention the dates of your arrival and eviction and attach the proof documents to your application when you submit them at the Iswar Nagar PWD office. Keep a copy of your application and inform us if they do not accept it.

The residents cheered the visitors with catcalls, thereby subverting the disciplinary strategies of the intermediaries, who complained about their conduct. In turn, the residents viewed the intermediaries' response as an example of nepotism and group-ism. To the annoyance of one particular *samaj sevak*, one of the residents got up and loudly argued that everyone present there deserved a resettlement plot. Another *samaj sevak* intervened and politely quelled the situation by agreeing with this resident, provoking more cheers by the residents. Their petty bickering reflects the palpable sense of condescension experienced by the residents. Nevertheless, the event provided an opportunity for sociality and allowed residents from diverse locations and with varying motivations to perform

FIGURE 4.1: *Delhi State Legal Services Authority's (DSLSA) meeting to resolve the issues of enumeration, proof documents, and eligibility in the* peepal *tree courtyard in Gautam Nagar. The Delhi High Court had recommended that DSLSA support the displaced residents in the resettlement process.*

their claims of urban citizenship. The residents informally evaluated the authenticity of the documents. Some were lucky enough to discuss the documents directly with the visitors, while others talked to intermediaries. The residents showed their readiness to register themselves and to collect a host of documents to prove their residency. While a list of 223 residents was annexed to the High Court petition in 2009, the self-survey list had swelled to 309 by this time. Many more residents, who claimed to be absent during the time of demolition, came armed with ration card numbers, voter ID numbers, and V. P. Singh card numbers. Many residents also initiated surveys on cardholder status with the help of activist groups. The quantification of various social indicators through state documentation practices may depoliticize the utilitarian measures of statecraft (see also Rose 1999: 198). Yet the struggles involving a parade of numbers in claims-making also constitute sites of citizenship struggles among the subalterns and activists.[11] Thus, in Gautam Nagar, a few residents were supportive of initiatives undertaken by activist organizations, such as Lok Raj Sangathan and Delhi Shramik Sangathan, to explore irregularities in the documents as supporting evidence to file with the RTI applications. Some enthusiastic residents, along with *samaj sevaks*, organized themselves into *samitis* (committees) and carried out a door-to-door survey about personal details, *jhuggi* numbers, residency status, and irregularities and errors in the documents. Similarly, the residents of the Azad resettlement colony organized to reveal missing persons in the survey and missing plots during the lottery, and they battled for joint surveys prior to relocation and for greater *jhuggi* representation in lotteries. Consequently, peculiar cases of negotiations, struggles, achievements, and failures related to the substantive realization of citizenship should be seen as a "work-in-progress" (Jayal 2013: 4).

The recent Right to Information (RTI) Act empowers the urban poor to interrogate the state's implementation of welfare objectives. Many collectively file RTI applications with the help of *samaj sevaks* and activists. These are used to question delays, uncover failures by the government to fulfill its obligations, and expose the shoddy state of affairs in the offices. I read through many such RTI applications and found they often contained highly subversive content. At times, the RTI applications inquired about the responsible authorities and punishment for the lapses in providing ration cards. The answers were most often standard, monotonous, and monosyllabic (see also Tarlo 2003: 79). Responses to substantive questions were often a mere "yes" or "no." One resident noted that phrases like "shall verify," "will be done in the due course of time," and "order has to come from above" often appeared in the responses. However, such politics of deferral are countered by the applications, appeals, and dogged perseverance of residents who follow the trail of letters and appeals. Thus, in March 2010, the residents of Gautam Nagar celebrated after sixty residents received their ration cards as a result of the Right to Information policy, and more residents followed that same course in later years.

Another vignette illustrates the apprehensions of the residents, dilatory tactics of the state, and politics of waiting that surround these aspirations. A *samaj sevak* from Gautam Nagar applied to renew his ration card in December 2007 and ultimately filed an RTI application in June 2009 when he still had not received a renewed document. The letter posed the following questions: Why did I not receive the renewed card despite submitting all the documents? Can you tell me if the application has been processed yet? What are the reasons for the delay? Can you kindly let me know the names and designations of the officials responsible for processing my application? Is there any action against these officials who did not fulfill their responsibilities? However, there was no response from the public information officer (PIO). As a result, the *samaj sevak* made his first appeal in July 2009. The First Appellate Authority (FAA) order (in English) was passed in August 2009. The order asked the appellant and PIO (for Consumer Affairs, Food and Civil Supplies, Government of National Capital Territory of Delhi) to be present during a hearing with all of the required documents. During the meeting, the appellant was told that his application was rejected. After the meeting, the FAA asked the appellant to file another application with the zonal assistant commissioner and suggested that the assistant commissioner "dispose of the case" in fifteen days.[12] The second appeal was filed in October 2009, as there was no compliance with the order of the FAA. During the subsequent hearing, the PIO promised that a ration card would be issued by the end of December 2009 if the appellant were eligible. To this response, the commission gently warned that action would be taken if the appellant did not receive the requested information. Finally, the appellant received his ration card in January 2010.

This particular case was ultimately resolved despite the delays. However, other serious questions relating to the navigation of the bureaucratic world remain unanswered. Why was his renewal application rejected? Why was he not notified about the rejection? What explains the long waiting period? In analyzing how "objective waiting become[s] subjective submission," Auyero argues, "the welfare clients become not citizens but patients of the state" (Auyero 2011: 8; see also 5). In fact, many of the experiences of poor people in Delhi revolve around waiting and its "uncertainty, confusion, and arbitrariness" (14). The *samaj sevak* is literate, has a grocery shop (self-employment), and has children who work to augment the family income. Thus, it could be argued that the effectiveness of RTI is dependent on literacy skills, relatively free or flexible time, an obstinate resolve to last through long waiting periods, and at times proximity to activists to help navigate the system. But the literacy skills of most of the urban poor are low; many of them are not even able to read Hindi, much less understand the technical nuances of written English. Even after the *samaj sevak* got his ration card, his problems continued. He visited ration shops but could not obtain his quota of grains and kerosene, which initiated another round of RTI applications. As a response during the hearing in October 2010, the commission tellingly noted that it was horrified by the "mockery of the government's scheme."[13] Similarly, a *samaj sevak* in the Sitapuri transit camp (a relatively new member of the neighborhood who had recently purchased a house) took recourse to RTI in an attempt to construe the neighborhood's entire story colored through his numerical aspiration of citizenship. The quantification of demographic profiles, the definition of legality, and eligibility based on a range of numerical criteria informed the recent state action in the Sitapuri transit camp. The *samaj sevak* carefully framed certain questions to unsettle the arbitrary invocation of particular readings of legality in the camp. Through his application, he queried the legal definition of a "transit camp" and also requested information about the original allottees and the documents they had received confirming their title. In other words, he challenged whether the state could define a neighborhood as transitory or temporary even after it had existed for more than twenty years. He also staked a claim to housing based on the legal documentation of the purchase of property from an original owner. The answer to his queries was that the requested information was not "traceable in this office and hence the same could not be supplied at this stage."[14] Thus, it can be argued that the endless wait and disdainful government interactions with poor populations are themselves the effects of power (see also Auyero 2011), as well as the residents' lack of resources to remedy the situation instantaneously. However, the tactics of self-enumeration and recourse to RTI belie an assumption of a monolithic state, and demonstrate how the apathetic and hostile state sometimes yields to the demands of the poor.

(COUNTER-)TACTICS OF ENUMERATION III: AUTHENTICATING AND COUNTERFEITING

Once the DUSIB decided in August 2017 to resettle the eligible residents of Gautam Nagar (subsequently endorsed by the Supreme Court in December 2017), the residents faced challenges with addressing the *kami* (lack) in their documents. The errors in the documents included spelling anomalies, overwriting, and inconsistencies between documents presented by the same person. At the DUSIB office in Raja Garden in late July 2017, I met many residents with various unresolved issues. Most of the errors were minor and thus provided ample room for negotiation and arbitration. While one resident claimed a resettlement flat as a legitimate heir upon the death of his grandmother before the demolitions and the allotment of flats, another claimed concessions (as stipulated for the oppressed castes in resettlement policies) in the amount of beneficiary contribution. Neither possessed the required documents—a death certificate of the eligible allottee for the former and a caste certificate for the latter. At the same waiting area of the office, an older citizen named PJ contended that a medical certificate would allow him to exchange the allotted flat on the top floor with a flat on the ground floor, as he anticipated restricted movements in the absence of elevator services. However, the medical certificate designated PJ with a 75 percent "disability" but the policy required him to be physically challenged by at least 85 percent in order to claim a flat on the ground floor. The residents could technically appeal to the Eligibility Determination Committees of DUSIB, but the resolution of these problems was seldom successful without mediation and the intervention of other actors. Unable to solve their problems after a lot of *bhaag daud*, they were keen to resolve the problems by *kharcha-pani* and even asked me if I had contacts in the office or with the *dalals* to fix their problems.

As discussed in the Introduction , in late August 2017 (and also in early September), the residents of Gautam Nagar had consulted their MLA and organized meetings in the neighborhood park to fix the *kami* (lack) in their documents. The residents had submitted their old ration cards and received new ration cards. However, they were required to produce photocopies of old ration cards to lay claim to existence in the city.

The common problems of legibility deemed many residents potentially ineligible for resettlement. The documents had endured the ravages of time; often the photocopies of the documents were too dark or light, or the documents were damaged or torn. Furthermore, the *sarkari* officials had also committed errors in various inscriptive practices.

At the early September 2017 meeting in the neighborhood park, Sita Devi was annoyed because the staff rejected her documents. Although her new ration card was error-free, the old ration card showed her name as Mita Devi and the staff required verification of the old document. She argued,

> Why do you need our old ration cards, especially when you are giving us flats instead of plots of land? The policy that required old ration cards issued before 1998 also assured us plots, but you are giving us flats. These are my documents; you can inquire and verify in the neighborhood if I am a genuine beneficiary or not. I am giving a legal affidavit that I am a genuine claimant. Seeing that I was correct in my arguments, the official kept his mouth shut. But he did not approve my application. What can I do? Should I just kill myself?

Sita Devi appealed the decision, but she still needed her neighbors to authenticate her presence and endorse her claim in front of the officials. She expected them to be present as *gawahis* (witnesses) in the office and a few residents present at the meeting concurred that they would do so if needed. Although a neutral and impersonal evaluation of demographic profiles and data worked against her, she nevertheless was keen to mediate, challenge, and reconstitute her inscribed personal data through affective relations and community sentiments. Subsequently, on a visit to Gautam Nagar in April 2019, the residents confirmed to me that the board eventually accepted Sita Devi's documents and deemed her eligible.

Similarly, while Raj Nand was inscribed as merely Raj in a document, Harvinder had become Maninder in another document. The correction of these problems was no longer a solitary or secret act. Instead, resolving these inconsistencies had become a community affair, thereby adding a moral force in the quest to provide proof of existence, evidence, and, ultimately authenticity. SB argued that he did not have proof documents, but he could authenticate his presence in the neighborhood. He remarked, "In 2002, my *jhuggi* was gutted due to a fire; I lost my wife and son in that fire. It was reported in *Rashtriya Sahara, Dainik Jagaran,* and *Punjab Kesari* newspapers. I had filed a police report and received new documents, but I could not produce old documents necessary for resettlement. But my neighbors could authenticate my genuine claim." A few of the residents with *kami* in their documents requested stamped letters from the MLA to add his endorsement of their claims of authenticity. The MLA, without giving any guarantee, promised that he would strive to include the genuine cases, especially those that were missing from the list of residents annexed to the 2009 petition to the court. He explained, "If the resident is genuine, then I would request the staff to ignore the minor errors in the documents or include the person as a beneficiary, but if the resident is a fraud, then we should take him out from the list." Thus, the residents navigated a world of friendships, relationships, emotions, and affect in their quest to prove their existence in the city. In this context, they goaded the *pradhans*, influential members, and other residents to endorse their presence in the city by various mnemonic tactics.

FIGURE 4.2: *Residents are verifying the eligibility list and addressing the* kami *(errors) in their documents. To prove their numerical presence, they deploy the mnemonic tactics of their authentic presence in the neighborhood since a particular date.*

Only about 150 residents (out of the 223 listed in the petition and 309 listed in the self-survey list) claimed resettlement flats. Furthermore, the board approved only sixty applications in the first round. In other words, the dilatory politics of the state caused significant attrition in the number of claimants. Without a modicum of housing after demolition of *jhuggis*, many families found it difficult to remain in the city. Their investments were lost upon demolition and they struggled to navigate impoverishment with uncertain hopes of fighting protracted court battles. Negotiations with various state officials and politicians allowed most of the residents who claimed flats to authenticate their claims. The rest of the applicants frantically negotiated with the MLA, councilor, and the lower-level bureaucracy to claim authenticity or rectify the *kami* in their documents. In October 2021, three of the residents told me (by phone) that the board finally approved the applications and documents of 94 out of the total of 223 residents who had petitioned the High Court for resettlement. There is also an active deliberation to procure *farzi* (counterfeit) documents through the work of *dalals*, who are embedded within the state structures of governance. Ironically, in this scenario, the forged documents without the errors may have greater force than the *asli* (genuine) documents with the errors. Furthermore, in this context, the acts of forgery and production of counterfeits are a force to contest the statist rule of proper documentation (Gupta 2012: 227).

The mandatory requirement of documents and proof IDs has created a market for counterfeit affidavits. One resident in the Azad resettlement colony asked me in 2011, "Tell me, how is one supposed to survive with twenty-four thousand two hundred rupees [around US$538] a year? Now, even if we earn slightly more, we are forced to produce documents attesting a lower income. Otherwise, we would not get subsidized rations. Moreover, you know how intricate and difficult it is to deal with bureaucracy, with their forms, offices, and officers." It is in this kind of scenario that the activities of *dalals* (brokers) play a large role in manufacturing counterfeit documents. The *dalals* (and also intermediaries) specialize in producing various documents and have specific contacts with government officials for producing a range of receipts, documents, and their counterfeits. They produce receipts at a fixed price per document. As C of

Gautam Nagar put it, "The intermediaries and the *dalals* are *jugaad lagane wale log* (people who carry out *jugaad*, or fixing) and carry out *jugaad lagane ka kaam* (work related to *jugaad*). We need some documents to amend mistakes. If you do not have a voter ID, you are not a citizen of this country. You must have it." The role of the *dalals* is ambiguous. *Dalals* not only facilitate making "authentic" documents but also forge documents and buy proof documents to exchange for a profit. Moneylenders and *dalals* work these schemes with sordid processes of coercing people to sell proof documents and by seizing proof documents. Their space for negotiation and maneuvering remains ethically uncertain, as discussed in Chapter 3. Some residents get their *haq* (rights), but those who are relatively more vulnerable are denied their *haq* as a result of others' *ghapla* (wrongdoings) and *hera pheri* (swindling). While it is politically impossible to distinguish between deserving and undeserving poor, these practices leave an impression among the excluded about the undeserving poor. Other policies regarding proper documentation had adverse effects. For instance, a policy requiring joint pictures of husbands and wives proved problematic because of the absence of matrimonial memorabilia among most of the residents of the Azad resettlement colony prior to relocation. The bourgeois notion of celebrating matrimony through framed photographs was suddenly tied up with urban planning policies regarding proof, evidence, and resettlement claims. How did the poor negotiate this dilemma? Some went to photo studios and quickly took pictures to produce for the authorities. But those whose spouses were in the village, were absent due to work, or had since abandoned them, improvised by pairing with friends (outside the *jhuggi* settlement) for the purpose of providing photo evidence. They were well aware that this subversion could help them procure plots integral to their survival in the city; then once the plots were allocated, these "proof documents" would rest only in the dusty files of key state offices.

Another issue arises when a particular family (especially families with adult members) tries to procure multiple plots. Although it may not violate a strict sense of morality in the community, the need to turn these plots of land or flats into tradable commodities invites censure in the neighborhood. Nonetheless, the fabrication of *farzi* documents is a complicated process in the neighborhood. Residents who have *kami* in their documents may attempt to fix the errors by producing additional *farzi* documents, but those who are not able to navigate the economy of *dalals* and intermediaries are left with bitter tales of dispossession in the city. Furthermore, few residents attempt to sell their allotment documents/flats/ plots because of economic desperation. The buyers are mostly people who attempt to buy an affordable house because they did not own a *jhuggi* or eligible documents. However, at times, some buyers attempt to invest in the speculative real estate in the city. Here, the genuine beneficiaries sell their plots/flats through a power of attorney—a quasi-legal contract— yet the resettled residents are prohibited from selling their plots/land according to state policy. The Delhi Development Authority can investigate the irregularity of selling and buying and even evict those buyers. As BK, a DDA official, remarked to me in early September 2017,

> We have a scenario of "genuine beneficiaries" and "ghost beneficiaries." We can conduct raids and evict the ghost beneficiaries. But the *dalals* and DDA officials, especially the field investigators, are hand in glove. They replace the documents of genuine beneficiaries stored in DDA offices with those of the fabricated documents of ghost beneficiaries. Once they have done this, the ghost beneficiaries file RTI applications to get details about their properties and also demand certified copies of the documents. We are forced to give these *farzi* documents back, as they have already made their way into the office files as genuine documents.

Thus, the genuine residents forgo their claims once they sell their properties through a power of attorney. Then the *dalals* and field investigators manage to replace the *asli* documents with *farzi* documents in order to turn the ghost beneficiaries into genuine beneficiaries. In 2017, during the time of my fieldwork, there was a massive government drive to identify *farzi* documents and cleanse the system of corruption and bribery. A few officers and staff in the DDA had already lost their jobs as a result of these bribery practices.

The improvisations producing counterfeit documents can forge neighborliness and a sense of community (Srivastava 2012). However, these improvisations, counterfeiting, and forgery practices often create an atmosphere of mutual suspicion, as the question of housing rights is over-shadowed by neighbors' purported misappropriation. Illustrations of the urban poor's improvisation tactics should be seen neither as romanticizations of rebellious law-breaking nor as indications of anarchy (cf. Scott 2009). Rather, they are acknowledgments of the state's inability to analyze the technicalities, strict legality, and notions of propriety in a setting where a sizable population is denied shelter, food, and human dignity. In fact, in recent times, surveyors have strictly followed the guidelines for taking pictures along with the façade of the *jhuggi* at the time of the survey. The more the state devises surveillance strategies, including demands for photographs, videos, thumbprints, signatures, iris scans, and other biometric identification (now required as part of Unique Identification Number or UID cards), without universal schemes of social housing and food security, the more repressive these strategies become for the poor, despite their improvisations and subversions of the strict norms of arbitrary legality.

Activists have already voiced concerns about insidious linkages between UID and surveillance. Ramanathan (2010: 10) argues that this connection may lead to the tracking and profiling of particular populations. Khera (2011: 39–40) interrogates the assumptions underpinning UID schemes that celebrate potential easy access to government services, cost-effectiveness, and curbing leakages, especially amid widespread misclassification, low allocation in the Public Distribution System, availability of alternative low-cost technologies, and lack of political will to fight corruption (see also Khera 2013). Ramanathan (2010: 13) notes that some people may be disenfranchised for their inability to provide biometric records, especially those with calloused hands, marred fingerprints, or corneal scars (see also U. Rao 2013a: 74). Yet despite the associated harms of surveillance and control, UID may also be empowering for the largely excluded homeless populations who are outside the "circuit of welfare distribution" and who face constant, everyday police harassment (U. Rao 2013a: 71). Successful attempts to enter the orbit of the state welfare imagination are conditioned by social relations and "a mixture of patronage, luck, and self-discipline" (74). In this, ethnography can reveal the trajectory of enumeration mechanisms, welfare objectives, and popular improvisations that foreground claims of citizenship in the city.

Indeed, the proliferation of counterfeits highlights "a dialectic of law and disorder, framed by neoliberal mechanisms of deregulation and new modes of mediating human transactions at once politico-economic and cultural, moral, and mortal," according to Comaroff and Comaroff (2006: 5). They argue, "With market fundamentalism has come a gradual erasure of received lines between the informal and the illegal, regulation and irregularity, order and organized lawlessness" (5). Long queues at the Food and Supply Office, struggles to obtain proof documents, daily rebuttals, and humiliation must be located in the ecology of scarcity of legible and "authentic" documents. In this kind of scenario, the lack of "proper" proof documents among the poor, as Gordillo (2006: 164) suggests in the Argentinean context, "[becomes] not only the emblem but also the cause of their poverty and political marginalization." Accordingly, the contours of legality and illegality and documents and their counterfeits have to be redefined as survival needs. In other words, "zones of deregulation are also spaces of opportunity, of vibrant, desperate inventiveness and unrestrained profiteering" (Comaroff and Comaroff 2006: 9). Whereas Marshall (2009) demonstrates the gradual progression from civil rights to social rights in the British context, the experience of citizenship in the post-colonial context in India remains uneven. Aspects of citizenship are realized without a natural progression toward egalitarian distribution of rights and the eventual predominance of social rights. Kaviraj (2005) describes such a scenario through his idea of a sequential trajectory of modernity and democracy (see endnote 13 of the Introduction).

This chapter engages with the moral force of mundane documentary artifacts and inscriptions among poor residents with precarious tenure and voting rights in Delhi. An analysis of documentary and inscriptive practices provides an understanding of how communities engage themselves with the state through their own imitative practices. In their claims of numerical citizenship, the residents forge relationships, establish and invent kinship ties, and subvert social hierarchies in unanticipated ways. Despite experiencing hardships and humiliation due to inadequate economic, social, educational, and cultural resources, the urban poor mount counter-tactics of enumeration by mobilizing neighbors, local politicians, intermediaries, the judiciary, activists, and NGO workers. These counter-tactics draw our attention to the layered and complex nature of the state and the heterogeneous outcomes for the poor. The state may appear hostile and indifferent, but it is also open to the influence and subterfuge of the poor. Moreover, the various organs of the state are amenable to the residents in different ways contingent upon particular circumstances.

The realization of citizenship entitlements is tied up with state governmentality, but it is also shaped by the unequal distribution of capital and the structural location of the poor, especially with state retrenchment from welfare objectives, such as social housing and other amenities. The formal aspects of citizenship, including the right to shelter and the right to food, contradict the substantive aspects of citizenship reflected in the abysmal levels of malnutrition and housing in the city. In the quest for these entitlements, the struggles to procure proof documents have necessitated imagination, aspiration, and politics around numerical citizenship. Documentary and inscriptive tactics spearhead claims of visibility and permanence in the city—the poor contest the idea that they are illegible and ineligible for citizenship entitlements. The efforts to authenticate documents, especially through manufacturing counterfeits and proving residence through mnemonic tactics, propel the performance of numerical entrenchment in the city. As this chapter shows, the urban poor's negotiations surrounding proof documents involve various organs of the state. The poor in Delhi also negotiate with the judiciary against demolition and for resettlement plots in their struggles of citizenship, an area examined in Chapter 5.

CHAPTER 5

THE JUDICIARY, THE MIDDLE
CLASS, AND THE POOR

HOW THE URBAN poor negotiate the judiciary is a critical part of their numerical citizenship struggles. The contingent circumstances under which law favors or disfavors the poor, as well as the social relations and alliances that shape the negotiation of law and legal outcomes, are analyzed in this chapter. This processual understanding helps us both analyze the limits of the law in advancing an emancipatory politics and understand how law can be a site of numerical citizenship struggles. Legal machinery has been at the forefront of urban restructuring in recent times. While issuing numerous verdicts, the judiciary has introduced a rationale for creating a "desirable" landscape for Delhi. In fact, most of the demolitions carried out since the 1990s have been backed by judicial regimes that promote pollution control, environmental aesthetics (Baviskar 2003; Bhan 2009; Bhuwania 2017), and the control of public nuisances (Ghertner 2008). Recent regimes have also deployed a narrow definition of "public interest" (Sharan 2002), and have framed the poor as illegal, despite their fundamental constitutional rights (Ramanathan 2006). Commenting on the emerging power of public interest litigations, Bhuwania (2017: 89) has aptly referred to them as constituting a "slum demolition machine." A summary of key verdicts discussed by scholars can provide a brief overview of the logic of judicial decision-making in recent times.

Here, I highlight some of the landmark verdicts that reflect some of the dominant motifs in judicial decision-making.

In the case of *Lawyers' Cooperative Group Housing Society v. Union of India* (CW No. 267 and CM 464/1993), the judge ruled that *jhuggi* dwellers were "trespassers on public land" who burdened the public exchequer with requests for alternative accommodation (cited in Ramanathan 2006: 3194). The judge also ruled that residents should be resettled on licensed rather than leasehold land. As Ramanathan argues, this case paved the way for denying the urban poor property rights in subsequent resettlement policies (Ramanathan 2006: 3194). The case of *Pitampura Sudhar Samiti v. GNCTD* (CWP 4,215 (1995)) argued that Delhi is a "showpiece" and should not be allowed to decay (Bhan 2009: 128). The cases of *M C Mehta v. Union of India* (Petition No. 13381 and 13029) argued for the closure and relocation of industries and the use of compressed natural gas (CNG) for vehicles (Bhan 2009: 133; Bhuwania 2017: 52). Similarly, *Almitra Patel v. Union of India* (WP 888 (1996)), regarding municipal solid waste disposal, also argued for treating Delhi as a "showpiece" (Bhan 2009: 134–135; Ghertner 2008: 60; Ramanathan 2006: 3194). The February 2000 verdict regarded the existence of slums as potentially "good business" and "well organized" (cited in Ramanathan 2006: 3194). Although the *Almitra* case connected questions of public health with public interest, it also argued against resettlement housing for the poor (Ramanathan 2006: 3195). In fact, the verdict in the *Almitra* case infamously argued that "rewarding an encroacher on public land with an alternative free site is like giving a reward to a pickpocket for stealing" (Bhan 2009: 135; Bhuwania 2017: 84; Ramanathan 2006: 3195). The verdict emphasized the illegality of the poor and called for "cleaning up the city" (cited in Ramanathan 2006: 3195). As Ghertner (2008: 61) argues, this was the first-ever case that "targeted slums as a city-wide public nuisance."

The cases of *Okhla Factory Owner's Association v. GNCTD* (CWP 4,441 (1994)) and *Wazirpur Bartan Nimrata Sangh v. Union of India* ruled on several violations of Delhi's Master Plan. These cases justified evictions of the urban poor in the interest of better solid waste management (Bhan 2009: 134). The judge in the *Okhla* case disagreed with what it considered an "arbitrary system of providing alternative land sites and land to encroachers on public land" (quoted in Bhan 2009: 135; Bhuwania 2017: 88; see also Ramanathan 2006: 3196). As Ramanathan (2006: 3195) notes, the *Okhla* judgment absolved the state of its obligation to provide housing for the poor by squashing the resettlement policy. The judge argued, "No alternative sites are to be provided in [the] future for removal of persons who are squatting on public land. . . . Encroachers and squatters on public land should be removed expeditiously without prerequisite requirement of providing them alternative sites before such encroachment is removed or cleared" (cited in Ramanathan 2006: 3196).

Although demolitions continue unabated in the name of "public purposes," the Supreme Court partially stayed the order on appeal (Ramanathan 2006: 3196). The case of *Delhi Pradesh Citizen's Council v. Union of India* (CWP 263, 264, and 266 (2006)) argued for the sealing (closing down) of authorized commercial units in residential neighborhoods (Bhan 2009: 134). These verdicts and their calls for strict adherence to the Master Plan contradicted the 1985 *Olga Tellis v. Bombay Municipal Corporation* judgment and many later judgments, which recognized the rights of urban "pavement dwellers" and other "slum dwellers" under the "right to livelihood" and "right to shelter," thereby overruling appeals for their arbitrary removal (Bhan 2009: 134; Ramanathan 2006: 3193). Various other verdicts have likened occupation of land by the poor to anarchy (Ramanathan 2006: 3197). For example, verdicts have distinguished between slum dwellers and non-slum dwellers as "unscrupulous citizens" and "honest citizens" (Ramanathan 2006: 3197). One judgment argued, "If they [the poor] cannot afford to live in Delhi, let them not come to Delhi" (cited in Bhan 2009: 135).

In their deliberations over public interest, public land, public money, public health, and public purposes, the courts have narrowly defined "public" to include property owners only (Ghertner 2008; Ramanathan 2005; Sharan 2002). These definitions rework the varying class logics of the judiciary by often overstating the preeminence of property ownership, thereby basing citizenship and rights on a person's ability to procure property in the city. Further, the reinterpretation of nuisance laws and the desire to manage nuisances occupy a preeminent place in urban governance regimes (Ghertner 2008; Sharan 2005). Ghertner's (2008) study argues that technical procedures prior to slum demolition are designed to generate evidence of nuisance and demonstrate a public threat. Tracing various verdicts over time, he argues that nuisance law has shifted from being a "positive technology of building municipal infrastructure" to a "negative and disciplinary technology of elimination and displacement" (Ghertner 2008: 61). As a consequence, "nuisance has become the key legal trope that has driven the slum demolitions in Delhi." Various judges have interpreted nuisance law and have argued that slums are filthy spaces that compromise the health, hygiene, and moral rectitude of citizens(Ghertner 2008: 59). The confluence of planning regimes, middle-class aspirations to control urban space, and judicial activism to clean up the city reflects the current political economy of Delhi.

Debates about the relationship between law and society provide critical insights into the limits of law, class interests that underpin law, and how legal discourse shapes urban order.[1] In the Indian context, Chatterjee (2011: 17) argues that the tyrannical power of law is tempered by popular practices in the domain of political society. Chatterjee's theorization of "political society" illustrates an emancipatory space, especially insofar as the Indian legal system mirrors the worldviews of the planners, the bourgeoisie, and the powerful elites. Chatterjee has effectively critiqued the normative parameters of liberal abstract law. However, an ethnographic study of India's judiciary, like the one proposed here, allows for a more complex analysis. Some legal attempts to prevent demolitions or to claim resettlement rights have been successful and others futile. Most of the Azad resettlement colony residents' legal challenges to demolition were unsuccessful. However, some used the courts to favorably procure resettlement plots when the planning regime did not recognize their right to resettlement. Thus, legal machinery presents yet another option for the poor in addition to the activities in the domain of "political society." In fact, numerical citizenship is expressed as a *rann-niti* of "political society" in legal battles. Here, the intermediaries, especially *samaj sevaks*, continue to play a significant role in negotiations with the judiciary.

One must address how the structural limits of the law and the legal apparatus may advance emancipatory politics. In other words, it is necessary to acknowledge the exigencies, social relations, and the wider social and political settings within which the law operates. In doing so, we can be attentive to the dynamics of how legal discourses, practices, and verdicts attain their characteristic meanings and come into force in a particular historical conjuncture. This approach facilitates an understanding of the dynamic aspects of the intersection of planning, legal, and political regimes. Therefore, this chapter explores how law is lived, challenged, encountered, and produced in the machinations of numerical citizenship struggles. Legal verdicts are produced by the constraints of social and political settings and through the dynamics of social struggles over legal meanings. Two court cases illustrate the "judicial palimpsest of popular assertions" (Routray 2018). The case studies are developed from my archival research on the cases and the neighborhoods, ethnographic fieldwork in neighborhoods and courtrooms, and interviews with officials from the Resident Welfare Associations (RWAs) and planning experts from the Delhi Development Authority (DDA). My intention is to "view archives not as sites of knowledge retrieval, but of knowledge production, as monuments of states as well as sites of state ethnography" (Stoler 2002: 87). Further, I argue that the production of legal verdicts in these two cases is a consequence of specific citizenship struggles and cannot necessarily be generalized for the rest of the cases.

THE CASE OF SITAPURI TRANSIT CAMP

The Sitapuri camp was established to temporarily accommodate residents displaced from "prime land" in various parts of the city, as discussed in Chapter 2. However, the residents were not later resettled on a permanent basis. Furthermore, the neighborhood was established in a designated "green zone," violating the zoning protocols in the city. The ad hocism and tentativeness of the planning regime shaped the precarity of the neighborhood, which could potentially be demolished for planning violations. Relatively better-off residents gradually moved into the transit camp after buying properties. Along with other members of the neighborhood, they slowly campaigned for "regularizing" the settlement as a planned colony along the lines of resettlement colonies elsewhere in the city. A delegation met with the prime minister in 1991 to request permission to renovate the asbestos roofs. Subsequently, they wrote letters between 1991 and 1994 to complain of unbearable heat and difficulties during inclement weather due to deteriorated asbestos sheets on their roofs.[2] These residents even proposed to change the transit camp's name[3] because the term "transit camp" reminded them of their precarious status.

Political lobbying yielded dividends. The DDA deliberated on changing the land-use plan of the area from "recreational" to "residential" in order to regularize the colony and relieve the residents of any uncertainty over possible demolition. Support from the Indian National Congress party—especially DDA members of the party (Sitapuri residents have been loyal supporters of the party since its establishment)—expedited the case. In 1992, after several intricate bureaucratic procedures and moving files between various departments and committees, the technical committee recommended changing the land-use designation from "recreational" to "residential."[4] This recommendation was consistent with the DDA's flexible approach to land-use designations in recent years. Strict zoning and layout plans have not yielded desired results because of factors including inadequate provision of housing and other infrastructural facilities in the city. In fact, building bylaws are often flouted numerous times before land-use changes are initiated to accommodate increasing family sizes or the construction of schools and recreational centers in urban green areas. The proposal to change the designated land use was approved by the authority on July 27, 1993. Only afterward was the Ministry of Urban Development (MoUD) asked to seek public input, as required by the DDA.[5]

Once they became aware of these plans, residents of Lakshmi colony (a middle-class "planned" colony adjoining Sitapuri) initiated negotiations with the DDA through their RWA. In 1997, one particular association filed a letter with the DDA requesting that it remove the transit camp and use the land for district parks instead.[6] There is no mention of the Lakshmi colony RWA in the DDA files regarding this letter. However, it is likely that the Lakshmi colony RWA also actively participated in this petition. It was obvious that the DDA could not remove the thirteen-year-old transit camp just to satisfy the middle-class residents without major protests. After all, it was the DDA's own irresponsible decision to resettle a population in an area designated as non-residential, violating its own norms and considerably delaying the resettlement of a population it considered "transitory." After a lot of deliberation, calls for clarification, and exchanges with the Ministry of Urban Development, the DDA convinced the ministry to change the land-use designation again in 1999.[7] The DDA published a notice in major national newspapers and the *Gazette of India* to invite policy objections and suggestions from the public. It also informed major planning regime stakeholders, such as the Delhi Urban Arts Commission (DUAC), Government of National Capital Territory of Delhi (GNCTD), Municipal Commission of Delhi (MCD), Ministry of Urban Development (MoUD), and the Town and Country Planning Organization (TCPO).[8]

In response to the public notice, the Lakshmi colony RWA filed objections in 1999. They argued that the area occupied by the transit camp was "vital lung space" and thus any "reduction in recreation areas and open spaces therein [would] be tantamount to exponential deterioration in the living and working conditions of middle income, low income, and *janta* flats occupants and residents of this area." Moreover, they argued that the authorities, "for the sake of justice and human value," should "distribute congestion and overcrowding uniformly." The RWA argued that their 306 flats existed amid a dense area of slums, commercial establishments, and cottage industries. Being surrounded by a "large number of garment factories, smelling *nallas* [drains], defecating fields, unauthorized shops and workshops, all adding to congestion, over-crowding, pollution, crime, and finally unhealthy and insecure living," was evidence of "uncontrolled growth and development." In fact, they urged authorities not to "choke [their] lives" and called the proposal to change land use a "betrayal of trust."[9]

Thus, the RWA associated physical deterioration and overcrowded municipal facilities with crime and insecurity in urban settings. They remained oblivious to the predicament and insecurity of the population living next door, even though the poor provided them with essential services and subsidized their lifestyles through petty trades and services in the area. Further, the RWA insisted that a particular population should not be patronized at their own cost. Thus, middle-class aspirations and anxieties (see also Mankekar 1999) about a clean environment, safety, open spaces, and ideal urban living—especially during the obsession with becoming a "world-class city"—were even more acute as a result of what the RWA considered to be populist initiatives of planning bodies.[10] Furthermore, the Lakshmi colony residents' inability to place themselves properly in an idealized spatial and cultural location in the city created discomfort.

Representative N of the RWA assumed the challenge of controlling what he called "the mafia outside the fences of Lakshmi colony." In my conversation with him in late May 2011, he argued,

> If we are limited to our own colony, we will be claustrophobic. I am a whistleblower and I demand accountability. I crusade against unauthorized construction, illegal parking, vegetable vendors who jam the roads, and slaughterhouses in the area. We have a socialist system—the government is not responsible here, and the officials get away with anything. There should be a policy of hire and fire, just like the Western world. Nobody should be subsidized; you should find out why you are poor and act accordingly.

The representative put the blame squarely on the poor and insisted that overcrowding due to densification had caused urban living standards to deteriorate. The policies of resettlement and minimal subsidized welfare services also induced his fear of socialism.[11] Another RWA representative voiced a similar view:

> REPRESENTATIVE A: Increased density in the area puts pressure on the infrastructure. This area is a big scam. You cannot accommodate public grievances of a certain population by betraying the trust of another that was promised a certain standard of urban living. The poor have gone on to build two- to four-story buildings on those tiny plots of land. In fact, money meant for our amenities is also diverted towards ghettoes, slums, and villages [urban villages]—in other words, to vote banks. When I bought property here, I also paid for the district park, open spaces, and other earmarked resources. But then I did not get them; instead, I witnessed encroachment by the poor. This is nothing but the theft of my money.

The physical urban spaces of ghettoes, slums, and villages create imaginative social categories that stigmatize the poor as mafia, encroachers, and criminals.[12] This is evident in the views expressed by the RWA representatives, who overlook the unequal distribution of municipal facilities in the city and the social relations that reproduce poverty in these physical spaces. The representatives stuck to their objections when I interviewed them in 2011. However, by then they had become more tolerant of their neighbors, as discussed later. Their expectations and aspirations of urban living had been compromised because of vote-bank politics, which contributed to what they viewed as the "choking" of their lives.

Similarly, DUAC and MCD objected to the proposed land-use change, insisting that it would bring about general environmental deterioration.[13] MCD filed an objection to the land-use change by reiterating the position of the RWA, adding that a large number of fully grown trees in the area would be threatened.[14] However, it is not clear how the existing trees would have been threatened by the change of land use since the transit camp already coexisted with those fully grown trees. These objections delayed the land-use change plans, but the technical committee met again and decided that they could not simply remove the Sitapuri residents and that they should instead work on changing the land use again. Consequently, various agencies of the state disagreed over the proper course of action, thus reconfirming the argument that the state is not a distinct political agency or structure but, rather, "the unified symbol of an actual disunity" (Abrams 1988: 79). The above observation challenges a unified conception of the state and demonstrates the divisions between political institutions, which lack a "sustained consistency of purpose" in their collective practices (79). Despite the numerous discussions and deliberations among various institutions of the state, including planning bodies, there was almost a stalemate on the question of land-use change in this case.

In early 2003, the Ministry of Urban Development asked for a survey of the Sitapuri transit camp.[15] The field investigators surveyed the condition of houses, families, and additional floors that had been built. The DDA was convinced that it could not remove the residents without facing a major backlash. In 2003, the DDA decided to redevelop Sitapuri expeditiously by upgrading the open spaces, as well as developing a park that separated Sitapuri from the Lakshmi colony.[16] The member of the legislative assembly (MLA) of Sitapuri was also facing a tremendous amount of pressure to upgrade the available facilities. A team visited the site again and carefully surveyed the single- or double-story houses separated by narrow lanes.[17] The visiting team was convinced that the poor had invested considerable amounts of money into their houses. For that reason, they recommended "augmentation and improvement" of the drainage system, development of open spaces and community facilities, and accommodation of numerous existing automobile and repair workshops to provide employment opportunities in the area.[18] By this time, the DDA had started unequivocally arguing for land-use change and community facilities provision. The residents—especially newcomers and Sitapuri traders with substantial economic, social, and cultural capital—started aggressively campaigning to regularize the neighborhood. They initiated plans to build a primary school in the park separating their neighborhood and the Lakshmi colony. The Lakshmi colony RWA sent representatives to the DDA in July 2003 to inform them that they considered the school construction illegal. In response, the DDA replied that it had transferred two acres of land to MCD for the school.[19] At this juncture in 2003, the RWA took the issue to the court.

THE ANTAGONISM OF CLASS RELATIONS, THE JUDICIARY, AND THE POLITICS OF LAND USE

The RWA argued that the greenery and open spaces lost to what it deemed "encroachments" by slum dwellers should be restored by canceling plans to build a school, and it even requested an inquiry into this matter.[20] The petition argued that the park belonged to the Lakshmi colony and was developed as a "green area for the welfare and use of all the residents ... and the public in general."[21] It further argued that the park had existed for twenty-three years and had acted as a buffer against noise and air pollution from the adjoining industrial area and the arterial road.[22] In a nutshell, the residents expressed their desire for "fortified enclaves" as a condition of urban living, in the terminology of Caldeira (1996).[23]

The RWA petition asserted that running a school in the park was "malafide," and opposed land-use and layout plans that put an environmental burden on residents. The petition criticized what it considered the modus operandi of regularizing temporary structures by changing land-use policies.[24] Thus, though the RWA's initial purpose was to check the construction of the MCD school in the park, it soon after demanded the complete demolition of Sitapuri. The RWA pitted its case against what it called encroachers and illegal occupiers who carried out illegal activities in the camp's vicinity.[25] The Lakshmi colony residents primarily wished to "live only among equals" as a symbol of status (Caldeira 1996: 309). Banishing and bullying the poor were natural consequences of this symbolic struggle.

The High Court directed the DDA to produce the Lakshmi colony development plan and to ascertain if there had been encroachments onto the green space.[26] The DDA gathered evidence, counter-evidence, files, letters, and documents, which in essence produced its own archive.[27] Further, the court case drew on recent judgments concerning pollution, aesthetics, and demolitions. In its judgment, the High Court invoked the 1996 Supreme Court case *G. N. Khajuria v. DDA* and argued, "The Supreme Court held that their Lordships could never conceive of a residential area without having green lungs. Their Lordships were appalled when confronted with a layout of a residential colony, which did not show the existence of a space reserved for [a] park."[28] The judgment further argued that the DDA should not allow the slum dwellers to encroach on green space with impunity. It accused the DDA officers of colluding with the slumlords.[29] In 2004, the High Court of Delhi directed the land "to be revert[ed] back to the park within eight weeks" of its order.[30] The court halted construction of the MCD school and accused the DDA of negligence for allowing fraud and the unauthorized occupation of property.[31] A mandamus was issued to remove the transit camp and to use the vacated area for a district park. The DDA was also directed to withdraw its proposal for the land-use change pending approval by the MoUD.

The court judgment accused poorer residents of encroaching on the land with impunity in the city, exemplifying Bourdieu's (1986-87) point that "law consecrates the established order by consecrating the vision of that order which is held by the State." Unlike private speech and insults, which lack great symbolic efficacy, "the judgment of the court . . . proclaiming the truth . . . belongs in the final analysis to the class of acts of naming or of instituting." Bourdieu argues, "The judgment represents the quintessential form of authorized, public, official speech which is spoken in the name of and to everyone." In other words, "Law is the quintessential form of the symbolic power of naming that creates the things named, and creates social groups in particular" (Bourdieu 1986–87: 838). In this case, by calling a population "criminal," the court neither interrogated public housing provisions nor interrogated the basis of planning that led to such a scenario. Instead, the court remained unaware of a significant poor population, their urban living and material conditions, and of impromptu planning to bring about adjustments in urban settings. The judgment consecrated a social order that simultaneously designated the poor as criminal and the middle-class residents as legitimate subjects with grievances in the neighborhood. As resident RK of Sitapuri explained to me in late September 2010, "A Lakshmi colony lawyer argued that we belong to the *bhoo*-mafia (land mafia). I attended most of the court proceedings but could hardly understand what was going on. But I know that the DDA lawyer who spoke super fast English considered us *badmaash* (bad) people and repeatedly made distinctions between allottees and purchasers. To be honest, they consider us dirty people, just like garbage." Resident SB added, "Tell me, do they eat gold? Are Lakshmi colony people 'gold-plated'? They argue that we drink and gamble in the parks, but the reality is that they are uncomfortable with our presence next to their neighborhood. They forget that we serve them in various ways by being here."

The court case complicated the matter further, as the directors and commissioners of various departments deliberated with the DDA vice chairman and the lieutenant governor of Delhi on what course of action to take. They vacillated between demolishing the entire area as per the court order or appealing the decision.[32] MoUD, which had reluctantly agreed to the land-use change, seized the opportunity and directed the DDA to comply with the High Court orders within the stipulated time and to file a final report with the ministry.[33] The DDA's land management, planning, and legal departments requested the lieutenant governor's intervention via the DDA vice chairman because the decision to remove the camp would require that approximately two thousand houses be demolished.[34] As the letters and files moved up and down the hierarchy, various actors collected signatures and offered recommendations for alternative courses of action. This combined consultation process displaced the blame from any particular agent (Hull 2003: 300), but it also opened up a site of active negotiation.[35]

This view of bureaucratic agency as collective agency (Hull 2003: 300) is mirrored in the letters and files involved in the establishment of the Azad resettlement colony against planning specifications (as discussed in Chapter 2), the efforts to convert land use in favor of the Sitapuri residents, and the deliberations about complaints concerning the provision of basic resources. This standard bureaucratic process involved the circulation of letters between various DDA departments and documents sent to and from the MoUD. The circulation of letters produces "truth effects," in which meetings and deliberations with various DDA departments are presided over by senior officers summoned by the ministry to arrive at collective resolutions.

After the consultations, the DDA decided to appeal the court decision and also to prepare a note with the necessary maps and a ground survey.[36] It produced a report about the major green areas and the magnitude of encroachment around Sitapuri.[37] In its review application against the order, the DDA argued that twelve hundred plots from the total allotment had been sold by the original allottees and explained that the buyers had also filed a writ against demolition.[38] However, the court did not agree to the stay order against demolition sought by the DDA.[39] The most vulnerable are often compelled to sell allotted plots because of debt, lack of work opportunities near their new place of residence, and family and health emergencies. Holistic planning that integrates work opportunities, health facilities, and structural changes that lift people out of poverty can prevent the need to sell. In contrast, current resettlement policies, which sever people from their economic and social contexts and dump them into new, inhospitable city precincts, only further their marginalization.

It must be emphasized that resettlement does not benefit undeserving residents, as is often claimed. In fact, new residents in resettlement colonies or transit camps are only marginally better off than the original allottees. The purchasers merge their assets to meet their housing needs in the absence of adequate housing options for the poor. The fact that some *jhuggi* residents sell their resettlement plots after relocating reflects their desperation, not their venality, as is often argued. The purchasers told me time and again about the desperation of the sellers, who had no savings to tide them over in the initial years of resettlement or to meet the exigencies of life later on. Except for a few residents who have managed to achieve significant upward mobility and move out of the area (but still hold property for their businesses in the area), most of the residents, including purchasers, still manage with bare minimum wages, basic amenities, and desperately small 10-square-meter plots. In other words, only desperately poor populations will purchase property measuring just a few square meters without basic amenities and legal tenure in these socially stigmatized neighborhoods.

Back at Sitapuri, the DDA did not carry out the demolitions as suggested. In 2005, the court issued a contempt notice.[40] Initially, the DDA maintained that sufficient green space was maintained in the area. It argued that compared with specifications of 8.03 and 6.92 hectares according to Master Plans I and II, respectively, the existing green area was 13.03 hectares, much larger than the specifications required in the plans.[41] This plea did not impress the court, and in 2005 the DDA issued an "unconditional apology" and promised to remove the transit camp.[42] In court, the DDA counsel insisted that the area would be maintained as a green area and would not be put to any other use.[43] In response, the court acknowledged that it had dismissed the contempt notice issued to the DDA earlier following the DDA's unconditional apology for not removing the encroachers. However, the court was dismayed by the developments and noted, "Today, in 2006, we are again back to the same situation where no effective steps have been taken to restore the character of neighborhood park, as well as the district park."[44]

The judge argued that most of the original occupants in Sitapuri "sold away their rights" and dubbed the buyers "encroachers" who destroyed the "environmental balance and ecosystem." The court granted the DDA three more weeks to "remove the encroachment from the district park."[45] The court further accused the DDA of "rampant misuse of land in complete disregard and violation of [the] Master Plan in the area."[46] It recognized the "grievance of the petitioner" by arguing that the green spaces, district parks, and neighborhood parks earmarked for the area were encroached upon by the Sitapuri transit camp.[47] By agreeing with the RWA's environmental concerns, the court reinforced middle-class concerns about neighborhood aesthetics. As this example shows, aesthetic judgments also influence the legality of slums and provoke actions against them (Ghertner 2010).[48]

Subsequently, the boundary wall facing Sitapuri was consolidated and the gate on the side of Sitapuri was permanently locked to prevent people that RWA representative N of the Lakshmi colony described as "unscrupulous and bad characters" entering from Sitapuri into the Lakshmi colony. When I walked around the boundary walls separating the park in early 2009, the gate was still locked and I was told that the Sitapuri residents did not use the well-maintained park anymore. Women made a detour around the wall to go to the Lakshmi colony to work as domestic workers and the gardeners guarded the park.

Thus, the Lakshmi colony RWA and the High Court expressed similar concerns about the violations of the Master Plan and zonal plan specifications. Ecological, aesthetic, pollution-control, and environmental concerns were paramount in numerous rulings. As mentioned, the RWA argued that its members had legitimately spent money for the land and houses, but that they were prevented from accessing some resources provided for in the plans for the area. As a result, both the judiciary and the RWA insisted that green spaces, open spaces, and district parks—all integral components of healthy urban living—were missing from the area. Instead, patronage and violations of legal and planning strictures benefited the "encroachers," who destroyed the environmental order of the area. However, the residents of Sitapuri pleaded that they were resettled and could not be displaced again after living and investing in the area for so long. Further, the purchasers were keen to demonstrate the sale-purchase affidavits, especially the power of attorney documents, which established their legal or quasi-legal claim to their property. As Tarlo (2003) demonstrates, "The power of attorney papers . . . function simultaneously as proof that an illegal purchase had taken place and as evidence of the purchaser's right to become officially recognized as an 'unauthorized occupant'" (74). The judiciary, RWA, and the residents of Sitapuri reprimanded the DDA for this reason. The strictly temporary nature of the transit camp in the mid-1980s lost its meaning over the years. A nebulous zone of legality was created through the residents' efforts to regularize the "camp," the sale and deeds of properties, and investments in construction of concrete structures.

THE INTERSECTION OF POLITICS AND LEGAL REGIMES (1)

When the bulldozers arrived in early May 2006, the residents sat on the arterial road adjacent to the neighborhood. The road blockade generated a tremendous amount of media attention in this heavily trafficked area. A former prime minister of India, Mr. V. P. Singh, stood in front of the bulldozer. The police and DDA officials were warned that there would be arson and violence if they touched the houses. Women stood on the rooftops and threatened to jump with their children. Residents blockaded the road for four days, patrolling the entire area. The protests that ensued each time the DDA attempted demolition made it impossible for them to comply with the court orders.

Meanwhile, the transit camp residents formed their own RWA and urged the MLA and the area councilor to meet with the RWA office members of the Lakshmi colony (cf. Banda et al. 2014; Kamath and Vijayabaskar 2014). Sitapuri residents harassed the Lakshmi colony residents with requests to withdraw the case, cursed the office members in public, and attempted to appeal to their conscience. It is also believed that the office members of the Lakshmi colony received threatening phone calls in the middle of the night from anonymous people linked to Sitapuri. The residents of the Lakshmi colony often encountered their class enemies on the streets, in the neighborhood, and at several different shops. They frequently came to the Sitapuri area to buy cheap vegetables and once, when a key office member of the Lakshmi colony RWA was buying vegetables, he was shamed by a group of Sitapuri residents for being anti-poor. Several Lakshmi colony residents knew the residents of the Sitapuri transit camp, as they depended on them for cheap labor and various services. A priest from Sitapuri, who often went to conduct *puja path* (religious ceremonies) in the Lakshmi colony, urged the residents not to "kick on their stomach" (*pet pe laat mat maro*). In other words, he urged them not to deprive Sitapuri residents of their livelihoods and housing in the area. A few of the residents of the Lakshmi colony even confirmed in public that they would be cursed if they pursued the court case any further. A Sitapuri resident, ML, commented that he once overheard one of the office members of the RWA of the Lakshmi colony publicly utter, "*Baddua lagega hamare bacchon ko*" (Our children will be cursed). A group of Muslim residents invited their religious leader, the imam of Jama Masjid, to brief the residents about the problem. The *sarkari karmacharis* (in this case, those working in the court) persistently raised the issue with the lawyers and representatives of the Lakshmi colony, urging them to drop the case.

The Sitapuri battle coincided with violent protests by shopkeepers against shop demolitions in the city (for details, see Mehra 2012). The Delhi Law (Special Provisions) Act of 2006 suspended initiation of demolitions for a year in the city. The one-year moratorium announced in May 2006 (Ramanathan 2006: 3197) was subsequently extended and is still in effect as this is written. Sitapuri is covered as part of this moratorium and there is no immediate threat of demolition. However, as Ramanathan notes, other lower-income neighborhoods have been demolished despite being under the act for public purposes (3197). This is evident in the case of Gautam Nagar and the displacement of many *jhuggi* residents in the city, some of whom received plots in the Azad resettlement colony. Thus, it must be emphasized that the Delhi administration has inconsistently enforced the law. Continued demolitions of various poorer neighborhoods exemplify the class logic of the state, as discussed in Chapters 1 and 2.

In 2007, the time came to draft Delhi's third Master Plan. A policy decision concerning the fate of the Sitapuri transit camp was needed in order to finalize the Master Plan and zonal plans. Once the Master Plan came into effect, the president of the Sitapuri RWA sent a representative with the MLA to the DDA in August 2007. The DDA initiated a review and forwarded a report to the MoUD about its position. Around this time, the DDA decided that transferring plots was illegal, as the allotment was on a license basis. This rationale was used to justify its proposal to seize the plots that were sold or transferred. However, the DDA had to abandon this plan because it escalated into what an official called "a major law and order problem" after the first few houses were seized. A vocal activist originating from a *jhuggi* neighborhood and representing Lok Raj Sangathan had a refrain: "*Jagah* illegal *hai*, *log* illegal *hai*, *lekin unke* votes *se* legal *sarkar ban ta hain!*" (The place is illegal, people are illegal, but their votes make a legal government!) This sentiment epitomized the moral outburst produced against any attempt at demolition.

In 2008, the DDA reinvigorated its efforts to change the land use as a result of persistent pressure from the local MLA. However, land-use changes were not feasible at this time because the matter was sub judice (before a court). Nonetheless, the DDA attempted to demarcate the actual areas of the park, encroachment, and reclamation before finalizing the zonal plan for the area.[49] The DDA reminded the MLA and the delegation from Sitapuri that no immediate relief could be provided, as the case was still sub judice.[50] Sitapuri residents also started to file Right to Information (RTI) applications to pressure the DDA to explain the administrative lapses that had occurred since the time of their settlement.

The DDA's efforts were successful and the residents of the Lakshmi colony effectively resigned themselves from the case. They seemed satisfied after the MCD school was removed and the park separating the neighborhoods was redeveloped. Opinions about the court case were divided. Representatives previously at the forefront of the crusade experienced a change of heart. While one representative stood by his position, others were much more tolerant of their neighbors by this point:

REPRESENTATIVE A: The demolition threat was an eyewash. Why would anyone want to remove a vote bank? And as for law, in reality, the funny interpretation of law prevails.

REPRESENTATIVE S: They are not a nuisance, so we are fine with it. In fact, my maidservant has a permanent structure there and she has been working with us for the last twelve years. The only problem is that they use and also dirty our parks. I will be glad if the government can provide them alternative accommodation and we can have a cleaner neighborhood.

REPRESENTATIVE N: I would not ask for complete demolition, as poor people who have put all their money into these structures would lose everything. It is human to construct more rooms for accommodating an expanding family or to earn money by renting. But the DDA should not have allowed this to go on unchecked.

REPRESENTATIVE P: We do not want the poor to be driven out of this place after they have lived here for so long. The government can redevelop the area; it can start an awareness campaign so that they can conduct themselves better. It's the fault of the government, which has not provided any housing for the service class who provide various kinds of services in the city. If they provided housing for them, there would not have been any *jhuggi* cluster.

Thus, while one representative mocked the events that unfolded and blamed them on what he viewed as "funny" aspects of the Indian judiciary and democracy, others were much more tolerant of their neighbors. These excerpts reveal the shift in the Lakshmi colony residents' thinking, approach, and attitude toward their neighbors in 2011. The dynamics of sociability, shaming, and *dabaab* (pressure) tactics altered perspectives from a desire to discipline to a didactic impulse. The poor ceased to be a nuisance but rather required education about civic life in order to better conduct themselves according to the standards of the middle-class residents.

In 2010, the court dismissed the case on the basis of non-prosecution when the petitioner did not appear in court, and the DDA again initiated efforts to change the designated land use.[51] The local MLA was quick to send a copy of the court orders to the DDA. During the same period, the residents gently threatened the MLA that they would defect en masse to other parties—the Bharatiya Janata Party or Bahujan Samaj Party—in the next elections. The DDA was not certain whether the earlier ruling was invalidated by the current one and sought a legal opinion.[52] It also argued that it might have to maintain the area's recreational designation after the "protection of the act [Delhi Law Special Provisions Act] goes away."[53] A faction of the DDA favored the land-use change policy, but it largely remained non-committal because of legal and planning ambiguities. Overall, normalcy was restored after a few years of uncertainty, demolition threats, and upheaval.

My fieldwork culminated in the summer of 2010, when I would often walk around the neighborhood and wait in the park before appointments. The park was well maintained in a lush green. The gate and its lock had rusted. A segment of the gate had been breached by this time. In an evocative piece, Kaviraj (1997) argues that the poor resort to the defilement of public spaces and subversion of municipal rules as a symbol of everyday insubordination and as a practical measure to reclaim spaces. The process of "plebianisation of the park" was not complete in the case considered here (107). However, Sitapuri residents had begun to use the park again, and women crossed the breached gate as a passage to the Lakshmi colony, where they worked as domestic workers. After successfully resisting demolitions through violent protests and threats of arson, the poor now resorted to spatial practices that subverted the

FIGURE 5.1: *Law as symbolic power: The gate separating Sitapuri transit camp and Laxmi colony was locked after the RWA of Laxmi colony had petitioned the High Court to demolish Sitapuri transit camp. By the summer of 2010, a segment of the gate had been breached by the residents to access the park and Laxmi colony.*

regulations regarding movement in and around the park (see de Certeau 1984: 96).

Officials previously discussed two options. The first was to demolish Sitapuri, develop the area as a district park, and allot eligible residents alternate plots. The second option was to rehabilitate the residents at the same place according to an in situ upgrade scheme and redevelop the reclaimed land as green space.[54] The removal of such a large population was neither feasible nor easy given the residents' zealous resistance *rann-nitis*. The DDA also discussed the possibility of high-rise buildings and public-private partnerships that were in vogue in neo-liberal planning. The developer would build high-income group houses to sell at market prices (as Sitapuri is in a prime location) while providing affordable housing for the "Economically Weaker Section."[55] The DDA modeled this policy after Jawaharlal Nehru Urban Renewal Mission (JNNURM) projects undertaken in many Indian cities. However, it did not elaborate on the beneficiaries' costs and financial burden.[56] After surveying the additional floors on allotted plots in Sitapuri, the DDA estimated that around six thousand families lived in the area.[57] Unless all the residents were rehabilitated, the DDA would very likely face major protests as it had before. The successful resistance of the Sitapuri residents is a daring story amid massive demolitions around the city. The policy of dividing the buyers from the original allottees failed to challenge the unity of the residents. The original allottees, now few in number, knew that they had to involve and support the buyers if they wanted to sustain forceful resistance.

For this reason, the residents have challenged charges that the buyers and original allottees were divided and consistently forged collective solidarity and strength in the neighborhood. The residents question the existence of a clear-cut policy preventing tenements from being sold or purchased.[58] They use the terms "resettlement colony" and "transit camp" interchangeably to emphasize that *jhuggi* residents were indeed resettled, not temporarily accommodated. The Sitapuri RWA office members insist that there are twelve neighborhood parks in the area already and that the DDA must refrain from compromising the lives of the twenty-five thousand to thirty thousand people living in Sitapuri. The Sitapuri RWA has strategically reiterated that both the DDA and MoUD have shown interest in the past in changing the land use to accommodate neighborhood needs. Moreover, residents have expressed reservations about court rulings and argued that courts should not interfere with executive policies.[59] The RWA has accused the court of advancing a flawed and unsustainable logic. In their push for regularization, they have cited a number of land-use changes, regularization of unauthorized constructions, and land encroachments.[60] Citing numerous cases of regularization, they insist that the residents paid license fees regularly, did not encroach on any land, and thereby were better positioned legally. Thus, the residents expand the scope of democratic politics and foreground their citizenship struggles by challenging the technicalities of planning and law.

The residents regularly petitioned DDA officials, politicians, and various ministers, and even organized signature campaigns for regularizing their neighborhood. In a 2007 letter to the minister of state for urban development, residents claimed that most people living in the area had been supporters of and workers for the Congress party.[61] They insisted that they had even successfully lobbied the prime minister's office to install electricity in the entire area.[62] Referring to a government notice in major newspapers dated June 11, 1999, they further claimed that the government had extended freehold rights to residents in transit camps, thereby legally entitling them to live in the neighborhood. In 2016, the RWA members of Sitapuri again petitioned the lieutenant governor and the minister of urban development to extend freehold rights to the residents after they had officially changed the name of their neighborhood to avoid stigma and bolster their legal claim (as discussed in the Introduction). In July 2017, RWA member A remarked to me, "We changed the name of the neighborhood when you came last time in 2010–11. But it is the responsibility of the residents to change their address in various documents." In fact, the RWA members have actively instructed the residents to change the documents with the new address as soon as possible in their claim of legitimacy and demand of freehold rights. Meanwhile, the residents have started using the park that separated Sitapuri and the Lakshmi colony. By August 2017, the middle-class residents of the Lakshmi colony had almost abandoned using the park, thereby ceding it to the residents of Sitapuri.

This case supports Chatterjee's (2011: 17) thesis that politics may counteract the tyrannical tendency of law. As the evidence presented here has shown, the legal system was subverted by popular practices of street blockades, unruliness, and political mediation in various forms. More importantly, it demonstrates how law is negotiated on the streets and rooftops, around walls and boundaries, and within neighborhoods in attempts at asserting numerical strength. Legal rulings and outcomes are not just produced in the court or through party politics, but through constant negotiation and resistance with respect to planning and legal regimes.

THE CASE OF GAUTAM NAGAR

The politically loaded terms "encroachment," "Right of Way," and "ineligibility" remain central in discussions concerning the predicament and struggles of the poor displaced from Gautam Nagar. As discussed before, a section of Gautam Nagar was demolished to construct an underpass as part of the urban restructuring projects prior to the Commonwealth Games. The roles of intermediaries, the *rann-nitis* of the poor, and resistance efforts are described in Chapter 3. As pointed out, these activities in the domain of "political society" did not yield many results after a part of Gautam Nagar was demolished. In response, the residents envisioned alternate routes of mediation, negotiation, and resistance. With a lack of coherent leadership, there were many suggestions on how to move forward, especially when the poor were resurrecting their lives from the rubble. The *pradhans* lost some support because the politicians had not helped them much. The *samaj sevaks* led the fight and quickly founded an organization called Gautam Nagar Sangharsh Samiti (Gautam Nagar Struggle Committee). As discussed previously, the poor carried out a self-survey as part of their struggle and the organization also met with some activists for advice.

Some conversed with the activists from Delhi Shramik Sangathan, who had visited the neighborhood earlier during a bicycle rally to disseminate information about government policies, the fundamental rights of the urban poor, and resistance strategies. Others met activists from Lok Raj Sangathan, who were engaged with various worker-related issues in the neighborhood. Two residents also invited an American medical anthropology student conducting doctoral fieldwork in the neighborhood to accompany them during their visit to a prominent activist from Sajha Manch (a coalition of organizations fighting for the rights of the urban poor). After deliberating on the suggestions of these three different activists and a lawyer, the residents launched a case against the Government of National Capital Territory of Delhi (GNCTD) in the High Court of Delhi with the backing of Delhi Shramik Sangathan. A lawyer volunteered to represent the case pro bono. Fortunately for the residents, two High Court judges known for their sympathy for the urban poor presided over the case.

The residents petitioned the court for resettlement plots according to state resettlement policy (see Chapters 1 and 2). They argued that they had lived there for more than thirty years, were provided with basic amenities by the government, and, more importantly, possessed two critical residency proof documents: ration cards and voter IDs. The petitioners fought the case on the grounds of their right to shelter.[63] The petitioners argued that demolition violated not only the right to shelter enshrined in the Constitution of India, but also a cluster of rights championed by various national bodies, as well as supranational bodies of which India is a member. The petition argued that the affected were indispensable to the city, constituted a marginalized population, and were protected by the current resettlement policy. More importantly, they asserted that they did not inhabit the area earmarked as the road, arguing that the government demolished the area beyond the limit of the road. They contended that there was no clear policy of Right of Way and that failure to compensate the poor by invoking this clause was "completely baseless, arbitrary, and discriminatory."[64] In response, GNCTD argued that the residents were not eligible for compensation because they had encroached on a road and violated the Right of Way municipal bylaw. Furthermore, the defendant maintained that it was within its mandate to acquire additional land beside the road and that it could decide on the "end limits of the land" at the time of construction.[65] Thus, the GNCTD opposed the petitioners' argument and argued that it could not compensate them.

The judges asked critical questions about Right of Way and about the measurement and definition of the road. They challenged the respondents' assumption that the road was encroached upon deliberately. Rather, it was argued that a vacant plot of land was used for building residential huts. During the hearings on December 17, 2009, the judge asked some probing questions:

> Can you claim that the land was a street after allowing a settlement for twenty to thirty years? On what basis do you decide to discriminate between the deserving and undeserving poor? What is the logic behind designating the poor living beside the road as eligible and the poor living on what you consider an existing road ineligible after allowing a settlement and providing services for so long? How would they know about the road? I think the road was contemplated but was not built. What is appalling is that you did not carry out a survey about the existing settlement nor did you provide them with adequate notice. You neither allowed them to go to court, nor did you provide them any compensation or accommodation.

The judges were critical of the agencies' definition of a street. The respondents argued that they had carried out a survey, but they did not

FIGURE 5.2: *Right of Way versus Right of Shelter 1: The demolished site of Gautam Nagar in 2009.*

FIGURE 5.3: *Right of Way versus Right of Shelter 2: A new road under construction on the demolished site of Gautam Nagar in 2010.*

FIGURE 5.4: *Right of Way versus Right of Shelter 3: A functional new road bisecting the undemolished parts of Gautam Nagar in 2017.*

produce the results. The judges were baffled by the policy's provision to arbitrarily demolish settlements without compensation for the residents.

THE INTERSECTION OF POLITICS AND LEGAL REGIMES (II)

Gautam Nagar residents demonstrated remarkable political acumen in their pursuit of judicial recourse. They approached three different organizations for advice, formed their own political organization focused on fighting for resettlement plots, and consulted a sympathetic lawyer who argued the case for free. As Comaroff and Comaroff (2006) note, law is often fetishized in attempts to attain rights and entitlements in postcolonial states. Without relinquishing their right of resettlement, the residents turned to the judiciary in their struggles for numerical citizenship. Unlike the Sitapuri case, legal outcomes were not shaped through constant negotiations with a variety of agencies and bodies and violent opposition on the streets. Nevertheless, the political activities of the residents shaped the contours of their legal struggles. They ensured they could present the documents, their self-survey list, and other legal paraphernalia to the lawyers as a collective to prove their numerical presence in the city. Tasks were divided among key representatives and funds were raised for the representatives who carried out these activities.

After deliberating, the High Court gave an unusual landmark verdict on February 11, 2010, that upheld the petitioners' right to shelter. This verdict was historic, as most recent cases in Delhi have ruled against the poor. The decision demonstrated a holistic understanding of the nature of urban poverty, including the lack of basic amenities, loss of dignity, rural-urban migration, and the government's duty to uphold basic human rights. It invoked multiple national laws as well as "international declarations, conventions, and agreements."[66] Commenting on slum demolitions' devastating effects on the poor, the court noted that displaced families lose a "bundle of rights—the right to livelihood, to shelter, to health, to education, to access to civic amenities and public transport, and above all, the right to live with dignity."[67]

The verdict ruled against the respondents' Right of Way argument, calling it contrary to the state's relocation and rehabilitation policies. The respondents could not provide any clear-cut Right of Way policy that would deprive eligible residents of resettlement plots. Even if there was a Right of Way policy, the court ruled that it should apply to existing roads only and not to open spaces where the poor had lived for decades. In other words, the verdict dismissed the respondents' retrospective claim that the land was earmarked for a road and the idea that the "encroachers" inhabiting that land could not be compensated. The court agreed with the petitioners' claim that demolition without compensation violated their right to shelter and other fundamental rights and called on the state to provide the constitutionally guaranteed right of decent shelter. It also argued that the state could not wish away the presence of the poor through demolitions or by effacing government records. Rather, the poor build cities, are citizens of the country, and have guaranteed constitutional rights. In its final argument, the court deemed the Right of Way "illegal and unconstitutional"[68] and ordered government agencies to relocate residents and provide them basic amenities within four months.

Even though they were suspicious of the agencies' subsequent willingness to relinquish their case, the residents rejoiced in the court decision. It galvanized the activities of Gautam Nagar residents. They invited the lawyer to their neighborhood to celebrate and recognized his pro-poor position in the presence of local politicians (see also Chapter 6). Their earlier cynicism gave way to enthusiasm; the old cry *"Kucch nahin hoga!"* (Nothing will happen!) was no longer the common refrain. Even the most cynical residents, previously suspicious of the volunteers, intermediaries, and the judicial process, changed their minds. Residents who had formerly expressed guilt for living on *sarkar*'s (government) land began to articulate their rights in the city. Bourdieu theorizes a relationship between the perception of harm and injustice and one's location in social space. He argues, "The conversion of an unperceived harm into one that is perceived, named, and specifically attributed presupposes a labour of construction of social reality which falls largely to professionals." A sense of injustice arises from the feeling that one has rights and entitlements (Bourdieu 1986–87: 833). In this case, the political mobilization by the residents and renewed interpretations of law, Right of Way, and urban entitlements politicized even the least optimistic of the residents.

After the successful verdict, the state delayed in allotting plots and the poor waited endlessly for their resettlement plots. The residents filed a contempt case against the agencies and the agencies issued a review petition against the order. The judge who had delivered the verdict retired and the review was transferred to Court Number 13. As we sat for the hearing on January 14, 2011, the respondent lawyer explained to another lawyer, "Unlike earlier days, the Court has become bad for MCD lately. We did not expect the verdict to go against us." The residents of Gautam Nagar were relieved to learn that one of the judges of the double bench that had delivered the earlier verdict would also be delivering the judgment in this case. However, the agencies introduced some new arguments this time:

LAWYER: There was a road of forty meters in 1980, and money was sanctioned to fortify the road. The metaled road was built in 1983. The road ends at the railway line and there are two walls beside the road, which barricade an industrial area. [The lawyer went on to show a map, which was apparently approved in 1981.]

JUDGE: Do you have a picture of the road? You did not dig the area to build the road, did you? How would people know that a road was earmarked there? Why did not you remove them [Gautam Nagar residents] for all these years?

LAWYER: If we compensate them then it becomes an attractive thing for the encroachers. We do not have much land in the city.

JUDGE: But we have a housing policy. These people you call "encroachers" are building your Delhi—the expressways, malls. They were working day and night for the Commonwealth Games. The contractors exploit them and we enjoy the fruits of their labor. Let's have an overall perspective about development.

LAWYER: The state is giving an incentive to them to go back [to their place of origin]. There is a problem of space and overpopulation.

JUDGE: These are your people. They are Indian citizens. You have money for land acquisition and middle-class residential neighborhoods, but no money for resettlement.

Road demarcation, surveys, and arbitrary fortification are not merely physical features of urban restructuring. Rather, they are suffused with power relations. As Blomley (2003) argues, "Certain spatializations—notably those of the frontier, the survey, and the grid—play a practical and ideological role." Space and property are produced through enactments that may be symbolic, practical, material, or corporeal (121). Thus, in the case of Gautam Nagar, the enactments of demarcation, fortification, and mapping are not inert processes for reconfiguring physical spaces, but are instead outcomes of social relations, legitimation procedures, and power dynamics in the city.

The Gautam Nagar representatives who attended the proceeding remained alienated from the language of the court. On our way back to Gautam Nagar, we discussed the court proceedings. I was asked to explain the court proceedings so the representatives could brief the "public" back in their neighborhood. We discussed and also disagreed on our interpretations of the proceedings. A representative noted, "When we are in the court, we feel as if we are in a foreign land. Many of us are illiterate, what will we understand if you debate our issues in English? Sometimes, I do not even know if my own lawyer is scolding or praising us." Thus, the poor are disadvantaged by the language of the modern legal system and dependent on English-speaking interpreters or lawyers to clarify the status of their case. The language barrier restricts their options for action, for maneuvering in the system, and for collecting favorable evidence. Instead, the system forces the poor to depend on the beneficence of activist lawyers. Moreover, they seldom possess requisite knowledge to understand and interpret legal rules, policies, remedial measures, and laws about their own entitlements.

The review petition filed by the government against the favorable judgment for resettlement in the High Court was dismissed in early 2011 and the verdict initiated debates among DDA officials regarding Right of Way. Furthermore, the lieutenant governor of Delhi also called for abrogation of the Right of Way–related ineligibility for resettlement.[69] Meanwhile, the residents grew restless with the lackadaisical attitude of the DUSIB in taking appropriate steps to resettle them. They sent contingents of representatives to various ministers with petitions and letters endorsed by numerous political leaders. Without much success in the High Court, the agencies went to the Supreme Court to appeal the case in early 2012.[70] It seems that the government vacillated even after it filed a Special Leave Petition at the Supreme Court of India, considering that it explored the possibility of rehabilitating the residents during this time. Even the government counsel argued that the Council of Ministers considered measures to resettle the residents in the court once. Finally, in July 2013, the government withdrew the case, thus allowing the judge to dismiss the case later. It is not apparent why the government did so, but the residents claim that their *dabaab* (pressure) on the ruling Congress party leaders and ministers had contributed to the decision of the government. However, in a bizarre move, the government started conversations about resettling only the petitioners and not all the displaced residents in the list attached to their petition. In other words, out of the 223 residents who claimed resettlement, the government decided to only resettle the four petitioners who had approached the court. In late 2013, the board sent letters to the petitioners to appear with the requisite documents for verification.

The selective extension of resettlement rights to only four residents created animosity in the neighborhood. The residents called for a meeting with the support of Delhi Shramik Sangathan. During the meeting, they collectively suggested that they should wait until the board agreed to resettle all the eligible residents. The petitioners disagreed, arguing that they would claim the flats while continuing to fight the court battle for the rest of the residents. Subsequently, they met the lawyer for suggestions. The lawyer argued that the case would be even stronger for the rest if these four petitioners accepted the resettlement flats. By this time, the lawyer had already decided to file a contempt petition in the court. In response, a resident argued that the petitioners should give a written commitment that they would support the court case even if they were allotted the flats. He wondered, "What if the board made the petitioners sign a letter that they did not have anything to do with the case anymore?" However, the petitioners were not interested in signing such a letter because they feared possible punitive action on the part of the board. One of the petitioners argued, "What if they reject our claims as well if we write such a letter?" The *dalit* residents of the Kabadda camp, who largely remained alienated from the upper- and intermediate-caste leadership in fighting the case, expressed their disgruntlement. A few of the residents of Gautam Nagar also demanded the return of the money they had contributed for fighting the case. One of the petitioners confided in me that he understood the anger of other residents, as they had lost homes, contributed money, and fought this struggle together. But he was also desperate to claim whatever the government actually offered at that stage. The residents aggressively argued that the petitioners should write such a letter and not appear *lalchi* (greedy). The residents even joined them at the board office when the petitioners went to submit the requisite documents. After a protracted debate, the petitioners provided a letter that they would continue to support the court case even if they received the resettlement flats.

In early 2014, the selected four residents submitted their documents, including photocopies of old ration cards, new ration cards, voter IDs, and Aadhar cards (identity cards), for verification. The board rejected the documents of one of the petitioners because of inconsistencies in the spelling of her name between her old and new ration cards. Subsequently, three petitioners deposited a sum of 68,000 rupees each as a beneficiary contribution in 2014. The board allotted them flats in a far-off neighborhood named Baprola. However, the board also demanded 30,000 rupees more from each petitioner as maintenance fees. The residents decided not to deposit the maintenance money. Additionally, the board could not give them possession letters, as the land-owning agency, PWD, did not pay for the expenses. The petitioners slowly realized the difficulty in fighting their battles alone. Furthermore, the petitioners wished to be resettled along with their previous neighbors. Without those social ties, they risked losing the relationships that were integral to survival in the city. They also collectively wished to fight for resettlement flats in a better neighborhood than moving into Baprola. Thus, the petitioners tempered their self-interested motivations with a desire for a collective struggle.

In late 2013, the residents filed a contempt petition[71] claiming the board violated the February 2010 judgment of the High Court of Delhi. The petition accused the contemnors of "willful disobedience of judgment"[72] of the High Court judge. It argued that the petitioners represented other residents named in the list attached to the petition and a "bare perusal of the writ petition would make it apparent that the Writ Petition was filed by the Petitioners on behalf of all the *jhuggi* dwellers."[73] The petition accused the government of misconceiving and misconstruing the judgment. In a February 2014 order,[74] the judge noted that the petitioners had consistently argued that the petition was filed to rehabilitate all of the 223 residents listed with the petition, not only the four petitioners. Thus, the judge directed notices to be issued to the government respondents "as to why contempt proceedings be not initiated against them." The High Court of Delhi website has uploaded eight different orders involving four different judges for this case. Later, in a twist of fate, the December 2014 order/judgment dismissed the contempt petition.

In early 2015, the residents collected 50,000 rupees for court expenses and filed a petition at the Supreme Court of India for Special Leave to Appeal against the decision of the High Court.[75] In its impugned judgment of the contempt case, the High Court only allowed for rehabilitation of the petitioners instead of all those who were displaced.[76] The High Court had interpreted the February 2010 High Court judgment in a way that made a distinction between eligible petitioners and ineligible non-petitioners.[77] The High Court had further argued that none of the 219 displaced residents (excluding the petitioners) had either expressed any grievances or approached the court for rehabilitation.[78] While the residents fought protracted battles in the Supreme Court, they also mobilized political support. Unfortunately, the grassroots activists of Delhi Shramik Sangathan who had actively organized the residents had already quit the organization by this time. Additionally, the leaders of the Sangathan had grown preoccupied with other activities in the city. However, the leaders of the Sangathan continued to extend their moral support and to speak to the board members about the issue occasionally. The regime change in 2015 created a favorable "political opportunity structure"[79] (Tilly 2008: 91), thereby creating an expectation of a decision of the board in favor of the residents. The residents had predominantly voted for the ruling populist AAP in the legislative election, and their MLA, who was also a board member, belonged to the party. Furthermore, the activists of

Delhi Shramik Sangathan had close activist friends who were nominated to serve as members of the board. They knew the chief minister personally because of his activist background. Unfortunately, despite these ties, the board failed to make a decision, as the matter was in the Court.

The residents also argued that the ego tussle between the lawyer and the chief minister contributed to this stalemate. The lawyer who fought their case was an ex-AAP party worker who was expelled from the party over disagreements concerning the leadership style of the chief minister. The residents continued their campaign by holding multiple protest rallies and by petitioning the ministers and leaders of AAP. Lok Raj Sangathan supported them in this endeavor. The grassroots leader of the Sangathan, who originated from an adjoining neighborhood, had maintained relationships and periodically campaigned and mobilized the residents over various issues. In June 2017, the organization successfully carried out a major demonstration in front of the residence of the chief minister to demand resettlement. The residents also pointed out that the petitioners had not received the flats even after depositing their beneficiary amount. The residents had active support from their MLA, who spent a considerable time in the neighborhood on an everyday basis, as mentioned in the Introduction. The MLA consistently apprised the chief minister of this particular case. Nonetheless, the residents showed disagreement over the *rann-nitis*. While some argued for strictly legal tactics, others argued for campaigning and putting *dabaab* on politicians.

On August 6, 2017, the petitioners (the three of the four petitioners whose documents the board had accepted) decided to visit Baprola and I joined them on their trip. The petitioners were disheartened about the new neighborhood, especially after the residents of Baprola compared the quality and surroundings of the buildings in Baprola to Dwarka. The eligible displaced residents of Delhi preferred resettlement flats in Dwarka to Baprola. In the February 2010 judgment, the High Court had jointly analyzed four different yet similar petitions of displaced residents from four distinct neighborhoods. One of the petitions represented the case of Gautam Nagar. The residents representing another petition had recently obtained resettlement flats in Dwarka. Consequently, the petitioners of the Gautam Nagar case decided to visit the co-petitioners in Dwarka to evaluate the quality of the buildings there. We arrived at the Dwarka resettlement neighborhood, inspected the quality of the buildings, and conversed with the resettled residents. After that visit, the petitioners of Gautam Nagar decided that they must campaign to get flats in Dwarka now; the flats in Baprola were unfit for human habitation, they opined. Apparently, the co-petitioners in Dwarka had belonged to a *jhuggi jhopri* settlement in Patparganj and a few of the residents knew the chief minister and deputy chief minister when those officials ran their NGOs in the area. They had received flats in Baprola, but they visited the office of the deputy chief minister to convince him of the difficulties there and had successfully campaigned to be resettled in the flats in Dwarka.

The petitioners of Gautam Nagar returned home reinvigorated. As C remarked, "I will sit on a hunger strike until my death but will not accept resettlement flats in Baprola." Furthermore, they had positive news for the residents of Gautam Nagar. If all their co-petitioners had received flats, all of them in Gautam Nagar must surely receive them soon. Subsequently, I met the activists of Delhi Shramik Sangathan on August 17, 2017, to learn about the developments and struggles of the residents' court cases. Once I informed them of the resettlement of the co-petitioners, activist A made a phone call to one of the board members (an activist friend) in order to confirm that the co-petitioners had already been resettled. She then requested, "*Ek hi jhaddu main usse bhi saaf kardo*" (Sweep them [Gautam Nagar residents] off with the same broom). The party symbol of AAP is a broom and her remark was a suggestion that the residents of Gautam Nagar should be resettled just like the party/government had resettled the co-petitioners. She added, "If you have resettled the co-petitioners, then you have to resettle the residents of Gautam Nagar as well." The board member discussed the ongoing conversation with the MLA of Gautam Nagar and the forthcoming board meeting. He also requested a brief of the events along with the list of the residents for him to present during the board meeting. The activists of DSS asked me to prepare a brief detailing the chronology of the events concerning the court cases. I sent them a brief along with the list of residents, which they forwarded to the board member. Meanwhile, the petitioners explained the rehabilitation of the co-petitioners to the residents and even met with the MLA about these developments. As discussed in the Introduction, on August 22, 2017, the board decided to resettle all the residents listed with the petition, subject to the verification of documents. Following the decision, the MLA called for a meeting to inform the residents about the future plan of action and to address issues related to minor errors in the documents. In December 2017, four months after the decision of the board, the final judgment of the Supreme Court emphasized that the High Court had been mistaken in arguing that the contempt petition was misconceived. It further contended that it was a "well-accepted principle of class litigation" that all the affected parties need not be petitioners in the public interest litigation.[80] In its final judgment, the Supreme Court extended the benefits to all the listed residents, even as the decision required verification of their requisite documents. However, as mentioned, the land-owning agency, PWD, did not deposit its share of resettlement costs, thereby delaying the process of resettlement. This compelled the petitioners, who had deposited their shares of fees but had waited to receive resettlement flats along with the rest of the residents, to accept their flats in Baprola. While one of the petitioners accepted his resettlement flat after he fell chronically ill in early 2020, the other two petitioners accepted their resettlement flats at the end of September 2021.[81]

For the time being, the case remains a unique example of the legal machinery working to rescue the poor. One could argue that the final Supreme Court judgment in 2017 was shaped by the political decision of the government to resettle the residents. However, the negotiations with the government and the protracted battles in the courts were only possible because of the favorable February 2010 High Court decision. The case demonstrates the limits of "political society" and the costs of political opportunism. Instead of being tyrannical, the judiciary acted as an alternative resource for the poor to assert its political interests. This example also shows how the working of political society is dependent on political regimes (Routray 2014: 2305). Nevertheless, the legal outcomes were shaped and the verdict was produced through the courts. Legal outcomes were not shaped on the streets or through violent protests, but through careful deliberation. Moreover, taking self-surveys, contesting road measurements in court, putting *dabaab* on the government, negotiating with activists, and felicitating (ceremoniously congratulating) a lawyer shaped the legal outcomes. This example demonstrates how law is not solely a weapon of the dominant class but is also a site of political battles in numerical citizenship struggles.

The contrasting cases of Sitapuri and Gautam Nagar alert us to the contingencies of legal interpretations, mediations, and the class interests of various social groups. In highlighting the labyrinthine nature of legal tactics, the cases also allow us to historicize the events central to numerical citizenship struggles that unfolded in the city. These events are intertwined with restructuring projects, RWA activism, a change in political regime, and the presence of certain political organizations like Jan Chetna Manch, Lok Raj Sangathan, and Delhi Shramik Sangathan. The cases illustrate how the political economy of urban space manufactures particular variations in the legal template. The cases shed light on how a multitude of insurrections shape legal outcomes despite structural difficulties in negotiating with the state and alienation from the judicial system. In other words, the cases demonstrate the social locations and relationships of various actors. In Sitapuri, the negotiations and resistance also involved traders and entrepreneurs, who ran businesses in the locality, and politicians, who enjoyed massive support. Media coverage and the promulgation of the Delhi Law (Special Provisions) Act of 2006 provided respite to the residents of Sitapuri. In Gautam Nagar, the poor received valuable support from activists, lawyers, and politicians.

Thus, a nuanced, historical, contingent, and contextual understanding of legal discourses and practices can provide an understanding of the politicized, relational, and embodied nature of the judiciary and its role in shaping urban spaces. In fact, legal verdicts are relationally produced. The marshaling of legal resources is contingent on the nature of the state and its policies, the social location of the actors, and subaltern political mobilization and organizing. Furthermore, the decisions of various organs of the state are a result of the variety of negotiations involved, thereby drawing our attention to the heterogeneous nature of the state. While I build on the literature discussed at the beginning of the chapter, which focuses on discourses and procedures of law that contribute to urban dispossession, I depart from these approaches to examine how law constitutes a site of conflict and struggle for the poor in their claims to a home and life in the city. By deploying an ethnographic approach, I examine how court cases help us understand the residents' struggles for recognition in the city. The residents contest state classificatory categories and designations such as transitory, land mafia, ineligible purchasers, and ineligible non-petitioners. Instead, I show how the residents deploy the *rann-nitis* to be counted, remapped, and reclassified in the courtrooms and beyond in their quest of numerical citizenship entitlements. The two cases discussed in this chapter demonstrate the poor's negotiation of the judiciary in their numerical citizenship struggles. Another approach, explored in Chapter 6, is for the poor to resist policies when most other institutional avenues are exhausted.

CHAPTER 6

CULTURAL IDIOMS AND
PERFORMANCES OF RESISTANCE

NUMERICAL CITIZENSHIP STRUGGLES draw on distinct repertoires of resistance (Tilly 2008) and cultural idioms of protest and resistance, along with the political mediations, documentary contentions, and legal negotiations discussed in earlier chapters. Resistance, political participation, and negotiation are overlapping arenas. In fact, the *rann-nitis* of numerical citizenship engage a variety of resistance demonstrations and performances. The poor are likely to resort to such contentious politics as protests and outright resistance when other avenues of problem solving are unavailable. This chapter explores the contingent resistance— the context-specific tactics of the poor—that shapes claims, entitlements, and outcomes in the city. It also explores the broader alliances, interests, constraints, and opportunities that shape the urban poor's *rann-nitis* of resistance and cultural expressions. The poor encounter multiple and intersecting social structures by deploying cultural schemas and accumulated resources (Sewell 1992) at particular historical conjunctures.[1]

While the question of resistance is built into the dominant and hegemonic types of spatial forms and exclusions, the forms of resistance seen in Delhi draw on cultural repertoires of protests and a shared history of political mobilizations. Throughout this book, I attempt to present the ambiguities in various negotiations without reifying the category of "urban poor" by analyzing how the urban poor embody power structures, cultural milieu, the possession of capital, and practical wisdom. I attempt to document "conflicted, internally contradictory, and affectively ambivalent" political practices on the part of the urban poor (Ortner 1995: 179). This conceptual stance continues here as I examine a range of speech acts, performances, and spectacles of resistance as one of the modalities of machinations of numerical citizenship. The ethnographic focus attempts an analysis of "actually existing politics" in its richness and unexpectedness, as suggested by Spencer (1997: 15). In so doing, this chapter is attentive to the vernacular idioms (Michelutti 2007) of "contentious performances" (Tilly 2008). My approach concentrates on producing nuanced accounts of historical events and examining patterns, repertoires, and cultural expressions of "contentious performances" within the given "political opportunity structure" (Tilly 2008: 91).[2] Furthermore, as I show, the specific cultural idioms and performance of resistance have particular meanings (Guha 1999) and cannot be easily translated into English. These modalities of resistance employed by Delhi's urban poor range from peaceful demonstrations to militant struggles in the three neighborhoods under study.

Although my attempt is to examine the politics of the poor on their own terms, I show throughout the book that the *rann-nitis* of the poor intersect with the activities of politicians, political parties, well-meaning activists, and NGO workers in a major way. As shown in this chapter, the leaders and intermediaries affiliated with various politicians and political parties mediate and play a significant role during the protest performances of the poor. For instance, I analyze how leaders and residents affiliated with V. P. Singh (a former prime minister) participated in local protests, and how the Congress party participated in the felicitation (celebratory) ceremonies after Sitapuri transit camp was renamed. However, unlike in other contexts the political parties do not explicitly and systematically participate in local protests as much as they could (cf. Auerbach 2020). Nevertheless, my ethnographic insights examine the involvement of the political parties if that involvement intersected with the local protests of the poor. In this regard, we can gain more insight if we research political parties and their involvement in local protest activities in a systematic way in Delhi.

In contrast, the involvement of activists and interlocutors is pronounced during protest events and performances. Before I analyze how the cultural idioms epitomized in distinct speech acts and everyday and spectacular performances contribute to claims of numerical strength, legibility, visibility, and recognition for citizenship entitlements on the part of the poor, let me further clarify the intersection of the activities of the urban poor and the activists with respect to their protest activities, difficulties in building broader alliances, and grassroots organizing in the city. In so doing, I analyze the fraught relationships, issues of trust and mistrust, nature of advocacy work, and unity and disunity concerning the activists to reemphasize the ambiguities and contradictions in these collaborations.

DUKANDARI VERSUS ADVOCACY, TRUST VERSUS MISTRUST, AND UNITY VERSUS DISUNITY

Most residents identify, classify, and even blur the activities undertaken by a range of activists and interlocutors who take on roles as advocates or service workers in the neighborhoods. While some residents note the usefulness of service-providing NGOs, the work of these project-based NGOs is largely critiqued as *dukandari* (running of shops). Their work is seen as neither contributing substantially to the improvement of the situation nor helping to put pressure on the state to deliver social goods. Often, the residents summarized the work of service-providing NGOs as follows: NGOs "develop" their own group of people, distribute medicines, click pictures, and receive foreign money. The Azad resettlement colony was flooded with NGOs providing token services during my fieldwork between 2010–11 and 2017. The NGOs provided drinking water, adolescent education, daycare services for children, maternal and child health facilities, support for battered women, and training for physically challenged persons, and some also initiated micro-finance self-help groups.

The residents viewed the omnipresence of service-providing NGOs with ambivalence. The dominance of policies arguing in favor of NGO-led interventions has depoliticized development, which has accompanied massive cuts in public spending (Harriss 2001: 8). It looks rather odd for the proponents of the NGO-led model of development that the poor refer to it as *dukandari* (running of shops). Further, the "NGO-ification of civil society" has diminished protest-oriented strategies to demand re-distribution of resources (see also Bayat 2010: 45; Ray and Katzenstein 2005: 9). In Delhi, the NGOs providing services in the low-income neighborhoods have not contributed much to the protest-oriented activities of the poor. However, the advocacy organizations have definitely contributed positively to the protest-oriented demands for redistribution of urban resources.[3] The residents acknowledge the advocacy work carried out by various middle-class activists and interlocutors. Often the residents developed their own *rann-nitis* based on *marg-darshan* (path-showing) and *chetna badhana* (consciousness-raising) work of advocacy groups. Nonetheless, the poor engaged with these advocacy organizations based on their own calculations and affective considerations.

For example, many residents in Sitapuri praised the *marg-darshan* work of V. P. Singh. They concurred that V. P. Singh and his organization organized events against demolition, referred the displaced poor to MCD officials to claim resettlement, addressed their everyday challenges, and suggested the routes of problem-solving in the city. Similarly, feminist organizations, such as Jagori in the Azad resettlement colony and elsewhere, have carried out advocacy work by training women in legal clauses and resources. Thus, women in particular were informed about their possible legal recourse if they encountered violence, if they received threats from neighborhood big men, or if the police failed to register their complaints. One can clearly distinguish between *mahila mandals* (women's organizations) that focused on advocacy work and those focused on service provision. In fact, advocacy work provides inspiration to the residents and is an important ingredient in resistance activities. The advocacy mediation, however, also puts the activists in difficult situations, as they receive threatening phone calls from politicians, industrialists, and ration shop owners. As activist A noted to me in May 2010, "After we were seen coming to Gautam Nagar repeatedly, I received a phone call from an anonymous caller threatening me to stay away from the area. I was told that if he saw me around again, he might beat me up. He was clearly worried about our consciousness-raising activity in the neighborhood."

The residents argue that they are compelled to seek support from anywhere in moments of utter desperation, especially when there is a plan to protest in either a peaceful or militant manner. A Sitapuri resident explained the role of activists during resistance against demolition, "*Doobte ko tinke ka sahara*" (A drowning person may even seek a straw to save himself/herself). Here, the plight of demolition is compared to drowning, and the activists are sought after even if they provide the flimsiest of support. The poor turn to activists only after the option of seeking aid from politicians and political parties is exhausted. Further, residents are aware that the activists could be contacted if there is harassment, police brutality, or repression in the wake of political mobilization and demonstrations. Activists' validation of the residents' resistance assures the residents of additional moral, political, and legal support in the wake of troubles.

The work involved in *chetna badhana* increases poor people's awareness of slum policies and workers' entitlements in the city. In 2006, the residents of Gautam Nagar organized cycle rallies for *chetna badhana* along with the Delhi Shramik Sangathan (DSS), which had been organizing similar rallies in many parts of the city. Despite having largely ignored DSS after the cycle rally, following demolition the residents sought out the organization to be part of their *rann-niti* in early 2009. Similarly, the activists also regularly organize protest demonstrations, rallies, and public meetings at Jantar Mantar. For instance, the activists of Jan Chetna Manch (JCM), led by V. P. Singh, organized routine protest meetings regarding ration supplies, demolitions, and electricity privatizations. The activists often deployed rhetorical language to draw the attention of media and politicians. They gave fiery speeches about the inhuman conditions in which the poor lived and the need for political mobilization, and they also called for celebration of *Garib Diwas* (Day of the Poor).[4] These mobilizations were aimed at increasing the enthusiasm for political resistance in the city. JCM activists organized campaigns against summary displacements, non-issuance of allotment slips, lack of basic amenities, relocation during children's annual school examinations and inclement weather, and contentions over eligibility requirements. V. P. Singh also called for the creation of the "Delhi Slums Removal and Resettlement Monitoring Committee" to monitor the resettlement process.[5]

Additionally, activist groups perform in street theaters around the neighborhood in order to raise awareness about the predicament of the poor, providing information about the political and legal resources available for the poor. These activities build a body of supporters in the neighborhoods, who advocate for the involvement of activists during a specific *rann-niti*. Once they are part of the neighborhood *rann-nitis*, the activists with literary skills play a significant role during office visits and filing RTI applications, as was the case in Gautam Nagar. The activists' cultural capital puts them in an advantageous position with respect to the social space of office set-up. As a consequence, the poor are less likely to be mistreated when accompanied to the offices by middle-class interlocutors to seek redress for their grievances. Further, the activists provide *tasalli* (consolation/solace) to the residents during difficult and uncertain times.

The activists' knowledge of government schemes, expenditure details, and future proposals informs collective action in the city. For instance, prior to the revision of resettlement policies, the activists from the DSS organized the urban poor to petition the DDA and a range of prominent politicians, ministers, and Delhi government officials to extend the eligibility date. As discussed in Chapter 4, eligibility can be established by producing proof documents (ration card and voter ID) that demonstrate that the person has been a domiciled resident in the city since a particular date. The DSS organized people to write letters and to send faxes about extending the cut-off date of eligibility for resettlement plots until 2010. At a monthly meeting in Gautam Nagar on July 25, 2010, the activists informed people that the cut-off date had been extended to 2002. As activist A of the DSS in the meeting noted, "There were letters from ninety settlements. Your neighborhood had thirty letters alone. The government did not extend the cut-off date until 2010 as requested, but our letters definitely put *dabaab* (pressure) on the government to at least extend the date until 2002." As discussed in Chapter 2, the cut-off date for resettlement eligibility has been periodically revised since 2010; it was extended from 1998 to March 31, 2002, in 2010,[6] and then again to January 1, 2015, for the time being.

There is a lack of definite evidence that the letters and faxes shaped the Delhi government's decision to extend the eligibility date. Nevertheless, it also cannot be said that there was absolutely no effect when the residents of ninety neighborhoods petitioned the government for the extension. Even an extension of a month necessarily means housing entitlements for a significant population in the city. The petitioning processes make a "gradual shift in the power structures" (Cody 2009: 349); the petitions and letters of the urban poor can be seen as performative devices that initiate shifts in power and the redistribution of urban resources in contemporary Delhi.

While the activists are welcome, their tendency to discipline "errant" local leaders and intermediaries is met with opposition in the neighborhoods and breeds mistrust of the activists. However, the activists originating from the neighborhoods and affiliated with the advocacy organizations speak passionately about how to build unity, fight untrustworthy leaders and intermediaries, challenge injustice, and build alliances to survive in the city. The local leaders and intermediaries may challenge the activists' condescension by tracing their struggles alongside earlier sources of support before the activists arrived on the scene. Thus, the poor acknowledge the support of the activists but time and again refer to the alternate sources of support they have received in their struggles. This reinforces the poor's sense of independence and undermines the monopoly on credit-taking attitudes among the activists. In other words, the poor concede the usefulness of the activists' role but underline their own strategies, intelligence, and alliances in specific *rann-nitis*.

Poor people also develop mistrust for well-intentioned middle-class activists because of the unbridgeable gap between them in terms of social location and lived realties. It is difficult for activists to leave social inequalities aside or even "bracket status differentials" (overcome status differences) (Fraser 1992: 117, 121). Once, a resident in Sitapuri remarked, "I know these activists; they are all government agents. The government only responds to their RTI applications and funds their upkeep." While this statement is definitely not entirely true, the diverse cultural and social worlds of both these classes create ample room for misunderstandings. State policies (including the Right to Information [RTI] policy) seldom materialize in the way conceived, thereby increasing the poor's suspicion. In fact, it was only after two years of sustained work in Gautam

Nagar that residents started to trust the DSS, though they continued to question its strategies, point out its merits and demerits, and remain affiliated with other organizations, such as Lok Raj Sangathan (LRS). Furthermore, as discussed in Chapter 5, the petitioners' ambiguity around seeking resettlement, after the court passed a judgment calling for the resettlement of only the petitioners listed in the case in 2013, created disunity among the residents of Gautam Nagar. The petitioners viewed the perspectives of the activists of DSS unfavorably, especially their insistence on refusing resettlement until the government provided the flats to the rest of the eligible residents.

The activists' credit-taking attitude is also easily challenged by the lack of unity among those working even in the same area. At times, activists compete to recruit residents and build a following in the neighborhood. However, the residents maintain memberships and affiliations with multiple organizations. As resident M of Gautam Nagar put it, "So what if I am a member of three or four organizations? One organization may help me in my struggles to get a ration card, and some other could help me get electricity. I do not create problems for these organizations. I should have the freedom to choose membership in multiple organizations." Thus, the residents are not bound by particular affiliations with activist organizations. Activists' attempts to take credit for a specific intervention also divide the residents and foster disunity. Sometimes, the residents become suspicious of how the nominal membership fees of particular organizations are spent, further increasing mistrust in the area. Some of the residents may not necessarily appreciate the organizations' attempts to expand their followings in the neighborhoods.

As discussed in the course of this book, three advocacy organizations— Jan Chetna Manch (JCM), Lok Raj Sangathan (LRS), and Delhi Shramik Sangathan (DSS)—have carried out advocacy work in the neighborhoods in my research. JCM's interventions almost stopped after the death of V. P. Singh in 2008. LRS has been active in Gautam Nagar, but its activities have declined significantly in Sitapuri. As discussed later in this chapter, LRS's role was quite significant during the *rasta roko* (road blockade) struggle in Sitapuri. While DSS was active in Gautam Nagar after the demolition in 2009, its role in neighborhood politics and advocacy had significantly declined by 2017, as discussed in Chapter 5. Further, activists from Jagori have trained local volunteers to take up feminist issues in the Azad resettlement colony. It should also be noted that the Azad resettlement colony has a wide range of NGOs and political groups, although I have not explored their dynamics as part of my research.

Building a common platform to carry out advocacy work for the poor is fraught with dilemmas, difficulties, and contradictions. There have been instances when like-minded activists have come together to fight jointly with the poor in the city. In fact, Sajha Manch, a coalition of activist organizations, is an example of mass organizing among middle-class activists in the city, though the independent organizations working under the banner of Sajha Manch also recruited a huge number of activists from the low-income neighborhoods in Delhi. Sajha Manch intervened in many important issues in Delhi but had almost disbanded by the time I started fieldwork in late 2009. By then, the activist groups that were previously part of the Manch worked independently. It requires further study to understand the difficulty of mass organizing in a city like Delhi. However, I provide some preliminary arguments about the difficulties and complexities of grassroots mass organizing in Delhi.

Often organizations, activist groups, and NGOs working in the same neighborhoods are divided by their ideological persuasions, political affiliations, protest strategies, and views on acceptable sources of funding. As one activist argued, "Activists working in the same area have different opinions about what strategies to adopt and engage in turf battles and competing claims over territory." In fact, ideological standpoints and tactical differences are two critical elements that divide organizations working in the poor neighborhoods. Thus, advocacy groups may lack unity despite working on common issues. For instance, the strategies of DSS and LRS differed significantly despite the residents choosing to work with both organizations depending on the context. As a resident in Gautam Nagar contended in March 2010, "DSS works within the framework of law but LRS does not necessarily work within the framework of law. For instance, LRS may have demonstrations without notifying the government and carry out road blockades too." DSS's strategy of petitioning and monthly meetings works within the legal framework. In contrast, LRS's strategy of effigy burning, road blockades, and militant sloganeering, discussed below, challenges the state more aggressively. Further, as illustrated throughout the book, the organizations gained influence depending on the context, local contingencies, and historical conjunctures as part of the general *rann-niti* of neighborhood politics. Residents also welcomed the help of politicians and lawyers as part of the *rann-niti*. Without completely undermining the role of various activists and interlocutors, the residents imply that the poor have become a constituency even for well-meaning activists, students, and researchers. "People come here for their own (*swarth*) selfish reasons: they receive money, salaries, scholarships, and recognition because of us," noted one resident in Sitapuri.

Having discussed the challenges of resistance demonstrations and the intersection of the activities of the urban poor and the activists, I turn to an analysis of the repertoires and idioms of protest demonstrations in the city.

THE IDIOMS OF PEACEFUL DEMONSTRATIONS

The repertoires discussed below do not strictly fall under peaceful or militant protests. Nevertheless, I discuss them under these labels to point out the varying intensity of protests, frustration, and worldviews among the poor at different conjunctures in the city. The repertoire of peaceful protests includes *bhook hartal* (hunger strike), *dharna* (peaceful gatherings), rallies (also cycle rallies), street theaters, and felicitation ceremonies. These repertoires were adopted in resistance to privatization of services and the demolition of neighborhoods. The following discussion is specifically attentive to the modalities, logics, and cultural expressions of three forms of peaceful resistance: *dharnas*, rallies, and felicitation ceremonies.

The Rann-niti of Dharnas

Dharnas typically entail congregating peacefully at various sites and expressing grievances through sloganeering, distributing pamphlets, and silently sitting with placards or holding hunger strikes. *Dharnas* are also carried out alongside more militant struggles like *rasta roko* (road blockades) and *gherao* (encirclement). Demands for public accountability through letter-writing campaigns and office visits are another tactic, discussed in Chapter 4. In many instances, delegations may produce a letter with a set of demands at the relevant office prior to organizing a *dharna*. Most often, intermediaries lead the contingent, collect residents' signatures, and produce a list of demands for immediate relief. The residents carefully collect signatures and endorsements from influential people, particularly politicians, to be presented during a *dharna*. Endorsements not only increase legitimacy and recognition but also provide a semblance of protection against arbitrary hostility at the office gates. Photographic and written documentation of the existing state of affairs sometimes accompany the letters. For instance, at one *dharna*, residents of Sitapuri produced photographic evidence of undeveloped parks, overflowing garbage dumps, and clogged drains from their auto-archive. *Dharnas* are most often held in front of the ruling party's offices. The strategic display of numerical strength conveys the magnitude of suffering and provides a moral justification for collective resistance. It also suggests that the politician may win the support of a substantial population by attending to the issue. The poor fill auto-rickshaws, trucks, and other vehicles to visit various politicians with their grievances. Most often they congregate in front of the politician's office or residence as a sign of protest, as well as to demonstrate their numerical strength.

The residents of Gautam Nagar consistently held *dharnas* in their neighborhoods and in front of political offices to protest the demolition and spatial restructuring of their neighborhood, and to express demands for "collective consumption" (Castells 1983). Gautam Nagar residents collectively spent approximately 20,000–30,000 rupees (US$444–$666) to organize *dharnas* at politicians' offices before and after the demolition in 2009. However, this palpable unity is subject to change as the residents vote for various parties, pursue different ideologies, and are divided by social cleavages. For example, the residents held a peaceful *dharna* in front of the MLA's house, aimed at securing resettlement plots. They also held a *dharna* in front of the urban development minister's house for three consecutive days after the *jhuggis* were demolished. Some residents continued to live on the streets or rent houses in the vicinity after demolition. The municipality stopped sending the water tanker, which was a major source of water in the area, thereby dramatically increasing the post-demolition hardships of both displaced and un-displaced residents.

Responding to this water scarcity, the residents held *dharnas* at the traffic crossing to register their resistance peacefully. To the embarrassment of the government, these *dharnas* sometimes continued unabated for many days despite threats of arrests. Gautam Nagar residents have continued to stage *dharnas* periodically, especially in front of the residence of the chief minister of Delhi. As discussed in Chapter 5, the residents organized a major demonstration (as part of a *dharna*) to claim resettlement in June 2017—barely a few weeks before the favorable decision of the government and also the favorable verdict of the Supreme Court of India. The residents disbanded only after receiving an assurance that the chief minister had agreed to investigate the lapse in providing resettlement plots as soon as possible. Thus, through their disruption of the "social-psychic peace" (Ramaswami 2012: 63), *dharnas* call attention to injustice in the neighborhoods.

Similarly, the Sitapuri residents staged a *dharna* at the Congress party office once they heard about the impending demolition:

RESIDENT J: After the failed first attempt to demolish, the demolition was rescheduled for early May 2006. We informed everyone to join us at Akbar Road once we heard about this. There were approximately five hundred of us—both men and women—who gathered in front of 24 Akbar Road. We had a *dharna* in front of the building for twenty-four hours. Meanwhile, key politicians came from inside and tried to placate our anger by asking us to meet this or that politician or minister. We chanted, '*Sonia Gandhi Zindabad! Jo hum se takrayega, chur chur ho jayega!*' (Long live Sonia Gandhi! Whoever will collide with us, will be broken into pieces!) The media covered it because it was near [Congress party President] Sonia Gandhi's residence. The police barricaded the area to keep watch on us. Activists from Jan Chetna Manch were also present. We returned back to our place only after we received assurance that our houses would not be demolished.

Thus, the residents' initial strategy involved protesting at the ruling party's national office. The contradiction of simultaneous praise and threat in their protest chants reflects their circumstantial predicaments. On the one hand, they selected the most powerful leader of the party to praise, as they knew that she could successfully intervene if she wished to stop the demolition. On the other hand, the threat of demolition was real as a result of court orders, and threatening the unnamed enemy was their last resort. The unnamed enemy here is the *sarkar* (government) in abstract terms, and the officials who embodied state power to demolish, such as bulldozer operators, police personnel, and paramilitary force, were the concrete figures of the unnamed enemy. Further, the threat might have indicated a subtle suggestion that the party could be voted out of power in subsequent elections if it failed to prevent the demolition. Similarly, staging *dharnas* and displays of numerical strength have been the most essential components of everyday *baghawat* (rebellion) against state officials for Azad resettlement colony residents. Sometimes, the residents embarrass the politicians for their unresponsiveness during these *baghawats*. At one such *dharna*, Azad resettlement colony residents carried a bottle of the undrinkable water available in their neighborhood and asked the member of Parliament to have a drink.

The Rann-niti of Rallies

Dharnas are most often conjoined with rallies and *juluses* (marches). Because the features of *dharnas*, rallies, and *juluses* overlap, residents use them interchangeably at times. Nevertheless, each form of "contentious performance" (Tilly 2008) has its own distinctive features. The rallies typically involve a small march (*julus*), sloganeering, and speeches by key leaders of the neighborhoods or guest activists. *Dharnas* do not involve a parade and may not necessarily involve speeches by key leaders. As I discussed earlier, the contingent, or context-specific, mobilization of collective resistance in the neighborhoods at various points in time may include the involvement of outside activist groups. The contingent formation of collective organizations is much more common in the Azad resettlement colony, which has a significant population. The leaders of the erstwhile displaced *jhuggi jhopri* settlements continue to fight to gain legitimacy in the resettlement colony. They immediately draw on supporters who come from their earlier places of residence in the *jhuggi jhopri* settlements, but they face difficulties mobilizing the majority, as the resettlement colonies are so vast and diverse. The initial anonymity of leaders, social divisions, and earlier neighborhood alliances pose tremendous barriers to organization. Nevertheless, I came across many collective organizations in the Azad resettlement colony. All had gradually built their organizational strength over several years. Some of the notable organizations included the All India *Soshit* Front, the New *Janheet* Welfare Association, the Kalam Welfare Society (Registered), and the Dr. Baba Saheb Nagarik Sudhar Samiti.[7] These organizations routinely organize *dharnas*, rallies, and other forms of public demonstrations both collectively and independently. Many specifically attended to the needs of the most marginalized sections of the resettled populations, including Dalits and Muslims. Their members also regularly held protests at Jantar Mantar (a place in Delhi designated by the state for public demonstrations).

The Kalam Welfare Society in particular has campaigned[8] for water supply, a sewage system, electricity connections, Delhi Transport Corporation bus service, a primary health center, burial grounds, and a primary school in the resettlement colony. In response to this campaign, the chief minister of Delhi visited the Azad resettlement colony in mid-June 2004 and requested that the DDA build a burial ground, multipurpose community facilities, parks, and shopping facilities in the area.[9] In the initial years of resettlement, Kalam Welfare Society voiced the concerns of approximately two thousand Muslims in the neighborhood, especially their need for a local *masjid* (mosque) and burial ground.

The society argued that Muslim residents incurred an expenditure of 2,000–3,000 rupees (US$44.44–$66.66) in order to transport their dead to the nearest burial ground.[10] The Kalam Society activists petitioned a former governor, the lieutenant governor of Delhi, the DDA vice chairman, Muslim leaders, and the local MLA to request the provision of a burial ground. Thus, these campaigns not only demanded redistribution of social goods but also the recognition of community-specific needs. In general terms, Fraser (2000) analyzes the displacement of redistributive demands into reified identities as a result of conflicting and multiple counter claims (108). However, in this case, recognition neither displaced redistributive demands nor reified identities. The society conjointly advocated the redistribution of basic amenities in the language of poverty, urban dispossession, and class inequality, while also asserting the recognition of community identities and the representation of their needs (see also Fraser 2009) by campaigning for a *masjid* and burial ground. The campaigns and *dabaab* (pressure) forced the government to allocate land for a cemetery for Muslims along with a cremation ground for Hindus.

The Rann-niti of Felicitation

Felicitation or congratulatory ceremonies may not qualify as part of the conventionally understood protest activities of the poor, at least in the same way that rallies and *dharnas* can. However, I argue that these ceremonies comprise significant resistance events that not only provide ideological impetus for resistance but also contribute to the reinvention of community solidarity for future collective action. The ceremonies also inaugurate renewed legitimacy through the demonstration of numerical strength. Most often, the celebration of small victories includes the felicitation of key actors, who in turn reinvigorate protest strategies. A short ethnographic vignette of one such occasion follows.

The High Court verdict concerning Gautam Nagar (discussed in Chapter 5) reaffirmed the need to resist certain urban policies that aim at erasing the poor from the government records in the city. The occasion necessitated deliberation of the verdict, discussion of future resistance tactics, and the felicitation of the lawyer who fought the case pro bono. On March 7, 2010, I arrived early in the morning in Gautam Nagar and met some key persons co-organizing the felicitation ceremony with DSS. The volunteers (along with *pradhans* and *samaj sevaks*) who had taken interest in the court case had dressed up and prepared their own speeches for the occasion. They had also collected flower garlands for the guests. A cultural group from the neighborhood rehearsed *bhajans* (devotional songs) to perform during the celebration.

I accompanied the residents slowly streaming into the neighborhood park, which was the venue for the celebration. The residents sat on the

FIGURE 6.1: *Felicitation ceremony: The residents of Gautam Nagar are felicitating the lawyer and celebrating the favorable High Court judgment.*

green carpet spread on the lawn facing the stage in the cleaned-up park. Behind the stage hung the banners and posters of DSS. The guests included not only the lawyers and activists associated with the case but also the councilor. The leaders of the neighborhood joined the guests on the dais. I was also asked to join the guests but declined and sat on the carpet. The leaders were not happy with my decision and were perplexed by what they perceived as inexplicable aloofness after being with them during the court proceedings. They contested my claim that my mere presence to collect data during their struggles did not qualify me to sit on the dais and speak on the occasion. I extended solidarity, felt euphoric during the celebration of the victory, but I still collected data during the event. More importantly, a section of the residents was unhappy with the decision to invite the councilor and other neighborhood leaders not directly associated with the legal struggle onto the dais. In fact, the residents sitting down along with me continued to debate the judiciousness of inviting guests not directly associated with the struggle.

The occasion started with the singing of *Ram Bhajan* (devotional song for Hindu god, Ram) followed by Bhojpuri folk songs. These cultural expressions not only highlight Hindu upper-caste hegemony but also point to the disproportionate representation of the interests of one particular community in the neighborhood. Nevertheless, passions, cheers, and socialist sloganeering overtook the occasion. The reinvention of a community, expressions of solidarity, and counter-discourses were clearly affective, mobilizing sensations and emotions among the crowd (see Warner 2002: 88). The residents frequently chanted "*Awaaz do, Hum Saath Hai!*" (Say it aloud, we are together!) Each leader spoke for a few minutes and exhorted the people to fight hard, maintain unity, claim their rights, and not retreat. The leaders eulogized the activists and the lawyer as part of the felicitation and invited them to share a few words:

> ACTIVIST A: The poor have not been able to resist the displacement policies despite their numerical strength in the city. But look at the shop owners and traders; they could successfully resist sealing and the demolition of their properties. You need to unite and resist.

> ACTIVIST R: The poor do not have land titles in the city, even in the resettlement colonies. The poor must organize!

> LAWYER P: The Supreme Court of India has reiterated time and again that the Indian constitution guarantees the poor certain rights. But look at the scenario today. The rural poor are coming into the cities due to distress migration. And the urban poor are living on the streets due to lack of housing. This judgment has given us a glimmer of hope. Let's hope that we are successful in fighting for the housing rights of the poor in the city.

The occasion reinvented community solidarity and reinvigorated the poor for political action. The residents' decision not to involve political parties was debated even though the residents knew that the involvement of the local MLA or MP would have generated more interest among the residents. In fact, one faction was even opposed to the idea of inviting the local councilor. The councilor knew that it was a hard-fought battle without the support of politicians. He remained a mute spectator and merely thanked the leaders, activists, and the lawyer for fighting the case. It was not a usual case of demagoguery, bragging about one's own political party, or pro-poor sloganeering. Nevertheless, the councilor's anxiety about retaining legitimacy in the neighborhood was obvious. The councilor did not object to the residents' scathing denunciation of politicians. He had instructed the gardeners to clean the park prior to the event and had also circulated *swagat samaroh* (welcome ceremony) notices to the residents, thereby leaving behind traces of his involvement in the felicitation ceremony.

However, the role of the councilor changed dramatically subsequent to the government delaying resettlement of the residents and also because the councilor went on to become the MLA of the ruling party. While the residents had almost deserted what they perceived as the powerless councilor in their legal struggles, the ensuing developments provide a longer temporal view of the numerical struggles in the city. The temporal unfolding of the struggles allows us to understand how the complex and contingent roles of various state agencies, intermediaries, and activists differ across space and time in particular conjunctures.

FIGURE 6.2: *The politics of renaming and reclassification: Stone unveiling and felicitation ceremony on the occasion of renaming of Sitapuri transit camp.*

Similarly, as discussed in the Introduction, the residents of Sitapuri organized a felicitation ceremony after the renaming of their neighborhood in August 2010. The residents celebrated the removal of the label "transit camp" and the addition of the name of the prime minister along with the label "colony" to their neighborhood. As discussed earlier, the label "transit camp" implied their lack of numerical entrenchment in the city. The label "colony" reaffirmed legitimacy, as the "planned" neighborhoods are often suffixed with "colony." Furthermore, the addition of the name of the former prime minister reaffirmed the political backing of their neighborhood. Thus, the renaming and felicitation ceremony reconfirmed that the residents had lived in the neighborhood for a long time, possessed numerous documents, and had voted en masse for the Congress party in the elections. As argued throughout the book, the state policies of housing and the provision of basic amenities, as enshrined in the policies of demolition and resettlement, are bound up with the numerical strength of a neighborhood and the number of years spent in the city.

The political divisions in the neighborhood were apparent once the Congress politicians changed the name of the neighborhood, as demanded by the residents. The minority of BJP supporters circulated notices around the neighborhood asking if the fate of the neighborhood had also changed as a result of these renaming circuses. While most Sitapuri residents advanced their rightful claim over space by reassuring themselves through this little *rann-niti* of renaming, a minority besieged them with questions regarding land-use changes, planning regime ambiguities, and uncertainty over the neighborhood's fate. In fact, as discussed in previous chapters, land-use policy changes do not merely reflect the political wills of the local politicians. They also involve legal and administrative ambiguities and interference, class interests (especially illustrated in the activism of the Lakshmi colony RWA), and beautification drives, such as the urban restructuring projects envisioned in the current Master Plan, which has been ratified by the political class at the national level. Nevertheless, the felicitation of the politicians at the renaming ceremony helped to reinvigorate solidarity among the residents and bolstered claims of visibility.

THE IDIOMS OF MILITANT DEMONSTRATIONS

In addition to the *dharnas*, rallies, and felicitation ceremonies discussed above, the urban poor also enact several other context-specific forms of peaceful resistance. For example, after their ration cards were confiscated, Gautam Nagar residents gathered on the main arterial road near the traffic crossing to form a *manav shrankhala* (human chain) by holding hands and wearing on their chests posters about the right to food. In times of dire need, however, the poor may also resort to the option of more militant protests by targeting public property and vehicles (see also Guha 1999: 71). The forms of militant protests include *gherao* (encirclement) and *rasta roko* (road blockades). I add *julus* (march or parade) to these forms of more militant struggles; although a *julus* usually entails peaceful demonstration, at times it may be combined with militant sloganeering and threats. Most of these militant protests are symbolic in nature, but they may entail direct confrontations and verbal or physical attacks on their targets. It should be noted that militant struggles involving arms to protest demolition or to demand basic amenities are unheard of in Delhi.

The Rann-niti of Julus

Once the residents of Sitapuri had learned about the April 2006 court decision and imminent demolition, they called on leaders, politicians, and activists for consultations, deliberations, and suggestions. The residents had to make a *rann-niti* and organize a campaign to contest the court decision. The residents developed a fresh *rann-niti*. LRS joined and helped them plan a *julus* (march) in the neighborhood in early May. The residents carried out a massive march and chanted angry slogans along with the activists of LRS, most of whom originated from around the neighborhood. The march comprised a significant number of residents from the neighborhood.[11] The residents of the Lakshmi colony observed the march from their neighborhood. Subsequently, the residents roamed around their neighborhood—both of the blocks—to encourage residents to join the struggle.

One of the banners at the *julus* read: *Agar* transit camp *bachana hai, sab ko bahar aana hai!* (If you want to save the transit camp, then all of you need to come out!)[12] In other words, the residents actively at the forefront of the struggle called out their fellow residents to display their numerical strength to thwart the demolition of the neighborhood. On most occasions, the *juluses* followed public meetings. In fact, the residents met in small groups in the parks every fifth day to provide updates about their activities through the month of May. On May 5, 2006, about one thousand residents attended a public meeting in a park.[13] This great numerical turnout reconfirms the success of *juluses* at mobilizing and organizing the residents. The residents defied police harassment during public meetings in the parks. Participants in the *juluses* and public meetings displayed and enacted what Tilly (2008: 72) would call their "WUNC—collective Worthiness, Unity, Numbers, and Commitment." The participants also informed the media about their story of struggle amid uncertainty.

The *juluses* accompanied the effigy burning of government officials (discussed later). Perhaps the most significant *julus* in this period involved the effigy burning of an RWA representative of the Lakshmi colony by a section of the protesters. The residents went out on a *julus* to burn an effigy after much sloganeering in the neighborhood. It was a solemn occasion, as people marched to conduct the symbolic funeral procession and last rites of this particular RWA representative. The entire Lakshmi colony watched the effigy burning from their rooftops. As resident ND observed during a group discussion, "The RWA representative was scared and even sought police protection." This event initiated acrimonious debates in the Lakshmi colony. As discussed in Chapter 5, the shaming of RWA representatives for being anti-poor and appealing to their conscience definitely contributed to their lack of further interest in the court case. As ND argued, "See, the fight was between an elephant and an ant, so the ant had no other option but to take any measure possible to save itself." Clearly, the elephant and the ant metaphors are used to represent the strong versus the weak and to emphasize the latter's valiant efforts at resistance. Tilly (2008: 4) argues that collective contention involves "learned and historically grounded performances ... [changing] ... incrementally as a result of accumulating experience and external constraints." Similarly, Della Porta (2005: 178) in another context argues that movements blend "path dependency and learning processes." The peculiar form of protest discussed above drew on modes of symbolic protests entailing

FIGURE 6.3: *The symbolic funeral procession of the dead (unresponsive) Delhi government in Gautam Nagar.*

effigy burning in the city. But the performance simultaneously innovated and improvised on this repertoire of protest so as to pressure the middle-class residents publicly at the same time. There are perceptible divisions between allottees and purchasers, residents who owned plots facing the road and the ones who suffocated in the *gallis* without ventilation, and supporters of Congress and the BJP. Nevertheless, the residents quickly realized that unity was needed, as demolition would not be beneficial to any segment of the population. Even if some became eligible for resettlement, the aftermath of their resettlement remained uncertain. Thus, the common refrain at the *juluses* in the neighborhood was *"Ek Pe Hamla, Sab Pe Hamla!"* (Attack on one is attack on all!)

Similarly, the residents organized *juluses* regularly with the leaders of LRS in Gautam Nagar. On a Sunday morning, December 6, 2009, I arrived early to participate in one of these processions. The procession was planned to protest against scarce facilities (including water and electricity provisions, garbage collection, subsidized food, and other essential services) and inflation that affected the poor. The *julus* was called the *antim yatra* (funeral procession) of the Delhi *sarkar* (government). An effigy representing the Delhi *sarkar* was paraded along with the contingent of marchers. The procession started from the local Ravidas temple. A *samaj sevak* known for his deep commitment to the ideology of LRS had canvassed the night before to inform the residents about the *julus*. The final destination was a dirty drain that bisected the neighborhood. The procession proceeded through the narrow *gallis* of *jhuggi jhopri* settlements in the area. The muddy roads full of potholes and rotten garbage created obstacles for the contingent to march together. Nevertheless, the contingent swelled in numbers as it marched in the neighborhood to the amusement of onlookers, reciprocal sloganeering among the residents, and the embarrassment of the police officials.

Throughout the march, leaders took turns standing on a cycle trolley to make speeches about the predicament in the neighborhoods. Most of the speakers spoke passionately about the rising costs of essential commodities and the confiscation of ration cards. They urged the residents to resist these urban policies in large numbers. Finally, the last rites of Delhi *sarkar* were performed and the effigy was dumped in a drain after an extended period of sloganeering. The leaders cheered on the participants creatively. As one speaker explained, "We would not burn the effigy of Delhi *sarkar*, as kerosene is too expensive in times of inflation. We would also not bury the dead [unresponsive] Delhi *sarkar*, as there is no land in Delhi [alluding to the lack of land for housing for the poor]. So, we will drown Delhi *sarkar* in a *gandi nali* (dirty drain)." Therefore, a *julus* is mostly a peaceful demonstration but may be accompanied by fiery speeches and symbolic attacks on the government authority or powerful interests, and followed by public meetings or other more strident forms of demonstration.

The Rann-niti of Gherao

Gherao (encirclement)[14] is a milder form of militant protest to register one's grievances. It may entail preventing a particular person or group of people from entering or leaving certain premises. For example, the residents of Sitapuri were successful after they *gheraoed* their entire neighborhood, as neither the police force nor the bulldozers could enter. This form of resistance was performed along with *rasta roko* (road block- ade). Similarly, Gautam Nagar residents *gheraoed* the politicians, MLA, MP, and the minister of urban development during the ceremony to lay the foundation stone for the underpass that was to be built as part of the road-widening project. Usually the *netas* (leaders) unveil the foundation stone that has their names inscribed on it. In this case, residents let the *netas* leave the area only after the *netas* had promised that the residents would be adequately compensated with resettlement plots (although, as matters unraveled, the politicians later reneged on this promise). *Gheraos* are usually mildly militant events, but sometimes they include *hata pai* (roughing up) or *tu tu mein mein* (argument) with the target, which might also involve bringing in the police.

Gherao is a strategy to bring urgent issues to the fore when politi- cians visit these neighborhoods on behalf of the poor. According to resi- dent A of Sitapuri, "We *gheraoed* the MLA during the sealing of com- mercial activities in the neighborhood. One of us was even arrested for four hours that day." In fact, the MLA in this particular case was forced to order the officials to stop sealing the commercial establishments. The Sitapuri residents also used a narrow *galli* to *gherao* a politician who had come to canvass for votes ahead of elections. Resident G recalled, "We wanted him to see what *jan suvidha* (public utilities) he had provided us during his tenure. We told him that we neither possessed arms nor planned to harm him physically. We just wanted him to experience what we experienced in the area. He shouted at the staff and asked them to immediately note down our grievances regarding *nali, kharanja, bijli aur pani* (drainage, brick-road, electricity, and water)." Thus, *gherao* tactics during election canvassing caused trouble for the politicians attempt- ing to campaign in the narrow lanes of free-flowing drains, temporarily effecting shifts in the balance of power between residents and politi- cians. These strategies also remind the politicians of their responsibili- ties. Most often, the politicians renege once they win elections, as is evident in the continuing state of affairs. Still, through *gheraos* they are made uncomfortable, asked to admit faults, and forced to promise solu- tions. Further, as Ramaswami (2012: 69) observes, these events provide us insights into the "non-absolute weakness of migrant workers [the urban poor] in Delhi."

The Rann-niti of Rasta Roko

Resistance through *rasta roko* (road blockade) was the primary factor that prevented the demolition of Sitapuri, as discussed in Chapter 5. The first attempt to demolish the neighborhood in April 2006 was unsuccessful, partly foiled by the intervention of the former prime minister, V. P. Singh, who stood in front of the bulldozer even though, according to one resident, he was on dialysis. Another resident noted that *raja-ji* (V. P. Singh is fondly remembered as *raja-ji*, or "king") put a lot of pressure on the government. V. P. Singh employed the *rann-niti* of sleeping in front of bulldozers to stall demolitions successfully in other neighborhoods as well. In response, the DDA informed the court that extra police support was required and postponed the demolition. In early May, the DDA circulated notices informing the residents that the demolition would be carried out from May 9 to May 11, 2006.[15] A huge number of people gathered on the arterial road adjoining the neighborhood on the night of May 8, 2006, anticipating the arrival of bulldozers the following day. May is the hottest month of the year, when temperatures hover around 45°C. However, the heat did not deter the residents from waging a *rasta roko* for four consecutive days, which completely paralyzed traffic in the area.

When asked if they organized under any particular banner, the residents vaguely referred to Transit Camp Sangharsh Morcha, Sitapuri Transit Camp Bachao Sagharsh Samiti, and their RWA as the organizations that fought against the demolition. However, members of the transit camp RWA claimed that they spearheaded the campaign. The RWA is composed of residents, *pradhans*, and traders who owned businesses in the area. However, my attempts to follow up on interventions made under each banner were not successful, as the residents mostly could not describe the structure, membership, and functioning of the organizations. Rather, they had participated as a unit and had not formalized the event under banners, despite fighting a well-coordinated battle. Nevertheless, the *rasta roko* became a major collective event in the community with the support of LRS, as the following exchange indicates:

RESIDENT K: We went to the street and slept right in front of the bulldozer. It was the month of May. Our feet developed boils and lesions.

RESIDENT B: It was like a *qayamat* (judgment day). The residents of block A guarded one end of the road and block B the other. We placed cut trees, branches, stones, and other things on the road as obstacles. We informed many people about our fight.

RESIDENT A: They [the government] even stopped supplying water to the neighborhood, but we asked the MLA to intervene and made a path for the water tanker to come into the neighborhood while continuing the road blockade.

RESIDENT S: Approximately two hundred police officers provided protection to three or four bulldozers that were brought to carry out the demolitions. And there were between twenty-five thousand and thirty thousand people on the street. My husband died due to heatstroke while protesting against the demolition. Another person also died due to heatstroke during this time, but I did not know him personally. Many developed health complications and a few never recovered from it.

Women protested angrily at the forefront so as to evoke sympathy from the police, but instead they took the blows of the police, who attempted to breach the blockade.[16] During the blockade, men, women, youth, and children sang revolutionary songs, staged mock funeral processions, and burned effigies of various officials.[17] There was a common belief that the residents had to unite across differences in order to resist the demolition, even though the neighborhood remained divided according to places of regional origin, caste, religion, language, and political allegiance. The solidarities based on the above loyalties pitted one against the other in the neighborhood. However, they had to forge a common class solidarity to have a chance of saving their neighborhood from being bulldozed.

The class-based solidarity drew on the movement's cultural idioms or practices. The Muslim residents sought out their religious leader to address the public during these struggles. Moreover, intra-community solidarities contributed to the creation of general class solidarity (see also Guha 1999: 170–77). For instance, it was easier for the members of various communities to mobilize each other for the protection of the general class interest of the neighborhood. During my fieldwork, one Muslim resident told me how he could mobilize members along community lines for the general interest of the neighborhood. His sister-in-law gained tremendous respect for participating in the hunger strike and for mobilizing Muslim women in the neighborhood during the *rasta roko*. Further, his own family mobilized the Muslims from eastern Uttar Pradesh to join the struggle. In fact, I was able to draw on his community networks in order to speak to the Muslim residents of Sitapuri in the initial part of my fieldwork.

V. P. Singh came twice to the neighborhood, though a resident noted his ill health prevented him from participating actively during the second series of events. The poor seek support from various politically and ideologically diverse constituencies. In Sitapuri, community leaders sought various activists for support, invited media to cover the issue, and frantically called politicians with updates about the situation. Despite the backing of LRS and its militant appeal to resist, the residents continued to reach out to diverse constituencies. Some residents narrated their stories about lacking much *pahunch aur pakad* (reach and hold). Resident A once told me, "If you [middle-class students] had a problem, you would organize a candlelight procession of one hundred people and the government would listen to you. But if we [the poor] turned out in the thousands, the government would not listen. So, we have to have some *pahunch aur pakad* to begin with." In fact, the cultivation of *pahunch aur pakad* in everyday life comes in handy during these grievous situations. Here, *pahunch aur pakad* implies the community's extent and the solidity of its social network.

The road blockade to resist demolition lasted four to five days, from May 8 to 12, 2006. The activists from LRS, who mostly belonged to the low-income neighborhoods of the area, participated passionately. While the agitations continued for four to five days, the residents were cautious not to engage in unnecessary violence. Activist B of LRS noted,

"We discussed prior to the blockade that stone pelting, burning, or *tod phod* (breaking) of government property may give the police an excuse to attack us." The residents used a combination of tactics but were aware that targeting police officials or arson might result in their movement being crushed. However, a government bus parked near the locality was pelted with stones on one day of the *rasta roko*. Many residents I spoke to claim that it was a clear case of sabotage on the part of miscreants. At one point, the police officials warned the residents that they would open fire unless the residents cleared the road. In response to this, the residents threatened to blow up the nearby gas station, which would endanger a densely populated area.

Women spearheaded the *rasta roko* struggle. While some guarded the ends of the road, others went onto rooftops and threatened the police and DDA officials that they would pour acid and kerosene if the latter attempted to demolish the area. As resident K reported, "We were also prepared to jump from the rooftops with our kids if they demolished our neighborhood." This was a strategy to put the blame squarely back on the *sarkar* for eventual deaths, violence, and arson. Moreover, the residents pleaded with the police officials to spare them and recognize their just cause.

Guha (1999) makes a useful distinction between rebellion and crime. He argues that rebellion is an open, public event, while crime is individualistic or operates in small groups and relies on secrecy to be effective (Guha 1999: 109, 115). The public event of *rasta roko* was organized, articulated, and expressed as a rebellion against the unjust demolition drive. It was reported time and again in the court that the police could not take action, as they feared the situation was getting out of control. However, the situation was quelled after the bulldozers were removed from the area. Following the removal of bulldozers, the *rasta roko* was withdrawn; the residents, however, continued with a relay hunger strike for four more days. The DDA filed a report in the court stating that it could not demolish the neighborhood because of large-scale protests. The court again postponed the verdict by another three months.[18] In this case, the *rasta roko* was a successful means of resistance. The struggle was well coordinated and involved alliances with activists, politicians, and media. More importantly, the struggle had numerical strength. Although the assertion of numerical strength primarily shaped the outcome and mode of *rasta roko*, the spatiality of the Sitapuri transit camp precipitated a distinctive mode of politics. The abstract representation of the Sitapuri camp as transitory, coded as such in the policy documents of planners, shaped the social relations between the middle-class residents of the Lakshmi colony and the residents of the camp. The gradual entrenchment of the Sitapuri residents—both the allottees and the purchasers—reflected the imagination of claims-making processes in the city.

It should also be emphasized that Sitapuri was a rare case (perhaps the only one in Delhi) of successful resistance against demolition through the mode of *rasta roko*. In fact, the "political opportunity structure" (Tilly 2008: 91) in Delhi may allow contentious performances but does not allow outright contestations of demolitions. In a sense, the *rasta roko* significantly modified the "political opportunity structure" for the benefits of the *rasta roko* activists. While the dominant political configuration in Delhi is opposed to demonstrations against demolition, as evident in other instances of police brutality, the *rasta roko* was perceived as a tolerable event. Further, the residents could create new allies by canvassing a former prime minister, politicians, activists, and the media. *Rasta roko* is not always such an effective strategy, however, especially if the demonstration involves fewer people. This is why the residents of the Azad resettlement colony have not used *rasta roko* to successfully call attention to their problems accessing electricity and water. According to resident BC, "We gave a notice to the police station about a *rasta roko* we planned to organize in 2004. The police came and arrested twenty-five of us, forcing the small group who had gathered for the protest to disperse." However, the steady, peaceful, and militant demonstrations carried out by the residents of the Azad resettlement colony yielded favorable results after a few years. While the provision of a water supply was conspicuously absent in 2017, the neighborhood had received electricity connections by 2012. The government had also built concrete roads by 2012 and opened a dispensary by 2016–17 in the neighborhood.

Other, disparate forms of militant protests are intended to preserve the basic amenities already available in the area. On December 20, 2009, while the Gautam Nagar residents deliberated on court-related issues on a Sunday morning, a young man came charging toward the collective, informing people there that the toilet vans were being removed. The neighborhood has a common toilet complex but the facility is very limited, so the removal of toilet vans was a significant concern for the residents. The collective dispersed immediately and charged toward the MCD workers trying to remove the vans. After considerable shouting, frantic phone calls to the councilor, and threats to the MCD workers, the residents were assured that the vans would only be removed if the councilor brought new replacements. Once the young man heard this, he enthusiastically climbed up the wall adjoining the vans to demolish part of it in order to make way for the new toilet vans. He screamed, "*Jai* (hail) *Bajrangbali!*" (*Bajrangbali* is a synonym for a Hindu god named *Hanuman*, known for his physical prowess), and the gathering rejoiced. While the councilor is usually the closest politician, spatially and socially (see also S. Benjamin 2000), he or she does not wield much political power beyond addressing local basic needs, and thus is unable to intervene in major decision-making processes in the city. As one resident described, "He is the *nali-kharanja* (drain and brick-road) person—he cannot do much. *Bade bade dhol jahan shor kare timki*" (The small drum makes noise in the midst of bigger drums). The drum analogy was meant to suggest that the councilor's actions were insignificant compared to those of MLAs, MPs, and ministers. This sentiment expresses the lack of effective local avenues to campaign for major entitlements in the city, including social housing, resettlement, and land-use changes. Nevertheless, as I demonstrate throughout the book, the local councilors remain pivotal in making pro-poor decisions and interventions because of their own electoral calculations and the poor's *dabaab* (pressure) tactics (S. Benjamin 2000; S. Benjamin and Raman 2001; Oldenburg 1976).[19]

The *dharnas*, rallies, felicitation ceremonies, *juluses*, *gherao*, *rasta roko*, and other "contentious performances" bring residents together and help them articulate their right to be counted. The cultural idioms and performances of resistance contribute to invocation of community sentiments, display of numerical strength, and reinvigoration of solidarity in the neighborhoods. Further, the planning of various *rann-nitis* becomes effective during resistance demonstrations. The resistance activities result from various historical configurations (Heller 2000). The historical configuration considered here includes the dire situation of demolition, the numerical and organizational strength of community members, the spatiality of the neighborhood, the commitment of activist groups, the integrity of intermediaries in the neighborhoods, proximity to state officials or politicians, and the effective formulation as well as enactment of *rann-nitis* that determine the course of resistance.

The performances of resistance "become embedded in particular cultural and social practices" (Michelutti 2007: 639). The performances embedded in such vernacular idioms as *antim yatra* (funeral procession), rhetorical linguistic expressions, effigy burning, and symbolic attacks on government and powerful groups spearhead the claims to be recognized in the city. The poor deploy various performative devices including fiery speeches, performances in street theaters in the neighborhoods, and demonstrations in front of the houses of the politicians to systematically claim their right to be counted. A whole host of factors shape the relative success and failure of particular modes of resistance in particular historical conjunctures. The poor invent various *rann-nitis* of resistance in engaging with the calculative governmentality of the state, as discussed in this chapter. The resistance repertoire draws on various context-specific cultural idioms and performances. Along with participation and negotiation, resistance activities constitute an integral aspect of numerical citizenship struggles in Delhi.

NUMERICAL CITIZENSHIP AND THE POLITICAL AGENCY OF THE URBAN POOR

THE RIGHT TO BE COUNTED examines the neo-liberal urban restructuring processes, consequent dispossession and impoverishment, and the *rann-nitis* of the poor in forging their right to the city.[1] While the abandonment of passive revolution in urban planning—the reformist agenda that secured minimal redistribution in the city—deepens urban dispossession, the poor have deployed a range of improvised and ingenious tactics to reclaim the city. In foregrounding "the right to be counted," I argue that the idea of numerical citizenship contributes to a theory of substantive citizenship that challenges the formal aspects of citizenship (Chatterjee 2004; Holston 2008: 22; Holston and Appadurai 1996: 190; Jayal 2013; Marx [1843] 2000). The struggles associated with the right to be counted expose the contradiction between a "theoretical embrace of equality" and an "acute polarization of real-life opportunities and satisfactions" (Wallerstein 2003: 650). While the state policies espouse normative and liberal principles of inclusion, the poor are systematically excluded from accessing their citizenship entitlements in the city. In response, the poor develop an extraordinary array of *rann-nitis* to lay their claim to the city.

As a theory and practice of citizenship (see Anand 2017; Anjaria 2011; Ong 1999: 32; Zhang 2002: 313), the framework of the right to be counted resonates with popular struggles in other megacities of the world. My approach draws on but also departs from James Holston's (2008) theory of "insurgent citizenship." Holston analyzes how the poor in the Brazilian context make persistent attempts to participate in urban governance by demanding equal rights to the city, extending horizontal solidarities, and challenging patron-client relationships in accessing services (Holston 2008: 248–49). In the Brazilian context, the poor put forth their demands as "contributor/stakeholder rights" (Holston 2008: 260); that is, they claim public services and social welfare as taxpayers, consumers, and property owners. This formulation of insurgent citizenship cannot be wholly extended to the Indian context, however, where urban politics are frequently forged solely in terms of patron-client relationships. While the poor often articulate their rights as citizens by developing horizontal solidarity, they do not usually articulate their rights as property owners and taxpayers in Delhi since they would lose the right of resettlement if they possessed properties in the city.[2] To a large extent, my approach to understanding collective struggles among the poor in Delhi resonates with Asef Bayat's work on housing and livelihood options in noninstitutional arenas in the Middle East, although I address institutionalized activities of the poor as well (see Bayat 1997: 58). Furthermore, the poor in Delhi do not claim their right to the city primarily through atomized and non-collective struggles but by forging collective solidarity (compare Bayat 2010).

To attend to the contextual specificity of Indian cities, I draw on the work of Sudipta Kaviraj and Partha Chatterjee in pushing for a situated understanding of citizenship—an understanding that is sensitive to a sequential view of democracy. However, I depart from Chatterjee's tendency to treat "the poor" as a heuristic category of enumerable "populations" that are mainly amenable to state calculations (Chatterjee 2004; Chatterjee 2011; see Routray 2014). In contrast, I examine the nuances and complexities of the political agency of the poor as they encounter state calculations and complex institutional and non-institutional arrangements. Chatterjee has argued for the need to theorize the critical salience of "community" to understand the peculiar nature of democracy in the non-Western world. While this book shows that collective solidarity is critical in mobilizing for the political right to be counted, I differ from his philosophical argument that the community does not represent "the body of citizens" but, rather, constitutes an instrumental category for the developmental machinations of the state (Chatterjee 1998: 281). Nevertheless, in the spirit of Chatterjee and Kaviraj, I have formulated the framework of numerical citizenship in a way that contests an abstract and universal conception of citizenship in an effort to foreground a more nuanced and contextual theory of citizenship struggles, processes, and relationships. In so doing, I illustrate how the poor build numerous relations and alliances across the political, social, and economic spectrum in their fight for recognition and visibility. This book details how the poor forge collective solidarity by embedding themselves in a myriad of relationships as they invent kinship networks and build alliances to claim their right to the city.

By detailing ethnographic engagements in multiple sites, I show how the poor foreground their claims as citizens, and how their claims of substantive citizenship entitlements are gained outside the conventional terms of liberal theory. In demanding services, contesting displacement, and claiming resettlement, the poor engage in a range of performative politics. They resort to political mediations via a range of intermediaries, and they deploy institutional means to demand services and basic infrastructure. They fight legal battles not just in the courts but also through the *rann-nitis* of petitioning and shaming, and by using pressure tactics to contest their displacement or to claim resettlement. They invoke not only moral claims (Chatterjee 1998: 281; V. Das 2011: 324) but also constitutional rights—they visit offices, petition the authorities through letters, carry out self-surveys, contest state arbitration by invoking the Right to Information, and engage in practices of authentication and counterfeiting in order to prove their eligibility for various services and rights. As I argue throughout this book, the agency of the poor is entwined with state practices: the poor respond to the contradictory intentions and goals of various state agencies by either partaking in or subverting the quotidian practices of the state. Furthermore, I have shown how changing political regimes shape the citizenship struggles of the poor. The *rann-nitis* of numerical citizenship operate in the context of democratic passive revolutions, where the state advances a reformist agenda in taking care of the poor (see Chatterjee 2008b; Gramsci 2000; Kaviraj 1988). While the neo-liberal model of state intervention continues to erode the redistributive claims of citizenship, I have also examined how the rise of populist parties like the AAP upended neo-liberal policies. In particular, I have shown how the policy of the AAP has redistributed wealth by subsidizing a range of public goods in the city.

In short, I have argued that numerical citizenship, which entails the forging of a collective solidarity, is articulated in terms of a demographic calculus. I have also examined how the dynamic nature of social spaces, the temporal dimensions of everyday struggles, and social divisions shape the *rann-nitis* of the poor, and it is to these issues that I turn below.

THE *RANN-NITI* OF DEMOGRAPHIC CALCULUS

The politics of numbers constitutes a pivotal aspect of democracy in the Global South. Instead of focusing on illegality, I foreground how demography itself is constituted as a *rann-niti* in the realm of urban citizenship. The demographic calculus—the strategic deployment of the numerical strength of a political community—does not merely convey an additive force of atomized individuals who show their numerical strength at an event or demonstration. I argue that the demographic calculus also turns the passive processes of state calculations—monitoring, surveillance, and bureaucratic documentation—into an active process of building community and forging solidarity. In this vein, the right to be counted is a struggle for legibility, visibility, and enlisting; it is a contingent and contextual struggle to lay claims to space and infrastructure in the city. In their attempts to be identified, the poor engage in *rann-nitis* that include processes of locality-building and recognition, as well as court battles to contest planning, legal erasure, and exclusionary classifications, and they employ numerous idioms of negotiation and resistance in the form of inscriptive strategies, public speech acts, and popular performances.[3]

Despite divisions and cleavages, the poor deploy local intermediaries who belong to their own communities in order to build *jhuggis* (hutments) in the abandoned and vacant niches of the city. By forging *ristedari* (relationships) and *bhai-chara* (brotherhood), they overcome the hostility of the police, the bureaucratic apparatus, and host populations.

Fighting real and putative threats as a community often leads to efforts that favor the residents' induction into the electoral database. State recognition of the community becomes the threshold for undertaking a range of political performances in mobilizing for numerical citizenship. For instance, the poor forge and invent village, caste, community, and kinship networks to demonstrate their numerical strength in organizing against demolitions. They then draw on affective ties and community sentiments to mobilize demonstrations in their fight for basic services and resettlement in the city.

The deployment of numerical strength as a *rann-niti* to lay claims to space and infrastructure implicitly or explicitly draws on three overlapping premises: (1) demonstration of strength is a bargaining power in electoral democracy, which in turn (2) builds collective solidarity, and which often entails (3) improvisations to establish numerical documentation of residence in the city. As I show, the intermediaries mobilize a kind of arithmetic calculus to engage in vote-bank politics, which catalyzes demands for differential treatment through patron-client relationships, instead of appealing to abstract principles of liberal justice. The intermediaries demonstrate numerical strength by canvassing and sloganeering during elections, and they display strength by carrying out rallies and *dharnas* and by organizing road blockades to contest demolitions or to demand services. As I argue in Chapters 5 and 6, one common *rann-niti* is to threaten the ruling establishment that the residents will defect en masse to other political parties if they do not receive their citizenship entitlements. Despite *bhed bhav* (discrimination) and social fault lines in the community, the poor forge locality-based identities and collective solidarity, often by tempering their individualist motivations with a sense of the need to forge collective struggles. The residents engage in both peaceful and militant performances of resistance in the neighborhoods, chanting slogans such as *"Awaaz do, Hum Saath Hai!"* (Say it aloud, we are together!) or *"Ek Pe Hamla, Sab Pe Hamla!"* (Attack on one is attack on all!) to demonstrate their numerical strength and to reinvent the bonds of community solidarity. The *rann-niti* of documenting their numerical presence is pivotal as residents collect and preserve, authenticate and counterfeit documents that systematically address the *kami* (lack) of documentary resources in their community.

THE SPATIAL AND TEMPORAL UNDERPINNINGS OF URBAN CITIZENSHIP

The political *rann-nitis* of the poor differ with respect to their urban status and degree of emplacement in different social spaces, as this book shows. The dynamic process of the production of social spaces includes the everyday activities of people across the socio-economic spectrum, the abstract imagination of experts and urbanists, the concrete deployment of city plans and policies, and the political struggles over claims to urban space (Lefebvre 1991). Urban social spaces such as Gautam Nagar *jhuggi jhopri* settlement, Sitapuri transit camp, and Azad resettlement colony embody and express concrete social, economic, legal, and political relations. Although Delhi's poor experience similar exigencies of life, the *rann-nitis* they employ vary across social spaces. The primary *rann-nitis* in these social spaces include activities that help them negotiate and secure livelihoods in the informal and formal sectors of the economy (see also Routray 2021). They struggle to build *jhuggi*s, forestall demolitions, and demand basic services and resettlement.

The social reproduction of life in the city is contingent on the legality and relative permanence of social spaces, such as when residents entrenched themselves in an incremental manner in the social space of Gautam Nagar. Their labor sustained the industries in their locality and contributed to the social reproduction of middle-class neighborhoods adjacent to their neighborhood. Gradually state recognition obtained at least in part from the *rann-nitis* of the poor had afforded them relative permanence and some basic services. The foremost *rann-niti* in Gautam Nagar involved struggles to delay or stall demolitions and pursue basic activities for their livelihood. Neo-liberal restructuring aimed at capital accumulation and beautification of urban space has led to the demolition of a portion of Gautam Nagar, after which the main *rann-niti* was aimed at demanding resettlement through struggles with politicians, activists, interlocutors, lawyers, and government officials.

Similarly, the abstract imagination of planners has shaped the contours of the social space of Sitapuri, where the relocation of a displaced but state-defined "eligible" population in a green zone has made their lives even more precarious. The spatial practices of the planners, judges, and middle-class residents in the adjoining Lakshmi colony have overlapped and also conflicted with one another at different conjunctures. Most importantly, the *rann-nitis* of the residents laid claims to permanence and infrastructure, stalled demolitions, and allowed the residents to carry out production and social reproduction activities in the vicinity. In a similar way, the production of the social space of the Azad resettlement colony was also an upshot of the abstract imagination of the planners and judges. The eligible displaced population from elsewhere was resettled in the Azad resettlement colony, which had been developed on a damp and marshy riverbed. The production of the Azad resettlement colony was marked by dispossessions and deaths in the margins of Delhi. Following political negotiations and struggles, especially through the *rann-nitis* waged on behalf of numerical citizenship, the residents demanded infrastructure and services and transformed the topography of the social space of the resettlement colony in an incremental way (cf. Katz 2002). In other words, the topography of Azad resettlement colony tells us how social space is produced through the intersection of abstract planning, dispossessions due to displacement and resettlement, the spatial practices of everyday life, and the lived politics of numerical citizenship.

My argument about the production of these social spaces is coterminous with a temporal frame of analysis. When describing the temporal dimensions of social practices and struggles, I have analyzed how different social spaces are produced through the processes of incremental entrenchment. Thus, I have gone beyond a "sedentarist bias" (V. Das 1996: 1512), in which the situations described are assumed to be stable or static, to illustrate the dynamic nature of social practices of the poor that shape and are also shaped by spatial-temporal transformations (see Massey 2005; Soja 1989). As I have argued, the citizenship project of the poor is premised on their incremental quest for legibility, visibility, and the numerical documentation of existence in the city. I show how the primary struggle of the poor entails changing their urban status from being migrants without claims to space and infrastructure to that of citizens with state-recognized entitlements in the city. I adopt an extended temporal frame to address the historical conjunctures that shape the political economy of urban planning, the shifting character of state calculations, changing political regimes, transfigurations of the roles of multiple interlocutors, and the permutations and combinations of the *rann-nitis* of the poor. In emphasizing how these struggles unfold over time, I show how the poor deploy incremental tactics to entrench themselves in various spaces and establish their presence and eligibility for citizenship claims. In redressing the *kami* (lack) in their proof documents, for example, the poor narrate their own biographies, especially those fragments which attest to their belonging in the city. Proving their presence and cultivating a sense of belonging with respect to state authorities is central to their claims of citizenship. In the process, they invoke the memory of co-residents in their neighborhood to authenticate the temporal sequence of events as part of a coherent life-story (cf. Carsten 2000). Their presence is interlaced with their sense of the temporal sequence of events, such as the precise moment of their arrival in the city,[4] participation in political events and elections, efforts at claiming state services, and experiences of upward or downward mobility as well as accidents or misfortune. Their ability to co-narrate their experiences with neighbors and kin members and to prove their presence at such events become salient in their demands for recognition, especially if there is any *kami* in their "proof" documents.

My emphasis on the temporal dimensions of struggles should not be understood to suggest that the progression of citizenship rights is inevitable, as liberal thinkers such as Marshall (2009) have been understood to argue. Instead, I show how citizenship is instantiated in uneven, incremental, and heterogeneous ways, such as when *rann-nitis* counteract the tyranny of neo-liberal accumulation, beautification, and state power. Likewise, protracted citizenship projects are often ruptured by demolitions; loss of status; forfeiture of claims among ineligible residents; the withdrawal of political patronage; the hostile policies of municipal, planning, and the judiciary apparatuses; and missing documents, as well as both voluntary and involuntary relocation to native villages. Thus, while these struggles are incremental, the outcomes are contingent on the nature of state policies, patronage structures, social locations and divisions in the neighborhood, the spatial layout of the settlement, and the involvement of a range of actors engaged in political, bureaucratic, and legal struggles. As a consequence, the citizenship project of the poor is "never cumulative, linear, or evenly distributed" in Delhi (see also Anand 2017; Holston 2008: 15).

GRADED LEGITIMACY AND THE CONUNDRUMS OF COLLECTIVE SOLIDARITY: *HUM KAGAZ NAHIN DIKHAYENGE* (WE WILL NOT SHOW THE PAPERS!)[5]

My primary focus in this book is to capture the full range of *rann-nitis*—not only the resistance tactics—of the poor. I have shown how the *rann-nitis* are dependent on particular historical contexts and contingencies. In showing these complexities and contradictions, I have analyzed the transformations of *rann-nitis* over an extended period. While the poor participate in and negotiate with the policies of the state, especially when they seek infrastructure and subsidized food in their neighborhood, they also contest and at times militantly resist threats of demolition and withdrawal of services. At times they draw on the support of a range of middle-class activists and interlocutors, but at other times they evade the advice and suggestions of others. As a result, the *rann-nitis* of the poor are constantly negotiated and evolving, and so they do not exhibit uniformity in thought and action.

While the poor draw on inter-community and intra-community solidarity in their claims for citizenship entitlements, the category of urban poor is never stable or monolithic. Collective solidarity is often tenuous and arrived at based on various contingencies, since the experience of urban dispossession and negotiated political outcome is never a universal or uniform experience (see Collins 2000; Crenshaw 1989; Tharu and Niranjana 1994). Rather, solidarity is refracted through specific social locations based on income, caste, gender, religion, regional origin, political affiliation, and, as I have shown, urban status based on possession of documents. Furthermore, there are divisions between allottees and purchasers, and among residents who own houses in better-serviced parts of the neighborhood versus those who suffocate in congested parts. As a result, the assertion of numerical strength is often tenuous. In the name of unity, solidarity, and strength a particular section of the poor may mobilize struggles that have differential effects across the social spectrum. As this book illustrates, the most marginalized among the poor often lose out on receiving decent plots, scarce urban resources, and a range of basic entitlements.

The efforts to forge collective solidarity and the *rann-nitis* of the poor recently received a jolt when the Government of India passed the Citizenship Amendment Act (CAA) on December 12, 2019.[6] The act offers an option for persecuted religious communities in Afghanistan, Bangladesh, and Pakistan—any person belonging to a Hindu, Sikh, Buddhist, Jain, Parsi or Christian community—to obtain Indian citizenship. But the act does not include persecuted sects within the Muslim community, including Ahmadiyya, nor does it include atheists and persecuted non-religious minorities in these countries. Moreover, the act does not address the persecution of minority religious communities including Christians, Rohingya Muslims, and Tamil Hindus in the respective neighboring countries of Bhutan, Myanmar, and Sri Lanka.[7] Along with the passing of this act, the government has planned to prepare the National Population Register (NPR) to build a database of residents in India. Furthermore, the government has initiated a plan to follow the NPR by preparing the National Register of Citizens (NRC) for Indian citizens,[8] along the lines of the NRC in the northeastern state of Assam. Assam has witnessed the immigration of many Bangladeshi people since Indian independence, with many arriving as religious refugees and others coming in search of a better economic livelihood. As the number of Bangladeshi migrants increased, Assamese people have mobilized and carried out violent struggles against this migration in order to retain their distinct ethnic identity and to secure the scarce state resources for natives of the region. In 1985, with the signing of the Assam accord, anyone who migrated into Assam after March 24, 1971, just two days before Bangladesh declared independence from Pakistan, had to be deported back to Bangladesh.[9]

The NRC in Assam is aimed at purging the "illegal" migrants by differentiating between citizens and non-citizens on the basis of proper documentation and family legacy data (Birla, Jha, and Kumari 2020). As a result of this exercise, approximately 1.9 million people have been rendered stateless—ironically, a majority of them, approximately 1.2 million, turned out to be Hindus.[10] Although the Hindus have the option of obtaining citizenship on the basis of the CAA, Muslims do not have such an option. The government has also proposed to build detention centers across the country for people who are unable to prove their citizenship in the country.[11] Extending citizenship to non-Muslim minorities and excluding Muslim migrants who have lived in the country for a long time will undermine the secular fabric of the Indian nation-state. Commentators have remarked that the CAA aims at the "first *de jure* attempt to make India a Hindu Rastra [nation-state]."[12] Furthermore, as the political theorist Niraja Jayal (2019) argues, the act marks a shift from the principle of jus soli (birth-based citizenship) to the consolidation of the principle of jus sanguinis (descent-based citizenship) within the current policy of granting Indian citizenship.[13]

The act has precipitated unprecedented anxieties among Muslim populations all over India. The apprehensions of Muslims in Delhi, especially poor Muslims, is warranted as it is difficult to distinguish between Muslims who have migrated from neighboring countries and Indian Muslims who have migrated from other states in India. It is likely that poor Bengali Muslims (Bangla-speaking Muslims from both Bangladesh and the Indian state of West Bengal) will experience dispossession and marginalization disproportionately. Irrespective of their origin, poor Bengali Muslims, especially women systematically identified as "Bangladeshis," are harassed and are exploited by state agencies, and police routinely extort their earnings and savings to simply allow them to live in the city (D. Das 2021). Moreover, even though some Muslim residents in *jhuggis* may come from Bangladesh, there is still a need to address their rights in the city. Bangladeshi Muslims have lived in the city for a long time— some have acquired proof documents, voted for various political parties in both the assembly and parliamentary elections, contributed to the profitability of capitalist businesses, or done a variety of work in middle-class households.

All over Delhi poor Muslim residents have mobilized and demonstrated against the trio of CAA-NPR-NRC, culminating in the famous Shaheen Bagh protests among primarily poor and lower-income Muslim women from mid-December 2019 until the COVID-19 lockdown in late March 2020 in Delhi.[14] These events have already fractured the unity and solidarity of the residents of Gautam Nagar, Sitapuri, and Azad resettlement colony. The residents I spoke to since the Shaheen Bagh protests have deliberated over the call for a Hindu Rashtra (nation), their experiences with xenophobia and Islamophobia, and the predicament they face in obtaining documents and family legacy data. Speaking to me by phone in early May 2020, JR argued, "We do not have many who oppose the CAA in Gautam Nagar. Only the Muslim *samaj* (society), especially in Jamia area, oppose this and proclaim their own law there. The country was partitioned on the basis of religion. The Muslims created an Islamic state in Pakistan. But we have not been able to create a Hindu Rashtra so far. Wherever Muslims are a majority, say for instance in Jamia, they drive you out from there. You cannot find a single Hindu house there. They are producing twelve children per household. There is too much freedom for them in India." Having made his point about the need for a Hindu Rashtra, JR then recited statistics about the suffering of Hindus in Pakistan, the decreasing Hindu population in Pakistan, and the increasing Muslim population in India. JR has been an active member of the Hindu nationalist organization Rashtriya Swayamsevak Sangh (RSS) since he arrived in the city in the early 1990s. When he spoke to me over the phone, he had just returned from distributing food on behalf of his organization during the COVID-19 lockdown in the neighborhood. Much of what JR (and also his friends who prompted him) argued constituted the standard invectives that one associates with the hyper-nationalist rhetoric of the RSS. JR is convinced that the *ghuspaithiyas* (infiltrators)—a term that Home Minister Amit Shah contributed to the everyday nationalist political lexicon—must be ousted from India.

Similarly, P argued, "People support CAA-NPR-NRC in Sitapuri. Muslims are unnecessarily getting alarmed. The politicians and *maulanas* (Muslim religious leaders) are provoking them. This law is to evict illegal

Bangladeshis out of this country and not allow any new Bangladeshi Muslim immigrant in the country. Muslims are a numerical minority in the transit camp. Wherever they are in the majority they protest." P went on to argue that this is just a political gimmick on the part of the Congress party and the AAP—the parties that treat the Muslims as their vote bank. "If everyone has to live in this country," he queried, "then why did they carve out Pakistan from India?" Similarly, C of Gautam Nagar argued, "There is a religious war waging in the entire world. People who belong to our own faith suffer elsewhere and must come into our country." By drawing distinctions among Hindus and Muslims, the residents attempt to mark what Ann Stoler describes as the "internal frontier" (Stoler 2000: 325, drawing on Johann Fichte and Etienne Balibar). Stoler argues that internal frontiers "nurture intimately held dispositions of difference" that morally police the nation and the self against pollution (Stoler 2017: 3). Here, Hindu residents participate in hegemonic attempts to amplify anxieties about unfamiliar Muslims who threaten the safety and purity of self and nation.

Residents opposing CAA-NPR-NRC have argued that the *mahol* (ambience) in the neighborhoods has been vitiated. Hindus tease Muslims in front of their houses by pronouncing pro-Hindu and supposedly nationalist slogans during election campaigns and processions. Today even children display stereotypical prejudices against Muslims in the area. Residents have said that Muslims are derogatorily referred to as *katwa* (the cut one), referring to the practice of circumcision among Muslims, without any hesitation. Others note that people have distributed relief materials within religious lines during the COVID-19 crisis. There have also been attempts to spread rumors and initiate riots in Sitapuri transit camp and Azad resettlement camp. As JA notes, "People have turned into *andha bhakts* [blind followers]. There have been riots in the northeast of Delhi [Shiv Vihar, Gokulpuri, Mustafabad]. They have destroyed the entire belt, and most of the victims have been Muslims. The official figures indicate that approximately 50 died during the riots. But around 400 people are missing from the area. I have relatives and acquaintances there. I know the situation. Luckily, we did not experience any riots in Sitapuri despite numerous rumors."

Sinister propaganda from various sources suggests that the CAA protects Hindus and also provides them an ideal space for their prosperity in India. While some Hindus have celebrated the law, Muslims in these neighborhoods witnessed this jubilation in silence. As B summarized, "Muslims did not openly demonstrate against the act because they are a minority in the Hindu majority areas of Gautam Nagar, Sitapuri, and Azad resettlement colony. Today, anybody who protests against any state policy is seen as a traitor of the country." JP, living in Azad resettlement colony, avers, "Muslims are feeling threatened and selling their houses and buying properties in Muslim areas." The purported numerical insignificance of Muslims in these field sites have further pushed them to the margins. While poor and lower-middle-class Muslims of Shaheen Bagh, which is approximately 4 kilometers from Azad resettlement colony, staged demonstrations against the law, Muslim residents in Azad resettlement colony felt intimidated about expressing their anxiety and fears. Muslims recognize the *bhed bhav* (discrimination) in this particular law that proclaims the extension of citizenship to non-Indian Hindus, and they question the ability of the state to provide food, work, and medicines to Indian citizens. In contrast, some Hindus celebrate the aim to reduce the Muslim population of India, which they believe will open up better employment opportunities and balance competition over scarce resources and infrastructure in the neighborhood.

A multitude of documents were not accepted as proof of Indian citizenship during the initial exercise of building the NRC database in Assam.[15] Muslim residents all over India and particularly in Shaheen Bagh in Delhi led the movement against CAA-NPR-NRC. The common refrain was "*hum kagaz nahin dikhayenge*" (We will not show the papers!). As AR of Azad resettlement colony notes, "Whatever happened in Assam spun their [government representatives'] heads. The same thing will happen if NRC is implemented all over India. A greater number of Hindus than Muslims will struggle to produce proper documents. They will regularize the Hindus by invoking CAA, but Muslims will suffer and only find their place in the detention camps. We fought against the white people for the independence of this country. But our own people are hurting us now." AR argued that the government has been spreading venom on a continuous basis, along with the "the *godi* media" (a common way of referring to the media as being on the "lap" of the ruling establishment and advancing the agendas of the government rather than reporting on issues in India in a critical or neutral way). He reminisced that people used to live in relative peace and harmony and shared *dukh* and *taklif* (sorrows and difficulties) in their *jhuggi* neighborhoods and in the Azad resettlement colony after they were resettled. Detesting the loss of a time when people could live in *talmel* (in sync), he loathed the toxic *mahol* (ambience) in his neighborhood.

As I have argued in this book, the ability to produce documentary evidence has remained central in the struggles for citizenship in the city. However, the citizens must now produce proof documents in addition to providing family legacy data. As MB of Sitapuri exclaimed, "The government has hung swords over our heads, which will threaten us forever." Many Muslims in Delhi, especially those who do not have ancestral land anymore, fear that they will be kicked out of the country. Before the COVID-19 crisis, many poor Muslims scampered back to their villages to collect documents, especially land documents. As B argues, "The *patwaris* [state officials who maintain the land records] have hit a purple patch; they are making loads of money as the residents are clamoring to receive land records and ancestral legacy data tracing back several generations." In addition to fighting for everyday survival, the poor must now engage with the tedious and arbitrary bureaucratic procedures of proving legacy and producing documents. In the words of JA, "People who do not fight for *buniyadi* [fundamental] problems, including housing, electricity, water, and school education for their children, may have the time to collect documents and prove family legacy. But the poor will get mentally tortured." While many residents complain about the difficulties of collecting documents, JR of Gautam Nagar argued otherwise. "It is very easy to collect four or five documents in this country," he asserted. "Do you not think the village headmen can authenticate their identity if they cannot produce any documents?" Ironically, JR's own documents were rejected by the state when he had applied for a resettlement flat, and he only succeeded in becoming an eligible beneficiary after a lot of *bhaag-daud* (running around) and *kharcha-pani* (bribe-related spending).

While collective solidarity and sharing *dukh taklif* (sorrows and difficulties) among residents have dissipated considerably in the aftermath of the enactment of CAA, repressed anxiety and hatred have raised their ugly heads in transforming the *mahol* (ambience) of the neighborhoods. An optimistic assessment of events as they unfold may emphasize the impossibility of evicting all the Muslims in the country. However, it is likely that many Muslim residents of the city will be targeted and harassed to prove their citizenship. It is ironic that people of Gautam Nagar, Sitapuri transit camp, and Azad resettlement colony did not resist the CAA and the implementation of the NRC. It is obvious that there is considerable dissensus among the residents in the three neighborhoods. While the majority of Hindu residents do not anticipate any difficulty in enlisting and recording themselves on the NRC, Muslims have grown increasingly suspicious and anxious about this project. As I argue in the Introduction and demonstrate in subsequent chapters, collective solidarity is often a tenuous project. However, the current political climate and the enactment of the law have disrupted the unity of the people. Nevertheless, it is misleading to interpret CAA-NPR-NRC as merely anti-Muslim. While it is very likely that the act will disenfranchise Muslim communities in a disproportionate way, it will also create tremendous difficulties for the poor in the city. As discussed in Chapter 4, the poor, most of whom are non-Muslims, struggle to produce proper documents to obtain a plethora of rights in the city. In particular, their experiences with waiting and humiliation, orthographic anxieties, and state condescension as they strive to document citizenship are described. But the design of the NRC confers graded legitimacy on different communities in their claim to social rights, political belonging, and citizenship (cf. Jayal 2019).

To sum up, in this book I have offered an analysis of extant urban dispossessions and the *rann-nitis* of the poor in Delhi. Although numerical citizenship struggles have only socialized collective spaces to a limited extent and have not been able to reorder land relations in any substantial way, the poor continue to forge their right to be counted. Furthermore, the increasing marginalization of Muslims foregrounds urgent and persistent questions about achieving equality of citizenship status and political belonging while highlighting what is at stake in struggles for the right to the city.

GLOSSARY OF HINDI TERMS

abadi	inhabited/homestead
aham	false ego
ahankar ki laxmi or ghamand ki devi	adjectives for "arrogant" women
andha bhakts	blind followers
antim yatra	funeral procession
antyodaya	poorest of the poor
asli	genuine
aukaad	one's social location determined by a range of capital or identity
babu	state official
badmaash	bad
baghawat	rebellion
behena	sister
bhaag-daud	running around
bhadra mahila	genteel woman
bhagidari	partnership
bhai	brother
bhai-chara	brotherhood
bhajan	devotional song
bhangi	a person from an oppressed caste engaged in scavenging work
bhed-bhav	discrimination
bhook hartal	hunger strike
bhoo-mafia	land mafia
bhram	misconception
bidi	a cigarette filled with tobacco and wrapped in a leaf
bijli	electricity
biradari	community
buniyadi	fundamental

chamchagiri	sycophancy
charpai	woven jute cot
chetna badhana	consciousness raising
dabaab	pressure
dada	bully
daftar	office
dalal	tout/broker
daldal	marshy
dhakka khao	shoving and pushing/struggling
dharma	right conduct
dharna	peaceful gatherings
dikhawa	showing off
dukandari	running of shops
dukh-dard/dukh-taklif	sorrows-suffering/sorrows-difficulties
farzi	counterfeit
galli	lane
gandh	dirt
gawahi	witness
ghapla	wrongdoings
gharelu samasya ka kaam	work related to domestic problems
ghat	riverbank
gherao	encirclement
ghuspaithiyas	infiltrators
girwi	mortgage
godi	lap
guldasta	bouquet
hafta	extortion of rent
haisiyat	capacity/status
halwai	an Indian confectionary
haq	rights
hata pai	roughing up
hera pheri	swindling
himmat	strength
jaan pehchaan	acquaintance
jagran	nighttime prayer meeting
jal	water
janamdata	creator
janata (or janta)	the people

jan suvidha	public utilities
jhuggi jhopri	improvised hutments made up of bricks, bamboo, iron railings, asbestos, and a variety of other materials
jhuggiwala	jhuggi resident
-ji	suffix commonly attached to names/titles as a mark of respect
jugaad	fixing
julus(es)	march(es)
kabadda	scrap
kabaddi	a team contact sport
kami	gaps or errors
katwa	the cut one
khaas aadmi	special man
kharcha-pani	bribe-related spending
kiraya	rent
kothi	mansion on gigantic plot
kshyamata	capability
lakh	one hundred thousand
lalchi	greedy
lal dora	red thread
leher	wave
likhai-padhai ka kaam	work related to writing and reading
mahila mandal	women's organization
mahol	ambience
manav shrankhala	human chain
manmani	arbitrary decision
marg darshan	path-showing or guidance
maulanas	Muslim religious leaders
milne julne wale aadmi	men who mingle
mohalla	neighborhood
mota dimag	low intelligence
naarabaazi	sloganeering
nakli	counterfeit
nali-kharanja	drain and brick-road
nalla	drain
nasbandi	sterilization
naya neta	new leader

neta	leader
neta-giri	activities of leaders
niti	political policy or tactics
padhe-likhe	literacy
pahunch aur pakad	reach and hold
panchayat	council
pani	water
patwaris	state officials who maintain the land records
police ka chakar	dealings with police
pradhan	chief
pradhan-giri	activities of chiefs
puja path	religious ceremonies
pyraveekar	fixers
qayamat	judgment day
rahan-sahan	way of living
raja	king
Ram Bhajan	devotional song for Hindu god Ram
rann-niti	tactics or counter-tactics
rashtra	nation-state
rasta roko	road blockade
ristedari	relationships
saashan	rule
samadhi	tomb/mausoleum
samaj	society
samaj sevak	social worker
samiti	committee
sangharsh samiti	struggle committee
sarkar	government
sarkari karmachari	government worker
seva	service
sevak	worker
sunwai	hearing/trial
swagat samaroh	welcome ceremony
swarth	selfish reasons
talmel	to be in sync
tasalli	consolation
tehkikat	investigation

thekedari	contract work
tod phod	breaking
tu tu mein mein	argument
vikas ka kaam	development-related work

NOTES

INTRODUCTION

1. In addressing the agency of the poor, I analyze the complexity of individual as well as collective political imagination and action, the building of social relations and allegiances, everyday improvisations, and the public performance in which the urban poor engage in the face of state power and agencies of urban governance. In other words, the poor participate and negotiate with and even resist state ideas, calculations, and practices in order to subsist and claim citizenship entitlements in the city.

2. The phrase "the right to be counted" has also been used in academic and media debates and in church sermons to address the extent of undercounting of various communities during census recording in the US. My use of the phrase is to underscore the quest of poor migrants in the city to attain visibility, legibility, and eligibility to obtain citizenship rights. In doing so, I also show how the poor assert their numerical strength and demographic calculus to obtain welfare rights. I owe the phrase "demographic calculus" to Ajantha Subramanian and other participants in my book workshop at the Political Anthropology and Political Ecology Working Group meeting at Harvard University.

3. I deploy the idea of governmentality as understood and used by Foucauldian scholars. Thus, I analyze the techno-bureaucratic ensemble of discourses, calculative interventions, and practices of the state that are aimed at governing, improving, and rehabilitating the urban poor in Delhi (see Ferguson 2006; Sanyal 2007). See also endnote 9 for a discussion of Foucault's theory of governmentality.

4. The *jhuggi jhopri* hutments are made up of bricks, bamboo, iron railings, asbestos, and a variety of other materials. The terminology assigned to settlements inhabited by the poor is often derogatory and politically loaded. Nevertheless, I retain the state-designated terms—such as *jhuggi jhopri*, transit camps, and resettlement colonies—to illustrate ambiguities in planning discourse and distinct modalities of struggles and in order to avoid confusion.

5. I formally started my ethnographic research in April 2010. However, I also draw on my interactions and experiences during court proceedings, public events, and meetings from November 2009 through March 2010.

6. I use pseudonyms or abbreviations of names for my research interlocutors to protect their privacy throughout this book.

7. I discuss the category of unauthorized colony in more detail in Chapter 2.

8. There is a growing body of scholarship on the politics of urban restructuring in Delhi. Amita Baviskar (2003) has analyzed "bourgeois environmentalism" and middle-class activism, and Veronique Dupont (2011) has addressed neo-liberal reforms shaping the space and politics in Delhi. Additionally, many scholars have investigated the role of

the judiciary (Bhan 2016; Bhuwania 2017; Ghertner 2015; Ramanathan 2006; Sharan 2002) in "slum" demolitions in the city. The changing logic of the judiciary has been analyzed in great detail. For instance, Asher Ghertner (2015) analyzes the aesthetic codes promoted by planning organizations and the judiciary that contribute to disenfranchisements in the city, and Gautam Bhan (2016) examines the "emergent rationalities" of the judiciary, which in turn are shaped by the planning protocols of Delhi Development Authority. In a thorough examination of public interest litigations (PILs), Anuj Bhuwania (2017) provides an analysis of the procedural departures and peculiarities that characterize the arbitrary vision of the judiciary, which make possible both progressive and regressive judgments with respect to the urban poor. Similarly, Usha Ramanathan (2006) has analyzed how the judiciary has invented a legality that turns the poor into encroachers without any rights in the city, and Awadhendra Sharan (2002) has questioned the notion of "public interest" proffered by the judiciary to legitimize slum demolitions in the city. Furthermore, the accumulation strategies in real estate development and the building of malls, expressways, and metro railways have exacerbated land conflicts and dispossession in the city (Dupont 2011; Bon 2016; Searle 2016). Thus, the poor have endured enormous suffering as a result of "slum" demolitions, industrial closures, and resettlement in Delhi (Batra and Mehra 2008; Menon-Sen and Bhan 2008; Nigam 2001; Padhi 2007; D. Roy 2000).

9. Drawing on Foucault's conceptualization of governmentality, critical scholars have shown how the generation of bureaucratic statistics constitutes a "technology of power" that establishes classifications, regularity, and probability (Hacking 1990: 181). Governmentality encompasses the "art of government" of every aspect of life, including the moral conduct of the self, with continuity between different kinds of government such as the economic management of resources and the political regulation of populations (Foucault 1991: 90–91). As Foucault argues, "We find at once a plurality of forms of government and their immanence to the state" (Foucault 1991: 91). Thus, Foucault's conceptualization of government is also a relational theory of how various spheres of life interact with each other both inside and beyond state control. In Foucault's conceptualization, population is the object of government of various spheres and kinds of government (Foucault 1991: 100). Thus, utilitarian measures, enumeration procedures, and welfare distribution aimed at populations all constitute tactics within the art of government. In Foucault's schema, statistical prediction techniques employed by modern state systems and arts of government weave a complex web of power relations that define deviant, vagrant, and criminal populations. Similarly, Ian Hacking (1990: 185) argues that statistics establish laws around probability, which he describes as the "taming of chance" that has eroded assumptions about natural and social determinacy while contributing to information and population control.

10. Foucault's insights offer critical perspectives on seemingly innocuous utilitarian measures that promote "pedagogical and disciplinary" doctrines (Appadurai 1996: 125) and the objectification of social life tendencies (Cohn 1987: 230) in modern state systems. It is also useful to explore the cultural practices of populations as a reflection of "the legitimation project of the state," as Cohn and Dirks (1988: 227) suggest.

11. Nikolas Rose (1999) also argues that the perspectives on "regimes of authority . . . share with Marxism and critical theory a profound unease about the values that pervade

our times. . . . They share a suspicious attention to the multitude of petty humiliations and degradations carried out in the name of our best interests" (60). In this sense, statistics are "one of the key modalities for the production of the knowledge necessary to govern" (209).

12. In the concluding chapter, Legg (2007) alludes to an analysis of resistance against colonial governmentality by analyzing both violent and non-violent protests in nationalist and also communal politics.

13. Chakrabarty and Chatterjee challenge the historicist idea of an empty, homogeneous time that defines capital and Western modernity and thereby direct our attention to the need for an ethnographic understanding of the lifeworlds of people in various cultures and settings (Chakrabarty 2000: 23; Chatterjee 2004: 6). Their attention to the peculiarity of practices addresses the heterogeneity of space-time against the inexorable march of capitalist modernity. Partha Chatterjee and Sudipta Kaviraj discuss the contradictions inherent in the norms of universal citizenship and how disadvantages and vulnerabilities shape the demands of particular groups (Chatterjee 2004: 4; Kaviraj 2005). Kaviraj argues for a sequential understanding of democracy and modernity that is accountable to historical difference (Kaviraj 2005: 497). Such an understanding challenges the commonplace view that the typical processes accompanying modernity—such as capitalist industrialization, the centralization of state power, and secularization in politics—emerge symmetrically and are functionally related (Kaviraj 2005: 508). In contrast to this historicist idea of modernity, he argues that the trajectories of capitalist modes of production, levels of wealth, poverty, literacy, universal suffrage, and processes of secularization and individuation are markedly different in post-colonial societies like India (Kaviraj 2005: 513). In general terms, "differences in historical conditions" give rise to differences in the nature and pattern of democracy, as epitomized in the improvisational character of "unprecedented features and institutional idiosyncrasies in different historical settings" (Kaviraj 2005: 522; see also Chatterjee 2011).

14. With a focus on the specificity of Indian democracy and drawing on the work of Kalyan Sanyal, Chatterjee (2008b) asserts that there is simultaneously a process of capitalist disenfranchisement and a reversal of the effects of these accumulation strategies through certain welfare policies for populations in India.

15. For instance, Chatterjee develops a Gramscian perspective to analyze how civil society is synonymous with bourgeois society, which in turn has taken on a hegemonic role in protecting the interests of the dominant class and also the middle class in India (Chatterjee 2004; Chatterjee 2008b). In the Gramscian definition, hegemony epitomizes a dynamic kind of class alliance wherein the dominant classes represent their own particular interest as the universal interest by securing the active consent of other groups of subordinated and exploited people (Gramsci 2000). Thus, according to Chatterjee, the dominant class is invested in the rapid growth of capital and metropolitan lifestyle, but the state has provided certain concessions by transferring a fraction of the accumulated resources to address the concerns of the subaltern classes in order to create the necessary political conditions for the functioning of capitalist democracy (Chatterjee 2008b).

16. Ananya Roy (2011: 224) provides the framework of "subaltern urbanism" to provide "accounts of the slum as a terrain of habitation, livelihood and politics."

17. In commenting on statecraft, Chatterjee (2011) distinguishes between *dharma* and *niti*. He refers to *dharma* as "right or appropriate conduct" and *niti* as political policy or tactics (54–55). Chatterjee notes a gradual preponderance of the principles of *niti* over *dharma* in Indian democracy. In turn, *niti* ties in well with his concept of political society. The poor deploy their *rann-niti* in dealing with the politicians and political parties in ways that often correspond with some of the *niti* aspects of statecraft. However, the poor also use the term *rann-niti* to refer to their negotiations with a range of state, para-statal, and non-state actors.

18. See Bjorkman (2014b) for a summary of the debates between liberal and post-colonial scholars on the theme of vote-bank politics. On the one hand, Bjorkman contests the liberal perspective that the process of vote banking manipulates and victimizes the poor by offering particularistic goods and by departing from programmatic politics of government provisioning and services (see also Breeding 2011: 74). On the other hand, she also departs from post-colonial scholars who celebrate the redistributive dynamics of political and legal exceptionalism inherent in vote-banking politics. Instead, she aptly suggests that vote banking constitutes the "very stuff of democratic politics" (Bjorkman 2014b: 180) wherein the poor successfully navigate the political and legal opacities to secure their entitlements in the city. In another perspective, Mary Breeding argues that vote banking has ceased to socially protect the poor; instead, it provides an opportunity for "conspicuous consumption on the part of political parties . . . during electoral canvassing" (Breeding 2011: 71). However, it can be argued that the reduction of vote banking to electoral canvassing does not provide insights into the everyday and complicated nature of the relationship between politicians and voters and social provisioning in the city (see also Auerbach 2020; Auerbach and Thachil 2018; Berenschot 2010). Furthermore, scholars have argued that vote-bank politics has furthered redistributive claims, but also deepened the vulnerabilities of the poor in the cities (Edelman and Mitra 2007). In this respect, as S. Benjamin and Raman (2001) argue, it is important to distinguish between party-based vote-bank politics (commonly associated with vote buying and trucking people to attend political rallies) and vote-bank politics that democratize access to resources, make local bureaucracy more responsive to everyday problems, and support claims against demolitions.

19. DUSIB, Agenda for the First Meeting of the Board, December 23, 2010, p. 17, http://delhishelterboard.in/dusib_board_agenda/1st_board_meeting_agenda_and_minutes.pdf, accessed May 18, 2020.

20. The political preferences in low-income neighborhood are not static. As I demonstrate throughout the book, the residents vote for various parties and often change their preferences in different points of time. However, various parties assess their political strength during elections and during a political tenure subsequently. If the elected members of a ruling party realize that a particular neighborhood did not vote for the party in a major way, then they may show lukewarm interest in extending services to the neighborhood. This was often asserted to me by the residents themselves.

21. US$1 was equivalent to approximately 45 Indian rupees in 2010–11 and 65 Indian rupees in 2017.

22. *Dalit* means oppressed. *Dalits* are at the bottom of the caste hierarchy in India.

23. For more information, visit Lok Raj Sangathan's website at http://www.lokraj.org .in/, accessed March 14, 2018.

24. For more information, visit Delhi Shramik Sangathan's website at https://delhidss .com/, accessed March 14, 2018.

CHAPTER 1

1. See Corbridge and Harriss (2001) for an analysis of development planning during the 1950s and early 1960s under the leadership of Prime Minister Jawaharlal Nehru.

2. The governance structure of Delhi is complex as it is a quasi-state with a multiplicity of governance structures. The Delhi Development Authority, which reports to the urban development ministry of the Government of India, is responsible for formulating land-use plans, including the city's Master Plan. Thus, both subjects of "land" and "law and order" remain within the jurisdiction of the Government of India (Planning Commission 2009: 31). The Municipal Corporation of Delhi carries out civic functions and comes under the jurisdiction of the Government of National Capital Territory of Delhi (GNCTD)—a quasi-state with its own assembly and council of ministers (Ghosh et al. 2009: 26). The Municipal Corporation of Delhi was divided into three municipal bodies in 2012 such as North Delhi Municipal Corporation, East Delhi Municipal Corporation, and South Delhi Municipal Corporation. The New Delhi Municipal Corporation and Delhi Cantonment are two additional local bodies maintaining two significant areas in Delhi. Other para-statal bodies in Delhi provide water (Delhi Jal Board) and mass transit (Delhi Transport Corporation) services (Ghosh et al. 2009: 26).

The multiplicity of governance structures has caused confusion and blatant indifference while allowing various agencies to conveniently bypass the issues. Furthermore, the resettlement colonies have been under the purview of different agencies at different times. Between 1962 and 1974, the Municipal Corporation of Delhi provided various services in the resettlement colonies. However, between 1974 and 1992, the resettlement colonies were under the purview of DDA. Then again, between 1992 and 2010, MCD was in charge of providing services in resettlement colonies. And since 2010, the resettlement colonies are under the purview of Delhi Urban Shelter Improvement Board—an agency specifically established to address the housing and infrastructural issues of the urban poor.

See Oldenburg (1976) for an analysis of the origin and development of MCD and its governance structure. Oldenburg also provides an illuminating analysis of power sharing and conflicts between councilors and administrators regarding administrative and civic responsibilities in the first two decades after Indian independence.

3. For an elaborate discussion of planning prior to the 1960s, see Sundaram (2010) and Mehra (2013). Mehra provides an account of the institutional power and speculative logic of the state that guided urban planning policies between 1936 and 1959 in Delhi. She also examines how world events including World War II, transfer of power, partition of India, and the subsequent refugee issue underpinned the urban transformations in Delhi.

4. Patrick Geddes was instrumental in drawing up plans for many cities in pre-independent India (see Gooptu 2001; N. Khan 2011; Priya 1993: 833). N. Khan (2011) analyzes the Geddesian apolitical and utilitarian logic of cooperative evolution of humans,

non-humans, and cities. Similarly, Gooptu (2001) analyzes Geddes's rejection of eugenicist policy and emphasis on character building and transformation of society (78). In another perspective, Rao-Cavale (2017) shows the limits of Geddesian thought by questioning the assumptions of civic participation, harmony, and cooperation among the residents, assumptions that do not consider racial and caste-based segregation and conflicts in urban milieus. He then goes on to examine how Indian nationalists negotiated with Geddes's ideas to advance their own notions of civic politics in pre-independent India.

5. The word "slum" is discredited because of its pejorative connotations (Gilbert 2007). However, in Delhi's planning parlance, "slum" is defined as an area "unfit for human habitation." Slums are designated according to the Slum Improvement and Clearance Areas Act of 1956. Therefore, slums are legal in status and eligible to receive a range of services. *Jhuggi jhopri* settlements are seen as "illegal" encroachments on public and private land. See DUSIB, "Present Policies and Strategies," http://delhishelterboard.in/main/?page _id=128, accessed May 23, 2014.

6. *Busti* and *jhuggi* are used interchangeably in state parlance. See DUSIB, Agenda for the First Meeting of the Board, December 23, 2010, http://delhishelterboard.in/dusib _board_agenda/1st_board_meeting_agenda_and_minutes.pdf, accessed May 18, 2020.

7. When Indira Gandhi was prime minister, a state of emergency was declared on June 25, 1975, under Article 352 of the constitution. After two years of excessive abuse of power during the period of Emergency, the newly constituted Central Government appointed the Commission of Enquiry on May 28, 1977. The Commission of Enquiry, also known as the Shah Commission, published three reports on the "abuse of authority, excesses and malpractices committed and action taken or purported to be taken in the wake of the Emergency" (Shah Commission 1978a: 1).

8. Unauthorized colonies have been developed on private land, often violating planning protocols (see Bhan 2013; Lemanksi and Lama-Rewal 2013). In contrast, the authorized colonies have supposedly been developed on land earmarked by a Master Plan and zoning regulations (Bhan 2013; Sheikh and Banda 2016). As Lemanski and Lama-Rewal's (2013) study shows, there is a "missing middle" in the studies of urban governance in Delhi. Underlining the cases of unauthorized colonies, which house between one-fourth and one-third of the city's population, they argue that most of the citizens in these neighborhoods are neither rich nor poor, thereby raising critical issues about class composition and urban governance (91). The residents of unauthorized colonies have fought long-term battles to get their settlements regularized. Recently, the *bhagidari* (partnership) program was opened to some of the Resident Welfare Associations of unauthorized colonies (94). Thus, as Lemanski and Lama-Rewal argue, the unauthorized colonies contest the binaries between the settlements of the poor and the rich.

9. Doreen Massey (2005: 82) provides some useful general critiques of current processes of globalization by underlining its integral inequalities and "power-geometries." This is not to argue that cities of the Global South like Delhi are converging along the lines of the cities of the Global North. As Shatkin (2007: 2) argues, one has to examine local agency by focusing on the diversity of experiences and the negotiated nature of the

effects of these processes by drawing on actor-centered perspectives. A contextual analysis can unravel the "actors, institutions and interests" that shape the interaction of global and local experiences and viewpoints (1). Nevertheless, the role of macro-level changes related to capital accumulation in shaping the cities in the global economy cannot be ignored completely, as illustrated in the planning protocols discussed above. In other words, as Shatkin notes, there is a common ground with the broad expansion of the new global economy and the consequent social and spatial inequality on a local scale (8).

10. The liberalized economic policy and entry of multinational corporations, especially in real estate development in the national capital region (Searle 2016; Srivastava 2014), are connected to the geographical dispersal of capitalism in times of a crisis of over-accumulation (Harvey 1996: 295). The transforming design, architecture, and lifestyles in cities reflect flexible capitalist accumulation and the predominance of a "postmodern cultural fabric" (Soja 1989: 3).

11. The NCRPB summarizes the major changes in economic policies as follows: reduction of the public sector; abolition of licensing and quotas; foreign equity investment; automatic approval of FDIs in high-priority industries; establishment of a Foreign Investment Promotions Board to facilitate FDIs; easier foreign technology agreements; introduction of convertibility; changes in the Foreign Exchange Regulation Act removing restrictions; lowering of customs duties; reduction of custom and central excise duties; and removal of blanket bans on imports (NCRPB 2005: 36).

12. As Harvey (1996: 298) notes, "Investment in consumption spectacles, the selling of images of places, competition over the definition of cultural and symbolic capital, the revival of vernacular traditions associated with places as a consumer attraction, all become conflated in inter-place competition."

13. I have paraphrased the experts' comments when they spoke in both Hindi and English.

14. Scholars have analyzed similar processes of economic restructuring that emphasize "privatization, deregulation, and digitalization" (Sassen 2001: xviii) and "informational economy" (Castells 2002: 126).

15. Scholars have commented on the established link between consumption and citizenship in India (Fernandes 2006; Rajagopal 1999: 135; Srivastava 2009). Fernandes (2006) analyzes the relationship between the production of middle-class identity and spatial restructuring processes in Indian cities. Similarly, Zukin (1998: 825) in a different context argues that urban lifestyle is marked by visual consumption and the pursuit of accumulation of cultural capital. The "phantasmagoria of capitalist culture" (W. Benjamin 1968: 83) and unrestrained "conspicuous consumption" on the part of the "leisure class" (Veblen 1994) have alienated the poor in the city, despite the opening up of a few work and consumption opportunities.

16. The earlier of these studies, Dupont's in 2011, noted thirty-four shopping malls in Delhi.

17. In general terms, "the intricate circuits of cultural intensification" have accompanied "interconnected mechanisms of economic expansion" (Kemple 2007: 156; see also Mazzarella 2003).

18. The idea of efficiency and market-based solutions has not eroded the presence of paperwork and red tape (Graeber 2015: 9); rather, it has enhanced the intricacies of bureaucratic rules of eligibility and legibility, as shown throughout the book.

19. Similar cases of restructuring aimed at the dissolution of informal land tenures and the regularization of low-income settlements based on the creditworthiness of the beneficiaries have been documented in Jakarta (Kusno 2012). As Kusno argues, these practices are not only technical and managerial but also social and political as they involve the displacement of people not considered creditworthy (Kusno 2012: 27).

20. DUSIB, Third Board Meeting Agenda and Minutes, No. PA/DIR (Admn)/2011/D-733, June 21, 2011, http://delhishelterboard.in/dusib_board_agenda/3rd _board_meeting_agenda_and_minutes.pdf, accessed May 18, 2020.

21. Neo-liberal state policies have combined "roll-back" and "roll-out" tactics. "Rollback" tactics include "deregulation, devolution, and even democratization" and their associated processes of "attacks on labor unions, planning agencies, entitlement systems, and public bureaucracies." In contrast, "roll-out" tactics include "intervention, amelioration, and reregulation" and their associated processes of community participation, publicprivate partnerships, and devolution of governance structures (Peck 2010: 22–23).

22. DUSIB, "About Us," http://delhishelterboard.in/main/?page_id=148, accessed May 18, 2020.

23. DUSIB, "Draft Protocol for Removal of Jhuggis and JJ Bastis in Delhi," June 14, 2016, no. D-231/ DD (Reh.) HQ/2016, http://delhishelterboard.in/main/wp-content/up loads/2012/01/Protocol-1.pdf, accessed May 18, 2020.

24. Ibid.

25. Government of National Capital Territory of Delhi, http://www.delhi.gov.in/wps/ wcm/connect/DoIT_Revenue/revenue/home/, accessed October 11, 2019.

26. DUSIB, "Office Order," no. DD/Rehab/II/DUSIB/2017/D-1082, January 4, 2017, http://delhishelterboard.in/main/wp-content/uploads/2016/07/order-9.3.17-1.pdf, accessed May 18, 2020.

27. DUSIB, "Delhi Slum and JJ Rehabilitation and Relocation Policy, 2015," no. D-232/ DD(Reh.) HQ/2016, June 14, 2016, http://delhishelterboard.in/main/wp-content/up loads/2012/01/Policy-2015.pdf, accessed May 18, 2020.

28. Ibid., 3.

29. DUSIB, "Present Policies and Strategies."

30. DUSIB, "Delhi Slum and JJ Rehabilitation and Relocation Policy, 2015," no. D-232/ DD(Reh.) HQ/2016, June 14, 2016.

31. DUSIB, "Agenda Notes for the Twentieth Meeting," October 27, 2017, http://del hishelterboard.in/main/wp-content/uploads/2017/11/20th-BM-Agenda.pdf, accessed on May 18, 2020.

32. DUSIB, Agenda for the First Meeting, December 23, 2010.

33. DUSIB, "Agenda Notes for the Twentieth Meeting," October 27, 2017.

34. The eligible residents were required to pay resettlement fees of 5,000 rupees (approximately US$110) for 12.5-square-meter plots or 7,000 rupees (approximately US$155)

for 18-square-meter plots. The currency conversions here are based on the exchange rate of US$1 = 45 Indian rupees prevalent at the time of fieldwork, 2010–11.

35. DUSIB, Agenda for the First Meeting of the Board, December 23, 2010, p. 175.

36. DUSIB, "Delhi Slum and JJ Rehabilitation and Relocation Policy, 2015," no. D-232/DD(Reh.) HQ/2016, June 14, 2016.

See S. Roy (2014) for a discussion of the history of the Aam Aadmi Party, and the promises and pitfalls of democratic and anti-establishment party politics. In analyzing the process of recruitment and mobilization of the party members for the Aam Aadmi Party, she discusses how ordinary people engaged in expressive and performative politics to fashion preferred political selves in Delhi.

37. Ibid. Dalit residents are required to pay 1,000 rupees and a maintenance fee of 30,000 rupees.

38. DUSIB, Agenda for the First Meeting of the Board, December 23, 2010.

39. GNCTD, Department of Urban Development, "Order," no. F.18(7)/UD/DUSIB/2011/Vol-I2350, February 25, 2013, http://delhishelterboard.in/main/wp-content/uploads/2013/04/relocation_and_rehabilitation_policy_25_02_2013.pdf , accessed May 18, 2020.

40. DUSIB, Agenda for the First Meeting of the Board, December 23, 2010.

41. Ibid.

42. DUSIB, "Delhi Slum and JJ Rehabilitation and Relocation Policy, 2015," no. D-232/DD(Reh.) HQ/2016, June 14, 2016.

43. Ibid.

44. In fact, the list did not even mention that Gautam Nagar—one of the sites where I conducted ethnographic research—was demolished in early 2009.

45. DUSIB, Agenda for the First Meeting of the Board, December 23, 2010.

46. DUSIB, "JJ Basti Details," http://delhishelterboard.in/main/?page_id=3644, accessed June 4, 2014.

47. DUSIB, JJ list, http://delhishelterboard.in/main/wp-content/uploads/2017/01/jjc_list_for_website.pdf, accessed May 18, 2020; DUSIB, "List of Additional JJ Bastis," http://delhishelterboard.in/main/wp-content/uploads/2017/02/List_of_additional_jj_bastis.pdf, accessed May 18, 2020.

48. DUSIB, Agenda for the First Meeting of the Board, December 23, 2010, p. 17.

49. Ibid., pp. 6–7.

50. High Court of Delhi, W.P. (C) 4713/2014 and CM APPL. 5424/2017, Judgement of March 10, 2017, http://delhihighcourt.nic.in/dhc_case_status_oj_list.asp?pno=714188, accessed October 19, 2019

51. Apart from the above resettlements, DUSIB has carried out in situ rehabilitation of 1,060 residents in Sultanpuri. It is also arranging the allotment of 7,620 flats in Savda Ghevra to residents who had applied for low-income housing under Residential Flats Registration Scheme in 1985.

52. Relocations used to be carried out by the Slum and JJ Department of the Municipal Corporation of Delhi (MCD). The Slum and JJ Department has also been part of the

DDA at various points in time, giving rise to confusion about the nodal agency responsible for relocation work. However, since 2010, the Slum and JJ Department has been with the Delhi Urban Shelter Improvement Board (DUSIB). DUSIB was established by an act of the Legislative Assembly of the National Capital Territory of Delhi in 2010. See DUSIB, "About Us," http://delhishelterboard.in/main/?page_id=148, accessed June 4, 2014.

53. DUSIB, "Seventeenth Meeting and Agenda Notes," September 28, 2016, http://delhishelterboard.in/main/wp-content/uploads/2012/02/Agenda.pdf, accessed May 18, 2020. See the same web address for cases against DUSIB officials (pp. 41–72).

54. High Court of Delhi, see WP (C) 11616/2015, Judgment of December 16, 2015, http://delhihighcourt.nic.in, accessed October 11, 2019.

55. In July 2019 the estimated contribution of the landowning agency (LOA) per flat was 900,000 to 1,000,000 Indian rupees. The financial contribution of the LOA varies depending on the location of the resettlement flats. Planner AD (July 2019) had noted that "the liability of LOA increases if the eligibility requirements are revised in favor of the displaced residents. Then the LOA agency has to revise their budgetary provisions in order to be able to contribute their share of the resettlement expenses."

56. See note 55.

57. For these reasons, various commentators have expressed varying amount of sympathy for the party and have termed the political stance of the party as "ideology-agnostic," "post-ideological," and "non-ideological." See, for example, the following three sources: Apoorvanand, "Why Delhi Poll Results Are to Be Seen as Polarized Despite AAP's Huge Win," February 11, 2020, *Business Standard*, https://www.business-standard.com/article/elections/why-delhi-poll-results-are-to-be-seen-as-polarised-despite-aap-s-huge-win-120021101180_1.html, accessed May 1, 2020; Prathama Banerjee, "BJP vs. AAP Is a Battle of Two Political Imaginaries—One of Identity and the Other, Politics of Infrastructure," January 30, 2020, *Indian Express*, ttps://indianexpress.com/article/opinion/columns/delhi-elections-2020-modi-kejriwal-bjp-aap-6241609/, accessed May 1, 2020; and Satish Deshpande, "The Other Delhi Is Distant Yet," February 12, 2020, *The Hindu*, https://www.thehindu.com/opinion/lead/the-other-delhi-is-distant-yet/article30795276.ece, accessed May 1, 2020.

58. DUSIB, "Delhi Slum and JJ Rehabilitation and Relocation Policy, 2015," no. D-232/DD(Reh.) HQ/2016, June 14, 2016.

59. The third Master Plan was approved and notified on February 7, 2007. It was published by the Delhi Development Authority in 2010.

CHAPTER 2

1. In 2010, there were only about 148 night shelters, including eighty-four temporary shelters in tents, providing temporary relief to approximately 17,485 people across the city. DUSIB, Agenda for the First Meeting of the Board, December 23, 2010, p. 178, http://delhishelterboard.in/dusib_board_agenda/1st_board_meeting_agenda_and_minutes.pdf, accessed May 18, 2020.

In 2015, the DUSIB claimed to have provided 200 night shelters for the homeless in Delhi. DUSIB, "Public Notice: opportunity to serve extremely poor people in Delhi by setting up and operating temporary night shelter in Delhi, during winters," http://del hishelterboard.in/main/wp-content/uploads/2012/01/Advertise_16-11-2015.pdf, accessed May 18, 2020.

Between 2016 and 2017, the DUSIB claimed to have provided 269 night shelters for approximately 22,309 homeless in Delhi. DUSIB, "Annual Report 2016–2017," p. 1, http://delhishelterboard.in/main/wp-content/uploads/2012/01/Annual-Report-2016-17.pdf, accessed May 18, 2020.

2. See Chakravarty (2016) for an examination on the emergence and establishment of unauthorized colonies in Delhi. Approximately four million people live in unauthorized colonies in Delhi (Sheikh and Banda 2016: 138).

3. Pati (2019: 262) notes that a recent official order claims that the building regulation exemptions applied only to rural rather than urban villages.

4. In recent years the populist Aam Aadmi Party in power in Delhi has attempted to extend housing rights to the renters in *jhuggi* settlements. DUSIB, "Draft Protocol for Removal of Jhuggis and JJ Bastis in Delhi," June 14, 2016, no. D-231/ DD (Reh.) HQ/2016, p. 5, http://delhishelterboard.in/main/wp-content/uploads/2012/01/Protocol-1.pdf, accessed May 18, 2020. However, most renters have difficulty obtaining proof documents. The owners seldom allow them to apply for voter IDs and ration cards, as they fear that the renters may seize their properties.

5. DUSIB, "Application Form and Guidelines for the Scheme for Grant of Freehold/ Ownership Rights to the Residents of 45 Resettlement Colonies of Delhi," http://del hishelterboard.in/main/wp-content/uploads/2014/03/application_form_guidelines.pdf, accessed May 18, 2020.

6. These social spaces are not clearly defined in state parlance, which indicate fuzzy boundaries between various kinds of spaces. Through the efforts of residents, the unauthorized colonies are regularized when the property titles are registered and legalized by the state (Bhan 2013: 61; Bhan 2016; Heller et al. 2015). See Sheikh and Banda (2016) for an analysis of legal and policy protocols in the regularization politics of unauthorized colonies.

Rural villages are usually at the periphery of the city limits and are designated as rural in the Master Plans (Bhan 2013: 64). In contrast, urban villages are those rural villages which eventually get incorporated into the urban limits of the city (Bhan 2016: 68; Chakravarty 2016). Both urban and rural villages are marked by inhabited or homestead (*abadi*) areas and farmland areas (Chakravarty 2016; Heller et al. 2015; Pati 2019). The *abadi* areas were extended to accommodate the growing population of the villages and the newly arrived migrants into the city after the enactment of the Delhi Land Reforms Act of 1954 (Chakravarty 2016: 114). An *abadi* area is also referred to as a *Lal Dora (LD)*, or "red thread," area to indicate the boundary of inhabited land that was drawn in red ink in the village maps. The owners of the plots in the *abadi* area do not have clear-cut rights or registered deeds to the land—they merely possess the land (Heller et al. 2015: 6; Pati 2019: 255). In contrast, an Extended *Lal Dora* (ELD) area is the extended inhabited area of a village, which houses plots that are recorded in the revenue records of the state (Heller et al. 2015: 6). The poor living in these social spaces are largely not able to claim a "legal" home under the resettlement policy in the city.

7. DUSIB, Agenda for First Meeting of Board, December 23, 2010, p. 14.

8. Transit Camp Files, 29 April 1994, document no. F-631 (additional commissioner's [DC and P] notes on transit camps), Delhi Development Authority (DDA), Delhi; Transit Camp Files, 8 August 1995, document no. F-544 (discussion notes of additional commissioner and joint director), Delhi Development Authority (DDA), Delhi. See also Transit Camp Files, 7 April 2005, "Background Note about the Transit Camp, . . ." document no. F 20 (7)91/ MP, Delhi Development Authority (DDA), Delhi.

9. Transit Camp Files, 13 April 1998, document no. 211 AC (AP) (correspondences among various officials regarding change of land use), Delhi Development Authority (DDA), Delhi. See also Transit Camp Files, 7 April 2005, "Background Note," F 20 (7)91/ MP, DDA.

10. Transit Camp Files, 29 April 1994, document no. F-631 (additional commissioner's [DC and P] notes on transit camps), DDA.

11. Ibid. See also Transit Camp Files, 7 April 2005, "Background Note," F 20 (7)91/ MP, DDA.

12. Right to Information (RTI) applications filed by a resident in Sitapuri establish that an education society paid approximately 8,205,000 rupees for the allotment of land in the neighborhood. Delhi Development Authority (DDA), O/o Director (Lands), 26 July 2010, "Compliance of CIC Order, . . ." document no. F. 18 (31) 89/IL/257, received in person by author from Sitapuri residents during fieldwork, 2010–11.

13. Resettlement Colonies Files, 28 February 2005, "Provision of Community Facilities/Utilities and Burial and Cremation Ground at, . . ." document no. F3 (21) 2001/MP, Delhi Development Authority (DDA), Delhi.

14. Resettlement Colonies Files, 10 May 2000, "Resettlement of Squatters at, . . ." document no. OSD (AP)/ Misc/2000/118, Delhi Development Authority (DDA), Delhi, p. 2.

15. Ibid., p. 4.

16. Ibid., pp. 4–5.

17. Resettlement Colonies Files, 30 April 2002, "Change of Land Use or 37.0 Ha. (91.4 acres) in Zone 'O' from Agricultural to Water Body (A-4) to Residential," document no. F3 (21) 2001, Delhi Development Authority (DDA), Delhi.

18. Ibid.

19. It is beyond the scope of this work to analyze conflicts among various stakeholders in the urban expansion process in the outskirts of the city.

20. Resettlement Colonies Files, 17 April 2001, "Development of Land for Relocation of Jhuggi Dwellers at, . . ." document NO. EM. 6(31) 2000/Est. /Pt. I/3349–53, Delhi Development Authority (DDA), Delhi. (Minutes from a meeting with the vice chairman describing difficulties associated with land development are enclosed with the above document.)

21. Ibid.

22. Resettlement Colonies Files, 10 July 2000, "Temporary/ Transit Accommodation at, . . ." document NO. F 2 (111)/Eld.10/799, Delhi Development Authority (DDA), Delhi.

23. In recent years, an array of theoretical and empirical insights has emerged on the factors shaping social suffering in the contemporary world (Bourdieu 1999; J. Davis 1992;

Farmer 2003; Farmer 2004; Kleinman, Das, and Lock 1997; Scheper-Hughes 1992). As Farmer (2003: 41) notes, "To explain suffering, one must embed individual biography in the larger matrix of culture, history, and political economy." And as Kleinman, Das, and Lock (1997: ix) argue, "Social suffering results from what political, economic, and institutional power does to people." Where J. Davis (1992: 155) examines various forms of social suffering as social products, Bourdieu (1999: 4) calls for an analysis of specific features of the social world rather than taking recourse to "subjectivist relativism" in order to understand social suffering.

24. In 2017, the vendors made approximately 400 to 500 rupees per day. But in Sitapuri, the earnings went down to 200 to 300 per day when the police raided these vendors, especially in early August 2017 in preparation for Independence Day celebrations.

25. However, the street hawkers have some political agency and ability to negotiate. They negotiate with various state agencies in multiple ways, eliciting varying state responses (Schindler 2014; Schindler 2016). Anjaria (2016) shows how the street hawkers carry out dynamic negotiations—which also entail varied political co-option and compromise with state officials—in claiming space and rights in Mumbai. Similarly, in the context of Manila, Recio (2020) examines how the hawkers evade state regulations in multiple ways, and how they draw on their network of family and kin members, local state officials, and grassroots organizers in carrying out their trades. In another view, Rao-Cavale (2019) provides a historically nuanced account of legal mobilizations of hawkers by considering their associations with political regimes and parties, unions, and social movements in Mumbai and Chennai.

26. The new residents each spent approximately 200,000 Indian rupees (US$4,444) between 2010 and 2011 to purchase homes in the Sitapuri neighborhood after selling everything they had back in their villages. In 2017, residents claimed that the houses (often with two or three floors) were bought or sold for between 500,000 and 800,000 rupees on average. However, the houses facing the road, strategically important for commercial purposes, were sold or purchased for hefty prices, which amounted to 2,000,000 or 2,500,000 rupees on average. Thus, the relative security and steady entrenchment of the neighborhood over the years have contributed to the appreciation of real estate value in the neighborhood.

27. A two-room *jhuggi* cost between 150,000 and 250,000 rupees on average in 2017 in Gautam Nagar. In the area, the *jhuggis* with considerable investment and no immediate threat of demolition cost between 500,000 and 700,000 rupees.

28. Residents rented one-room houses for approximately 2,000 rupees in 2017.

29. As discussed earlier, Henri Lefebvre's (1991) insights have helped us understand the processes underpinning the production of space, especially in the urban context of contemporary capitalism (see also Soja 1989: 127). As Soja (1989: 129) argues in general terms, spatiality embodies and presupposes social relations and social structure, and the forms of spatiality give rise to conflicts and crises.

30. High Court of Delhi, W.P. (C) 4713/2014 and CM APPL. 5424/2017, Judgement of March 10, 2017, http://delhihighcourt.nic.in/dhc_case_status_oj_list.asp?pno=714188, accessed October 19, 2019.

31. Ibid.

32. Each container carried 15 liters of water and was sold for 10 rupees at a discounted rate in 2011. Otherwise, the residents bought 1 liter by paying 1 rupee.

33. The residents claimed that there were approximately forty privately run filtration systems in the neighborhood.

34. In Marxist thought, there is a presumption that class relations encompass social relations. Critiquing this notion, Doreen Massey (1994: 2) shows that gender relations are integral to the spatiality and geography of capitalist and post-colonial class formations. In other words, the social relations of space are experienced differently not only along class lines but also according to a multiplicity of other social relations, including gender relations (3–4).

35. Women spent 25 rupees (US$0.55) per day on transportation traveling to middle-class colonies to earn a monthly salary of 1,500 to 3,000 rupees (US$33 to US$67) in 2011. In 2017, they earned approximately 7,000 to 8,000 rupees per month but incurred a daily expense of 40 rupees on transportation. The populist AAP-led government implemented a policy of free bus transport for women in October 2019. This policy promises to provide a huge respite for women in Azad resettlement colony who daily commute to work in various parts of Delhi. See "Free Bus Ride Scheme for Women Begins in Delhi," October 29, 2019, *Economic Times*, https://economictimes.indiatimes.com/news/politics-and-nation/delhi-free-rides-for-women-in-dtc-cluster-buses-from-today/articleshow/71800064.cms?from=mdr, accessed May 18, 2020.

36. Resettlement Colonies Files, 12 April 2001, "V.C.'s Inspection of . . . J.J. Resettlement Sites," document no. F. 2(1)/2001/LM (C)- Pt./ 57, Delhi Development Authority (DDA), Delhi. Sewer lines were absent even in 2017 during the second round of my fieldwork in the Azad resettlement colony.

37. DUSIB, "Fifth Meeting, . . ." no. D-05/AD (Meeting Cell)/DUSIB/2011, December 17, 2011, http://delhishelterboard.in/dusib_board_agenda/5th_board_meeting_agenda_and_minutes.pdf, accessed May 18, 2020.

38. Even in 2017, the DUSIB was not able to maintain and service a phase of MKRC as it lacked funds and infrastructure. However, the municipality had developed roads by 2017 in the neighborhood. See DUSIB, "Agenda Notes for the Twentieth Meeting," October 27, 2017, http://delhishelterboard.in/main/wp-content/uploads/2017/11/20th-BM-Agenda.pdf, accessed May 18, 2020.

39. The Aam Admi Party government has turned the government schools around by improving the infrastructure and standard of education. The government schools primarily target the poor and low-income residents in Delhi. In the 2018–2019 fiscal year, it invested approximately 26 percent of the total budget in the education sector. See "APP Govt Allocates Nearly Rs 14,000 cr for Education Sector in Its Budget," March 22, 2018, *Economic Times*, https://economictimes.indiatimes.com/news/economy/policy/aap-govt-allocates-nearly-rs-14000-cr-for-education-sector-in-its-budget/articleshow/63413527.cms, accessed May 18, 2020.

Furthermore, the government facilitated the establishment of a School for Excellence in Azad resettlement colony in 2018. As the residents note, the middle-class people in surrounding areas also attempt to enroll their children in the school in a "slum" area. The residents negotiate with their *pradhans* and leaders to make sure that the students from the neighborhood are able to enroll in the school. The chief minister also runs coaching institutes for students in low-income areas. See Sagar, "A Day with AAP Volunteers Who Reflect the Party's Convoluted Social-Justice Politics," February 7, 2020, *The Caravan*, https://caravanmagazine.in/politics/a-day-with-aap-volunteers-who-reflect-the-partys-convoluted-social-justice-politics, accessed May 18, 2020.

40. Resettlement Colonies Files, 12 April 2001, "V.C.'s Inspection of . . . J.J. Resettlement Sites," F. 2(1)/2001/LM (C)- Pt./ 57, DDA).

CHAPTER 3

1. As M. Khan (2005) argues, the persistence of patron-client relationships can be traced to structural factors characteristic of capitalist development in post-colonial societies. Without resources to redistribute, these structures give rise to competitive factional politics. India's economic structure is marked by an "informal economy, presence of nonmarket accumulation processes (often described as primitive accumulation), and the use of state power to create a range of rents that directly benefit the factions in power" (M. Khan 2005: 712). In other words, the "economic characteristics of developing countries make patron-client politics both rational for redistributive coalitions and effective as strategies for achieving the goals of powerful constituencies within these coalitions" (704).

2. See Hansen (2005b) for an analysis of the assertion of plebeian identities with respect to scarce material and symbolic resources in the context of changing political cultures in India.

3. Bourdieu (1991: 59) argues that the dispossession of the dominated classes is "inseparable from the existence of a body of professionals, objectively invested with the monopoly of the legitimate use of the legitimate language." He further argues that linguistic competencies can be "signs of wealth" and "signs of authority" (66).

4. This is not to argue that only ethnic factors shape the interactions between intermediaries and residents in Delhi. While I contend that the affective equations between residents and intermediaries—especially based on caste, regional origin, and gender backgrounds—underscore collective problem-solving dynamics, my ethnographic insights attest that the residents also reach out to various intermediaries based on the latter's perceived efficacy and ability to distribute welfare goods in the informal neighborhoods, as Auerbach and Thachil have argued (Auerbach 2020; Auerbach and Thachil 2018).

5. James Holston (2008) argues that such a process of land occupation subverts entrenched urban inequalities through "insurgent citizenship movements" (313). Though Holston's Brazilian context is different, his empirical findings concerning what he calls "auto-constructions" that involve "the hardships of illegal residence, house building, and land conflict" (4) resemble the gradual home construction process in Delhi.

6. As Appadurai (2002: 29) argues, the activities of the urban poor in collaboration with grassroots NGOs represent a "logic of patience" and a "politics of accommodation, negotiation, and long-term pressure rather than of confrontation or threats of political reprisal." It can be argued, however, that the involvement of NGOs is not a prerequisite

for these activities, and that the practices can at times involve outright confrontation with and rejection of state policies.

7. Appadurai contrasts the notion of locality to that of neighborhood and argues that the latter includes "the actually existing social forms in which locality, as a dimension or value, is variably realized" (Appadurai 1996: 178–79).

8. Krishna, Rains, and Wibbels (2020) provide an insightful analysis of how the intermediaries help the residents obtain documents, property deeds, and titles in informal settlements in Bangalore. They emphasize that the process of obtaining proof documents, gaining notification or regularization, and accessing service provisions is neither sequential nor seamless. However, the *jhuggi* residents do not receive any state-sanctioned property deeds or titles in Delhi.

9. The extension of a panoply of basic amenities is contingent on various factors. As Chidambaram underlines, the factors including built environment, infrastructural nature of the public amenities, and institutional contexts (especially bureaucratic and political arrangements) underscore the intra-slum variations in the provision and access of different public goods (for example, water and toilet facilities) in Delhi (Chidambaram 2020).

10. See the Government of National Capital Territory of Delhi website, http://www.delhi.gov.in/wps/wcm/connect/doit_power/Power/Home/About+Us, accessed November 28, 2018.

11. The Aam Admi Party–led government provides subsidized electricity and water bills to the residents in Delhi. While the poor in *jhuggi jhopri* neighborhoods, transit camps, and resettlement colonies do not usually possess a water connection at home but must rely on public water hydrants, they benefit from free electricity or reduced bills on their electricity consumption. As pointed out by many commentators, the government has redistributed its revenues from taxes and duties in subsidizing essential goods and services in the city. The revenues escalated by 31 percent from 2014–2015 to 2017–2018 and the government has used most of the increase for salaries for staff in government schools, neighborhood clinics, and subsidized goods including subsidized electricity and water and free bus rides for women in state-run Delhi Transport Corporation buses. See Kaushal Shroff, "The Mathematics behind the AAP's Subsidies for Electricity and Water," February 6, 2020, *The Caravan*, https://caravanmagazine.in/government/delhi-elections-2020-aap-bjp-budget-campaign, accessed May 18, 2020.

CHAPTER 4

1. The Office of the Registrar General and Census Commissioner, Ministry of Home Affairs, Government of India, collects demographic and socio-economic data of Indian citizens. The data collected is used to formulate policies at the state and national level. The delimitation of the election constituencies is also carried out based on this data. The residents are issued acknowledgment slips during enumeration, which are required for biometric authentication and enrollment. Furthermore, the Unique Identity Authority of India issues a unique identity number to the Office of the Registrar General and Census Commissioner, which maintains the National Population Register database. The authority also issues identity cards, which are referred to as Aadhar cards, based on biometric

authentication and demographic data of people. The Revenue Department of Government of National Capital Territory of Delhi maintains the lists and also addresses grievances related to enumeration and documentation. It is responsible for maintaining and periodically revising the voters' list and issuing voter IDs along with the office of the Chief Electoral Officer, Delhi. The Revenue Department also issues domicile and citizenship certificates and marriage certificates. Apart from proving voting rights for citizens, voter IDs are also used as proof documents for claiming resettlement flats. Similarly, the Department of Food Supplies and Consumer Affairs is responsible for issuing ration cards. Ration cards enable people to procure subsidized food and other household items and can also be used as proof documents in claiming resettlement flats. I discuss the politics shaping access to these documents in Delhi, but the politics concerning these documents varies across states in India. The above account draws on information available on the following websites: http://censusindia.gov.in/?q=economic+survey, http://www.delhi.gov .in/wps/wcm/connect/doit_revenue/Revenue/Home/Services/Introduction, http://www .ceodelhi.nic.in/Content/home.aspx, http://nfs.delhi.gov.in/Home.aspx, accessed February 26, 2018.

2. This account of Delhi's resettlement policy draws on information available on the DUSIB website, http://delhishelterboard.in/main/, accessed February 26, 2018.

3. Similarly, Ranganathan (2014) has shown how the preservation and demonstration of property tax receipts, proofs, and rosters of payment for water pipes and connections have been used by lower-middle-class residents to claim legal tenure of their "peripheral" neighborhoods in Bangalore.

4. I use *babus* as a generic term for all government officials, regardless of their location in the bureaucratic hierarchy.

5. See "Letter to the Group of Ministers on Caste Census," August 14, 2010, *The Hindu*, http://www.thehindu.com/todays-paper/tp-opinion/letter-to-the-group-of-ministers-on-caste-census/article569547.ece, accessed November 17, 2013; and "Caste Census: Senseless Separation," September 13, 2010, *The Hindu*, http://www.thehindu.com/todays -paper/tp-opinion/caste-census-senseless-separation/article627987.ece, accessed November 13, 2013.

6. Jan Chetna Manch Files, 22 May 2006, document no. D.O. No. 538/PA/VC/06 (Tajdar Babar's letter to additional commissioner [slum and JJ], Municipal Corporation of Delhi), Jan Chetna Manch, Delhi.

7. Jan Chetna Manch Files, 11 January 2002, "Transparency in Relocation Operations," document no. NO. PA/ADDL Commr (S and JJ)/2002/D-32 (additional commissioner's letter to joint director, SUR), Jan Chetna Manch, Delhi.

8. Berenschot (2010) has observed similar idioms of expressions related to the difficulties in dealing with the bureaucracy in Ahmedabad, Gujarat. Gujaratis use the phrase *dhakka khaavadave chhe* to explain getting pushed around in offices (Berenschot 2010: 889).

9. My experience also corroborates Harriss's (2006: 453) findings that the poor often visit the government offices accompanied by others or by influential persons.

10. Graeber (2015: 32–33) argues that we are experiencing a phase of "total bureaucratization" today. He emphasizes that numerous technologies of scrutiny and the menacing

tactics of surveillance by uniform-clad staff guide all aspects of our lives in the contemporary era.

11. As discussed in the Introduction, Chatterjee (2004) distinguishes between citizens and populations in order to illustrate the career of citizenship in India. According to him, citizens share in the sovereignty of the state while populations are enumerable entities amenable to state welfare objectives (34). However, the urban poor articulate their rights through legal and constitutional language along with an emancipatory vocabulary. Even so, Chatterjee's distinction is useful to map the trajectory of the urban poor, who are neither well equipped to participate in civil society nor well placed to navigate the bourgeois procedures of the state apparatus.

12. Office of the First Appellant Authority, Department of Food Supplies and Consumer Affairs, 21 August 2009, document no. RTI (Appeal)/ ID-0029/ FAA/2009/179, received in person by author from Gautam Nagar residents during fieldwork, 2010–11.

13. Central Information Commission, 29 October 2010, decision no. CIC/ SG/A/2010/002578/9954 (response to RTI application, appeal number CIC/ SG/A/2010/002578), received in person by author from Gautam Nagar residents during fieldwork, 2010–11.

14. Delhi Development Authority (DDA), O/O Director (LM), 4 July 2006, "First Appeal Filed by . . . under RTI Act," document no. Dy. NO. 33/ LM/SEZ/55 CO (response to first appeal filed by "resident" under RTI Act), received in person by author from Sitapuri transit camp resident at Sitapuri Transit Camp.

CHAPTER 5

1. Tomlins (2007: 45) reviews the debates between formalists, who regard law as "the product of internally constructed rules, procedures," and instrumentalists, who consider law to be "rationales or an effect of external social forces and interests." In his classic review of Marxist perspectives on law, Spitzer (1983) demonstrates how deterministic legal economism gave way to Althusserian theoretical accounts. These theoretical accounts emphasize the "relative autonomy" of law, although law was still accounted for by an economic logic in the last instance. Recent Marxist theory aims to broaden the law with insights into politics, history, and struggles to understand the judicial system (Spitzer 1983: 107–108). While Spitzer recognizes the theoretical promise of treating law as practice, he also argues that law always operates within the framework and limits of institutions (109). Tomlins notes that social-legal scholarship today recognizes the interpenetration of the social and legal fields. In other words, there has been an intellectual move from "autonomy to mutuality" (Tomlins 2007: 47). Similarly, Bourdieu (1986–87) breaks away from Althusserrian perspectives on law as an apparatus of the state and instead engages with the juridical field as a "structure of symbolic systems" (815). He argues that the "social practices of law are in fact the product of the functioning of a field" (816). The field is structured by ongoing conflicts over competence and the power struggles among actors possessing specific and unequal amounts of judicial capital. In this respect, Bourdieu demonstrates how the internal logic of judicial functioning limits possible actions and solutions in the juridical field (816). Bourdieu's approach has been criticized for being static

and quasi-structuralist, and for not accounting for dynamic processes involving conflicts and contestations over law, society, and the knowledge relations that constitute it (Valverde 2006). Valverde adds that "with Bourdieu's work we can shed a lot of light on what lawyers do and are, but we do not actually know much about law and its knowledge dynamics" (595). However, Bourdieu also provides subtle insights into the symbolic struggles that inform the establishment of technical competence, conflicts between professionals, the politics of rationalization, and the categorization of professional and lay knowledge systems.

2. Sitapuri Resident Welfare Association, 3 February 1994, document no. K.T.C.R.W./ N.D./ 94/92 (letter to prime minister), received in person by author from Sitapuri transit camp residents during fieldwork, 2010–11.

3. Sitapuri Resident Welfare Association, 13 December 1993, document no. K.T.C.R.W./N.D./93/79 (letter to prime minister), received in person by author from Sitapuri residents during fieldwork, 2010–11.

4. Transit Camp Files, 13 November 1992, document no. F 1265 DC and P (notes on six transit camps), Delhi Development Authority (DDA), Delhi. See also Transit Camp Files, 7 April 2005, "Background Note about the Transit Camp, . . ." document no. F 20 (7) 91/ MP, Delhi Development Authority (DDA), Delhi.

5. Transit Camp Files, 2 March 1994, document no. F189, Delhi Development Authority (DDA), Delhi; Transit Camp Files, 28 March 1994, document no. F-264 (discussion notes about the change of land use), Delhi Development Authority (DDA), Delhi.

6. Transit Camp Files, 22 October 1997, document no. 493 AC (AP) (notes about a letter from the general secretary of an association), Delhi Development Authority (DDA), Delhi.

7. Transit Camp Files, 9 June 1999, "Change of Land Use of an Area, . . ." document no. K-13011/17/93-DDIB, Delhi Development Authority (DDA), Delhi. See also Transit Camp Files, 7 April 2005, "Background Note," F 20 (7)91/ MP, DDA.

8. Transit Camp Files, 19 July 1999, document no. P-193-95/COM (letter issued to Government of India Press), Delhi Development Authority (DDA), Delhi; Transit Camp Files, 21 July 1999, document no. P-196-98/COM (letter issued to National Book Trust and National Herald), Delhi Development Authority (DDA), Delhi.

9. Transit Camp Files, 18 August 1999, "Objection to Change in Land Use," Residents Welfare Association (Regd.), Delhi Development Authority (DDA), Delhi.

10. Various scholars have commented on issues of fear, safety, security, and elite identity concerning spatial restructuring in cities. As M. Davis (1992: 224) notes, security and safety have "less to do with personal safety than with the degree of personal insulation, in residential, work, consumption and travel environments, from 'unsavoury' groups and individuals, even crowds in general." Similarly, Nair (2005) argues that high-income groups are "protected by an architecture of fear—high walled compounds, twenty-four-hour security, and restricted single point access" (163). Architectural insulation produces social homogeneity and restricts plebeian assertions and practices in the neighborhoods. The desire for "social homogeneity" and an "architecture of fear" are conjoined by the preference for an agreeable visual, olfactory, and civic order (134). Further, Fernandes (2006: xviii) argues

the new middle class in India is in the process of producing a "distinctive social and political identity ... and lays claims to the benefits of liberalization."

11. His sentiment brings to mind a remark by Marx ([1852] 1978: 21): "Every demand of the simplest bourgeois financial reform, of the most ordinary liberalism, of the most formal republicanism, of the most shallow democracy, is simultaneously castigated as an 'attempt on society' and branded as 'socialism.'"

12. Scholars like Huey and Kemple (2007) illustrate how the poor are criminalized in skid row in the North American context. They argue that skid row in Western contexts is seen as a "social container for transient or ambiguously located individuals marked as uniquely immoral, pathological, delinquent, or simply deviant" (2306). In an analysis of how social categories are invented through place, Pigg (1992: 507) similarly argues, "The village becomes a space of backwardness—a physical space that imprisons people in what is considered an inferior and outmoded way of life."

13. Transit Camp Files, 15 November 1999, document no. 474/Dir (AP) I (discussion notes of director and joint director regarding suggestions and objections to proposed land use change), Delhi Development Authority (DDA), Delhi. See also Transit Camp Files, 4 October 1999, "Publication of Public Notice Regarding Change of Land Use," document no. 11 (1)/98, Delhi Urban Art Commission, Delhi Development Authority (DDA), Delhi.

14. Transit Camp Files, 5 October 1999, "Suggestions/ Objections of Municipal Corporation of Delhi to Public Notice," document no. TP/G/99/2267, Delhi Development Authority (DDA), Delhi.

15. Transit Camp Files, 7 March 2003, document no. DDA- F 452-AC II (notes about transit camp upgrading scheme), Delhi Development Authority (DDA), Delhi.

16. Ibid.

17. Transit Camp Files, 6 January 2003, "Regarding the Site Visit, . . ." document no. PA/Dir (AP) I- D-2, Delhi Development Authority (DDA), Delhi.

18. Ibid.

19. Transit Camp Files, 2003, "In the High Court of Delhi at New Delhi, Civil Writ Petition No. . . . of 2003 in the Matter of Residents Welfare Association . . . Petitioner versus Delhi Development Authority and Others . . . Respondents," Delhi Development Authority (DDA), Delhi, p. 3. See also Transit Camp Files, 22 September 2004, "In the High Court of Delhi at New Delhi WP (C) Number 6324/2003," Delhi Development Authority (DDA), Delhi, p. 3–4.

20. Transit Camp Files, 2003, "High Court Civil Writ Petition No. . . . of 2003 in the Matter of Residents Welfare Association versus Delhi Development Authority and Others," DDA, p. 6.

21. Ibid., p. 2.

22. Chandola (2012) examines what constitutes a "sensorial vocabulary" in shaping Delhi's materiality (392). In her analysis, she examines how low-income neighborhoods are represented as "spaces of [an] overwhelming sensorial overload." In particular, she provides an interpretation of how "dirt, noise, and smell of these spaces" are invoked to denounce the people residing in these neighborhoods (395).

23. Caldeira (1996: 303) argues that upper-income groups today desire "fortified enclaves" that are "privatized, enclosed, and monitored spaces for residence, consumption, leisure, and work."

24. Transit Camp Files, 2003, "High Court, Civil Writ Petition No. . . . of 2003 in the Matter of Residents Welfare Association versus Delhi Development Authority and Others," DDA, p. 4.

25. Ibid., pp. 1–6.

26. Transit Camp Files, 3 August 2004, "In the High Court of Delhi at New Delhi, W.P. (C) 6324/2003," Delhi Development Authority (DDA), Delhi.

27. In a recent article, Mawani points out that law is a "locus of juridico-political command that is . . . operative through . . . a double logic of violence: a mutual and reciprocal violence of law as symbolic and material force and law as document and documentation." The legal archive constituted through this process thus erases law's provenance and naturalizes its "meanings, authority, and legitimacy" (Mawani 2012: 337).

28. Transit Camp Files, 22 September 2004, "High Court WP (C) Number 6324/2003," DDA, pp. 7–8.

29. Ibid., p. 9.

30. Transit Camp Files, 18 October 2004, document no. F-544-AC II (director's planning notes on High Court order), Delhi Development Authority (DDA), Delhi. See also Transit Camp Files, 22 September 2004, "High Court WP (C) Number 6324/2003," DDA, p. 12.

31. Transit Camp Files, 4 April 2005, "In the High Court of Delhi at New Delhi . . . CM No. 14278/ 2004 in LPA No. 1063/2004," Delhi Development Authority (DDA), Delhi. See also Transit Camp Files, 22 September 2004, "High Court WP (C) Number 6324/2003," DDA, pp. 11–12.

32. Transit Camp Files, 18 October 2004, F-544-AC II (director's planning notes on High Court order), DDA.

33. Ibid.

34. Ibid.

35. Hull (2003) shows how "successful bureaucratic processes result in action that is not dissolvable into the agency of distinct individuals" (288). The collective agency of bureaucracy by a simultaneous diffusion of individual agency (290) thereby creates an ambiguous and ill-defined arena of bureaucratic action. Hull argues that the "contingent achievement of movement up and down the chain of command and laterally to other departments produces on the notesheet a representation of collective agency" (303).

36. Transit Camp Files, 8 December 2004, document no. F-544-AC II (handwritten notes of the commissioner, planning), Delhi Development Authority (DDA), Delhi.

37. Transit Camp Files, 10 December 2004, document no. F-544-AC II (handwritten notes of various officials indicating encroachment), Delhi Development Authority (DDA), Delhi.

38. Transit Camp Files, 27 April 2005, document no. F-10-AC II (notes of the director, planning, on the High Court orders), Delhi Development Authority (DDA), Delhi.

39. Ibid.

40. Transit Camp Files, 4 May 2005, "DDA's Land Officer Gets Court Notice," *Hindustan Times*, Delhi Development Authority (DDA), Delhi.

41. Transit Camp Files, 7 April 2005, "Background Note," F 20 (7)91/ MP, DDA.

42. Transit Camp Files, 23 November 2010, document no. F-202 (remarks of the commissioner, planning, and the deputy chief legal advisor on the High Court orders), Delhi Development Authority (DDA), Delhi. See also Transit Camp Files, 24 May 2005, "In the High Court of Delhi at New Delhi . . . LPA No. 1063/2004 and CM Nos. 14278/2004 and 7372/2005," Delhi Development Authority (DDA), Delhi.

43. Transit Camp Files, 24 May 2005, "High Court LPA No. 1063/2004 and CM Nos. 14278/2004 and 7372/2005," DDA.

44. Transit Camp Files, 1 March 2006, "In the High Court of Delhi at New Delhi . . . W.P. (C) 6324/2003," Delhi Development Authority (DDA), Delhi.

45. Transit Camp Files, 26 April 2006, "High Court W.P. (C) 6324/2003," Delhi Development Authority (DDA), Delhi.

46. Transit Camp Files, 1 March 2006, "In the High Court of Delhi at New Delhi . . . W.P. (C) 6324/2003," DDA.

47. Ibid.

48. Ghertner (2010: 188) argues that a normative aesthetic has shaped governmental processes in Delhi and has led to slum demolitions. Surveyors no longer establish the legality of slums through mapping, scientific data compilation, and survey logs, but instead on the basis of a "settlement's appearance" (203).

49. Transit Camp Files, 19 April 2010, document no. F-242- Director (AP)-I (notes of director, area planning, on the Zonal Plan), Delhi Development Authority (DDA), Delhi.

50. Transit Camp Files, 11 June 2010, document no. F-202 (comments of various officials on the status of the High Court case), Commissioner (Planning), Delhi Development Authority (DDA), Delhi. See also Transit Camp Files, 12 March 2010, "In the High Court of Delhi at New Delhi, W.P. (C) 6324/2003," Delhi Development Authority (DDA), Delhi.

51. Transit Camp Files, 14 January 2011, "Change of Land Use in Respect of Transit Camp, . . ." document no. F-20 (7) 91/MP/2011/D-9, Area Planning Unit I, Delhi Development Authority (DDA), Delhi. See also Transit Camp Files, 20 April 2010, "In the High Court of Delhi at New Delhi, W.P. (C) 6324/2003," Delhi Development Authority (DDA), Delhi.

52. Transit Camp Files, 25 October 2010, document no. F-124/ Dir (AP) I (handwritten notes of the director, planning), Delhi Development Authority (DDA), Delhi.

53. Transit Camp Files, 23 November 2010, F-202 (remarks of the commissioner, planning, and the deputy chief legal advisor on the High Court orders), DDA.

54. Transit Camp Files, 29 January 2008, "Minutes of Meeting held by Secretary (UD), . . ." Delhi Development Authority (DDA), Delhi, pp. 1–3.

55. Ibid.

56. Ibid.

57. Ibid.

58. Transit Camp Files, 12 April 2006, "Prayer for Interim Relief of Residence of Transit Camp, . . ." Transit Camp Residents Welfare Association (Registered), document no. KTCRWA/N.D./025/2006, Delhi Development Authority (DDA), Delhi.

59. Ibid., p. 6.

60. Ibid., pp. 8–9.

61. Transit Camp Files, 9 May 2007, unnumbered and untitled letter to the minister of state for urban development from the transit camp Residents Welfare Association, Delhi Development Authority (DDA), Delhi.

62. Ibid.

63. High Court of Delhi at New Delhi, WP (C) Nos. 8904/2009, 7735/ 2007, 7317/2009 and 9246/2009, February 11, 2010. Collected from Gautam Nagar residents during fieldwork, 2010–11. Subsequent summaries of arguments from petitioners and defendants are drawn from this court order.

64. Ibid., p. 12.

65. Ibid., p. 11.

66. Ibid., p. 25.

67. Ibid., p. 40.

68. Ibid., p. 56.

69. DUSIB, Agenda for the First Meeting of the Board, December 23, 2010, http://delhishelterboard.in/dusib_board_agenda/1st_board_meeting_agenda_and_minutes.pdf, accessed May 18, 2020.

70. Supreme Court of India at New Delhi, Special Leave to Appeal (Civil) Nos. 445–446/2012. Record of proceedings available at http://supremecourtofindia.nic.in/case-status, accessed April 17, 2018.

71. High Court of Delhi at New Delhi, Contempt Case No. 884/2013. Collected from Gautam Nagar residents during fieldwork, 2017.

72. Ibid., p. 2.

73. Ibid., p. 4.

74. High Court of Delhi at New Delhi, Contempt Case No. 884/2013. Orders available at http://delhihighcourt.nic.in/dhc_case_status_oj_list.asp?pno=682337, accessed December 17, 2017.

75. Supreme Court of India at New Delhi, Special Leave to Appeal (Civil) Nos. 6626–6627/2015. Orders and the final judgment available at http://supremecourtofindia.nic.in/case-status, accessed December 17, 2017.

76. Ibid.

77. Ibid, p. 6.

78. Ibid.

79. Tilly (2008: 91) defines political opportunity structures in terms of six features: "openness of the regime, coherence of its elite, stability of political alignment, availability of allies for potential actors, repression or facilitation, and pace of change."

80. Supreme Court of India at New Delhi, Special Leave to Appeal (Civil) Nos. 6626–6627/2015, December 12, 2017, p. 7.

81. Unfortunately, the chronically ill petitioner passed away in the summer of 2021, and his heirs inherited his resettled flat.

CHAPTER 6

1. Sewell (1992: 27) theorizes structure "as constituted by mutually sustaining cultural schemas and sets of resources that empower and constrain social action and tend to be reproduced by that action."

2. See Endnote 79 of Chapter 5.

3. Bornstein and Sharma (2016) argue that the advocacy organizations mix "techno-cratic languages of law and policy with moral pronouncements" in asserting themselves as "righteous and rightful" (76). The advocacy organizations, including Delhi Shramik Sangathan (DSS), Lok Raj Sangathan (LSR), and Jan Chetna Manch (JCM), combine the vocabularies of law and policy and moral pronouncements in Delhi. However, their strategies and protest/resistance performances differ, as pointed out in the Introduction.

4. Jan Chetna Manch Files, 26 February 2003, document no. VPS/2003/Sabha Suchana (V. P. Singh's invitation to celebrate Garib Diwas), Jan Chetna Manch, Delhi.

5. Jan Chetna Manch Files, 5 May 2006, document no. A/791 (V. P. Singh's letter to Ajay Maken), Jan Chetna Manch, Delhi.

6. DUSIB, Agenda for the First Meeting of the Board, December 23, 2010, http://delhishelterboard.in/dusib_board_agenda/1st_board_meeting_agenda_and_minutes.pdf, accessed May 18, 2020.

7. I have not examined the ideologies, strategies, and dynamics of these organizations in my research. Nevertheless, I came across members of these groups in many collective struggles despite political and ideological differences. There was palpable unity and display of numerical strength whenever the residents engaged in a range of peaceful as well militant demonstrations.

8. I use "campaign" in this chapter in the sense used by Tilly (2008: 89) as "a sustained, coordinated series of episodes involving similar claims on similar or identical targets."

9. Resettlement Colonies Files, 21 July 2004, "Provision of Facilities at ... Resettlement Scheme," document no. F. 3 (21) 2001-MP/210, Delhi Development Authority (DDA), Delhi.

10. Resettlement Colonies Files, 7 March 2003, "Rehabilitation of 10,000 Families in the Year of 2000" (letter from Kalam Welfare Society to a former governor), Delhi Development Authority (DDA), Delhi.

11. During my interviews, the residents estimated that between 500 and 1,000 people joined the march in early May 2006.

12. Lok Raj Sangathan, "Long Live the Unity of the Residents of Transit Camp!," in *Lok Raj Sangathan Report* 1, no. 3 (April–July 2006), p. 9. Received in person by author from Lok Raj Sangathan activists during fieldwork, 2010–11.

13. Ibid., p. 10.

14. I also use *gherao* broadly to document instances when the poor did not technically encircle their target but barred a particular person from leaving the premises before answering them.

15. Lok Raj Sangathan, "Long Live!," p. 10.

16. Ibid.

17. Ibid., p. 11.

18. Ibid.

19. Oldenburg discusses how the councilors have historically been salient in maintaining everyday contacts and providing materials and civic benefits to city residents in India, especially in Delhi.

CONCLUSION

1. In this light, the book builds on and expands the analysis of critical urban theorists, especially Marxist scholars who have conceptualized struggles for the "right to the city" (Harvey 2008) and "collective consumption" (Castells 1983) as class struggles that defy the capitalist production of urban space (Lefebvre 1991), the contingent shaping of social struggles in the city (Merrifield 2012), profit-driven urbanization and the commodification of urban space (Brenner, Marcuse, and Mayer 2009), and the bourgeois assumptions underlying the use of public space in contemporary cities (D. Mitchell 2003). While I analyze how the poor claim their right to the city, I attend to the specific and contingent struggles of citizenship that go beyond a universal theory of citizenship.

2. The policy of resettlement requires that the poor do not possess any property in the city. See DUSIB, "Delhi Slum and JJ Rehabilitation and Relocation Policy, 2015," No. D-232/DD(Reh.) HQ/2016, June 14, 2016, http://delhishelterboard.in/main/wp-content/uploads/2012/01/Policy-2015.pdf, accessed May 18, 2020.

3. While the numerical strength of neighborhoods shapes the logics and outcomes of politics, I also examine various other factors including political regimes, neo-liberal state policies, judicial activism, spatial arrangements, and most importantly the ingenious *rannnitis* of the poor in providing a nuanced account of the right to be counted.

4. In stating the time of their arrival, residents invoke different periods; for example, the time surrounding the *nasbandi* (sterilization) during the Emergency (1975–1977), the time of the Asian Games (1982), the time of the death of Indira Gandhi and the anti-Sikh riots (1984). Their animated discussion of the event that meshed with their personal biography is itself a performance of their rightful belonging in the city. Similarly, they retrace their involvement in different political rallies in particular years, campaigns for gaining basic amenities in specific periods (for instance, before or after Delhi gained statehood), and experiences of fortune or misfortune (upswings in businesses, birth or wedding of a family member, death of a family or kin member, illnesses, accidents, and fires) in the city.

5. This section draws on my telephonic conversations with twelve research interlocutors across the three field sites in April and May 2020.

6. *Gazette of India*, No. 17, New Delhi, Thursday, December 12, 2019/Agrahayana21, 1941 (SAKA), http://egazette.nic.in/WriteReadData/2019/214646.pdf, accessed May 20, 2020.

7. See Parthasarathy (2020) for a discussion of other minorities in the neighboring countries that are ignored as part of CAA, and the recurring hierarchies and exclusions in the Indian subcontinent that are ignored by anti-CAA protesters.

8. "NPR Update Exercise to Begin on April 1, President to Be Registered First," February 17, 2020, *The Wire*, https://thewire.in/government/npr-update-april-1-ram-nath-kovind, accessed April 29, 2020.

9. Debarshi Dasgupta, Saba Naqvi, and Toral Varia Deshpande, "A Foreign Hand from the East," September 3, 2012, *Outlook*, https://www.outlookindia.com/magazine/story/a-foreign-hand-from-the-east/282075, accessed May 18, 2020. See also Sara Shneiderman and Sahana Ghosh, "New Laws Weaponize Citizenship in India," December 22, 2019, *The Conversation*, https://theconversation.com/new-laws-weaponize-citizenship-in-india-129027, accessed May 18, 2020.

10. "Exclusion of Hindu Bengalis from Assam NRC Changing Political," September 22, 2019, *Business Standard*, https://www.business-standard.com/article/pti-stories/exclusion-of-hindu-bengalis-from-assam-nrc-changing-political-119092200259_1.html, accessed May 18, 2020.

11. "Navi Mumbai to Have Maharashtra's First Detention Centre for Illegal Migrants: Report," September 7, 2019, *Scroll*, https://scroll.in/latest/936556/navi-mumbai-to-have-maharashtras-first-detention-centre-for-illegal-immigrants-report, accessed May 18, 2020.

12. Shadan Farasat, "A Patently Unconstitutional Piece of Legislation," December 11, 2019, *The Hindu*, https://www.thehindu.com/opinion/lead/a-patently-unconstitutional-piece-of-legislation/article30270128.ece, accessed May 18, 2020.

13. See also Niraja Gopal Jayal, "The Misadventure of a New Citizenship Regime," November 27, 2019, *The Hindu*, https://www.thehindu.com/opinion/lead/the-misadventure-of-a-new-citizenship-regime/article30090226.ece, accessed May 18, 2020.

14. Ahan Penkar and Amrit Singh, "AAP's Cynical Stance on the CAA Goes Only as Far as Its Electoral Posturing Allows," February 6, 2020, *The Caravan*, https://caravanmagazine.in/politics/aap-cynical-stance-on-caa-electoral-posturing, accessed May 18, 2020. The protests that ensued resulted in police brutality, incarcerations, arson, a witch hunt of activists, especially Muslim student activists, excessive abuse meted out to students on university campuses, and riots in the northeast of Delhi. Approximately fifty-three people, a majority of them Muslims, were killed in the riots orchestrated as a vengeance against the anti-CAA protests. See also Valay Singh, "India: Charged with Anti-terror Law, Pregnant Woman Sent to Jail," April 26, 2020, *Al Jazeera*, https://www.aljazeera.com/news/2020/04/india-charged-anti-terror-law-pregnant-woman-jail-200426100956360.html, accessed May 18, 2020.

Arvind Kejriwal, the chief minister of Delhi, embraced the politics of vacillation concerning CAA, which in retrospect proved to be a potent strategy in recruiting voting subjects from diverse political affiliations in favor of the Aam Padmi Party and ultimately winning the Delhi Assembly elections in February 2020. His political stance demonstrated a non-committal engagement with the Citizenship Amendment Act; the party did not address the anxieties of the Muslims, fearing polarization and withdrawal of support among communally charged Hindu voters. Nevertheless, the party raised pertinent questions regarding the ability of Purvanchalis (people from Eastern India, especially from the eastern part of Uttar Pradesh and the state of Bihar) to produce appropriate documents and legacy data to prove citizenship in the city.

15. Many citizens, especially women without legacy data, were declared foreigners. Faizan Mustafa argues that the Foreigners' Tribunals, quasi-judicial bodies that act as kangaroo courts, also rejected the documents. See "Why 15 Documents Are Not Enough for Citizenship?," Faizan Mustafa's Legal Awareness Web Series, https://www.youtube.com/watch?v=20nvqR3eNTs, accessed May 18, 2020.

REFERENCES

PRIMARY SOURCES & GOVERNMENT DOCUMENTS

DDA (Delhi Development Authority). 1962. *Master Plan for Delhi*. New Delhi: Delhi Development Authority.

———. (1990) 1996. *Master Plan for Delhi Perspective 2001*. New Delhi: Delhi Development Authority.

———. (2007) 2010. *Master Plan for Delhi—2021*. New Delhi: Delhi Development Authority.

Government of India. (1957) 2011. *The Delhi Development Act, 1957* (DD Act). New Delhi: Universal Law Publishing.

———. Ministry of Urban Development. 1992. *The Constitution (Seventy-fourth Amendment) Act 1992 on Municipalities*. New Delhi.

Jan Chetna Manch Files. Jan Chetna Manch office, Delhi.

NCRPB (National Capital Region Planning Board). Government of India. 2005. *Regional Plan 2021—National Capital Region*. New Delhi: India Habitat Centre.

Planning Commission, Government of India. 2009. *Delhi Development Report*. New Delhi: Academic Foundation.

Puri, V. K. 2010. *New Zonal Development Plans of Delhi under MPD 2021*. New Delhi: JBA.

Resettlement Colonies Files. Delhi Development Authority (DDA), Delhi.

Shah Commission of Inquiry. 1978a. *Interim Report I*. New Delhi.

———. 1978b. *Interim Report II*. New Delhi.

Transit Camp Files. Delhi Development Authority (DDA), Delhi.

SECONDARY SOURCES

Abrams, Philip. 1988. "Notes on the Difficulty of Studying the State." *Journal of Historical Sociology* 1 (1): 58–89.

Anand, Nikhil. 2011. "Pressure: The PoliTechnics of Water Supply in Mumbai." *Cultural Anthropology* 26 (4): 542–64.

———. 2017. *Hydraulic City: Water and the Infrastructures of Citizenship in Mumbai*. Durham, NC: Duke University Press.

Anjaria, Jonathan. 2011. "Ordinary States: Everyday Corruption and the Politics of Space in Mumbai." *American Ethnologist* 38 (1): 58–72.

———. 2016. *The Slow Boil: Street Food, Rights, and Public Space in Mumbai*. Stanford, CA: Stanford University Press.

Appadurai, Arjun. 1996. *Modernity at Large: Cultural Dimensions of Globalization*. Minneapolis: University of Minnesota Press.

———. 2002. "Deep Democracy: Urban Governmentality and the Horizon of Politics." *Public Culture* 14 (1): 21–47.

———. 2004. "The Capacity to Aspire: Culture and the Terms of Recognition." In *Culture and Public Action*, edited by Vijayendra Rao and Michael Walton, 59–84. Stanford, CA: Stanford University Press.

———. 2012. "Why Enumeration Counts?" *Environment and Urbanization* 24 (2): 639–41.

Auerbach, Adam. 2018. "Informal Archives: Historical Narratives and the Preservation of Paper in India's Urban Slums." *Studies in Comparative International Development* 53 (3): 343–364.

———. 2020. *Demanding Development: The Politics of Public Goods Provision in India's Urban Slums*. Cambridge: Cambridge University Press.

Auerbach, Adam, and Tariq Thachil. 2018. "How Clients Select Brokers: Competition and Choice in India's Slums." *American Political Science Review* 112 (4): 775–91.

Auyero, Javier. 2000a. "The Hyper-shantytown: Neo-liberal Violence(s) in the Argentine Slum." *Ethnography* 1 (1): 93–116.

———. 2000b. "The Logic of Clientelism in Argentina: An Ethnographic Account." *Latin American Research Review* 35 (3): 55–81.

———. 2011. "Patients of the State: An Ethnographic Account of Poor People's Waiting." *Latin American Research Review* 46 (1): 5–29.

Banda, Subhadra, Varsha Bhaik, Bijendra Jha, Ben Mandelkern, and Shahana Sheikh. 2014. "Negotiating Citizenship in F Block: A Jhuggi Jhopri Cluster in Delhi." A Report of the Cities of Delhi Project. Centre for Policy Research, New Delhi.

Bandyopadhyay, Ritajyoti. 2011. "Politics of Archiving: Hawkers and Pavement Dwellers in Calcutta." *Dialectical Anthropology* 35 (3): 295–316.

———. 2016. "Institutionalizing Informality: The Hawkers' Question in Post-colonial Calcutta." *Modern Asian Studies* 50 (2): 675–717.

Bardhan, Pranab. 1988. "Dominant Proprietary Classes and India's Democracy." In *India's Democracy: An Analysis of Changing State-Society Relations*, edited by Atul Kohli, 214–224. Princeton, NJ: Princeton University Press.

Batra, Lalit, and Diya Mehra. 2008. "Slum Demolitions and Production of Neo-liberal Space: Delhi." In *Inside the Transforming Urban Asia: Processes, Policies, and Public Actions*, edited by Darshini Mahadevia, 391–414. New Delhi: Concept.

Baviskar, Amita. 2003. "Between Violence and Desire: Space, Power and Identity in the Making of Metropolitan Delhi." *International Social Science Journal* 55 (175): 89–98.

———. 2011. "What the Eye Does Not See: The Yamuna in the Imagination of Delhi." *Economic and Political Weekly* 46 (50): 45–53.

———. 2020. *Uncivil City: Ecology, Equity, and the Commons in Delhi*. Delhi: Sage.

Baviskar, Amita, and Nandini Sundar. 2008. "Democracy versus Economic Transformation?" *Economic and Political Weekly* 43 (46): 87–89.

Baxi, Upendra. 1988. "Introduction." In *Law and Poverty: Critical Essays*, edited by Upendra Baxi, v–xxx. Bombay: N. M. Tripathi Private.

Bayat, Asef. 1997. "Un-civil Society: The Politics of the 'Informal People.'" *Third World Quarterly* 18 (1): 53–72.

———. 2010. *Life as Politics: How Ordinary People Change the Middle East.* Amsterdam: Amsterdam University Press.

Benjamin, Solomon. 2000. "Governance, Economic Settings and Poverty in Bangalore." *Environment and Urbanization* 12 (1): 35–56.

———. 2008. "Occupancy Urbanism: Radicalizing Politics and Economy beyond Policy and Programs." *International Journal of Urban and Regional Research* 32 (3): 719–29.

Benjamin, Solly, and Bhuvaneswari Raman. 2001. "Democracy, Inclusive Governance and Poverty in Bangalore." Working Paper No. 26, Urban Governance, Partnership and Poverty. University of Birmingham.

Benjamin, Walter. 1968. "Paris, Capital of the 19th Century." *New Left Review* I/48: 77–88.

Berenschot, Ward. 2010. "Everyday Mediation: The Politics of Public Service Delivery in Gujarat, India." *Development and Change* 41 (5): 883–905.

Bhan, Gautam. 2009. "'This Is No Longer the City I Once Knew': Evictions, the Urban Poor and the Right to the City in Millennial Delhi." *Environment and Urbanization* 21 (1): 127–42.

———. 2013. "Planned Illegalities: Housing and the Failure of 'Planning' in Delhi: 1947–2010." *Economic and Political Weekly* 48 (24): 58–70.

———. 2016. *In the Public's Interest: Evictions, Citizenship and Inequality in Contemporary Delhi.* Delhi: Orient Blackswan and Athens: University of Georgia Press.

Bhan, Gautam, and Swathi Shivanand. 2013. "(Un)Settling the City: Analysing Displacement in Delhi from 1990 to 2007." *Economic and Political Weekly* 48 (13): 54–61.

Bhuwania, Anuj. 2017. *Courting the People: Public Interest Litigation in Post-Emergency India.* Delhi: Cambridge University Press.

Birla, Swati, Ragini Jha, and Rashmi Kumari. 2020. "A War with No Measure: The Indian State against Its People." *Antipode Online.* January 30, 2020.

Bjorkman, Lisa. 2014a. "Becoming a Slum: From Municipal Colony to Illegal Settlement in Liberalization-Era Mumbai." *International Journal of Urban and Regional Research* 38 (1): 36–59.

———. 2014b. "'Vote Banking' as Politics in Mumbai." In *Patronage as Politics in South Asia*, edited by Anastasia Piliavsky, 176–95. Delhi: Cambridge University Press.

———. 2015. *Pipe Politics, Contested Waters: Embedded Infrastructures of Millennial Mumbai.* Durham, NC: Duke University Press.

Blomley, Nicholas. 2003. "Law, Property, and the Geography of Violence: The Frontier, the Survey, and the Grid." *Annals of the Association of American Geographers* 93 (1): 121–41.

Bon, Berenice. 2016. "Megaproject, Rules and Relationships with the Law: The Metro Rail in East Delhi." In *Space, Planning and Everyday Contestations in Delhi*, edited by Surajit Chakravarty and Rohit Negi, 181–97. India: Springer.

Bornstein, Erica. 2012. *Disquieting Gifts: Humanitarianism in New Delhi.* Stanford, CA: Stanford University Press.

Bornstein, Erica, and Aradhana Sharma. 2016. "The Righteous and the Rightful: The

Technomoral Politics of NGOs, Social Movements, and the State in India." *American Ethnologist* 43 (1): 76–90.

Bourdieu, Pierre. 1986. "The Forms of Capital." In *Handbook of Theory and Research for the Sociology of Education*, edited by John G. Richardson, 241–48. New York: Greenwood Press.

———. 1986–87. "The Force of Law: Toward a Sociology of the Juridical Field." *Hastings Law Journal* 38: 814–53.

———. 1991. *Language and Symbolic Power*. Edited and introduced by John B. Thompson. Translated by Gino Raymond and Matthew Adamson. Cambridge: Polity Press.

———. 1998. *Practical Reason: On the Theory of Action*. Stanford, CA: Stanford University Press.

———. 1999. "The Space of Points of View." In *The Weight of the World: Social Suffering in Contemporary Society*, 3–5. Translated by Priscilla Parkhurst Ferguson and others. Cambridge: Polity Press.

———. 2003. "Participant Objectivation." *Journal of the Royal Anthropological Institute* 9 (2): 281–94.

Breeding, Mary. 2011. "The Micro-Politics of Vote Banks in Karnataka." *Economic and Political Weekly* 46 (14): 71–77.

Breman, Jan. 1996. *Footloose Labor: Working in India's Informal Economy*. Cambridge: Cambridge University Press.

———. 2004. *The Making and Unmaking of an Industrial Working Class: Sliding Down the Labour Hierarchy in Ahmedabad, India*. New Delhi: Oxford University Press.

Brenner, Neil, Peter Marcuse, and Margit Mayer. 2009. "Cities for People, Not for Profit." *City: Analysis of Urban Trends, Culture, Theory, Policy, Action* 13 (2–3): 176–84.

Caldeira, Teresa P. R. 1996. "Fortified Enclaves: The New Urban Segregation." *Public Culture* 8 (2): 303–28.

———. 2017. "Peripheral Urbanization: Autoconstruction, Transversal Logics, and Politics in Cities of the Global South." *Environment and Planning D: Society and Space* 35 (1): 3–20.

Carsten, Janet. 2000. "Knowing Where You've Come From: Ruptures and Continuities of Time and Kinship of Adoption Reunions." *Journal of the Royal Anthropological Institute* 6 (4): 687–703.

Castells, Manuel. 1983. *The City and the Grassroots: A Cross-Cultural Theory of Urban Social Movements*. London: Edward Arnold.

———. 2002. "An Introduction to the Information Age." In *The Blackwell City Reader*, edited by Gary Bridge and Sophie Watson, 125–34. Malden, MA: Blackwell.

Cerwonka, Allaine, and Liisa H. Malkki. 2007. *Improvising Theory: Process and Temporality in Ethnographic Fieldwork*. Chicago: University of Chicago Press.

Chakrabarty, Dipesh. 2000. *Provincializing Europe: Postcolonial Thought and Historical Difference*. Princeton, NJ: Princeton University Press.

Chakravarty, Surajit. 2016. "Between Informalities: Mahipalpur Village as an Entrepreneurial Space." In *Space, Planning and Everyday Contestations in Delhi*, edited by Surajit Chakravarty and Rohit Negi, 113–36. India: Springer.

Chandola, Tripta. 2012. "Listening into Others: Moralizing the Soundscapes in Delhi." *International Development Planning Review* 34 (4): 391–408.

Chari, Sharad, and Vinay Gidwani. 2005. "Introduction: Grounds for a Spatial Ethnography of Labour." *Ethnography* 6 (3): 267–81.

Chatterjee, Partha. 1998. "Community in the East." *Economic and Political Weekly* 33 (6): 277–82.

———. 2004. *The Politics of the Governed: Reflections on Popular Politics in Most of the World.* New York: Columbia University Press.

———. 2008a. "Classes, Capital and Indian Democracy." *Economic and Political Weekly* 43 (46): 89–93.

———. 2008b. "Democracy and Economic Transformation in India." *Economic and Political Weekly* 43(16): 53–62.

———. 2011. *Lineages of Political Society: Studies in Postcolonial Democracy.* Ranikhet, India: Permanent Black.

Chatterji, Roma. 2005. "Plans, Habitation and Slum Redevelopment: The Production of Community in Dharavi, Mumbai." *Contributions to Indian Sociology* 39 (2): 197–218.

Chidambaram, Soundarya. 2020. "How Do Institutions and Infrastructure Affect Mobilization around Public Toilets vs. Piped Water? Examining Intra-Slum Patterns of Collective Action in Delhi, India." *World Development* 132: 1–14. https://doi.org/10.1016/j.worlddev.2020.104984.

Cody, Francis. 2009. "Inscribing Subjects to Citizenship: Petitions, Literacy Activism, and the Performativity of Signature in Rural Tamil India." *Cultural Anthropology* 24 (3): 347–80.

Coelho, Karen, T. Venkat, and R. Chandrika. 2012. "The Spatial Reproduction of Urban Poverty: Labor and Livelihoods in a Slum Resettlement Colony." *Economic and Political Weekly* 47 (47–48): 53–63.

Cohn, Bernard S. 1987. "The Census, Social Structure and Objectification in South Asia." In *An Anthropologist among the Historians and Other Essays*, 224–54. New Delhi: Oxford University Press.

Cohn, Bernard S., and Nicholas B. Dirks. 1988. "Beyond the Fringe: The Nation State, Colonialism, and the Technologies of Power." *Journal of Historical Sociology* 1 (2): 224–29.

Collins, Patricia Hill. 2000. *Black Feminist Thought: Knowledge, Consciousness, and the Politics of Empowerment.* New York: Routledge.

Comaroff, Jean, and John L. Comaroff. 2000. "Millennial Capitalism: First Thoughts on a Second Coming." *Public Culture* 12 (2): 291–343.

Comaroff, John L., and Jean Comaroff. 1992. *Ethnography and the Historical Imagination.* Boulder: Westview Press.

———. 2006. "Law and Disorder in the Postcolony: An Introduction." In *Law and Disorder in the Postcolony*, edited by Jean Comaroff and John L. Comaroff, 1–56. Chicago: University of Chicago Press.

Corbridge, Stuart, and John Harriss. 2001. *Reinventing India: Liberalization, Hindu Nationalism and Popular Democracy.* New Delhi: Oxford University Press.

Corbridge, Stuart, John Harriss, and Craig Jeffrey. 2013. *India Today: Economy, Politics and Society*. Cambridge: Polity Press.

Crenshaw, Kimberle. 1989. "Demarginalizing the Intersection of Race and Sex: A Black Feminist Critique of Antidiscrimination Doctrine, Feminist Theory and Antiracist Politics." *University of Chicago Legal Forum*: 139–67.

Das, Dharashree. 2021. "Matters of the Womb: Muslim Women's Narratives of Fertility, Family, and the Indian State." PhD diss., Simon Fraser University.

Das, Veena. 1996. "Dislocation and Rehabilitation: Defining a Field." *Economic and Political Weekly* 31 (24): 1509–14.

———. 2011. "State, Citizenship, and the Urban Poor." *Citizenship Studies* 15 (3–4): 319–33.

Das, Veena, and Ranendra K. Das. 2007. "How the Body Speaks: Illness and the Lifeworld among the Urban Poor." In *Subjectivity: Ethnographic Investigations*, edited by Joao Biehl, Byron Good, and Arthur Kleinman, 66–97. Berkeley: University of California Press.

Das, Veena, and Deborah Poole. 2004. "State and Its Margins: Comparative Ethnographies." In *Anthropology in the Margins of the State*, edited by Veena Das and Deborah Poole, 3–33. New Delhi: Oxford University Press.

Datta, Ayona. 2016. *The Illegal City: Space, Law and Gender in a Delhi Squatter Settlement*. London: Routledge.

Davis, J. 1992. "The Anthropology of Suffering." *Journal of Refugee Studies* 5 (2): 149–61.

Davis, Mike. 1992. *City of Quartz: Excavating the Future in Los Angeles*. New York: Vintage Books.

———. 2004. "Planet of Slums." *New Left Review* 26: 5–34.

de Certeau, Michel. 1984. *The Practice of Everyday Life*. Translated by Steven Rendall. Berkeley: University of California Press.

Della Porta, Donatella. 2005. "Multiple Belongings, Tolerant Identities, and the Construction of 'Another Politics': Between the European Social Forum and the Local Social Fora." In *Transnational Protest and Global Activism*, edited by Donatella della Porta and Sidney Tarrow, 175–202. Lanham, MD: Rowman and Littlefield.

De Neve, Geert. 2008. "We Are All Sondukarar (Relatives)! Kinship and Its Morality in an Urban Industry of Tamilnadu, South India." *Modern Asian Studies* 42 (1): 211–46.

Deshpande, Satish. 2013. "Caste and Castelessness: Towards a Biography of the 'General Category.'" *Economic and Political Weekly* 48 (15): 32–39.

Deshpande, Satish, and Mary E. John. 2010. "The Politics of Not Counting Caste." *Economic and Political Weekly* 45 (25): 39–42.

Doshi, Sapana. 2013. "The Politics of the Evicted: Redevelopment, Subjectivity, and Difference in Mumbai's Slum Frontier." *Antipode* 45 (4): 844–65.

Dubey, Shruti. 2016. "Understanding Participation in a Heterogeneous Community: The Resettlement of Kathputli Colony." In *Space, Planning and Everyday Contestations in Delhi*, edited by Surajit Chakravarty and Rohit Negi, 35–56. India: Springer.

Dupont, Véronique. 2008. "Slum Demolitions in Delhi since the 1990s: An Appraisal." *Economic and Political Weekly* 43 (28): 79–87.

———. 2011. "The Dream of Delhi as a Global City." *International Journal of Urban and Regional Research* 35 (3): 533–54.

Dupont, Véronique, Subhadra Banda, Yashas Vaidya, and M. M. Shankare Gowda. 2014. "Unpacking Participation in Kathputli Colony: Delhi's First Slum Redevelopment Project, Act I." *Economic and Political Weekly* 49 (24): 39–47.

Edelman, Brent, and Arup Mitra. 2007. "Slums as Vote Banks and Residents' Access to Basic Amenities: The Role of Political Contact and Its Determinants." *Indian Journal of Human Development* 1 (1): 129–50.

Farmer, Paul. 2003. *Pathologies of Power: Health, Human Rights, and the New War on the Poor*. Berkeley: University of California Press.

———. 2004. "An Anthropology of Structural Violence." *Current Anthropology* 45 (3): 305–25.

Fassin, Didier, and Estelle d'Halluin. 2005. "The Truth from the Body: Medical Certificates as Ultimate Evidence for Asylum Seekers." *American Anthropologist* 107 (4): 597–608.

Ferguson, James. 1999. *Expectations of Modernity: Myths and Meanings of Urban Life on the Zambian Copperbelt*. Berkeley: University of California Press.

———. 2005. "Seeing Like an Oil Company: Space, Security, and Global Capital in Neoliberal Africa." *American Anthropologist* 107 (3): 377–82.

———. 2006. "The Anti-Politics Machine." In *The Anthropology of the State: A Reader*, edited by Aradhana Sharma and Akhil Gupta, 270–86. Malden, MA: Blackwell.

Fernandes, Leela. 2006. *India's New Middle Class: Democratic Politics in an Era of Economic Reform*. Minneapolis: University of Minnesota Press.

Flyvbjerg, Bent. 2002. "Bringing Power to Planning Research: One Researcher's Praxis Story." *Journal of Planning Education and Research* 21 (4): 353–66.

———. 2004. "Phronetic Planning Research: Theoretical and Methodological Reflections." *Planning Theory and Practice* 5 (3): 283–306.

Foucault, Michel. 1991. "Governmentality." In *The Foucault Effect: Studies in Governmentality*, edited by Graham Burchell, Colin Gordon, and Peter Miller, 87–104. London: Harvester Wheatsheaf.

Fraser, Nancy. 1992. "Rethinking the Public Sphere: A Contribution to the Critique of Actually Existing Democracy." In *Habermas and the Public Sphere*, edited by Craig Calhoun, 109–42. Cambridge, MA: MIT Press.

———. 2000. "Rethinking Recognition." *New Left Review* 3: 107–20.

———. 2009. *Scales of Justice: Reimagining Political Space in a Globalizing World*. New York: Columbia University Press.

Froystad, Kathinka. 2003. "Master-Servant Relations and the Domestic Reproduction of Caste in Northern India." *Ethnos* 68 (1): 73–94.

Fuller, Christopher J., and John Harriss. 2009. "For an Anthropology of the Modern Indian State." In *The Everyday State and Society in Modern India*, edited by C. J. Fuller and Veronique Benei, 1–30. New Delhi: Social Science Press.

Geertz, Clifford. 1973. "Thick Description: Toward an Interpretive Theory of Culture." In *The Interpretation of Cultures*, 3–30. New York: Basic Books.

Ghertner, D. Asher. 2008. "Analysis of New Legal Discourse behind Delhi's Slum Demolitions." *Economic and Political Weekly* 43 (20): 57–66.

———. 2010. "Calculating without Numbers: Aesthetic Governmentality in Delhi's Slums." *Economy and Society* 39 (2): 185–217.

———. 2011. "Gentrifying the State, Gentrifying Participation: Elite Governance Programs in Delhi." *International Journal of Urban and Regional Research* 35 (3): 504–32.

———. 2015. *Rule by Aesthetics: World-Class City Making in Delhi.* New York: Oxford University Press.

Ghosh, Archana, Loraine Kennedy, Joel Ruet, Stephanie Tawa Lama-Rewal, and Marie-Helene Zerah. 2009. "A Comparative Overview of Urban Governance in Delhi, Hyderabad, Kolkata, and Mumbai." In *Governing India's Metropolises*, edited by Joel Ruet and Stephanie Tawa Lama-Rewal, 24–54. New Delhi: Routledge.

Gidwani, Vinay, and Kalyan Sivaramakrishnan. 2003. "Circular Migration and Rural Cosmopolitanism in India." *Contributions to Indian Sociology* 37 (1–2): 339–67.

Gilbert, Alan. 2007. "The Return of the Slum: Does Language Matter?" *International Journal of Urban and Regional Research* 31(4): 697–713.

Gooptu, Nandini. 2001. *The Politics of the Urban Poor in Early Twentieth-Century India.* Cambridge: Cambridge University Press.

Gordillo, Gaston. 2006. "The Crucible of Citizenship: ID-Paper Fetishism in the Argentinean Chaco." *American Ethnologist* 33 (2): 162–76.

Graeber, David. 2015. *The Utopia of Rules: On Technology, Stupidity, and the Secret Joys of Bureaucracy.* Brooklyn: Melville House.

Graham, Steve, and Simon Marvin. 2001. *Splintering Urbanism: Infrastructures, Technological Mobilities and the Urban Condition.* New York: Routledge.

Gramsci, Antonio. 2000. "Passive Revolution, Caesarism, Fascism." In *The Gramsci Reader: Selected Writings 1916–1935*, edited by David Forgacs, 246–74. New York: New York University Press.

Guha, Ranajit. 1999. *Elementary Aspects of Peasant Insurgency in Colonial India.* Durham, NC: Duke University Press.

Gupta, Akhil. 2012. *Red Tape: Bureaucracy, Structural Violence, and Poverty in India.* Durham, NC: Duke University Press.

Hacking, Ian. 1990. *The Taming of Chance.* Cambridge: Cambridge University Press.

Hall, Stuart, and Doreen Massey. 2010. "Interpreting the Crisis: Doreen Massey and Stuart Hall Discuss Ways of Understanding the Current Crisis." *Soundings* 44: 57–71.

Hansen, Thomas Blom. 2005a. "Sovereigns beyond the State: On Legality and Authority in Urban India." In *Sovereign Bodies: Citizens, Migrants, and States in the Postcolonial World*, edited by Thomas Blom Hansen and Finn Stepputat, 169–91. Princeton, NJ: Princeton University Press.

———. 2005b. *Violence in Urban India: Identity Politics, "Mumbai," and the Postcolonial City.* Delhi: Permanent Black.

Hansen, Thomas Blom, and Finn Stepputat. 2001. "Introduction: States of Imagination." In *States of Imagination: Ethnographic Explorations of the Postcolonial State*, edited by Thomas Blom Hansen and Finn Stepputat, 1–38. Durham, NC: Duke University Press.

———. 2006. "Sovereignty Revisited." *Annual Review of Anthropology* 35: 295–315.

Harriss, John. 1986. "The Working Poor and the Labour Aristocracy in a South Indian City: A Descriptive and Analytical Account." *Modern Asian Studies* 20 (2): 231–83.

———. 2001. *Depoliticizing Development: The World Bank and Social Capital.* New Delhi: Leftword Books.

———. 2005. "Political Participation, Representation and the Urban Poor: Findings from Research in Delhi." *Economic and Political Weekly* 40 (11): 1041–54.

———. 2006. "Middle-Class Activism and the Politics of the Informal Working Class: A Perspective on Class Relations and Civil Society in Indian Cities." *Critical Asian Studies* 38 (4): 445–65.

———. 2007. "Antinomies of Empowerment: Observations on Civil Society, Politics and Urban Governance in India." *Economic and Political Weekly* 42 (26): 2716–24.

Harriss-White, Barbara. 2003. *India Working: Essays on Society and Economy.* Cambridge: Cambridge University Press.

Harvey, David. 1996. "From Space to Place and Back Again." In *Justice, Nature and the Geography of Difference,* 291–326. Malden, MA: Blackwell.

———. 2008. "The Right to the City." *New Left Review* 53: 23–40.

Heller, Patrick. 2000. "Degrees of Democracy: Some Comparative Lessons from India." *World Politics* 52 (4): 484–519.

Heller, Patrick, Partha Mukhopadhyay, Subhadra Banda, and Shahana Sheikh. 2015. "Exclusion, Informality, and Predation in the Cities of Delhi." *An Overview of the Cities of Delhi Project.* New Delhi: Centre for Policy Research.

Holmstrom, Mark. 1984. *Industry and Inequality: The Social Anthropology of Indian Labour.* Cambridge: Cambridge University Press.

Holston, James. 2008. *Insurgent Citizenship: Disjunctions of Democracy and Modernity in Brazil.* Princeton, NJ: Princeton University Press.

Holston, James, and Arjun Appadurai. 1996. "Cities and Citizenship." *Public Culture* 8 (2): 187–204.

Housing and Land Rights Network. 2010. *The 2010 Commonwealth Games: Whose Wealth? Whose Commons?* New Delhi: Habitat International Coalition.

Huey, Laura, and Thomas Kemple. 2007. "'Let the Streets Take Care of Themselves': Making Sociological and Common Sense of 'Skid Row.'" *Urban Studies* 44 (12): 2305–19.

Hull, Matthew S. 2003. "The File: Agency, Authority, and Autography in an Islamabad Bureaucracy." *Language and Communication* 23 (3–4): 287–314.

———. 2010. "Democratic Technologies of Speech: From WWII America to Postcolonial Delhi." *Journal of Linguistic Anthropology* 20 (2): 257–82.

———. 2012a. "Documents and Bureaucracy." *Annual Review of Anthropology* 41: 251–67.

———. 2012b. *Government of Paper: The Materiality of Bureaucracy in Urban Pakistan.* Berkeley: University of California Press.

Jayal, Niraja Gopal. 2013. *Citizenship and Its Discontents: An Indian History.* Cambridge, MA: Harvard University Press.

———. 2019. "Reconfiguring Citizenship in Contemporary India." *South Asia: Journal of South Asian Studies* 42 (1): 33–50.

Jeffrey, Craig. 2009. "Fixing Futures: Educated Unemployment through a North India Lens." *Comparative Studies in Society and History* 51 (1): 182–211.

Jeffrey, Craig, Patricia Jeffery, and Roger Jeffery. 2008. *Degrees Without Freedom? Education, Masculinities, and Unemployment in North India.* Stanford, CA: Stanford University Press.

Jha, Saumitra, Vijayendra Rao, and Michael Woolcock. 2007. "Governance in the Gullies: Democratic Responsiveness and Leadership in Delhi's Slums." *World Development* 35 (2): 230–46.

Kamath, Lalitha, and M. Vijayabaskar. 2014. "Middle-Class and Slum-Based Collective Action in Bangalore: Contestations and Convergences in a Time of Market Reforms." *Journal of South Asian Development* 9 (2): 147–71.

Katz, Cindi. 2002. "Vagabond Capitalism and the Necessity of Social Reproduction." *Antipode* 33 (4): 709–28.

Kaviraj, Sudipta. 1988. "A Critique of the Passive Revolution." *Economic and Political Weekly* 23 (45, 47): 2429–33; 2436–41; 2443–44.

———. 1997. "Filth and the Public Sphere: Concepts and Practices about Space in Calcutta." *Public Culture* 10 (1): 83–113.

———. 2005. "An Outline of a Revisionist Theory of Modernity." *European Journal of Sociology* 46 (3): 497–526.

———. 2010. "The Imaginary Institution of India." In *The Imaginary Institution of India: Politics and Ideas*, 167–209. Ranikhet, India: Permanent Black.

Kemple, Thomas M. 2007. "Spirits of Late Capitalism." *Theory, Culture and Society* 24 (3): 147–59.

Khan, Mushtaq H. 2005. "Markets, States, and Democracy: Patron-Client Networks and the Case for Democracy in Developing Countries." *Democratization* 12 (5): 704–27.

Khan, Naveeda. 2011. "Geddes in India: Town Planning, Plant Sentience, and Cooperative Evolution." *Environment and Planning D: Society and Space* 29 (5): 840–56.

Khera, Reetika. 2011. "The UID Project and Welfare Schemes." *Economic and Political Weekly* 46 (9): 38–43.

———. 2013. "A Cost-Benefit Analysis of UID." *Economic and Political Weekly* 48 (5): 13–15.

Kleinman, Arthur, Veena Das, and Margaret Lock. 1997. "Introduction." In *Social Suffering*, edited by Arthur Kleinman, Veena Das, and Margaret Lock, ix–xxvii. Berkeley: University of California Press.

Kothari, Rita. 2013. "Caste in a Casteless Language? English as a Language of 'Dalit' Expression." *Economic and Political Weekly* 48 (39): 60–68.

Krishna, Anirudh. 2007. "Politics in the Middle: Mediating Relationships between the Citizens and the State in Rural North India." In *Patrons, Clients, and Policies: Patterns of Democratic Accountability and Political Competition*, edited by Herbert Kitschelt and Steven I. Wilkinson, 141–58. Cambridge: Cambridge University Press.

———. 2013. "Stuck in Place: Investigating Social Mobility in 14 Bangalore Slums." *Journal of Development Studies* 49 (7): 1010–28.

Krishna, Anirudh, Emily Rains, and Erik Wibbels. 2020. "Negotiating Informality:

Ambiguity, Intermediation, and a Patchwork of Outcomes in Slums of Bengaluru." *Journal of Development Studies* 56 (11): 1983–99.

Kudva, Neema. 2009. "The Everyday and the Episodic: The Spatial and Political Impacts of Urban Informality." *Environment and Planning A* 41 (7): 1614–28.

Kumar, Sanjay. 2009. "Changing Face of Delhi's Politics: Has It Changed the Face of the Political Representatives?" In *Rise of the Plebeians? The Changing Face of Indian Legislative Assemblies*, edited by Christophe Jaffrelot and Sanjay Kumar, 419–36. New Delhi: Routledge.

Kusno, Abidin. 2012. "Housing the Margin: *Perumahan Rakyat* and the Future Urban Form of Jakarta." *Indonesia* 94: 23–56.

Lefebvre, Henri. 1991. *The Production of Space*. Translated by Donald Nicholson-Smith. Malden, MA: Blackwell.

Legg, Stephen. 2007. *Spaces of Colonialism: Delhi's Urban Governmentalities*. Malden, MA: Blackwell.

Lemanski, Charlotte, and Stephanie Tawa Lama-Rewal. 2013. "The 'Missing Middle': Class and Urban Governance in Delhi's Unauthorised Colonies." *Transactions of the Institute of British Geographers* 38 (1): 91–105.

Mankekar, Purnima. 1999. *Screening Culture, Viewing Politics: An Ethnography of Television, Womanhood, and Nation in Postcolonial India*. Durham, NC: Duke University Press.

Manor, James. 2000. "Small-Time Political Fixers in India's States: 'Towel over Armpit.'" *Asian Survey* 40 (5): 816–35.

Marshall, T. H. 2009. "Citizenship and Social Class." In *Inequality and Society: Social Science Perspectives on Social Stratification*, edited by Jeff Manza and Michael Sauder, 148–54. New York: W. W. Norton.

Marx, Karl. (1843) 2000. "On the Jewish Question." In *Karl Marx: Selected Writings*, edited by David McLellan, 46–70. Oxford: Oxford University Press.

———. (1852) 1978. *The Eighteenth Brumaire of Louis Bonaparte*. Peking: Foreign Language Press.

Massey, Doreen. 1994. *Space, Place, and Gender*. Minneapolis: University of Minnesota Press.

———. 2005. *For Space*. London: Sage.

Mathur, Nayanika. 2012. "Transparent-Making Documents and the Crisis of Implementation: A Rural Employment Law and Development Bureaucracy in India." *PoLAR: Political and Legal Anthropology Review* 35 (2): 167–85.

———. 2016. *Paper Tiger: Law, Bureaucracy, and the Developmental State in Himalayan India*. Delhi: Cambridge University Press.

Mawani, Renisa. 2012. "Law's Archive." *Annual Review of Law and Social Science* 8: 337–65.

Mazzarella, William. 2003. *Shoveling Smoke: Advertising and Globalization in Contemporary India*. Durham, NC: Duke University Press.

Mehra, Diya. 2012. "Protesting Publics in Indian Cities: The 2006 Sealing Drive and Delhi's Traders." *Economic and Political Weekly* 47 (30): 79–88.

———. 2013. "Planning Delhi ca. 1936–1959." *South Asia: Journal of South Asian Studies* 36 (3): 354–74.

Menon, Gayatri. 2018. "People Out of Place: Pavement Dwelling in Mumbai." *Economic and Political Weekly* 53 (12): 85–92.

Menon, Nivedita. 2010. "Introduction." In *Empire and Nation: Selected Essays 1985–2005*, edited by Partha Chatterjee, 1–20. New York: Columbia University Press.

Menon-Sen, Kalyani, and Gautam Bhan. 2008. *Swept off the Map: Surviving Eviction and Resettlement in Delhi*. New Delhi: Yoda Press.

Merrifield, Andy. 2012. "The Politics of the Encounter and the Urbanization of the World." *City: Analysis of Urban Trends, Culture, Theory, Policy, Action* 16 (3): 269–83.

Michelutti, Lucia. 2007. "The Vernacularization of Democracy: Political Participation and Popular Politics in North India." *Journal of the Royal Anthropological Institute* 13 (3): 639–56.

Misra, Girish K., and Rakesh Gupta. 1981. *Resettlement Policies in Delhi*. New Delhi: Indian Institute of Public Administration.

Mitchell, Don. 2003. *The Right to the City: Social Justice and the Fight for Public Space*. New York: Guilford Press.

Mitchell, Timothy. 1991. "The Limits of the State: Beyond Statist Approaches and Their Critics." *American Political Science Review* 85 (1): 77–96.

Nair, Janaki. 2005. *The Promise of the Metropolis: Bangalore's Twentieth Century*. New Delhi: Oxford University Press.

Nigam, Aditya. 2001. "Dislocating Delhi: A City in the 1990s." In *Sarai Reader 01: The Public Domain*, edited by Geert Lovink and Shudhabrata Sengupta, 40–46. Amsterdam: Waag Society for Old and New Media.

Oldenburg, Philip. 1976. *Big City Government in India: Councilor, Administrator, and Citizen in Delhi*. Tucson: University of Arizona Press.

Ong, Aihwa. 1999. *Flexible Citizenship: The Cultural Logics of Transnationality*. Durham, NC: Duke University Press.

Ortner, Sherry B. 1995. "Resistance and the Problem of Ethnographic Refusal." *Comparative Studies in Society and History* 37 (1): 173–93.

Padhi, Ranjana. 2007. "Forced Evictions and Factory Closures: Rethinking Citizenship and Rights of Working Class Women in Delhi." *Indian Journal of Gender Studies* 14 (1): 73–92.

Palshikar, Sanjay. 2009. "Understanding Humiliation." In *Humiliation: Claims and Context*, edited by Gopal Guru, 79–92. New Delhi: Oxford University Press.

Parthasarathy, D. 2020. "Citizenship (Amendment) Act: The Pitfalls of Homogenising Identities in Resistance Narratives." *Economic and Political Weekly* 55 (25). https://www.epw.in/engage/article/citizenship-amendment-act-pitfalls-homogenising-identities-resistance-narratives. Accessed September 7, 2021.

Pati, Sushmita. 2019. "The Productive Fuzziness of Land Documents: The State and Processes of Accumulation in Urban Villages of Delhi." *Contributions to Indian Sociology* 53 (2): 249–271.

Patnaik, Utsa. 2007. *The Republic of Hunger and Other Essays*. Gurgaon, India: Three Essays Collective.

Peck, Jamie. 2010. *Constructions of Neoliberal Reason*. Oxford: Oxford University Press.

Pigg, Stacy Leigh. 1992 "Inventing Social Categories through Place: Social Representations and Development in Nepal." *Comparative Studies in Society and History* 34 (3): 491–513.

Piliavsky, Anastasia. 2014. "Introduction." In *Patronage as Politics in South Asia*, edited by Anastasia Piliavsky, 1–35. Delhi: Cambridge University Press.

Postero, Nancy. 2017. *The Indigenous State: Race, Politics, and Performance in Plurinational Bolivia.* Oakland: University of California Press.

Priya, Ritu. 1993. "Town Planning, Public Health and Urban Poor: Some Explorations From Delhi." *Economic and Political Weekly* 28 (17): 824–34.

Raffles, Hugh. 2002. "Intimate Knowledge." *International Social Science Journal* 54 (173): 325–35.

Rajagopal, Arvind. 1999. "Thinking through Emerging Markets: Brand Logics and the Cultural Forms of Political Society in India." *Social Text* 60: 131–49.

Ramanathan, Usha. 2005. "Demolition Drive." *Economic and Political Weekly* 40 (27): 2908–12.

———. 2006. "Illegality and the Urban Poor." *Economic and Political Weekly* 41 (29): 3193–97.

———. 2010. "A Unique Identity Bill." *Economic and Political Weekly* 45 (30): 10–14.

Ramaswami, Shankar. 2012. "Forces of Truth: A Struggle of Migrant Workers in Delhi." *Ethnography* 13 (1): 57–70.

Ranganathan, Malini. 2014. "Paying for Pipes, Claiming Citizenship: Political Agency and Water Reforms at the Urban Periphery." *International Journal of Urban and Regional Research* 38 (2): 590–608.

Rao, Ursula. 2013a. "Biometric Marginality: UID and the Shaping of Homeless Identities in the City." *Economic and Political Weekly* 48 (13): 71–77.

———. 2013b. "Tolerated Encroachment: Resettlement Policies and the Negotiation of the Licit/Illicit Divide in an Indian Metropolis." *Cultural Anthropology* 28 (4): 760–79.

Rao, Vijayendra, and Michael Walton. 2004. "Culture and Public Action: Relationality, Equality of Agency, and Development." In *Culture and Public Action*, edited by Vijayendra Rao and Michael Walton, 3–36. Stanford, CA: Stanford University Press.

Rao-Cavale, Karthik. 2017. "Patrick Geddes in India. Anti-colonial Nationalism and the Historical Time of 'Cities in Evolution.'" *Landscape and Urban Planning* 166: 71–81.

———. 2019. "The Art of Buying Time: Street Vendor Politics and Legal Mobilization in Metropolitan India." In *A Qualified Hope: The Indian Supreme Court and Progressive Social Change*, edited by Gerald N. Rosenberg, Sudhir Krishnaswamy, and Shishir Bail, 151–83. Cambridge: Cambridge University Press.

Ray, Raka, and Mary Fainsod Katzenstein. 2005. "Introduction: In the Beginning, There Was the Nehruvian State." In *Social Movements in India: Poverty, Power, and Politics*, edited by Raka Ray and Mary Fainsod Katzenstein, 1–31. Lanham, MD: Rowman and Littlefield.

Read, Cressida J. 2012. "A Place in the City: Narratives of 'Emplacement' in a Delhi Resettlement Neighbourhood." *Ethnography* 13 (1): 87–101.

———. 2014. "Un-Settlement." *Home Cultures* 11 (2): 197–218.

Recio, Redento B. 2020. "Street Entanglements: Contestation, Collaboration, and Co-optation in Manila's Informal Vending Spaces." *Journal of Urban Affairs*. https://doi.or g/10.1080/07352166.2020.1798242.

Reddy, G. Ram, and G. Haragopal. 1985. "The Pyraveekar: 'The Fixer' in Rural India." *Asian Survey* 25 (11): 1148–62.

Rose, Nikolas. 1999. *Powers of Freedom: Reframing Political Thought*. Cambridge: Cambridge University Press.

Routray, Sanjeev. 2014. "The Postcolonial City and Its Displaced Poor: Rethinking 'Political Society' in Delhi." *International Journal of Urban and Regional Research* 38 (6): 2292–308.

———. 2018. "The Judge as an Urban Planner: Law, Interests and Politics in India." *Books and Ideas*, 12 February. ISSN: 2105–3030. http://www.booksandideas.net/The-Façade -of-the-Public.html.

———. 2021. "Timepass and Setting: The Meanings, Relationships, and Politics of Urban Informal Work in Delhi." *Urban Studies*: 1–17. https://doi.org/10.1177/0042098021103172 1.

Roy, Ananya. 2003. *City Requiem, Calcutta: Gender and the Politics of Poverty*. Minneapolis: Minnesota University Press.

———. 2005. "Urban Informality: Toward an Epistemology of Planning." *Journal of the American Planning Association* 71 (2): 147–58.

———. 2008. "Introduction." In *Calcutta Requiem: Gender and the Politics of Poverty*, xiii–1. Delhi: Pearson Longman.

———. 2009. "Why India Cannot Plan Its Cities: Informality, Insurgence and the Idiom of Urbanization." *Planning Theory* 8 (1): 76–87.

———. 2011. "Slumdog Cities: Rethinking Subaltern Urbanism." *International Journal of Urban and Regional Research* 35 (2): 223–38.

Roy, Dunu. 2000. "Organising for Safe Livelihoods: Feasible Options." *Economic and Political Weekly* 35 (52–53): 4603–7.

Roy, Indrajit. 2018. *Politics of the Poor: Negotiating Democracy in Contemporary India*. Cambridge: Cambridge University Press.

Roy, Srirupa. 2014. "Being the Change: The Aam Aadmi Party and the Politics of the Extraordinary in Indian Democracy." *Economic and Political Weekly* 49 (15): 45–54.

Saberwal, Satish. 1977. "Indian Urbanism: A Sociohistorical Perspective." *Contributions to Indian Sociology* 11 (1): 1–19.

Sadiq, Kamal. 2008. *Paper Citizens: How Illegal Immigrants Acquire Citizenship in Developing Countries*. New York: Oxford University Press.

Sanyal, Kalyan. 2007. *Rethinking Capitalist Development: Primitive Accumulation, Governmentality, and Post-Colonial Capitalism*. New Delhi: Routledge.

Sassen, Saskia. 2001. *The Global City: New York, London, Tokyo*. Princeton, NJ: Princeton University Press.

Scheper-Hughes, Nancy. 1992. *Death without Weeping: The Violence of Everyday Life in Brazil*. Berkeley: University of California Press.

Schindler, Seth. 2014. "Producing and Contesting the Formal/Informal Divide: Regulating Street Hawking in Delhi, India." *Urban Studies* 51 (12): 2596–612.

———. 2016. "Seeing and Governing Street Hawkers Like a Fragmented Metropolitan State." In *Space, Planning and Everyday Contestations in Delhi*, edited by Surajit Chakravarty and Rohit Negi, 21–34. India: Springer.

Scott, James C. 1998. *Seeing Like a State: How Certain Schemes to Improve the Human Condition Have Failed.* New Haven, CT: Yale University Press.

———. 2009. *The Art of Not Being Governed: An Anarchist History of Upland Southeast Asia.* New Haven, CT: Yale University Press.

Scott, James C., John Tehranian, and Jeremy Mathias. 2002. "The Production of Legal Identities Proper to States: The Case of the Permanent Family Surname." *Comparative Studies in Society and History* 44 (1): 4–44.

Searle, Llerena Guiu. 2016. *Landscapes of Accumulation: Real Estate and the Neoliberal Imagination in Contemporary India.* Chicago: University of Chicago Press.

Sennett, Richard, and Jonathan Cobb. 1972. *The Hidden Injuries of Class.* Cambridge: Cambridge University Press.

Sewell, William H., Jr. 1992. "A Theory of Structure: Duality, Agency, and Transformation." *American Journal of Sociology* 98 (1): 1–29.

Sharan, Awadhendra. 2002. "Claims on Cleanliness: Environment and Justice in Contemporary Delhi." In *Sarai Reader 02: The Cities of Everyday Life*, edited by Ravi Vasudevan, Ravi Sundaram, Jeebesh Bagchi, Monica Narula, Geert Lovink, Shuddhabrata Sengupta, 31–37. Delhi: Sarai, Centre for the Study of Developing Societies and Society for Old and New Media.

———. 2005. "'New Delhi': Fashioning an Urban Environment through Science and Law." In *Sarai Reader 05: Bare Acts*, edited by Monica Narula, Shuddabrata Sengupta, Ravi Sundaram, Ravi S. Vasudevan, Awadhendra Sharan, Jeebesh Bagchi, Geert Lovink, 69–77. Delhi: Sarai, Centre for the Study of Developing Societies.

Shatkin, Gavin. 2007. "Global Cities of the South: Emerging Perspectives on Growth and Inequality." *Cities* 24 (1): 1–15.

———. 2014. "Contesting the Indian City: Global Visions and the Politics of the Local." *International Journal of Urban and Regional Research* 38 (1): 1–13.

Sheikh, Shahana, and Subhadra Banda. 2016. "Unpacking the 'Unauthorized Colony': Policy, Planning, and Everyday Lives. In *Space, Planning, and Everyday Contestations in Delhi*, edited by Surajit Chakravarty and Rohit Negi, 137–61. India: Springer.

Simone, AbdouMaliq. 2015. "The Urban Poor and their Ambivalent Exceptionalities: Some Notes on Jakarta." *Current Anthropology* 56 (Supplement 11): S15–23.

Snell-Rood, Claire. 2015. *No One Will Let Her Live: Women's Struggle for Well-Being in a Delhi Slum.* Oakland: University of California Press.

Soja, Edward W. 1989. *Postmodern Geographies: The Reassertion of Space in Critical Social Theory.* London: Verso.

Soni, Anita. 2000. "Urban Conquest of Outer Delhi: Beneficiaries, Intermediaries and Victims: The Case of the Mehrauli Countryside." In *Urban Spaces and Human Destinies*, edited by Veronique Dupont, Emma Tarlo, and Denis Vidal, 75–94. New Delhi: Manohar.

Spencer, Jonathan. 1997. "Post-Colonialism and the Political Imagination." *Journal of the Royal Anthropological Institute* 3 (1): 1–19.

Spitzer, Steven. 1983. "Marxist Perspectives in the Sociology of Law." *Annual Review of Sociology* 9: 103–24.

Sriraman, Taringini. 2013. "Feeling the Rules: Documentary Practices of Rationing and the 'Signature' of the Official." *Contributions to Indian Sociology* 47 (3): 335–61.

Srivastava, Sanjay. 2009. "Urban Spaces, Disney-Divinity and Moral Middle Classes in Delhi." *Economic and Political Weekly* 44 (26–27): 338–45.

————. 2012. "Duplicity, Intimacy, Community: An Ethnography of ID Cards, Permits, and Other Fake Documents in Delhi." *Thesis Eleven* 113 (1): 78–93.

————. 2014. *Entangled Urbanism: Slum, Gated Community, and Shopping Mall in Delhi and Gurgaon.* Delhi: Oxford University Press.

Stacey, Judith. 1988. "Can There Be A Feminist Ethnography?" *Women's Studies International Forum* 11 (1): 21–27.

Stoler, Ann Laura. 1995. *Race and the Education of Desire: Foucault's History of Sexuality and the Colonial Order of Things.* Durham, NC: Duke University Press.

————. 2000. "Sexual Affronts and Racial Frontiers: European Identities and the Cultural Politics of Exclusion in Colonial Southeast Asia. In *Theories of Race and Racism: A Reader*, edited by Les Back and John Solomos, 324–53. London: Routledge.

————. 2002. "Colonial Archives and the Arts of Governance." *Archival Science* 2 (1–2): 87–109.

————. 2017. "'Interior Frontiers' as Political Concept, Diagnostic, and Dispositif." Hotspot, Fieldsights, January 18. https://culanth.org/fieldsights/interior-frontiers-as-political-concept-diagnostic-and-dispositif.

Stoller, Paul. 1989. *The Taste of Ethnographic Things: The Senses in Anthropology.* Philadelphia: University of Pennsylvania Press.

Sundaram, Ravi. 2010. *Pirate Modernity: Delhi's Media Urbanism.* New York: Routledge.

Swaminathan, Madhura. 2000. *Weakening Welfare: The Public Distribution of Food in India.* New Delhi: Leftword Books.

Tarlo, Emma. 2003. *Unsettling Memories: Narratives of the Emergency in Delhi.* Berkeley: University of California Press.

Tharu, Susie, and Tejaswini Niranjana. 1994. "Problems for a Contemporary Theory of Gender." *Social Scientist* 22 (3/4): 93–117.

Tilly, Charles. 2008. *Contentious Performances.* New York: Cambridge University Press.

Tomlins, Christopher. 2007. "How Autonomous Is Law?" *Annual Review of Law and Social Science* 3: 45–68.

Valverde, Mariana. 2006. "The Sociology of Law as a 'Means against Struggle Itself.'" *Social and Legal Studies* 15 (4): 591–97.

Veblen, Thorstein. 1994. *The Theory of the Leisure Class.* New York: Dover.

Verma, Gita Devan. 2002. *Slumming India: A Chronicle of Slums and Their Saviors.* New Delhi: Penguin.

Wacquant, Loic. 1997. "Elias in the Dark Ghetto." *Amsterdams Sociologisch Tijdschift* 24 (3/4): 340–48.

Wallerstein, Immanuel. 2003. "Citizens All? Citizens Some! The Making of the Citizen." *Comparative Studies in Society and History* 45 (4): 650–79.

Warner, Michael. 2002. "Publics and Counterpublics." *Public Culture* 14 (1): 49–90.

Weinstein, Liza. 2014. *The Durable Slum: Dharavi and the Right to Stay Put in Globalizing Mumbai*. Minneapolis: University of Minnesota Press.

———. 2017. "Insecurity as Confinement: The Entrenched Politics of Staying Put in Delhi and Mumbai." *International Sociology* 32 (4): 512–31.

Williams, Raymond. 1973. *The Country and the City*. New York: Oxford University Press.

Willis, Paul, and Mats Trondman. 2000. "Manifesto for Ethnography." *Ethnography* 1 (1): 5–16.

Yiftachel, Oren. 2009. "Critical Theory and 'Gray Space': Mobilization of the Colonized." *City* 13 (2–3): 240–56.

Zhang, Li. 2002. "Spatiality and Urban Citizenship in Late Socialist China." *Public Culture* 14 (2): 311–34.

Zukin, Sharon. 1998. "Urban Lifestyles: Diversity and Standardisation in Spaces of Consumption." *Urban Studies* 35 (5–6): 825–39.

Page locators in *italics* refer to figures and tables.

157, 162, 189–94, 266; and counter-tactics of enumeration, 44, 162; cut-off dates, 76–78, 86, 95–96, 164–65, 238–39; denial of in Argentina, 169; failed applications, 172; and gendered division of labor, 175–76; *jhuggi* number, 6; *kami* (gaps or errors) in, 5–8, 172, 186–88, 191, 271; lost during demolition, 108–9; mediated politics of, 142–44; medical certificates, 186; photographs of married couples required, 167, 190; and renters, 169; state practices vs. resident practices, 172–74; types of, 162; V. P. Singh cards, 162, 181, 182. *See also* documents
proof of presence, 6–8, 21
property rights, 78, 196
public decision-making, 29
Public Distribution System (PDS), 163–64, 192
public information officer (PIO), 184
"public interest," 195–97, 230, 288n8
"public," judicial definition of, 197
public-private partnerships (PPP), 60–61; *bhagidari* program, 69–74, 292n8; in situ development, 76–77, 83, 215
"public purposes," 61–62, 76–77, 98, 197, 211
Public Works Department (PWD), 85, 181
pyraveekar (fixers, rural areas), 128, 130–31

Rajiv Gandhi Awas Yojana, 78, 79
rallies, 37, 237, 242, 245–47
Ramanathan, Usha, 192, 196, 211
Ramaswami, Shankar, 256–57
Ram Bhajan (devotional song for Hindu god, Ram), 249
rann-nitis (tactics and counter-tactics), 1–3, 15; counter-tactics of enumeration, 174–94; cycle rallies, 37, 237, 242; of demographic calculus, 12, 19–21, 267–69; demographic calculus as, 19–21; *dharnas* (peaceful gatherings), 11, 12, 22, 242–45; felicitation ceremonies, 247–51, *248; gherao* (encirclement), 252, 255–57;

insubordination, everyday, 214; *juluses* (marches), 245, 252–56, *254*; letter writing and office visits, 174–80, 238, 243; marginalized communities forced out of negotiations, 18–19; non-institutional and institutional, 18; of numerical citizenship, 19–24; politicians and lawyers as part of, 242, 248–50; rallies, 245–47; *rasta roko* (road blockades), 37, 137, 210, 240, 252, 256, 257–63; renaming/reclassification, 8–11, 88, 200, 216, *250*, 251; songs as part of, 247, 249; state classifications undermined by, 21–22. *See also* activist organizations; intermediaries; numerical citizenship
Rao, Ursula, 115
rasta roko (road blockades), 37, 137, 210, 240, 252, 256, 257–63
ration cards, 6–7, 95, 98, 142–44, 161, 303n1; confiscation of, 111, 153, 176, 255; deaths due to loss of, 121; as loan collateral, 114; old, as proof, 186–87; renewal process, 170; and RTI process, 183–84
"recreational" land, 28, 62, 65, 200–201
recycling industry, 6, 34, 110, 139, 164
Reddy, G. Ram, 128, 130, 131, 135
redistributive politics, 20, 34, 85–86, 126–27, 247–48
reformist agendas, 56, 74–75, 264, 266–67
regularization attempts, 9–10, 72, 90–91, 97, 157; and judiciary, 199–200, 204–5, 210, 216
"relief roads," 101
religious communities, persecuted, 273–78
relocation and resettlement, 32–33; fees, 82, 114, 158, 230, 294–95n34; of industries, 55, 60; judicial rulings on, 196–97; legal heirs, 172, 186; marginally better off than original allottees, 207–8; selective judicial rulings, 225–26; slow pace of relocation, 79–83, *80*; of "squatters," 55, 56–57, 98; temporality of, 111–12. *See also* demolition; displacement of poor